The Restoration Economy

The Greatest New Growth Frontier

Immediate & Emerging Opportunities for Businesses, Communities & Investors

STORM CUNNINGHAM

BERRETT-KOEHLER PUBLISHERS, INC.
San Francisco
a BK Currents book

Berrett-Koehler Publishers, Inc.
235 Montgomery Street, Suite 650
San Francisco, CA 94104-2916
Tel: (415) 288-0260   Fax: (415) 362-2512   www.bkconnection.com

ORDERING INFORMATION
Quantity sales. Special discounts are available on quantity purchases by corporations, associations, and others. For details, contact the "Special Sales Department" at the Berrett-Koehler address above.

Individual sales. Berrett-Koehler publications are available through most bookstores. They can also be ordered direct from Berrett-Koehler: Tel: (800) 929-2929; Fax: (802) 864-7626; www.bkconnection.com

Orders for college textbook/course adoption use. Please contact Berrett-Koehler: Tel: (800) 929-2929; Fax: (802) 864-7626.

Orders by U.S. trade bookstores and wholesalers. Please contact Publishers Group West, 1700 Fourth Street, Berkeley, CA 94710. Tel: (510) 528-1444; Fax (510) 528-3444.

Berrett-Koehler and the BK logo are registered trademarks of Berrett-Koehler Publishers, Inc.

Printed in the United States of America

Berrett-Koehler books are printed on long-lasting acid-free paper. When it is available, we choose paper that has been manufactured by environmentally responsible processes. These may include using trees grown in sustainable forests, incorporating recycled paper, minimizing chlorine in bleaching, or recycling the energy produced at the paper mill.

Library of Congress Cataloging-in-Publication Data

Cunningham, G. Storm, 1951–
    The restoration economy : the greatest new growth frontier : immediate & emerging opportunities for businesses, communities & investors / Storm Cunningham.
      p. cm
    ISBN10: 1-57675-191-0; ISBN-13: 978-1-57675-191-6
    1. Construction industry—Management. 2. Building trades—Management. 3. Pollution control industry—Management. 4. New business enterprises—Management. 5. Public works—Maintenance and repair—Economic aspects. 6. Buildings—Repair and reconstruction—Economic aspects. 7. In situ remediation—Economic aspects. I. Title.
HD9715.A2 C86 2002
338.4'7624—dc21   2002071676

Project management, interior design, and composition: Shepherd, Inc.

First Edition
07 06 05   10 9 8 7 6 5 4 3 2

Contents

Part Two
The Four Growth Industries Restoring Our Natural Environment:
Ecosystems, Watersheds, Fisheries, and Farms   53

Part Three
The Four Growth Industries Restoring Our Built Environment:
Brownfields, Infrastructure, Heritage, and Misfortunes   129

Preface

During the '70s and '80s, my return trips to favorite islands, villages, SCUBA sites, and mountain jungles almost invariably broke my heart. Usually, they had significantly deteriorated—and often had been destroyed outright—since my last visit.

In many cities, their best assets (such as beautiful historic buildings) had been replaced with sterile, ugly monstrosities that would themselves be torn down in 30 years. Developers were increasingly desperate for new land to conquer and were taking whatever they could get . . . appropriate or not.

But then, in the late '90s, I began noticing a miraculous new trend: a number of places—both ecosystems and communities—were actually getting better, some spectacularly so. Rivers that had been devoid of fish were teeming with them. Blighted industrial waterfronts were becoming gorgeous, lively, economically thriving public areas. Devastated, clear-cut hills were becoming forests again—*real* forests, not just the typical tree farms that are devoid of wildlife.

I began investigating this seeming miracle and discovered a monstrously huge, almost entirely hidden economic sector. It was restoring our world—both our built environment and our natural environment—and it already accounted for over a trillion dollars per year. But nobody was paying it any attention! I found this incredible, and decided to expose these sneaky people.

I also wanted to help bring the millions of restorationists together. All were working in isolation, unaware that they were part of the fastest-growing economic sector on the planet. I wrote this book because I wanted the public to see them, wanted more businesses to partake in the profits they were making, wanted more communities to follow their example, and I wanted them all to "look up and see each other."

READ THE FOLLOWING SIX PARAGRAPHS, AND YOU'LL KNOW THIS BOOK'S MAJOR IDEAS

During the last two decades of the twentieth century, we failed to notice a turning point of immense significance. New development—the development mode that has dominated the past three centuries—lost significant "market share" to another mode: restorative development. Despite the fact that restorative development will dominate the twenty-first century, its phenomenal rate of growth has gone largely undocumented. This is hardly an unimportant transition: economic growth based primarily on the exploitation of new resources and territories is giving way to economic growth based on expanding our resources and improving our existing assets. How could we miss a story like that?

More importantly, why is it happening? Primarily, it's because we've now developed most of the world that *can* be developed without destroying some other inherent value or vital function of that property. The major driver of economic growth in the twenty-first century will thus be *re*developing our nations, *re*vitalizing our cities, and *re*habilitating and expanding our ecosystems. We'll be adding health and wealth, in a way that doesn't cause a corresponding loss of health or wealth elsewhere. (If that sounds like sustainable development to you, note that restorative development isn't about expanding our domain in a sustainable manner: it's about revitalizing the domain we already occupy. More on this in Chapter 14.)

Development activity comes in three life cycle "flavors": (1) new development, (2) maintenance/conservation, and (3) restorative development. Obvious? Sure. But we've failed to formally acknowledge these three modes of development in our economic and social dialogue. This failure substantially delayed our inevitable transition to the long-lasting "third" mode: restoration (the real "third wave"?). This has been a tragic oversight, because, of the three development modes, restorative development is the only one that can fuel continual economic growth without limit. Fortunately, the "restoration backlog" is creating such pressure that we seem to be making up for lost time.

We've been stuck in the first stage of development (new development) far too long. Like a homeowner who compulsively adds another floor to his/her house each year, this habit of continually "piling on," rather than restoring what we've already got, can only end in collapse. This has put us deep in the throes of three global crises: the Constraint Crisis, the Corrosion Crisis, and the Contamination Crisis. Together, they form the foundations of the Restoration Economy, and are good guides to business and community restoration opportunities.

The Restoration Economy can be divided into eight component industries (actually macro industries): four natural and four built. These eight industries are currently balkanized and inefficient—hamstrung by separation from one another—and therein lies great opportunity. Industries that restore the *built* environment have far more in common with those restoring the *natural* environment than either group realizes. The various restorative professions need to recognize, celebrate, and leverage what they have in common, for their mutual benefit. With integration, restorative development's displacement of new development as the dominant paradigm will occur far more quickly—possibly in just a few years, rather than a decade or more.

Restoration will soon account for the vast majority of development on this planet. It already rules in many U.S. cities, such as Chicago, Louisville, and Washington, D.C. Whether it becomes the dominant mode in 2010, or as late as 2020, will largely depend on how soon corporate and government planners wake up to the fact that restorative development is already the fastest growing of the three development modes. Those leaders who become aware of this vast new frontier of opportunity, and who guide their community, national, and company futures in this direction, will be the foremost leaders of the twenty-first century.

WHAT THIS BOOK IS, WHAT IT ISN'T, AND WHO IT'S FOR

This is not a technical book—and it's certainly not an economics book—despite the title and the plethora of technical subjects. Although the subject matter is deadly serious, I've chosen to write in an informal, anecdotal style. Restoration has become a very passionate subject for me, so I hope you'll forgive an occasional rant, personal story, or attempt at humor.

My goal is to catalyze, not catalog, so you won't be wading through copious footnotes (which might be frustrating for researchers and teachers, I know, but it's preferred by my principal target audience: organizational leaders). This is primarily a business book, for readers of every stripe: corporate leaders, investors, entrepreneurs, engineers, contractors, architects, scientists, environmentalists, students, developers, and government planners, to name a few. What these diverse readers have in common may relate to your reason for exploring these pages:

1. a professional need or personal desire for insight into the future of world economic development and investment trends.
2. a career that requires you to generate a constant flow of immediate growth opportunities.
3. a personal passion (or political agenda) for revitalizing human communities and/or ecosystems, in a way that produces dramatic, measurable results and healthy business or tax revenues.

Those factors apply to the world of business, nonprofits, and government alike.

This book is meant to launch a new dialogue, not to resolve or end one. We need to start talking about, thinking about, and researching the "whole" created by the myriad activities that are already restoring our built and natural environments worldwide.

> **Restorative development:** The process of adding new value to natural or built assets, ideally in a manner that detracts neither from their other preexisting values, nor from the value of other assets.
> —one of several working definitions (by author)

I hope you'll find this book not only exciting and useful, but sensitizing. One early reviewer reported that reading the manuscript of this book reminded him of taking a wilderness survival course, after which he suddenly perceived the wealth of edible and medicinal plants that had surrounded him all along. Likewise, before you've finished this book, you'll probably start seeing restorative development everywhere you look.

This is not some wistful vision of the future: it's already happening. Restoration comprises the largest new economic growth cycle since the beginning of the industrial revolution. Millions of people are already working at it and/or investing in it as you read this, and billions are already benefiting from it. What can you do with this newfound awareness of restorative development? You can revitalize your company, your land, or your community. In doing so, you may just revitalize your life.

Our "frontier-style" economic mode, in which we turn virgin land into farms, highways, and buildings—and irreplaceable virgin resources into products and waste—is reaching its natural terminus. Development has arrived at the ends of the Earth. Progress has nowhere to turn, except to revisit and restore what we've already wrought.

Most of us are at least vaguely aware of the eight industries of restoration that comprise the realm of restorative development, but we're only now beginning to perceive them as a discrete, multifaceted economic sector. Perception is seldom a linear progression: stare at the eight restorative industries long enough, and—like one of those "magic pictures"—all of a sudden the omnipresence of restorative development becomes startlingly clear, leaving us shaking our heads at our previous obliviousness.

THE THREE MODES OF THE DEVELOPMENT LIFE CYCLE

Maturing civilizations stand on three legs:
1. new development
2. maintenance/conservation
3. restorative development

Dominance periodically shifts from one leg to another, fundamentally altering technology, culture, and commerce. We are now in such a transition.

- **New Development** This crude pioneering mode launches most communities and civilizations, but destroys irreplaceable assets if prolonged. New development is fast becoming less profitable, less desirable, and less possible.
- **Maintenance/Conservation** This calmer mode is always present, seldom dominant.
- **Restorative Development** This dynamic, high-energy mode restores the existing built environment and natural environment. Restorative development is nearing dominance—in construction, ecology, government, and business.

Acknowledgments

Most authors acknowledge that they had help from others and that any errors are their own fault, rather than the fault of their benefactors. That was certainly the case here. I'm not an expert in a single restorative discipline, only in the integrative, big-picture stuff. So it's very likely I mangled some of the excellent information provided by my expert sources in the worlds of science, engineering, architecture, finance, and economic development.

I couldn't have made a better choice of publisher for my first book than Berrett-Koehler. My readings on the publishing industry had made me a bit paranoid; the nightmare accounts of projects orphaned by departing editors . . . arbitrary title, cover, and content changes made without author input . . . stylistic clashes with copyeditors, etc.

Everyone at Berrett-Koehler has been wonderful to work with: Thank you, Mike Crowley, Pat Anderson, Robin Donovan, Ken Lupoff, Heather Vaughn, Maria Jesus Aguilo, Marina Cook, Jenny Hermann, and Kristen Frantz! For instance, when we couldn't seem to agree on a cover, production director Rick Wilson invited me to recruit my own artist, at their expense. I was working at the Construction Specifications Institute at the time and had been hugely impressed with the work of our staff artist, Mel Zaldivar. She had never done a book cover before but hit a home run her first time at bat. Thanks, Mel!

Rick Wilson also did me the huge favor of recruiting the team at Shepherd Incorporated, in East Dubuque, Ill., to edit and lay out the book. Larry Goldberg was an absolute sweetheart to work with, and I couldn't possibly have had a finer copyeditor than Sharon R. Kraus. Any remaining grammatical or stylistic snafus are almost certainly those few instances where I ignored her advice.

I owe managing editor Jeevan Sivasubramaniam primary credit for bringing me to Berrett-Koehler: He immediately saw the proposal's potential and forced it on visionary publisher Steve Piersanti—insisting that he read it immediately—as Steve boarded a plane. I also owe Jeevan major thanks for recruiting absolutely first-class manuscript reviewers: Sheila Kelly, Charles Dorris, Mark Stewart, Kathleen Epperson, Barry-Craig Johansen, Jeff Mendelsohn, and Pam Gordon. Pam is the author of *Lean and Green*, and she gave generously of her time and energy when I was trying finalize the title, subtitle, and tagline. This diverse group of dedicated, conscientious reviewers provided a breadth, depth, and frankness of feedback that quite literally saved me from embarrassing myself on bookshelves around the world (I hope!).

On the home front, my biggest thanks must go to Maria MacKnight, L.Ac., Dipl. Ac., my gorgeous wife, my healer (she's a doctor of oriental medicine in Arlington, Va., whose web site is wellnessrestoration.com, of course), and my favorite traveling companion of two decades. She put up with four years of waking alone six days a week, as I began the writing portion of my day earlier and earlier, with each new realization of how huge a project I had taken on. For her patience, understanding, and loving support, I'll be eternally grateful.

I was immensely fortunate that my mother—Alma Cunningham, in Charlottesville, Va.—is a talented writer, and that one of my brothers—Andrew Cunningham, in Falmouth, Mass.—is a full-time freelance copyeditor. My mother, in addition to providing a lifetime of unfailing support, love, and grammatical "advice," patiently slogged through many clumsy early attempts to make this book readable, which must have pained her British sensibilities greatly.

Andrew always made himself available at the drop of a phone call or email for a wide variety of editorial questions. I must also thank Andrew's sons, my nephews Christopher and Trevor, for so nicely putting up with my constant intrusions on their father's attention.

My brother Scott Cunningham—along with his multitalented artist/paramedic/wife Samantha, and my other nephews, Rowyn and Thane—provided me with two essential ingredients for the completion of this book: relaxation and competition. Spending vacations with Scott and family—whether in Alaska or Belize—has been tremendously restorative for me.

I inflicted the first, God-awful version of this manuscript on a number of people and must thank Marie DeLucia, Joel Hirschhorn, and Roger Courtenay for their valuable critiques. Bill Hudnut, senior fellow at the Urban Land Institute, was especially gracious in his feedback and assistance, going far out of his way to ensure this book's success.

Greg Balestrero and the wonderful members and staff of CSI provided a supportive environment for six years that allowed this book to emerge and my learning to flourish. Don Ethier was a great help with marketing issues. Without CSI, I might never have conceived a book that included restoration of the built environment, since my previous knowledge and interest had been primarily in the natural environment.

John MacLean of Seattle, Wash.—long-time friend and energy consultant with the World Bank—encouraged me to verbalize and think through this project with him during its earliest, fuzziest stages. Ellen Glew, managing director of the Restoration & Renovation Exhibition and Conference, has helped in a variety of ways over the years, from supplying statistics to putting me in touch with the great folks at Restore Media, LLC—Paul Kitzke, Mike Tucker, and Peter Miller—who helped greatly in launching both the book and my speaking career.

Alemayehu "Alex" Mitiku, Abel, Tensae, and many other crew members at Fresh Fields store, Arlington, Va., provided the caffeine, the friendly ambience, and the patience with my extended presence in their café, where a significant portion of this book was written. Alex is probably the most universally adored employee—of any business—I've ever encountered. Thanks also go to the crews of the Starbucks at Harrison, Lee Highway, and at Lyon Village, all in Arlington. I also owe a huge thanks to the world's best chiropractor, Dr. Waleed Hawa of Riverside Chiropractic in Alexandria, Virgina, for undoing the damage done by that caffeine and by too many hours at the computer.

Paul Hawken's visionary use of the phrase "restorative economy" in 1992—when restorative development was only just emerging—was way ahead of the curve. I must confess to having missed its significance when I first read *The Ecology of Commerce,* but I'm sure the concept was planted in my subconscious, waiting to germinate when fertilized with the right data. His repeated use of the word "restorative" over the years—especially at the U.S. Green Building Council conference in Miami in 1997, where we first meet—definitely swayed my writing further towards restoration. I hope you like what sprouted, Paul.

Introduction

> The world's great age begins anew,
>   The golden years return,
> The earth doth like a snake renew
>   Her winter weeds outworn.
> > —**Percy Bysshe Shelley,** *Hellas,* 1822

Restoration is the business and the spirit of the twenty-first century. Let's now expand on the subjects mentioned in the Preface, so you'll understand why this opening sentence is accurate, rather than wishful. Part of that understanding will come from facts and figures, and part from grasping three key concepts:

1. The Trimodal Development Perspective Development has three modes of operation, corresponding to natural life cycles: new development, maintenance/conservation, and restorative development. Each category produces its own realm of players.

Communities and nations normally start with new development, for obvious reasons. The maintenance and conservation mode then kicks in, to service this newly built environment (and to save parts of the newly-threatened natural environment). When their creations get too old to maintain, when the "highest and best" uses of their structures change, and/or when they run out of room and have to start redeveloping the land they've already developed, then the final, and longest-lasting, mode becomes dominant: restorative development.

When viewed from this "trimodal" perspective, the causes of many "mysterious" national and community problems suddenly become conspicuous, and strategizing becomes far simpler. The most interesting fact for business and government strategists is this: restorative development is now the fastest growing of those three modes, and it will soon be the largest of the three realms of development.

1

2. The Interactivity of the Built and Natural Environments This concept should be painfully obvious, but you'd never know it from the way we plan and run our world today. Industries involved in new development are, by nature, generally exploitative. They normally ignore the negative impacts of their activities, chalking them off as "the price of progress" in a manner disturbingly similar to the "justify anything" style of fundamentalist religious fanatics. When we attempt to restore the aging products of new development, however, the importance of the interrelatedness of built and natural becomes startlingly clear.

For example, city planners now know that a key to restoring the quality of metropolitan life is restoring the surrounding watersheds. Watersheds are their major source of both clean air and clean water, not to mention mental-health-enhancing green spaces and recreational areas. (A recent poll of U.S. public works directors revealed water supplies to be their top concern.)

Combining watershed restoration with infrastructure restoration is now a proven path to metropolitan restoration. Add just one more element to the mix (such as heritage restoration) and a near-magical renewal often results, as businesses become attracted to the area because it's now healthier, more efficient, and more interesting.

3. The Eight Industries of Restorative Development Most restorative development can be divided into two sectors: restoration of the natural environment, and restoration of the built environment. For practical applications, though, the realm of restorative development must be sliced more finely.

Here, you'll find it divided into eight industries, four natural and four built. The four natural environment restoration industries address ecosystems, watersheds, fisheries, and farms. The four built environment restoration industries address brownfields, infrastructure, heritage, and disaster/war.

THE BIGGEST THING YOU'VE NEVER SEEN

This most vibrant new economic growth sector has been hiding in plain sight for over a decade, but has now become too large to ignore. More than a trillion dollars worth of restorative development takes place around the world every year, but it isn't yet perceived as an industrial sector—or as any kind of whole, for that matter.

(Actually, this trillion-dollar-plus figure I'm using is extremely conservative. Just one of those eight restoration industries—infrastructure restoration—probably accounts for over a trillion dollars worldwide each year, all by itself. The heritage industry probably comes close to another trillion, if one includes all of its facets: adaptive use of old buildings; historic district redevelopment; and rehabilitation of architectural treasures, old forts, monuments, ancient artifacts, classic homes, etc. I'm purposely understating the size of the Restoration Economy to avoid accusations of exaggeration, because no one (yet) has an accurate tally [as we'll see in Chapter 4].)

When formal recognition of the realm of restorative development begins, the Restoration Economy will accelerate its already impressive rate of growth. This heightened pace will encompass research, business, and technology. It will also spawn numerous new professional disciplines.

This book is designed to (1) help readers perceive the Restoration Economy, (2) stimulate the "gelling" of its multitudinous disciplines and organizations as a technical and economic community, and (3) guide business, investment, NGO (nongovernmental organization), and government leaders towards related revenue-generating opportunities.

OPENING OUR EYES TO THE RESTORATION ECONOMY

What does this restorative activity look like? Looking from the window of my riverfront Old Town Alexandria, Virginia office, I see Washington, D.C.'s National Airport being restored on my left. The airport project combines three types of restorative development: replacement, adaptive reuse, and historic restoration. The first phase—replacement of several old buildings with the gorgeous new main terminal—is complete and has put $450 million into a variety of deserving pockets. During that construction, an old hangar was adaptively reused for several years as an interim terminal. The second phase will be a complete restoration of the historic main terminal building, built in 1941.

Continuing this survey from my office window, we find, next to the airport, the 50-year-old Pentagon, which had started a 15-year, $3 billion renovation/reconstruction project even before terrorists plunged an airliner into it. On my right is the about-to-be-restored (via replacement) Woodrow Wilson Bridge, projected to cost around $2.5 billion. Just beyond the Wilson Bridge, at the mouth of the Potomac, is Chesapeake Bay, the world's largest (and once it's most economically valuable) estuary.

The collapse of the Chesapeake's fish, shellfish, and crab harvests over recent decades stimulated a number of "expensive" pollution reduction efforts over the years, with some measurable results. But on March 8, 2000, we moved beyond simple pollution control when the Clinton administration announced the $100 million Chesapeake Bay restoration program, jointly funded with Virginia. This first phase tackles 35,000 acres of land, streams, and rivers, and is just the start of a three-state effort to conserve and restore a million acres of Chesapeake watershed. I can't see the bay, though, so we won't include those funds in this visual accounting.

Now let's look at the *new* development around me. On a clear day, I can make out five distant cranes where new office buildings are going up in downtown D.C. But casting the net that far away would also pull in a cornucopia of restorative development, especially infrastructure, historic buildings, monuments, and museums. Included would be the $100 million restoration of the National Archives, begun in 2001, and the $8.5 million restoration of the gorgeous U.S. Botanical Gardens building, completed in 2001.

So let's stick to my immediate area, from the Pentagon to the north, and south to the Wilson Bridge. There's just one significant new office building going up (at a cost of about $40 million), plus a hotel and a few condos. Adjacent to the Wilson Bridge, on the Maryland side of the Potomac, 260 acres of riparian wetland is trying to become the problematic $560 million National Harbor hotel, retail, and convention center complex. And that's about it for new development visible from my office.

Here's the point of this superficial survey: despite the fact that the National Harbor complex is the largest single commercial development project in Maryland's entire history, the $6 billion of nearby restoration activity dwarfs the new development activity, by a factor of ten. Although this is a higher differential than you'll usually find west of the Mississippi, it's similar to many older eastern cities, even taking into consideration the unusually large size of the Pentagon and Wilson Bridge projects.

My visual inventory didn't mention the ubiquitous but less visible restoration activities in my local area. These include the sewer rehabilitation that's a monstrous problem over in D.C., the restorations of the Potomac and Anacostia Rivers, numerous eight- and nine-digit brownfield redevelopment efforts, and a multitude of historic residential restorations. The infamous "Mixing Bowl" interchange on I-95 (just south of D.C.) is also being rehabilitated, at a cost of about $700 million.

Of course, there are many less visible *new* development projects, but the 10:1 ratio is likely to hold up pretty well in this neighborhood after everything is factored in. Nor does my survey include the less visible aspects of restorative development, such as related educational activities. A 1995 survey of 51 U.S. universities revealed that 11 had graduate programs in restoration ecology (at that time, many European universities had undergraduate degrees in the subject, but no graduate programs). Bottom line: you'll be shocked to see how much restoration is going on around you, once you're sensitized to it.

What does this mean for you or your organization? If a sizeable portion of your business, your investments, or your community economic development plan is not related to restoration in some way, you're missing out on the greatest growth frontier of the twenty-first century. The good news is that, even though it already accounts for over a trillion dollars worldwide, many restorative development industries are not only still young, they are still being birthed.

Humankind seems to prefer change to derive from intelligent—or at least visionary—"leadership" at the top. But the low-profile, bottom-up emergence of the Restoration Economy is actually nature's way. Algae, invertebrates, and vertebrates were forming complementary relationships and communities millions of years before the structures and communities we call coral reefs came into existence. Trees grow thousands of root hairs, rootlets, subterranean fungal communities, etc., long before the first leaf breaks through the mulch. Even humans tend to build businesses, farms, and houses long before someone decides to identify a community and build public infrastructure, schools, churches, and other structures. (Modern exceptions are planned "smart growth" and "New Urbanist" communities. Historical exceptions include factory towns and nineteenth-century utopian experiments like Robert Owen's hybrid utopian factory town of New Lanark, Scotland.)

So, the fact that a plethora of restoration-oriented businesses and scientific disciplines already exist shouldn't make readers feel like they've been living under a rock. We've all been missing the big picture.

THE TURNING POINT

By opening an EcoDeposit account, individuals and institutions can support community development and ecosystem restoration in the coastal temperate rainforest of the Pacific Northwest.
—Shorebank Pacific, promotional material, 2001
[the bank's investments are increasingly focused on restoration
of ecosystems, watersheds, farms, brownfields, and communities]

Sometime during the late 1990s, possibly the most important turning point in the economic development of the United States (and most other industrialized nations) was reached, and almost nobody noticed. For the first time in U.S. history, the restoration portion of many key sectors of our economy exceeded that of new development, and that of maintenance/conservation.

Only idiots make predictions in print—especially with numbers attached—but I'm having a moment of lunacy: sometime between 2012 and 2020, restorative development will account for over 50 percent of all development-related expenditures in the United States and Europe. This means that it will be larger than new development and maintenance *combined*. There will also be a highly significant amount of peripheral economic activity, such as the products and services these restorative organizations will require.

We're reaching a "tipping point." We're on the verge of the inevitable transition from an economy based on new development to one based on restorative development—as have most long-lived civilizations before us. This shift is germinating a gargantuan new category of business opportunities that will dominate the rest of this century. Passing this tipping point might take another decade, but once we've entered a full-blown Restoration Economy, nothing will be able to reverse the momentum. As with all evolution, there will be winners and losers: those organizations unable to evolve out of new development mode will certainly be the losers.

Even more surprising than restorative development's current size is its rate of growth, by far the fastest of the three modes of the development life cycle. A few professionals are uniquely positioned to notice this new development–restorative development turning point. One of those is Ellen Glew, Managing Director of Restore Media LLC, the firm that produces the "Restoration & Renovation Exhibition and Conference" twice a year. Glew has heard estimates of restoration's market share growth that exceed 80 percent of the entire U.S. construction economy by 2010.

Whether the 2010 level turns out to be 65 percent or 85 percent, there is zero doubt that restoration is where the growth is. This situation will remain so until development of outer space, "the final frontier," exceeds our enterprise here on Earth. Therefore, holding one's corporate breath until new development regains the throne and this "restoration craze" is over will be a disastrous strategy. In fact, there are major areas of development—such as public infrastructure—in which reconstruction and restoration already account for over 75 percent of expenditures.

Future historians may designate the year 2000 (they like round numbers) as the birth of the global Restoration Economy; the point at which centuries of one-way development reversed direction. "One-way" means forest into farm; wetland into factory; clean air/water into toxicity; living soil into lifeless dirt, depletion of non-renewable resources, etc.—with no counterbalancing activity in the opposite direction. We're finally abandoning our addiction to building more of what we no longer want more of, while the desirable assets we already have, both built and natural, deteriorate, die, or disappear.

The new direction is to reverse that deterioration on all fronts, focusing on quality of function and diversity of components, rather than just more and bigger stuff. Businesses and governments are learning how to produce more assets and more health—not just more money—as a result of each profitable transaction. Of course, restoration itself isn't new; what's new is its adoption on such a massive, commercial scale, especially by developers.

Huge, burgeoning outlays of public and private funds are actively restoring our built and natural environments, and, in the process, our societies and economies. Defunct, century-old factories are becoming mixed-use retail and residence complexes. Flood-inducing denuded hills are being replanted. Fish are returning to rivers that have been freed of their engineered straightjackets. Decrepit inner cities are being revitalized. Decontaminated industrial sites are becoming parks, shopping centers, and residences. Decayed archaeological sites are being restored into vibrant tourism assets. And so on, all around the planet, even in countries that haven't yet been fully industrialized.

Less developed nations also have fast-growing restorative development sectors, though they are generally a decade or so out of sync with industrialized countries. Their nascent Restoration Economies also tend to have different foci, due to their fast-growing populations and lesser amount of industrial and public infrastructure.

We are now in the "Re" century, when redevelopment displaces development, reconstruction outpaces construction, redesign is more common than design, reuse betters use, repaving keeps more people busy than does paving, reengineering dominates engineering, renew dethrones new, and revitalization supplants devitalization. We're finally kicking our self-destructive addiction to sprawling new growth and replacing it with healthy, sustainable regrowth.

What's the big deal? Why is our transition to an economy based on restorative development, as opposed to new development, so important? Here are just three key factors:

1. Restorative development comprises the most efficacious remedy for many of our most pressing social and economic ills, addressing all spheres of activity: international, urban, rural, workplace, family, and individual.

2. Restorative development is the best way to breathe new life into both conservation (which is an insufficient balance to new development) and sustainable development (which has been progressing far too slowly). In the process, restorative development is becoming the solution to both our ecological crisis, and the economic/national security problems stemming from our impending natural resource crises.

3. Restorative development's coming dominance comprises the largest new category of business threats and opportunities, and is far more "real", more substantial, and more rewarding than the rise of the Internet and e-commerce ever were.

HOW RESTORATION'S GROWTH IS REFLECTED IN OUR PRINT MEDIA

The growth of restorative development has reduced new development's market share, and nowhere is that situation more apparent than in the pages of *Urban Land,* the excellent monthly magazine of the Urban Land Institute (ULI). ULI is an organization of private land developers, architectural/engineering firms, mayors, and other professionals interested in the future of our metropolises. If the forces of new development were going to rebel against restorative development's invasion anywhere, this is where you'd expect to see it, either in articles attacking the intruder, or simply in the publication's turning a blind eye to restoration's presence.

Instead, the contents of almost every issue are generally devoted to about two-thirds restorative development, and one-third new development. Themed issues are often closer to 100 percent restorative development. Adaptive reuse, historic restoration, infill, brownfields reindustrialization, waterfront revitalization, urban stream restoration, military base redevelopment . . . such articles comprise the majority of every issue, with just a token smattering of new development.

As we'll see later, this is why restorative development has exploded with so little controversy: rather than putting new developers out of business, it has seduced them via a combination of greater profits and more interesting projects. Industry leaders saw something better, and they abandoned new development with hardly a backward glance. New developers morphed into restorative developers.

The industries of maintenance/conservation have less of a "philosophical" clash with restorative development, so you'll find that most of their relevant publications are loaded with restorative content.

For instance, *Land and Water* magazine, founded in the mid-1900s, serves major landowners, contractors, government engineers (soil and water districts, departments of transportation, etc.), and landscape architects. It used to call itself "The magazine of water management and erosion control," but in 1992, its publishers saw the future. Reflecting the changing interests and activities of its readership, the magazine's slogan changed to "The magazine of natural resource management and restoration." Likewise, *Old-House Journal*, launched over three decades ago, changed its slogan in February 1999 to "The *Original* Restoration Magazine," in reaction to the recent onslaught of competition from other restoration-focused periodicals.

Looking at the table of contents of the average issue of *Land and Water*, the reality is even more obvious, because over half of the content is usually about restoration. It should be noted that this is not a "green" magazine: it's not normally read by environmentalists or ecologists. Many of the articles deal with engineering approaches from the bad old days, such as "controlling" floods with levees, and you'll still see titles like "Taming Those Urban Streams" (the trend is toward "rewilding"). The restorative impact is clear, though, in the titles of ten out of sixteen articles, taken from a randomly selected issue (Jul/Aug 2001). All deal with restoration or wildlife habitat creation, though that's not always evident in the titles:

- "Land Reclamation: Creation of Peck Farm Park's Dolomite Prairie"
- "A Beautiful Urban Tributary Stream Is Unearthed"
- "Pond Apple Habitat Wetlands Restoration"
- "Wetlands Mitigation Paves the Way for Pennsylvania Highway Project"
- "The Ideal Roadside Seed Mix: A Lesson in Native Seed Design"
- "Management of Invasive Species in Restoration Projects"
- "Illinois' Premiere Streambank Restoration"
- "Pueblo of Santa Ana Bosque Restoration"
- "50 Years of Land Improvement"
- "Rehabilitation and Revegetation of a Landslide"

The same goes for popular (as opposed to professional) publications. The August 1999 issue of *Islands* [travel] magazine had a "millennial" special section called "The Future of Islands," profiling 10 projects that demonstrated trends crucial to island development in the twenty-first century. It didn't have an explicit restoration theme, but

- the first article referred to "the *resurrection* of traditional culture" and described the use of indigenous materials to contain and *remediate* a disastrous oil spill at sea [all emphases added, including all below];
- the second and third dealt with conservation and passive *restoration* of fisheries and indigenous medicinal plants (and related knowledge);
- the fourth article profiled Stanley Selengut, the ecotourism developer who designed and was the original owner of Daniel's Head Village, a Bermuda resort based on *restorative development* (featured in Chapter 15 of this book);
- the fifth article, "*Restoring Rare Species*," contained this passage: ". . . the Soskos could become one of the greatest resorts-plus-wildlife sanctuaries on earth, because of its outstanding opportunities to *restore* muntjac deer, pangolins, civets, and ferret badgers." About biologist James Lazell, writer Susan Yim said, "He's also had great success *reintroducing* species to places where they once lived—in a sense, *restoring species back to the future.*" Lazell himself was quoted as saying, "The good news is that there are people out there besides me trying to save the natural diversity of islands and *restore* them";
- the sixth article profiled Desmond Nicholson's Antigua projects: "Nicholson has helped in the dockyard's *restoration* and is now . . . *rebuilding* a naval officer's [1855] house for use as the Nelson's Dockyard Museum [which] is a model for the *transformation of historic buildings* throughout the Caribbean";
- the seventh discussed conservation and passive *restoration* of fruit bats in Micronesia, because the trees need their pollination services, and increased trees would "*replenish* soil fertility";
- the eighth article dealt with heritage *restoration* and *adaptive reuse* on Dominica (one of my favorite places). Describing artist Lennox Honychurch, Yim said he might be found "directing the *restoration* of a historic 18th Century fortress . . . [or] *converting* an old marketplace into a craft market and museum . . .";

- the ninth profiled a story of preserving and *revitalizing* native arts via "increased respect for the few remaining women of Mindanao who maintain the body of textile skills and lore";
- tenth was an article on *restoring* native plant species—and *rehabilitating* military damage—on Lanai, Hawai'i, through commercial cultivation of indigenous species: "They're often rare and endangered," [Jon Kei] Matsuoka says, pointing out that these plants are intended for *reforestation* on the island of Kahoolawe, which for years was a U.S. navy bombing target. (Another wonderful project that I wish I had space to describe further.)

Whether or not *Island*'s editors noticed the continual thread of restoration in this issue, they certainly had picked up on our entry into "the Century of Restoration."

What Restorative Activities Is this Book Not Including?

Many restoration industries have appeared or expanded quite recently, but there are many old, stable restorative professions and industries. This well-established, slower-growth side of restorative development also includes rehabilitating paleontological or archaeological finds, restoring classic vehicles (boats, aircraft, cars, carriages, etc.), and so on.

One might wonder what such "trivial" hobbyist activities or luxury items have to do with revitalizing our world. Am I going to treat every restorative activity as a part of the Restoration Economy? If so, does that make it good or important? For the purposes of this book, the answer is twofold: (1) yes, almost every restorative activity can be considered part of the realm of restorative development, and (2) no, not all will be included in this book.

What is the conceptual difference between restoring an antique motorcycle and restoring a bridge, or between restoring an heirloom gold brooch and restoring an historic home? All add value to existing assets. Both increase wealth without significantly depleting wealth or health elsewhere. The main difference is the size of the project, and the number of people who benefit. That said, there will be few mentions of hobbyist-, art-, or museum-related restoration in these pages.

Professional and Organizational Opportunities Abound

> How wonderful it is that nobody need wait a single moment before starting to improve the world.
>
> —**Anne Frank**, *The Diary of Anne Frank*

Opportunities in restorative development are not limited to the biologists, contractors, doctors, civil engineers, and large companies that you'd expect to be associated with solving the problems of insufficient space, aged infrastructure, or deteriorating environmental (and human) health.

A wide range of restorative professions, products, and services is emerging: from software and seminars, to stoneworking tools and model ecosystems, to videos and tours. Also needed are entirely new inventions for performing restorative work, along with a profusion of new, restoration-related service companies, NGOs, professional societies, and consultants.

> We're good at taking things apart. We need to learn how to put them
> together. If you think you can't make money in restoration, [just] take your
> car into the shop or your body to the doctor.
> —**David Brower** with **Steve Chapple**, *Let the Mountains Talk, Let the Rivers Run*, 1996

Young and old, organizations and professionals, public and private— all are delightedly exploiting these lucrative new markets, these eight industries of restorative development. Around the turn of the millennium, Dr. Joseph Westphal, the assistant Army secretary for civil works (the civilian responsible for overseeing the Army Corps of Engineers) told the Corps' leaders, "I think our real next opportunity is to be ready to build the infrastructure man will need to settle the planets."

A new frontier such as outer space will certainly revive the new-development portion of our economy, but it won't happen tomorrow. To find today's unlimited frontier of opportunity, we must look "behind" us, at the territory we've already settled or exploited.

OTHERS HAVE SEEN THIS COMING

This is not the first book to mention the concept of a "Restoration Economy":

- Paul Hawken's wonderful *The Ecology of Commerce* (1994) discussed the theoretical possibility of, and need for, a "restorative economy" and offered a few early examples.
- In Stewart Brand's modern classic, *How Buildings Learn* (1994), he repeatedly demonstrates (in a chapter titled "Unreal Estate") how insufficient attention to the restoration and reuse of buildings has been undercutting our economy.
- William Jordan III, founder of the journal *Ecological Restoration* has long discussed how restorative activities often animate profound

changes in cultural values. In 1997, Eric Higgs (in an article entitled" What is Good Ecological Restoration?" that appeared in the Journal) posited restoration as a distinct cultural mode.

However, I believe mine is the first book to unite the restoration of both natural and built environments. I further believe this to be the first book to document the rise of a *real* Restoration Economy, rather than "merely" envisioning or hoping for one.

> Randy Stemler . . . is the program manager for the MRC Reforestation Program. It's part of what he calls the "restoration economy." "There's a lot of money being spent locally focused on natural resource reinvestment. We go in and identify sites where it's biologically appropriate to do reforesting. Then I arrange for financing, train the crews and plant trees where they were once growing." In its 10 years of operation the program has been sponsored by several northern California catalog companies. Smith and Hawken was the first.
> —**Bob Doran,** "If you rebuild it . . . will they come back?" *North Coast Journal Weekly,* March 2, 2000 [discussing the 18th Annual Salmonid Restoration Conference and the work of the Mattole (watershed) Restoration Council]

These first two decades of the new millennium comprise the greatest window of opportunity. During this period, healthy organizations will learn to perceive restorative development's often-camouflaged opportunities in their eight favorite hiding places:

- Ecosystem and species restoration
- Aquifer recharging and waterway/watershed "rewilding"
- Estuary, reef, and pelagic fishery regeneration
- Rural economic revival and farm redevelopment
- Brownfields remediation, and redevelopment of closed military bases
- Utility restructuring and public infrastructure rebuilding
X • Heritage site renovation/adaptive reuse of historical buildings
- War reconstruction, resettlement, and disaster recovery

As mentioned in the Preface, I've spent much of my last 20 years exploring our planet's last remaining healthy jungles, reefs, and other ecosystems. I must be a masochist, because I return to some of my favorite nature spots from time to time. This allows me to perceive their decline, which is often tragic to the point of lumpy throat and leaky eyes. I've simultaneously encountered almost universal degradation of communities and cultures. This, too, is deeply tragic, and profoundly moving.

After witnessing a lifetime of marginally successful environmental efforts, failed urban revitalization plans, and the general decrease of satisfaction with our lives and our world in general, a bright light has suddenly appeared at the end of the tunnel.

In every development-related industry I surveyed over the past four years, what has been most exciting to the investors and business planners has been the growth of restorative projects. This made me realize that tremendous untapped growth potential was awaiting the day that this immense economic sector came together and was recognized.

The first step towards this goal is giving it a name: the Restoration Economy. Come with me now on a guided tour of this unlimited new realm of economic growth, social revitalization, and planetary health.

Part One

The Transition from Our "New Development" Past to Our "Restorative Development" Future

> **Restorative development:** A mode of development that increases the health or value of existing assets without (or with minimal) destruction of other assets, and without significantly increasing the restored assets' geographic or ecological footprints.
>
> —one of several working definitions (by author)

The goal of Part One is to familiarize readers with the general nature of restorative development and its underlying history, dynamics, drivers, and cycles.

This section offers generalized, big-picture insights designed to help organizational and governmental leaders understand the basic nature and underlying causes of the dominant macrotrend of the twenty-first century: the growth of restorative development. This is the factor they can least afford to ignore when formulating their developmental strategies.

Chapter 1 will review the three global crises that are driving restorative development's rapid growth. I've labeled them the Constraint Crisis, the Corrosion Crisis, and the Contamination Crisis. Chapter 2 will explore the concept of looking at development from a life cycle point of view, which divides it into the three modes of new development, maintenance/conservation, and restorative development.

Chapter 3 will step back and provide a little historical perspective on restorative development. Chapter 4 will wrap up this first section by examining the question that, more than any other, seems to leave more people scratching their heads: how in the world did we accumulate such a broad expanse of related multibillion-dollar industries without noticing it much earlier?

Although you'll probably be surprised by the size of our existing restoration industries, the real eye-opener is that none of them is close to mature. Many are very, very new. Despite their already impressive rapid rates of growth, two new factors will accelerate these restorative industries at an even more astonishing pace in the coming decade.

The first factor is the simple recognition of the Restoration Economy's existence, its encompassing of both the built and natural environments, and its eight restoration industries. The second factor is the onset of integrated restoration, a practice that will spawn myriad new professional disciplines, research programs, design and consulting services, and entirely new industries. This book offers only brief flashes of the trend toward integration; this trend deserves its own book, and will get it.

The Restoration Economy will thus attempt to

1. raise awareness of why restorative development has emerged in such vast proportions, and why its advent has been both rapid and unheralded;
2. broadly define the restoration markets with the most growth potential; and
3. provide some insight into issues that must be addressed by organizations responding to restorative development's threats and opportunities.

The major activities of the twenty-first century will restore our natural world, our built world, our social world, our work world, our family world, and even our "inner world" (the realm of spirit). We are maturing from the "exploit and run" behavior of raiders, to behavior befitting of long-term natives of our planet. We're developing a sense of place, creating a present that forms a viable connection between our past and our future. Let's now explore the frontier of this global restoration.

The Three Foundations
of the Restoration Economy

To restore is to make something well again. It is mending the world. People have to believe there will be a future in order to look forward. To live in that future, we need a design. To pay the bills from the past, we need a means. . . . For those who say that times are tough, that we can ill afford sweeping changes because the existing system is already broke or hobbled, consider that the U.S. and the former U.S.S.R. spent over $10 trillion on the Cold War, enough money to replace the entire infrastructure of the world, every school, every hospital, every roadway, building and farm. In other words, we bought and sold the world in order to defeat a political movement. To now assert that we don't have the resources to build a restorative economy is ironic, since the threats we face today are actually happening, whereas the threats of the postwar nuclear stand-off were about the possibility of destruction.

—**Paul Hawken**, *The Ecology of Commerce*, 1992

The sudden growth of restorative development is rooted in three crises. These crises emerge whenever an economy—global or local—remains dependent on new development for too long.

THE TWENTY-FIRST CENTURY'S THREE GLOBAL CRISES

1. The Constraint Crisis　We're out of "painless" expansion room: every time we put property to a new use, we lose some other vital service it was providing. Wars and legal conflicts over territory and related natural resources are epidemic.

2. The Corrosion Crisis   Most of our built environment is aged and decrepit; is wearing out faster than expected; or is based on old, wasteful, dysfunctional designs.

3. The Contamination Crisis   The ecosystems that produce our air, soil, food, and water—and fueled our centuries of unbridled new development—are under great stress, as are the immune systems of both human beings and wildlife. Industrial, agricultural, and military contamination is largely to blame, and its damage is compounded, in a vicious cycle, by the reduced capacity of our damaged and destroyed ecosystems to cleanse the environment.

This chapter is an overview—not a thorough accounting—of these crises. Parts Two and Three, where we look at the restorative industries that are addressing these crises, contain a more detailed examination of these crises, and our restorative responses to them. This chapter scans the Three Crises from three perspectives: the U.S. economy, non-U.S. economies, and the global natural environment. The crises won't be segregated from each other: they are inextricably intertwined. Nor will we always label them or point them out, as each is easily recognizable.

The Three Crises at Work in the United States

> Almost all of our sewer and wastewater projects are rehabilitation these days. Even with urban sprawl, construction of new systems is a rarity. It's true nationwide, but especially so here in the Northeast, where everything is so old.
> —**Howard B. LaFever**, P.E., DEE, Executive Vice President, Stearns & Wheler Co., a 250-person engineering firm (conversation with author)

In 1998, the American Society of Civil Engineers (ASCE) issued a "Report Card on America's Infrastructure." It revealed, for the first time, the extent of one aspect of our built environment's deterioration: a $1.3 *trillion* backlog of desperately needed work on our public infrastructure. Our bridges, roads, sewage plants, solid/hazardous waste handling facilities, and educational institutions are crumbling before our eyes.

Although some of this $1.3 trillion is for maintenance, by far the majority of funding is needed for renovation and replacement. Even more importantly, while $1.3 trillion is a gargantuan number, it represents only public infrastructure—just one of eight major industries of restoration—and it's only the U.S. portion.

But this book isn't about bad news. Quite the opposite: Restorative development now accounts for hundreds of billions of dollars in the

United States alone, maybe a trillion, depending on how one defines it. Just two years after the first ASCE Report Card, a small but significant portion of the transportation renovation challenge had been funded. The June 1998 Transportation Equity Act (TEA-21), along with the TEA-21 Restoration Act of July 1998, addressed a significant chunk of the U.S. Corrosion Crisis. It increased spending over a six-year period by 70 percent, allocating over $200 billion in federal funds to U.S. transportation infrastructure. States will add significantly to this amount.

Only 20 percent of these funds is for "new starts," while about 25 percent is officially designated for restorative projects. But, almost the entire remaining 55 percent is allowed to be spent on restoration (as opposed to maintenance, like patching potholes), and most of it will be, according to conversations with several state Department of Transportation (DOT) officials.

There's good news for the Contamination Crisis, too. Restoration is being funded by reallocating the budgets of some of the most harmful, out-of-control agencies of new development. The U.S. Army Corps of Engineers' budget is being reallocated from new development to ecological, infrastructure, and watershed restoration, and the Corps is far from alone. The Department of Energy now spends billions cleaning up the petrochemical and radioactive mess it left all around the United States during the last half of the twentieth century.

The United States will account for more than its fair share of space throughout this book, so we won't focus more on it here. Suffice it to say that one would be hard put to stand on any piece of American soil without seeing (or detecting with instruments) at least one significant impact of the Constraint, Corrosion, and/or Contamination Crisis.

The Three Crises at Work Around the World

> Restoration ecology plays an important role in nature conservation policy in Europe today.
>
> —Jorg Pfadenhauer, *Restoration Ecology*, June 2001

The trillion dollar-plus annual bill for restorative development is no surprise when we consider the Three Crises globally, especially when we factor in the crushing needs of former communist bloc countries. Many of them are economic and environmental basket cases (the two usually go hand in hand), and their problems are affecting us "First Worlders" more than we like to think, in terms of our health and our wealth.

The United States leads the world in many categories of restoration, but all other industrially developed countries are now moving along the restoration track at a similar pace. As a result, most U.S. and European firms that continue to concentrate on *new* development are being forced to shift their focus to Latin America, Asia, and Africa. Even in regions where new development is still strong, such firms will be missing many, often better, opportunities if they ignore the developing world's fast-growing restoration markets.

Three recent announcements, one for each of the Three Crises, illustrate the magnitude of non-U.S. restoration.

1. Constraint (and Contamination) Crisis   At the Brownfields 2000 conference in Atlantic City, New Jersey, Detlef Grimski, a project officer with Germany's Federal Environmental Agency, revealed 304,000 (official) contaminated sites in Germany. The agency's studies show that restoring just 320,000 acres of these "brownfields" could provide 28 percent of Germany's housing construction needs, and 125 percent of its industrial construction needs.

However, both Germany's construction industry and its government are stuck in new-development mode, destroying some 300 acres of rare, precious greenfields daily, while ignoring the wealth of brownfields. ("Wealth of brownfields," a phrase I've heard at several conferences, is the sort of perverse language that's endemic in the dying days of a new development-based economy.)

2. Corrosion (and Constraint) Crisis   Developer Minoru Mori, President/CEO of Mori Building Co., Ltd., and a member of Japan's Economic Strategy Council, has proposed a *trillion*-dollar restorative development plan for Tokyo, one of the world's oldest and most crowded cities. "Revitalizing Tokyo and other major cities is the best way to revitalize the Japanese economy," he claims.[1] It is part of an "Urban New Deal" policy he has presented to the Japanese government. It is strongly focused on cultural renewal, calling for a "true urban renaissance."

3. Contamination Crisis   On June 5, 2000, Romania, Bulgaria, Moldova, and Ukraine signed the "Green Corridor" agreement for the Danube River, which has more riparians (countries that border it) than any river in the world. It is Europe's largest environmental restoration initiative ever, encompassing over 1.5 million acres of wetlands and riparian habitat. That's just a beginning: "It is our vision that other coun-

---

[1] Management Visions for a Changing World: Japan's CEOs Speak on the Record, "A Better Life: Revitalizing Japan," Forbes.com [Special Advertising Section].

tries along the Danube will join this initiative for a full-length green corridor, connecting Danube countries from the Black Sea to the Alps, including many EU accession countries," stated Romica Tomescu, Romania's Minister of Waters, Forests and Environmental Protection.[2]

Worldwide disaster recovery—both war and natural—is a category of restoration that accounts for over a hundred billion dollars annually. And then there are non-war, non-natural, human-caused disasters: literally hundreds of significant oil spills, industrial explosions, chemical spills, toxic fires, and radiation leaks occur daily, worldwide. Someone once said that CNN could devote a channel solely to natural and human-made disasters—giving each item 10 seconds and never repeating a story—to fill each day's programming.

Being more "real estate challenged" (Constraint Crisis) than the United States also puts Europe ahead on the new development vs. maintenance curve. Tim Broyd, Research and Innovation Director at the WS Atkins company in the United Kingdom, told me that his company had, ten years ago, about 2,200 employees and virtually all its business was in the design of new construction. Today, the company has about 7,500 employees, but 60 percent of its business is related to managing existing facilities, and much of what it counts as "new" construction is actually restorative work (or "refurbishment," as the Brits tend to call it). Broyd says that such growth and profitability paths—switching from new development to maintenance and restoration—are now the industry norm.

The 1998 Yangtze River floods, which were largely caused by the clear-cutting of surrounding forests, killed thousands, obliterated entire communities, and caused massive migration and waterborne sickness. To address the resulting Constraint and Contamination Crises, the Chinese government launched an emergency $12 billion reforestation program. That $12 billion figure exceeds the Gross Domestic Product of Panama, and that of Costa Rica. In fact, it's larger than the GDP of 113 of the 189 countries existing in 1999, and that sum represents only *one* of China's many deforested watersheds. Unlike conservation efforts, where million-dollar projects make headlines, the word "billion" is quite common in restoration circles, at least at the national level.

The similarly huge reforestation projects that are needed worldwide would take pages to list. In early 2000, when deforestation-related floods devastated Mozambique, Zambia, and Madagascar, Mozambique asked

---

[2] Worldwide Fund for Nature (WWF), press release, June 5, 2000.

world donors for $450 million to rebuild its nation. Millions are still suffering the effects of the floods—again greatly amplified by deforestation—caused by Hurricane Mitch in Honduras, El Salvador, and Guatemala, in October 1998. The more reforestation takes place, the fewer such devastating disasters. Reforestation fulfills many agendas beyond mere flood prevention: producing drinking and irrigation water, carbon sequestration, firewood-lumber-pulp supply, and recreational industries are just a few of the added benefits of reforestation. As the advantages of reforestation become better recognized, the funding for watershed restoration continues to increase.

Saying Goodbye to (Some of) New Development's Ethical Problems

As has been extensively documented in recent years—even by the bank itself—the World Bank's colossal dam, highway, and fossil fuel power projects almost unfailingly displace poor farmers. They also disrupt healthy portions of socioeconomic systems, and kill or degrade vital ecosystems, all while (usually) failing to provide the promised counterbalancing, short- or long-term benefits.

Further, the World Bank does not attempt meaningful remedies for people it has displaced, as many have noted. For example, Lori Pottinger of the International Rivers Network said in a *Wall Street Journal* article, "We've never had confidence in the World Bank's ability to restore these people's lives." MIT professor of Law and Development Balakrishnan Rajagopal refers to the "violence of development." He coined the term "development cleansing" to describe the way new development, such as dam building, usually takes place on the lands of poor and/or indigenous peoples, displacing them by the hundreds of thousands, in a process similar to ethnic cleansing, only with bulldozers instead of guns.

Trying to find ways to improve and revive the waning paradigm called new development is a recipe for frustration. The Constraint and Contamination Crises will provide development banks with many decades, even centuries, of work if they switch from new development to *re*development. As we'll see in Chapter 14, that's exactly where the World Bank's future may lie: restorative development.

On a cynical note, we could say that efforts in the first seven restorative industries—ecosystems, watersheds, fisheries, farms, brownfields, infrastructure, and heritage—decrease business in the eighth: disaster restoration. No worries, though: swelling (largely coastal) populations,

combined with global climate change, should ensure a burgeoning supply of lucrative disasters for the world's restorative A/E/C (architectural, engineering, contracting) firms. The fact that politically powerful
lumber companies still get away with clear-cutting ensures that many
fortunes will continue to flow from flood-related restoration for decades
to come.

The Three Crises Have Been Masked by Three Myths

> Men and nations do behave wisely, once all other alternatives have been
> exhausted.
>   —**Abba Eban**, *Vogue*, August 1, 1967

The environmental problems of new development derive from all three of
the Three Crises. The Corrosion Crisis contributes to environmental problems in the form of outdated, toxic industrial facilities, obsolete sewage
treatment facilities, antique fossil fueled power plants, etc. The Contamination Crisis's effects in this context are obvious.

But it's the Constraint Crisis that's most tightly linked to our ecological decline. If we keep expanding our population on a planet of finite
size, simple logic plots a clear path to Armageddon. Restorative development can greatly delay the collapse and can even increase quality of
life along the way, but there's no escaping the laws of physics. The universe might be expanding, but this planet isn't.

It took us only twelve years to go from five billion to six billion people. Several indicators show the rate of population growth decreasing,
"thanks" in part to increased death rates due to starvation, dehydration,
waterborne diseases, malaria, AIDS, cancers, and other health concerns,
most of which are directly or indirectly related to the Three Global Crises.
The average life expectancy in many African countries has plummeted in
the past decade, dropping from 62 to 40 years in Botswana, and from 61
to 39 in Zimbabwe.

Unfortunately, many anti-family-planning forces have jumped on
these lowered population growth estimates and said, "See? The population is going down!" They are confusing a slowing of increase with a
decrease. The most optimistic forecasters say we might see world population entering a period of net decline toward the end of this century. But
they are assuming that our current downward blip in birthrates is the
beginning of a long trend. Hopefully, this will prove to be the case, but
it's wise to remember that the largest group of youngsters the world has

ever seen—the children of the baby boomers—is entering its peak reproduction years.

Even if the trend toward smaller families continues, several factors
point to a less-than-rosy scenario: the Three Crises have *all* been worsen-
ing at a rate that's greater than the population growth rate. In the United
States, development of greenfields (Constraint Crisis) has outpaced population growth by a factor of three in most areas. This means that even if
the population froze at its current levels, all three crises would continue
to intensify. Another factor is that all real population growth (that is, not
driven by immigration) in the coming decades will take place in the
developing world, which has the least ability to handle it. Without an
equally intense growth of restorative development, this could lead to far
greater political instability than we currently experience.

The Constraint Crisis isn't driven solely by population growth. It's
partially driven by the increasing consumerism, and thus the larger
ecological footprint, of developing countries' citizens. But even U.S.
citizens—who already consume 10 times more than the average world
citizen—are *still* increasing our ecological footprints. The amount of real
estate "required" by each U.S. homeowner has been growing quickly and
steadily in recent decades and shows no signs of slowing.

Even if the most recent projections of a world population peak of
"only" nine billion around 2070 turn out to be accurate, a continuation of
this increasing-footprint trend means that the Constraint Crisis will follow a much steeper trajectory than that of population growth. And the
Constraint Crisis will continue to worsen, even after the population peak
has been reached. That's bad news for the world in general; good news
for real estate owners.

Our seeming inability to get a handle on our breeding, manage our
resources properly, eliminate toxic and wasteful industries, and effect
other reforms stems in large part from three common myths that cloud
our perception of the Three Crises.

Myth #1: We've got lots of land available for development Those who
oppose rational dialogue on the problems of human population growth
often point to the planet's enormous expanses of sparsely populated lands
as proof that we've got almost unlimited room for expansion. What they
don't understand is that the problem isn't that we don't have enough land
for more human residences and industries: there is *plenty*.

However, we've reached the point where new development usually
means destroying some other, often irreplaceable, use for the land that

we also consider important, whether for agriculture, watershed, species survival, indigenous peoples, or just sanity-inducing open space. Almost every acre of arable land on the planet is either already being farmed, or has been paved or housed over. The no-win situation of having to sacrifice food, wildlife, commerce, watershed, or housing to get just one of those five uses—being forced to define a "highest and best use"—is emblematic of the Constraint Crisis.

From California's Central Valley to the suburbs of Shanghai, houses are replacing farms, even while the world's hunger grows. Geographic expansion of communities is increasingly undesirable, even in those few cases where it's still possible. (The Earth's inventory of real estate is actually shrinking in real terms, due to rising sea levels.) Witness the multilateral war on urban sprawl and corresponding focus on smart growth.

Meanwhile, much of the land that's left is losing its value, due to desertification, salinization, contamination, and other ills. Both of these dynamics intensify a Constraint Crisis that's primarily caused by population growth and poor land use.

Such dynamics make it even more obvious that the solution to the Three Crises of our aged new development-dependent economy is not to stop, or even slow, economic growth, but to develop as rapidly as possible in the opposite direction: restoration. The price tag for repairing our world will be huge, but that's not a problem as long as it's a profitable, rather than charitable, activity. (Fully restoring a Victorian house, e.g., usually adds more to the economic and the cultural capital of a community than does building a new house, and uses far fewer resources.)

Myth #2: The prime economic value of ecosystems is their products For centuries, our accountants have measured only the timber, fish, nuts, deer, etc., harvested from ecosystems. But all systems, human and natural, are based on both goods *and services:* Just as our human economy has switched its emphasis from manufacturing to services, so too must we start focusing more heavily on the service side of the natural economy. The services provided by Earth's natural systems far exceed the value of their products.

Ecosystem services include air and water purification, genetic resource development/storage, healthful aesthetics, and carbon sequestration (turning atmospheric carbon dioxide into oxygen and nongaseous forms of carbon, such as wood, in order to mitigate global climate change). Were these systems to go "on strike" for even a few weeks, all human civilizations would quickly collapse. As long as our accounting systems are blind to the services provided by ecosystems, we will under-value them and will be unable to "manage" them intelligently (they've actually been managing us, without our knowledge or appreciation).

Myth #3: Our oil wells are almost dry, our mines almost empty   Looking at this book's Table of Contents, we might wonder why the text focuses so much on the natural environment, when most visible forms of restoration deal with the built environment. If it struck you in this manner, you might be the victim of a third common myth, one that hamstrings the "green" strategic planning of many organizations.

Many people, including many government and business leaders, think that our impending natural resource shortages primarily involve antediluvian, non-renewable materials such as metals, phosphate, coal, natural gas, petroleum, and others. The reality is that we still have vast supplies of such materials, at least for current generations. Despite the fact that our oil consumption went from 57 million barrels per day in 1973 to 73 million in 2000 (and is expected to reach 110 million by 2020), known reserves have remained at about a trillion barrels, thanks to new discoveries.

The resources that are *actually* disappearing—at a catastrophically rapid pace—are the assets we've always assumed were inexhaustible, such as topsoil, fisheries, fresh water, clean air, and genetic wealth (e.g., crop diversity). In other words, we're losing those things that are pro-duced only by complex living systems. As Saudi oil minister Ahmed Yamani famously said, the Stone Age didn't end because we ran out of stones, but because humans came up with better ways of doing things. Likewise, our switch to renewable, nontoxic sources of energy, raw mate-rials, pharmaceuticals, and chemicals will derive from our desire for healthier, more enjoyable lives, not from exhausted mines or dry oil wells.

> Human history becomes more and more a race between education and catastrophe.
> —**H. G. Wells**, *The Outline of History*, 1920

That's not to say excessive use of these buried treasures isn't a problem. Overuse of non-renewable resources is directly linked to the Contamina-tion Crisis: our dying ecosystems; our epidemics of asthma, cancers, depression, weakened immune systems, and other signs of toxicity. Present-day species and ecosystems evolved in a world where much of our carbon and metal ores were out of circulation. The carbon had been sequestered by ecosystems, millions of years ago. Putting it back into circulation so suddenly has been equivalent to transporting wildlife to a different planet, or to a much earlier Earth: most plants and animals can't possibly adapt quickly enough.

The apologists of the new development realm aren't always ill informed, or even influenced by material gain; they're just removed from natural reality. Even those in the life sciences sometimes have little concern for wildlife. Some biologists join the "brown" industrialists in singing "don't worry, be happy," claiming that it's arrogance for humans to think we can kill the Earth, and that nature has nothing to worry about.

> The only thing that ever consoles man for the stupid things he does is the praise he always gives himself for doing them.
> —Oscar Wilde

They're right on the planetary scale, of course, but such cavalier attitudes dismiss as unimportant the irretrievable loss of thousands of ancient species. This biological, aesthetic, and spiritual tragedy would occur (and is occurring) long before we snuffed ourselves. (Humans would likely be among the last of the larger life forms to go, because we share the adaptable super-survivor traits of cockroaches, starlings, and Norway rats.)

Even if a miracle occurred and we made a rapid switch to renewable resources, the ecosystems we're expecting to churn out these renewables— fish, fresh water, timber, etc.—have already lost much of their ability to do so. Many of these systems can't passively recover on their own, even if vigorously protected, at least, not quickly enough to address the needs and impacts of our fast-growing human population. These systems need *active* restoration, at local, state, national, and global levels, which is a huge job. The largest, in fact.

Environmental and lifestyle-related illnesses (e.g., heart disease, asthma, cancers, and depression) are raging, as are plagues old and new (tuberculosis, malaria, AIDS, to name a few). The reduced ability of human immune systems and wildlife ecosystems to perform under the massive load of industrial and agricultural contaminants is no small factor in this situation.

The good news is that there are many lucrative opportunities in the recapture, re-use, and/or resequestration of the metals, gases, and elements that don't belong in our air, soil, or water in such vast quantities. If we want a return to pure, unlimited fresh water; wide, clean beaches;

rich, deep topsoil; and other vital needs, the only solution is to revive the living systems that produce them. Bringing such dying "resource manufacturing systems" (to use the language of the new-development realm) back to a state of high productivity is spawning new industries of immense proportions.

The Three Modes of the Development Life Cycle and Their Three Realms of Development

If you're looking primarily for specific opportunities to grow or revitalize your organization, business, or community, you may not be interested in spending a lot of time on hypothesis or theory. But developing a new organizational strategy or vision requires a deeper understanding of underlying dynamics than does grubbing for contracts. If that's part of your purpose, this chapter is for you. Here, then, are two hypotheses to which we'll refer throughout the rest of the book:

1. Economic development can be divided into three modes, corresponding to the natural cycles through which all life passes: Birth/youth (new development), maturity (maintenance/ conservation), and rebirth (restorative development) (Death, although a part of all natural systems, is neither mode nor cycle; it's just an ephemeral, transitory moment.)

2. When confined by inelastic borders, growing civilizations, especially those dependent on nonrenewable resources, move through a predictable progression of dominance among the modes: first new development, then maintenance/conservation, and finally restorative development. *We are experiencing one of these transitions of dominance right now.*

[handwritten margin note: Rebirth = Restorative Development]

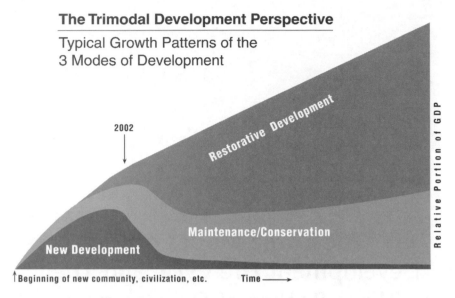

The Trimodal Development Perspective

Typical Growth Patterns of the
3 Modes of Development

Besides being more relevant than the traditional sequence of agrarian-industrial-service/information modes of economic development, this sequence of life cycle modes fosters easier and more effective development planning and decision making. Therefore, we will repeatedly reference this three-mode (or trimodal) development framework.

Assuming a civilization survives long enough—and earthquakes, volcanoes, tsunamis, wars, and other such phenomena don't destroy its creations—maintenance of its new development quickly becomes a substantial economic component of the economy. However, restorative development must arise, eventually achieving dominance, if a society is going to thrive in the long term. When everything is old and developed, only restoration can provide renewal, and the stability that comes with it.

Long-lived civilizations are those that make the transition to renewal before too many critical, irreplaceable assets have been destroyed. They recognize the limits of reasonable expansion, and restoration becomes the primary driver. In contrast, new development-oriented societies are always going "somewhere else," rather than becoming native to their land and looking forward to a long relationship with it. Like a poorly planned hike, new development-based economies exhaust their food and supplies (nonrenewable resources) and encounter unfordable rivers and unbridgeable chasms (insurmountable obstacles to growth).

One such obstacle: running out of virgin, uncontaminated real estate. Impossible, you say? Consider the city of Niagara Falls, New York. This economically depressed community has *zero* uncontaminated real estate available for development. It's not that their greenfields are off-limits; they *have* no greenfields. The city must either restore and redevelop previous industrial sites, or die. Restorative development is not one of the city's options. It's the only option. The situation in Niagara Falls is far from unique; many other industrialized (or formerly industrialized) cities are in the same boat, and many others are joining them.

Edmund Burke (1729–1797) said "All men that are ruined, are ruined on the side of their natural propensities" (Letter i. *On a Regicide Peace,* Vol. V). The observation applies to civilizations, and our new development-based civilization's propensities are to use nonrenewable resources and raw land. Our sprawl mentality focuses on more, rather than better; hardly wise in a finite world.

Countries that reach acute levels of resource depletion, pollution, infrastructure deterioration, etc., as most have today, usually find that merely strengthening the maintenance/conservation mode is insufficient. When maintenance of the built and/or natural environments is ignored or delayed too long, societies reach a crisis point that forks into two roads: inertia or mode reversal.

As we'll see in Chapter 3, inertia—getting stuck in new-development mode—leads to collapse from resource depletion, health problems, cultural rot, etc. It's sometimes a slow collapse, since belated restorative development can retard the descent.

The other fork, mode reversal, triggers a profusion of restorative development. Mode reversal means not just slowing depletion of resources by emphasizing maintenance and conservation, but switching to restorative development, which *increases* resources without taking up more room (even decreasing our ecological footprint in many cases), while generating goods, services, and profits.

New development isn't always the initial phase, of course. Many civilizations are birthed in the ashes of war, so their initial growth has a large restoration component. Similarly, a city or society based on new development needn't be old to find itself suddenly growing a hefty realm of restorative development. Examples would include many modern-day emerging nations (after wars for independence), Chicago after its Great Fire of 1871, and San Francisco after its 1906 earthquake/fire.

TRIMODAL RELEVANCE

> The Arkansas State Highway and Transportation Department (AHTD) used to award contracts for about 15 mi (24 km) of interstate highway work each year. This year, however, it expects to issue contracts worth about $415 million for 142 mi (228 km) of work—the latest in a series of what have been the largest contract awards in the department's history. The record-breaking contracts are part of the state's five-year Interstate Rehabilitation Program (IRP), which is designed to reconstruct 380 mi (611 km), or about 60% of the state's interstate highway system . . . [and] will cost approximately $950 million.
>
> —*Civil Engineering*, March 2002

For investors, business leaders, government planners, and nongovernmental organization (NGO) executives, the most relevant aspect of this trimodal development perspective is not how many modes the economy has, but which of the modes is entering a growth phase. The modes, regardless of their number, are never in stasis. Complex, healthy economies are, in fact, usually in a state of discomforting imbalance.

The relative energy of each mode tends to wax and wane with sporadic, unpredictable intensity, but in a predictable progression: a burst of new development, a mirrored bloom of maintenance, and then a long period of continuous restoration. Of course, entropic events, such as invasion, plague, or internal strife, sometimes hinder this natural progression.

One reason for the economic "passivity" of the maintenance/ conservation mode is that it's dependent on the other two modes for things to maintain and conserve. It's obvious enough that maintenance/ conservation industries need new development to expand the built environment and to threaten the natural environment. What's not so obvious is that the maintenance/conservation realm needs restorative development to bring decrepit parts of the built environment back to a useful condition, thus needing maintenance. It also needs restorative development to revive damaged portions of the natural environment to the point where they can be conserved.

All economies have at least some activity in all three modes at any given time. For the United States and other "First World" countries, the eighteenth and nineteenth centuries (the industrial revolution) were clearly dominated by new development, the twentieth century was dominated by new development and maintenance/conservation (those two modes were fairly balanced in overall expenditures in the latter half of the century), and restorative development is fast becoming dominant as the twenty-first century progresses. Lesser Developed Regions are basically on the same trajectory, but are often a decade or two out of phase with the More Developed Regions.

THE END OF THE BEGINNING

As new development loses momentum, it's fragmenting into a large collection of niche markets. Simultaneously, the currently fragmented industries of restorative development are moving in the opposite direction, coalescing into a whole.

New development is focusing on ever more remote geographic regions, primarily for the very wealthy and the very poor. Restorative developers are moving in exactly the opposite direction; for example, they are redeveloping, revitalizing, and repopulating the inner-city properties that new developers are "done with."

Like a pig in a python, the bulk of economic activity is moving inexorably from centuries of frenetic new development toward a frenzy of restoration. Even if we weren't living on a small world with a booming population (Constraint Crisis), the crumbling of our built environment (Corrosion Crisis) means the bulge can't help but move into restoration mode. If new development proceeded in a linear, gradual fashion, the transition to restoration wouldn't take us so much by surprise. But extended orgies of new development tend, as we've experienced, to be followed by economic ruin, pathological stagnation, or a sudden, healthful storm of restoration.

Without restoration, to continue the python analogy to its nasty denouement, it all turns to . . . well, you know (Contamination Crisis). Most of the energy produced by our national economic "digestive process" is wasted by a horribly inefficient industrial system (which also has a tremendous gas problem: witness global climate change), rather than being channeled into rebuilding the "body" of our civilization. We must either convert the "dead pig" of previous development into the "healthy python" of restored worlds—shedding our old ways in the process—or we're left with nothing but stinky excreta. Well, I've beaten that metaphorical snake quite to death, yes?

One caveat concerning the use of this trimodal development perspective: complex systems are messy, often to the point of enduring periods of chaos. The three modes described here are not meant to be viewed as a rigid linear progression. Indeed, there's a great deal of overlap.

Whatever predictive value the trimodal perspective might have goes little further than common sense: *of course* new development eventually declines and hits a point of decreasing returns on a planet of finite size; *of course* maintenance follows new construction; *of course* conservation kicks in when new development reduces natural areas to remnants; *of course* restoration follows age and damage.

Despite its obviousness, government policy and corporate strategy indicate that, amazingly enough, our organizations and institutions are only now starting to internalize this trimodal perspective.

Historical Perspectives on the Three Crises and on Restorative Development

> Every civilization when it loses its inner vision and its cleaner energy, falls into a new sort of sordidness; more vast and more stupendous than the savage old sort. An Augean stable of metallic filth.
> —**D. H. Lawrence** (1885–1930), *The Short Novels*, vol. 2, 1956

The Cambodian city of Angkor is so old that it died half a century before Columbus stumbled onto the "New World." It ruled the mighty Khmer Empire for more than twice as long as the United States has existed. Part of the reason for its power and long life was its location in one of the most resource-rich areas of Southeast Asia.

Experts long assumed the city was abandoned as a result of invasion, but archaeologists now realize, thanks in part to new data from satellite imagery, that its fall was probably due to the convergence of the Three Crises. Angkor's obsolete infrastructure and population growth, combined with its misuse of land and water resources, ruined the health of its ecosystems and probably the health of its citizens.

Angkor covered over a thousand square kilometers at its peak (Boston, by comparison, is about 67 square kilometers). Its growth resulted in massive deforestation and horrendous pollution of waterways (core samples from canal bottoms show them to have been the primary

recipient of household wastes and garbage). Area wetlands were disrupted by a latticework of roads and canals.

The 600 buildings uncovered so far reveal a pattern of low-density
development. In modern vernacular, the city sprawled itself to death.
Angkor's economy, culture, and armies were defeated by the same "three
horsemen" of new development's apocalypse that threaten us today: the
Constraint Crisis, the Corrosion Crisis, and the Contamination Crisis (in
Angkor's case, the contamination was primarily organic, such as fecal).

We like to think that such a fate couldn't happen to us, but isn't it
likely the citizens of Angkor were afflicted with similar hubris? They
enjoyed "king of the hill" status far longer than we have. The fact is,
human nature hasn't changed much, if at all; we're responding similarly
to similar situations and stimuli. New development almost always
remains on the throne too long, because humans (especially our institutions) react primarily to present crises—not future crises—no matter how
certain the latter may be.

The relevant lessons of Angkor don't end in the past, however. The
area around Tonle Sap, the largest lake in the area, has always been the
territory's primary economic engine, due to its fish harvests, productive
wetlands and forests, and rich soil. A millennium ago, Angkor's excessive new development almost killed the Tonle Sap ecosystem, shutting
off its flow of resources. Thanks to the resulting demise of Angkor, the
Tonle Sap wetlands were able to restore themselves in the subsequent
centuries. As a result, Tonle Sap eventually resumed its role as the economic core of the region. Once again, though, it's on the verge of collapse, for all the same reasons.

For the first time, economic and ecological data spanning over a
thousand years are being analyzed from a trimodal perspective. The
Mekong River Commission, a hybrid research and management entity
created in 1995 by the governments of Cambodia, Laos, Vietnam, and
Thailand, is performing this pioneering work.

The committee members believe that a better understanding of this
progression of overextended new development, lack of conservation,
environmental collapse, socioeconomic ruin, and eventual restoration
will help them avert a repeat performance. Rather than allowing a repeat
of the reflexive, natural, slow restoration that follows apocalypse, they
hope to make this period of restoration conscious, planned, and rapid.

The same patterns being revealed in ancient Angkor's development
are also showing up in recent research into the Maya, the Anasazi, the

Easter Islanders, and many other "mysteriously disappeared" civilizations: over-extended new development, followed by a failure to restore.

BACK TO THE WEST

> In the time of the Trojan wars . . . the land of Mycenae was in good
> condition. But now the opposite is the case . . . the land of Mycenae has
> become . . . dry and barren. Now the same process that has taken place in
> this small district must be supposed to be going on over whole countries
> and on a large scale.
> —**Aristotle** (384–322 B.C.), *Meteorologica*, Book 1, Chapter 14

Egypt, Rome, and Greece provide the best-documented series of declines and rebirths (in western civilization) for the study of restoration economies, and their cycles continue to this day. All three are busily restoring their heritage sites, both for their cultural value and their importance to the tourism industry. Egypt recently spent many years (on and off) restoring the Great Pyramid, the largest of the three Giza Pyramids, built as King Cheops' tomb about 4,500 years ago. Rome invested eight years in restoring the 1,500-year-old Coliseum, where classical Greek tragedies are now performed rather than the more traditional—but somewhat less socially acceptable—gladiatorial combat. And Greece is restoring the Parthenon. These are representative of the myriad restoration projects that, from ancient monuments to famous palaces to old mills, are occurring across the planet.

If restorative development is the only path to long-lived economic growth (other than constant conquest and pillaging of other societies), we must be able to look to the historical records of the greatest civilizations for documentation of restorative dynamics and characteristics, right? Possibly, but not likely.

The problem is that not many hard facts exist on ancient economies. Future research and analysis will likely provide more statistics related to the natural economic progression of new development, maintenance/conservation, and restorative development. For now, we largely have to rely on that least rigorous of tools, common sense, to support the legitimacy of the trimodal development perspective: new development, maintenance/conservation, and restorative development. What other modes could there be?

That each of the three modes of development cyclically enjoys star billing as the dominant mode is also a no-brainer. How else to grow a new civilization but by emphasizing new development, which creates a need for maintenance/conservation? Both of these modes, though, culminate in a need to renew the built assets when they reach the end of their useful life, and to restore the natural assets when they can no longer withstand humankind's impact without assistance.

> During the early Empire revenues were so abundant that the state was able to undertake a massive public works program. Augustus repaired all the roads of Italy and Rome, restored the temples and built many new ones, and built many aqueducts, baths and other public buildings. Tiberius, however, cut back on the . . . program and hoarded large sums of cash. This led to a financial crisis in 33 A.D. in which there was a severe shortage of money.
> —**M. K. Thornton** and **R. L. Thornton**, "The Financial Crisis of A.D. 33: A Keynesian Depression?" *Journal of Economic History*, 1990

We know that most long-lived civilizations suffered degradation and destruction of their natural and built environments, often due to factors we like to believe are unique to our modern times. Historically, these problems usually stimulated calls for conservation and restoration that echo today's Constraint, Corrosion, and Contamination Crises. Here are just a few examples:

- Socrates, Plato, and Aristotle all criticized their own (and earlier) generations for destroying the formerly beautiful landscapes and forests of Greece, and called for their restoration. The stark, stony landscape that tourists assume is Greece's natural, picturesque condition is actually the result of human-induced erosion (from deforestation and agriculture) during four seperate episodes of unsustainable new development: around 2500 B.C., 350-50 B.C., A.D. 950–1450, and modern times. Each of the earlier episodes was followed by a period of natural soil restoration due to societal collapse (and resulting disuse).
- Around 1758 B.C., the King of Babylonia, Hammurabi, enjoyed widespread public praise—and suffered attacks from powerful private development interests—for establishing extensive systems of public parks and forests.
- Archeologists Thorkild Jacobsen and Robert Adams have discovered evidence that the collapse of the Sumerian civilization—the world's first large agricultural society—was due to the salinization of its soils via irrigation. It took millennia to naturally restore the farmland. (Soil salinization is occurring again worldwide, and we can't afford to wait a thousand years for passive restoration.)

- Marcus Cicero (106–43 B.C.) issued a call that can be heard on Capitol Hill today: "The . . . budget must be balanced. The . . . treasury should be filled. Government indebtedness must be reduced. The arrogance of the authorities must be moderated and controlled. The people should learn to work again, instead of living off the public dole." Cicero called for revitalizing Rome's lethargic, lead-poisoned culture; restoring its crumbling infrastructure; and renewing its tired, new development-based (via conquest) economy.
- Emperor Majorian issued an edict in A.D. 458 to protect Rome's old buildings from demolition.
- In 45 B.C., Julius Caesar, sick of the dust, noise, and congestion of Roman streets, banned all chariots and wheeled transportation during daylight hours, as part of his effort to restore the quality of urban life.
- Two millennia later, scientists exploring Roman silver and lead mines (operated from 20 B.C. to A.D. 80) in Extremadura, Spain, reported, "There is as much as 20,000 ppm (2.0%) lead, 7000 ppm (0.7%) zinc, and 5000 ppm (0.5%) arsenic in the dump soils, much higher than . . . outside the mining area . . . [M]etals continue to be transported into the local drainage systems."[1]

Such historical examples of toxic, excessive, and/or poorly planned new development (and related restoration efforts) are legion. Of course, many Asian cities are far older than anything in the West, and have even longer data tails from which to glean insight into the trimodal development development "cycle."

Anthropogenic ecological collapses are obviously nothing new. What *is* new is the scale of the damage. Unlike Rome or Angkor, modern contamination sites and ecosystem collapses often are not limited to clearly defined areas. Compared to its condition three centuries ago, virtually our entire planet could be considered a brownfield. "Wilderness areas" are now those that are *less* contaminated, *less* radioactive, or *less* disrupted than urban and industrial areas; forget pristine. As a result, remediation and ecological restoration firms now enjoy a very broad range of expansion opportunities.

[1]Robert G. Schmidt, Cathy M. Ager, and Juan Gil Montes, adapted from poster presented at Metals in Antiquity Symposium, revised February 2001.

An Unprecedented Moment in Time

> . . . [W]e're the first generation with tools to understand the changes in the
> earth's system caused by human activity, and the last with the opportunity
> to influence the course of many of the changes now under way.
> —**Peter Vitousek**, Stanford University biologist, quoted by Gretchen C. Daily and
> Katherine Ellison, *The New Economy of Nature*, 2002

I offer the historical material of this chapter to provide perspective. We mustn't forget that the Three Global Crises in general, and restoration in particular, are nothing new.

The Corrosion Crisis has obviously been striking specific aspects of our built environment for millennia. Many societies have encountered the Constraint Crisis whenever their increasing population collided with a lack of new geographic frontiers. As with Rome, more than a few early European and Asian city-states went through their own Contamination Crises.

Even if we had copious hard data, these earlier examples, despite some similarities to our present situations, probably wouldn't offer us much insight or policy guidance, because OUR Restoration Economy is very different from any in Earth's history. Our Restoration Economy is a macrophenomenon that has been centuries (actually millennia) in the making. Ours is the first Restoration Economy that will be global, rather than national or regional, in scale:

- This is the first time in history that the planet has been mostly developed, rather than mostly wilderness, pasture, and small-scale agriculture.
- This is the first time in history that the vast majority of our structures has been in a deteriorated state (thanks in part to the nineteenth and twentieth centuries' sudden proliferation of built environment.)
- This might be the first time since the Yucatan meteorite strike 65 million years ago that species have been disappearing at such a high rate, and that ecosystems have been collapsing worldwide.
- This is the first Restoration Economy to occur subsequent to a population increase of four billion in just one century, after having taken hundreds of millennia to reach half that.
- This is the first Restoration Economy to occur in a world with tightly connected societies and economies, thanks to telephones, TV, airlines, the Internet, satellites, express freight, and international lending.

- This is the first Restoration Economy equipped with computers and biotechnology, making it easier (in theory) to functionally integrate our built, natural, economic, and personal environments.
- This is the first Restoration Economy to occur as we're just beginning to understand the complex adaptive systems that we are, and within which we co-evolve.

Bottom line: we humans are at a unique moment in our development. Throughout previous millennia, we frequently have called upon our individual and societal reserves to meet the challenge of restoring cities, and even entire countries. But never before have we been presented with the challenge of restoring our entire world, both built and natural.

Why Our Trillion-Dollar-Plus
Restoration Economy
Has Been Kept a Secret

It's a truism in our industry that over 50 percent of our budgets go to restoration. It's probably been that way since the early nineties, but no one has formally measured it.
—**Ed Sullivan**, Editor of *Building & Operations Management* magazine (conversation via phone with author, 2000)

Despite restorative development's ubiquity and impressive economic power, the fundamental transition from new development to restorative development has taken place almost entirely unnoticed. The presence of an invisible, trillion-dollar-plus sector of the world economy is especially incredible when we consider how many people earn their living churning out economic analyses. But this is, in fact, the situation.

This is not to say that the eight restorative industries haven't individually caught media attention on occasion, or that none of them is measured. Some, such as disaster/war reconstruction, and historic restoration, create dramatic visuals and human interest stories, and are therefore media darlings. Others, such as brownfields remediation, watershed restoration, and fisheries revitalization, are ignored in many regions but are frequently in the headlines in places with contamination, water, or fishing industry problems.

So, none of these component industries is totally invisible; some are *very* visible. But, even if all of these "parts" appeared on the evening news constantly, it's likely that the whole they create would remain as it is: largely invisible. Why? Because we don't perceive economic development from a lifecycle point of view. If we thought in terms of new development, maintenance/conservation, and restorative development, we'd instantly recognize that these eight restorative industries are clearly related to each other. We'd take our attention off of how different a highway is from a historic house, and focus instead on the dynamic: are we building it, maintaining it, or restoring it?

As a businessman, I imagine fellow businesspeople and other readers are asking right about now: So what? Who needs to see this whole, this so-called "realm of restorative development"? The answer is, leaders and investors; those who need to see its huge threats and opportunities sooner than their competitors. This chapter is designed to help readers begin to develop that perception.

THE GLOBAL RESTORATION ECONOMY

Not all societies launch restorative periods at the same point. While one country might not focus on restoration until its future is dark and gloomy, another might be more forward-looking, pulling in the reins on new development before its quality of life deteriorates to crisis levels.

So, how we can speak of a global, or even a national, Restoration Economy, when cities, states, and countries are all of different ages, have their own economic cycles, and display very different characters? The main factor that qualifies this moment as the starting point of a global Restoration Economy was described in Chapter 2: each of the three crises that are driving the growth of restoration—the Constraint Crisis, the Corrosion Crisis, and the Contamination Crisis—is truly global. At least one of the three crises exists in every community and ecosystem on the planet, regardless of size, age, or remoteness. In most cases, all three crises are rampant. If the need is global, the solution—restorative development—must also be global.

Restoration of historical structures has been a sizeable part of Europe's economy for ages, but it grew tremendously in the second half of the twentieth century. European restoration industries got a "great" boost from World War II, which, thanks to air power, destroyed far more infrastructure and buildings than had World War I. Europe's built environment is generally much older than that of the United States, so we shouldn't be surprised that this portion of its restorative development realm is better recognized there than in the United States.

For example, take a look at the website of Steensen & Varming (steensenvarming.com), a medium-sized consulting engineering firm in Copenhagen. At the time of this writing, it profiles almost four dozen restoration projects that the firm is working on simultaneously.

Or consider Edinburgh, Scotland, which is wall-to-wall restoration. Restoration activity is not limited to Scotland's ancient, picturesque castles and churches, either. A sign across from my hotel announces a revitalization of the retail corridor extending from the beautiful new convention center to the beginning of the "Royal Mile." The project also encourages local businesses to restore their centuries-old storefronts.

Europe tends to be ahead of the United States in the heritage and infrastructure restoration industries. When it comes to ecosystems, fisheries, brownfields, and most other industries of restoration, however, they seem to be lagging behind the United States. Individual U.S. projects tend to be larger on average than those in Europe, but that's not to say Europe has no big projects: the London Underground, for example, is being rehabilitated to the tune of $21 billion.

Restoration opportunities in China, Russia, and the not-so-newly independent states seem endless, despite the huge amount of new development surrounding the Chinese boom cities. Two decades of tight (or nonexistent) maintenance budgets in the former Soviet Union have left most infrastructure and buildings—historic and modern—in dire straits. Now, restoration is the only alternative to complete dysfunctionality. The recently-announced $3.1 billion rehabilitation/restructuring of Russia's rail system is just one example. For most communist countries, the last half of the twentieth century was typified by some of the most haphazard, wasteful industrial growth on the planet. It left their natural environment, and their citizens' health, in horrifying condition.

A STRANGELY SILENT REVOLUTION: WE DON'T TALK MUCH ABOUT RESTORATION BECAUSE WE'RE STILL DEVELOPING THE LANGUAGE

How did an elephant like the realm of restorative development sneak up on us? How could such a huge economic activity be so surreptitious, going largely unreported and uncelebrated? How did this happen without much public debate, and with a minimum of corporate bragging? Why don't we even know *when* restoration started "taking over"?

For centuries, our assumption has been that new development is the primary, almost the sole source of all wealth and progress. This long-standing worship of new development has blinded us to restorative development. We've built an entire belief system around new development, which has strongly influenced both our thought and our speech. This, in turn, created two factors that drape the Restoration Economy in a cloak of invisibility:

- each of the eight giant industries of restorative development has its own terminology and its own definition of restoration, as well as its own unique cycles, making the industries difficult to recognize and aggregate as a whole; and,
- restorative activities have no standardized classification language, so they appear almost anywhere in budgets and reports.

Restorative development hides behind a plethora of names, including: *reconstruction, modernization, rebuilding, replacement, capital improvement, refurbishment, reintroduction/return/repopulation/reestablishment/ recolonization (species and cultures), renewal, reuse, rehabilitation, regeneration, redevelopment, enhancement, alteration, greening, revitalization, retrofit, redesign, recovery, remanufacturing, reindustrialization, conversion, reclamation, revamping, revegetation,* and *remediation.*

This isn't just a list of synonyms I pulled out of a thesaurus: All are used as headings in corporate, NGO, and government reports describing restorative development. Restoration Economy terms are popping up across the entire spectrum of industrial activities. There are also informal terms such as *rebound, comeback, resurgence, re-creation, creation* (as in creation of wetlands, a form of ecosystem restoration), *revamp, extensive remodeling, economic rebirth, renaissance, complete overhaul, transformation, cleanup,* and *total makeover,* as well as industry-specific terms like *reforestation, mitigation,* and *infill.*

New development and maintenance—even combined—have less than a quarter as many synonyms. Why so many ways to say "restoration"? Linguists say the presence of numerous related appellations indicates a concept's true importance to a culture.

You'll notice that many of these synonyms begin with "re." "Re" will likely be the dominant prefix of the twenty-first century. The green movement has its "reduce, recycle, reuse," which might have helped spawn the profusion of "re's" listed above. One hundred percent reuse of resources is now the pinnacle goal in many industries, and it's usually far more profitable and ecologically sound than consumer-based recycling. Even organizations are "re" naming themselves with "re" names, such as the well-established Washington D.C. area charity "Christmas in April," which recently changed its name to "Rebuilding Together." We've finally realized that everything on our planet is (or must be) reused and revitalized: land, buildings, water, air, etc.

The people who do restoration are variously known as restorers, restorationists, restorators, preservers, preservationists, conservers, conservators, rehabilitators, rebuilders, developers, conservationists, and a host of other monikers. When the day comes that they unite under one descriptor (preferably restorationists, which, besides being more accurate, has an heroic timbre), all will derive great mutual benefit from the public's perception of them as a huge, dynamic, and oh-so-vital worldwide professional community. It's difficult to appreciate, honor, or reward those whom one can't talk about.

The resolution of this confusion can occur surprisingly fast, because a feedback loop is formed: Our vocabulary is shaped by our mental constructs, and our mental constructs are shaped by our vocabulary. The clearer our vocabulary becomes, the clearer our thinking becomes, which further clarifies our vocabulary, and so on.

Terminology is deadly boring for most people, so we won't belabor the point. Some terms apply to both new development *and* restorative development, in some cases even having opposite meanings. "Reclamation" to the U.S. Bureau of Reclamation, has long meant turning ecosystems into farmland. This "eminent domain"-style usage assumes that the *raison d'être* of all wild land is to serve humans, and that—by turning a forest into a farm—we are "reclaiming" what is ours. The forests' purification of our air and water—not to mention its production of wildlife and beauty—apparently isn't enough service to humanity already.

Now that restorative development is becoming the dominant paradigm, however, "reclamation" more commonly refers to the opposite: turning land damaged by industry or agriculture back into healthy, natural ecosystems. Further clouding our perception is that restoration can be partial, thorough, ongoing, or sporadic. The "reclamation" of industrial land could thus mean turning it back into the farmland it was before the factory moved in, or all the way back to the forest that was there before the farm.

CONFUSING MAINTENANCE WITH RESTORATION

> While sustainable new buildings often catch most of the limelight, far more
> square footage is renovated than built new in the U.S. each year. What about
> sustainable renovation? SWA [Steven Winter Associates] is exploring that
> issue in its work on the Brooklyn Children's Museum in New York, which is
> undergoing a major renovation and expansion.
> —*WinterGreen* newsletter, www.swinter.com, Vol. 3, Issue 10, April 2002

"Remodeling" is another term with multiple meanings. Here, confusion arises from the varying degrees of restoration that are possible. Remodeling is usually considered a form of maintenance, but at what point does an extensive remodeling enter the realm of restoration? Residential remodeling alone is a $180-billion-per-year industry—just in the United States—so properly defining it is hardly unimportant. Despite all of our new developments and sprawl, 85 percent of house sales in the United States are previously owned homes, over 550,000 of which are considered historic (over 50 years of age, very young by European standards).

Terminology issues may seem academic, but they have suddenly become crucial to the economic growth of industries and communities. Restorative development's vocabulary and measurement techniques are somewhat more sophisticated for the commercial (nonresidential) building industry. Commercial builders track renovation work separately from remodeling and other forms of maintenance, so they know that restoration brought them $128 billion in 2000 (United States only). This is up from $87.4 billion just five years earlier, a growth rate of some $10 billion per year. Hammering it home: just the annual amount of *increase* in this small sub-sub-sector of restorative development—and only the United States' portion at that—is larger than the GDP of over 100 countries.

Another form of (partial) restoration that gets confused with maintenance is modernization, such as retrofitting structures with more up-to-date components. As with renovation, it's sometimes just the extent of the project that determines whether it's labeled "maintenance" or "restoration." Retrofits are often extremely profitable for the contractor, especially the kinds that take owners by surprise. For example, when an area experiences an earthquake for the first time in recorded history, tall buildings and bridges are often required to get seismic retrofits.

More commonly, retrofits are simply the inevitable result of progress, such as the way our entire industrial complex has been getting upgraded with toxin and/or waste reducing technologies and processes. This could be considered a form of slow, "organic" restoration, similar to the way each component of animal bodies and ecosystems is constantly rebuilt, revitalized, or replaced.

Maintenance and restoration share the dynamic of returning assets to a healthier condition. One key difference is that most maintenance is regular and only takes the asset back a few increments of functionality or appearance, whereas restoration is much more widely spaced (chronologically). Restoration is more systemic, goes deeper, and tends to add new functionality, or make a far more significant improvement to existing functions. Another big difference is budgetary: maintenance is almost always budgeted for, but restoration usually involves special capital campaigns. When maintenance isn't properly budgeted, so-called deferred maintenance, restorative activity increases.

Without clear terminology, the eight industries of restorative development will have an exceedingly difficult time resolving their conflicts with each other. For instance, switching a farm from growing tobacco to growing cotton might contribute to the restoration of a society wishing to decrease its use of addictive, carcinogenic drugs, but it's certainly not farm restoration. Cotton is less profitable and more damaging to the land than tobacco. Switching instead to raspberries might be both more profitable and less damaging to the land, but it's still not farm restoration, only a change for the better. Switching to organic raspberries . . . now *that* might be restorative. All restoration is improvement, but not all improvement is restoration.

RETURNING TO THE REAL

> How do we know a society isn't sustainable? When its quality of life is decreasing.
> —**Joel S. Hirschhorn,** Ph.D., National Governors Association (lecture at George Washington University, Washington D.C., 2002)

Of course, most of the world's highly profitable businesses never left the physical realm of food, energy, medicine, travel, construction, and manufacturing. Our euphoria with the initial flowering of the "Information Economy" caused us to take the name too literally. Anyone who has studied Maslow's "hierachy of needs" knows that hunger, thirst, discomfort, danger, and disease tend to quickly reshuffle our priorities.

Most of the easily developable world is already developed, and most of the harder-to-develop world is already depleted or damaged. Hardly any territory is "virgin." This includes the poles, which are already radioactive, strewn with garbage, and more industrialized than most people realize. Our search for untouched frontiers, which is as old as humankind itself, has hit the point of diminishing returns . . . often to the point of crisis. Crises reshuffle our priorities, refocusing both individuals and society on "the real."

In the wake of the 2000–2001 dot-com implosion, Michael E. Porter's article in the *Harvard Business Review* said, "The creation of true economic value once again becomes the final arbiter of success."[1] It's a lot easier to strategize—and to execute—when one's business is based on real needs.

After nearly a decade of books and magazine articles (not to mention IPOs) promising vast opportunities in the "New Economy," most of them based either on new ways of connecting things, or on new ways of accessing information, most organizations are hungry to sink their teeth into a solid, *tangible* new frontier of growth. Few of us need to be reminded that the total cumulative profit earned by the 4,200 Nasdaq-listed firms between September 1995 and September 2001 was exactly zero.

> The next phase in tech is emerging—one that will be deeper, more complex and more thrilling, say venture capitalists, entrepreneurs, and CEO's in tech. . . . The next phase will mix the Internet with new and complex software, breakthrough discoveries in areas such as materials science and lasers, and *deep integration of technology with the real, nuts-and-bolts world* [emphasis added].
> —**Kevin Maney**, "Dot-Com Carnage Opens Door to Brighter Future,"
> *USA Today*, June 22, 2000

Even those few winners of the Internet revolution are finding their best opportunities in the "realm of the real." The November 2000 issue of *Wired* provided its web-frenzied readers with a reality check, reminding them that ". . . a handful of oil companies raked in more than a quarter of a trillion dollars in the U.S. last year, a take unmatched by the B2B and B2C markets combined."

Technology is probably the most untapped aspect of the Restoration Economy: For the most part, the industries of restorative development are adaptively using the tools of new development. Sometimes those tools serve the purpose well, but as restorative development becomes more sophisticated, it needs software, monitoring tools, field imple-

[1] Michael E. Porter, "Strategy and the Internet," *Harvard Business Review*, March 2001.

ments, chemicals, and other technologies designed specifically for the task of restoration.

Petroleum will continue to be fantastically profitable for a while longer, but even the oil companies acknowledge that this cash cow's udder is shriveling: they are the largest investors in alternative energy technologies, such as fuel cells, photovoltaics, wind, and hydrogen production.

> While science searched for technological solutions, what really stymied most
> of the world was frighteningly basic.
>   —**Laurie Garrett**, *Betrayal of Trust: The Collapse of Global Public Health,* 2000

But the petroleum firms are also focusing on nonenergy essentials, many of which are already harder to obtain than oil. Clean, fresh water is one of them. Water quality is often the issue that gets the most attention, which isn't surprising, given that impure water is the world's number one killer. But ask the mayors and public works directors of many growing metropolises, and they'll tell you water *quantity* is their top challenge for the coming decades.

The notorious takeover artist of the '80s, oilman T. Boone Pickens, purchased the water rights to 150,000 acres in Texas, hoping to make a killing selling the water to increasingly desperate cities like Dallas and San Antonio (which is expecting to run out of water by 2010). "We've got water, and they need it. Of all the deals I've done, this one is the most clear-cut," Pickens said in the October 16, 2000, issue of *Forbes.* Savvy investors should contemplate those words: the transition to a Restoration Economy is manna from heaven for both investors and business leaders, thanks to its targeting of "real" markets that won't—*can't*—go away, no matter what. Even if this politically dicey deal doesn't pay off for Pickens, he has certainly set his sights in the right direction.

Whether putting public water in the hands of for-profit firms is a good idea is an issue deserving extensive public debate, but one thing's clear: cheap water is the enemy of clean and abundant water. The price we pay for it must go up, way up, before more efficient, more healthful water systems can be effectively financed.

The dark night of impending doom from overdevelopment is waning, and the sun of restoration is rising. New development is withering, maintenance/conservation is insufficient, sustainable development (a hypothetical blend of new development and conservation) is struggling for an identity—and restorative development is wildly proliferating. Where does your organization's path fit into this scenario?

Part Two

The Four Growth Industries Restoring Our Natural Environment: Ecosystems, Watersheds, Fisheries, and Farms

Despite Part One's discussion of theory, history and crises, readers who aren't economists, historians, or survivalists needn't worry: *The Restoration Economy* is not an apocalyptic catalog. Nor is it an academic analysis of the three modes of development. It's an introduction to the crises that are creating the twenty-first century's greatest growth frontier, and a business guide to most dynamic mode: restorative development.

The Restoration Economy's eight restorative industries are divided into two groups, corresponding to the two environments that are being restored: natural and built. None of these industries is purely natural or purely built. For instance, farms primarily affect, and are affected by, the natural environment, but most have significant buildings and infrastructure. Likewise, placing the "brownfields" industry under the "built environment" category reflects its industrial basis (with factory sites, ports, dumps, and other human artifacts being the usual restoration target), but many of these cleanup sites are or will soon again be living ecosystems, with few—if any—structures.

Let's deal first with the four industries restoring the natural environment. I've defined them according to a rather economically driven taxonomy: the restoration of water production, fishing, and farming, plus one for all other types of ecosystems. This productivity-based perception is the most natural from the point of view of restorative *development.*

Throwing "all other ecosystems" together—as I have in the "ecosystem restoration industry" of Chapter 5—is not meant to imply that they are economically less important. These systems directly support fisheries, farms, and watersheds by producing clean air, clean water, and biodiversity. Without these functions, most living systems would soon die.

Many of the ecosystems discussed in Chapters 5, 6, and 7 are located in parks and other protected areas (national, local, and private). They provide recreation-based economic value, which can be both a blessing and a curse for the wildlife.

For example, Smoky Mountain National Park is the most popular (in terms of number of visitors) and the most biologically diverse of the U.S. national parks. In addition to the impact of hikers, campers, and drivers (and the infrastructure that serves them), it must contend with the worst air pollution of our national parks. It has more "dangerous smog" alerts than most large cities, and its rain is strongly acid. The restoration challenge here is more difficult because much of the air pollution is coming from coal-burning power plants hundreds of miles away.

All ecosystems are affected, often catastrophically, by human activities in the built and natural environment around them (even from a great distance). So, please don't let the chapter structure of this book compartmentalize your thinking about each restorative industry.

All four "natural" restorative industries share some dynamics, such as:

- restoring function(s) to the dysfunctional
- returning something to a previous state
- revitalizing—even resurrecting—the dead and dying
- rehabilitating the damaged or poisoned

Not every project meets all of these criteria, of course, but one dynamic *is* shared by all: when properly designed and executed, every restoration project will add value without producing a corresponding loss of value or health elsewhere. That is a defining difference between restorative development and new development.

Restoring Our Ecosystems: Lakes, Wetlands, Prairies, Shores, and Others

The wounds we have inflicted on the Earth can be healed . . . But if it is to be done, it must be done now. Otherwise, it may never be done at all.
—Jonathon Porritt, *Save the Earth*, 1991

"Isn't this an incredible woodland?" asked Sue Welles, Land Preservation Coordinator of the Delaware Nature Society. She was addressing Bob Oertel, who was reporting on the nature society's restoration success story in the September/October 2001 issue of *Land and Water* magazine, a leading publication for major U.S. landowners, engineers, and contractors. Just five years earlier, this gorgeous expanse of white and red oaks, tulip poplar, red maple, and white ash—most 10 to 15 feet tall—had been an unsightly 60-acre abandoned farm, largely devoid of wildlife.

In an article entitled "Model Reforestation Project," Welles continued: "This is a favorite nesting area for goldfinches, mockingbirds, indigo buntings, and the yellow-breasted chat. The chat is very uncommon for us here in Delaware. What we've seen is that there are birds here all year around, not just in the nesting season. Naturally, we're excited that the birds like our plantings." The society is also managing the reforested fields for the return of mammal, reptile, amphibian, and insect species, as well as encouraging natural seed-in of native pioneer tree species, such as wild black cherry.

From a thick catalog of degraded sites awaiting rescue, the society intelligently chose one located within the 815-acre Middle Run Natural Area Park. This location protected the restored area while giving the conserved park ecosystems room to expand. "Our main thrust is to increase the forest interior habitat, especially for neotropical migratory birds that nest in North America. . . . Secondly, we are increasing the forested buffer area along Middle Run Creek to improve the quality of its water. Thirdly, our aim is to develop cost-effective reforestation techniques that can be used by other individuals and groups," Welles continued.

The society's concern with increasing *interior* forest space demonstrates an understanding of ecosystem dynamics. A major enemy of indigenous bird species on the Atlantic coast is the brown-headed cowbird, which parasitically lays its eggs in the nests of other species; its chicks are larger and shove the mother's own babies out of the nest. But this mostly happens along the edges of forests, since cowbirds generally don't penetrate more than 300 feet into woodlands.

A high percentage of perceived U.S. "forests" are just roadside "beauty strips" masking hideous clear-cuts. This strategy was designed by the U.S. Forest Service (USFS) to help Americans maintain the comforting illusion that such irresponsible practices happen only in "primitive," lesser-developed nations. (It's not the USFS's fault: the agency was misnamed. It is under the aegis of the Department of Agriculture, which serves food and lumber companies, so the job of the USFS is to maximize logging. Trees are just another crop. It's *never* been the USFS's mission to protect forest ecosystems, only to expand commercial tree farms. Confusing a tree farm with a forest is like confusing a field of bioengineered, artificially stimulated corn with a meadow of wildflowers.)

THE BROWN-HEADED COWBIRD: PROBABLY
OUR MOST HATED *NATIVE* SONGBIRD

It's native to North America but an alien invader to the East Coast, having begun moving east from the Great Plains in the mid-nineteenth century (probably due to pioneer-induced habitat changes). Cowbird populations didn't explode until the 1950s and 1960s, but they have already seriously depleted 150 species of native eastern songbirds.

The pervasiveness of beauty strips makes for a dearth of nesting sites more than 300 feet from a road, development, pasture, or farm, so cowbirds gain access to the nests of most other songbirds. Even in a relatively simple restoration like Welles' Delaware project, that bit of research into species behavior makes a huge difference in biological outcomes. Such knowledge helps distinguish simple tree planting from forest restoration.

The Delaware Nature Society is just one of literally thousands of private nature groups around the world for whom restoration has recently become a key strategy. With each passing day, there are fewer opportunities to conserve pristine ecosystems, but unlimited opportunities to restore.

THE SCOPE OF THE ECOSYSTEM RESTORATION INDUSTRY

> **Restoration:** The return of an ecosystem to a close approximation of its condition prior to disturbance.
> —**National Research Council** [U.S.], "Restoration of Aquatic Ecosystems," 1992

The title of this chapter has "and others" at the end of it because this restoration industry aggregates all of the "less-commercial" ecosystems: those that don't "manufacture" commercially harvested water, vegetables, livestock, or fish. That's a terrible definition, because all ecosystems have tremendous—though not always obvious—economic value. What's more, many of the ecosystems in this chapter do create significant revenue, mostly from recreational usage, such as boating, hunting, and camping. Basically, this chapter catches all the ecosystems missed by the following three chapters. I present it first, because the principles of ecosystem restoration, some of which you'll learn here, apply equally to the restoration of watersheds, fisheries, and agricultural properties.

There is tremendous overlap surrounding this category, because most land, including farmland, is part of a watershed—including farms—and most bodies of water are related to a fishery. The most flagrant overlap is lakes, most of which are integral to a watershed. Lakes are discussed in this chapter because restoring them is often a discrete project due to their heavy residential development and recreational use. But that's more a function of how this book is structured: There's no reason why lakes shouldn't be part of a watershed restoration project, and many reasons why they should be.

Three common types of ecological restoration included in this industry are as follows:

- **Habitat restoration** This accounts for the vast majority of ecosystem-related restoration activity. One of the key challenges is to accurately establish the historical reference point for an ecosystem. (The first book on this subject, *The Historical Ecology Handbook: A Restorationist's Guide to Reference Ecosystems*, was just published in 2001 [see Restoration Readings].) "That's the holy grail of restoration—to know what habitats and species assemblages belong where, and what processes contribute to producing them," said Peter Baye, a U.S. Fish and Wildlife Service botanist. He was quoted in an article entitled "Resurrection" in the June 2, 2001, issue of the excellent U.K. weekly *New Scientist*. It profiled the ecosystem restoration efforts of the San Francisco Estuary Institute (SFEI), touted as "a leader in the worldwide trend toward deeper, more thorough use of historical sources in habitat restoration." SFEI's projects show how small remnant ecosystems, such as vernal pools, provide genetic resources for much larger restoration projects surrounding them.

- **Species reintroduction** In the United States, many states have active or proposed programs to restore locally extinct species, such as elk (Missouri, Kentucky, Arkansas, Tennessee, and Virginia), fishers (eight states and three Canadian provinces), grizzly bear (Montana and Idaho . . . but dropped by Bush administration), black-footed ferret (South Dakota), and bison. That's just a few of the mammals. Bald eagles, ospreys, and peregrine falcons have all been delisted as endangered species (U.S.) thanks both to the DDT ban, and to active restoration efforts. Reintroduction occasionally proceeds without prior habitat restoration when a local extinction has stemmed from a single, no longer active factor, such as trapping, bounties, or disease.

- **Habitat reconnection** Legendary Harvard biologist E. O. Wilson first proposed the importance of wildlife corridors in the 1980s; since then, corridors have been increasingly proven to be among the most cost-effective strategies. Sometimes it involves restoring interstitial habitat, such as finding a farm located between two isolated reserves, and linking the reserves by returning the farm to forest. In other cases, only the removal of barriers is necessary: farmers in Belize simply strung a rope ladder over a main road, allowing black howler monkeys to reach the riverside habitat that the farmers had restored.

Wallace Stegner once said that our national parks are "the best idea America ever had." If not the best, most Americans would agree that they are a very good idea. Yet our 379 national parks face maintenance and construction backlogs estimated at $4 billion. . . . At Acadia National Park in Maine . . . the non-profit Friends of Acadia is raising $9 million in private funds to match the park's commitment of $4 million [to] pay for restoration of Acadia's 130-mile trail system. The present National Park System receives one-tenth of a penny from each tax dollar. Increasing it to two-tenths of a cent would restore the parks in less than a decade and ensure their ecological, social, and economic vitality.
    —George J. Mitchell, former U.S. Senate majority leader, and W. Kent Olsen, President of Friends of Acadia, in a *Washington Post* editorial, September 4, 2000

The ecosystem types lumped into this industry include prairies, lakes, wetlands, and littoral (beaches, lagoons, saltwater marshes, etc.). Restoration is *the* hot subject whenever professionals involved in these ecosystems get together. For instance, approximately two-thirds of the presentations at the Third Annual American Wetlands Conference in Boston on May 6–8, 1999, fell into program tracks dealing with restoration.

PROBLEMS AND SOLUTIONS

Wilderness recovery, I firmly believe, is the most important task of our generation.
    —Dr. Reed Noss, founder, Conservation Biology Institute

Costa Rica has generated a lot of good press about being the nature tourism paradise of Central America in the past decade, but there's trouble in paradise. The country has the largest per capita acreage of national parks in the world, and the largest percentage of land set aside as "wild" (25 percent versus 10 percent in the United States). However, until very recently, it also had the highest percentage rate of rain forest deforestation—even higher than notorious Brazil—and this was happening during its ecotourism growth.

The deforestation was so bad, in fact, that it changed the country's weather patterns, reducing the rainfall in national parks hundreds of miles from the deforested land, with associated loss of species and degradation of ecosystems in the parks. Because tourism is Costa

Rica's second largest industry, restoring these treeless areas is vital to its economy.

"We're seeing that if you deforest the lowlands it impacts the environment several hundreds of kilometers away," reported Ron Welch, chairman of the Atmospheric Science Department at the University of Alabama in Huntville (*Research Review,* University of Alabama, Fall 2001), who conducted studies in Costa Rica. It's not just the well-known effect of losing the water that normally forms clouds through leaf transpiration. Welch's team found that the deforested area also becomes hotter, due to lack of shade and transpiration, and the rising hot air pushes clouds higher, so the rain misses the mainland and falls on the ocean.

That's the bad news. The good news comes from both a government program, and from a small restorative grassroots effort. We'll examine the large-scale government watershed project in the following chapter.

Arbofilia

The small-scale good news comes in the form of a forest restoration organization called Arbofilia, and its founder, Miguel Francisco Soto Cruz. Working with very limited (almost zero) funds, in less than ten years Cruz helped eight rural Costa Rican communities restore the devastated land they had created around themselves. Twenty more are on a waiting list, due to the funding shortage. Cruz's passion for restoration extends beyond ecosystems and watersheds to farms, disasters, and infrastructure: when an earthquake struck in nearby El Salvador, he spent a week there as a trainer, helping communities bring their water mains back to life.

In 2001, 20 years after founding Arbofilia, Cruz was presented the coveted Theodore M. Sperry award (named after the creator of the world's oldest restored prairie, a project initiated by Aldo Leopold) by the Society for Ecological Restoration at its Thirteenth Annual International Conference in Niagara Falls, Canada. Here are just a few of Arbofilia's many accomplishments leading to that award:

- Restored 40 springs for community drinking water
- Planted hundreds of thousands of trees, representing some 400 native species
- Restored rural economies by planting 200 varieties of tropical fruit trees to provide year-round diversified food and revenue
- Built schools and research facilities to disseminate restoration skills

- Created a refuge to restore a broad spectrum of native stingless bee species, which provide sustainable pollination for orchards and restored forests
- Removed over 100 tons of nonbiodegradable trash from rivers and beaches
- Restored scarlet macaw habitat to, in turn, help restore that magnificent, endangered bird by planting over 200 species of native trees important to its survival
- Acquired and restored (again with almost no funding) 50 acres to launch the reconnection of biological corridors between the Carara National Forest and the highland cloud forests

Grand Visions for the Great Plains

In the Great Plains of the United States, numerous groups and individuals are envisioning the restoration of vast expanses of restored prairie, complete with bison, elk, ferrets, and wolves. Several books, scientific and lay, have been written on the subject. The first on integrated bison/prairie restoration was *Where the Buffalo Roam: The Storm over the Revolutionary Plan to Restore America's Great Plains* (1992). Dan O'Brien's wonderful *Buffalo for the Broken Heart: Restoring Life to a Black Hills Ranch* arrived in 2001, telling the restoration story on a more intimate (and extremely entertaining) level.

Both books are as much about farm, ranch, and rural economic restoration as they are about ecosystems. Prairie restoration in Wisconsin and Minnesota was the birthplace of U.S. restoration ecology. The fact that the publication dates of the first book and the most recent book are less than a decade apart further indicates how recent this eruption of restoration has been.

One proposed Great Plains macroproject is that of Joel Sartore of Nebraska, whose Conservation Alliance of the Great Plains aims to restore between one and two million acres around the area where Nebraska, South Dakota, and Wyoming come together. It's not as crazy as it sounds, as a large portion of the land is already federally owned and would "only" require Congress to change its land-use designation. Sartore hopes the sustainable tourism revenues, tax benefits from private land trusts, and enhanced health and beauty of the area will benefit such a broad spectrum of local residents that politicians will be able to resist the mining and agribusiness lobbies.

You call it wild, but it wasn't really wild, it was free.
—**Leon Shenandoah,** from **Harvey Arden, Steve Wall,** and **White Deer of Autumn,**
Wisdomkeepers: Meetings with Native American Spiritual Leaders, 1991

While Sartore is dreaming grand visions, The Nature Conservancy [TNC] has launched the largest tallgrass prairie restoration in the United States, called the Glacial Ridge Project, after having purchased 25,000 acres in Polk County, Minnesota. The land is already home to the endangered western prairie fringed orchid, along with sandhill cranes, moose, Dakota skipper butterflies, and a wide variety of waterfowl, shorebirds, and grassland birds. Currently only one-third prairie, the restoration effort will also bring back native wetlands. Maybe most importantly, the project connects a number of private, state, and federal protected areas, which should produce many synergistic benefits. This integrated approach yields ecological values that none of the projects could provide in isolation. It also rebuilds topsoil, which used to be measured in yards and is now measured in inches.

In considering topsoil, we should explore some of the common misconceptions and assumptions regarding ecological restoration. For instance, prairie restorations seek to restore the natural topsoil-building grass, forb, and bison-based prairies encountered by Europeans. (Forbs are broadleaf plants lacking woody stems, such as most flowering houseplants, strawberry, milkweed, alfalfa, daisy, etc.) The settlers destroyed the prairies via plowing, fire suppression, bison extermination, and other such activities, creating the "natural" disaster of the "Dust Bowl," which turned topsoil into air pollution.

Topsoil regeneration is also a goal of restorative agriculture, farm-to-ecosystem reversions, and many other projects. It's only natural, then, that most laypeople assume that increasing the depth and quality of topsoil is a universal goal of terrestrial ecosystem restoration. Not true. Many ecosystems are naturally nutrient-poor, and centuries of nonintensive farming have built a layer of topsoil that is too nutrient-rich to allow these ecosystems to reestablish. Ecosystem restoration might thus start with topsoil *removal.* (The topsoil could be transferred to a restoration project requiring topsoil, such as a brownfield—one of many fringe benefits of integrated restoration initiatives.)

For example, topsoil removal was an element of the successful restoration of endangered fen meadows ecosystems in The Netherlands. But this example exposes another popular misconception. Those unique, topsoil-poor fen meadows were probably the product of unsustainable land use centuries ago. These beautiful, desirable fens, now considered "native," "natural," and "historic," which the modern Dutch seek to recreate, are actually the scars of earlier ecological devastation by humans. Such "revelations" about anthropogenic origins can cause confusion and undermine support. Goals and labels are inherently simplifying, so we should take care in formulating them, avoid getting attached to them, and avoid generalizing them across diverse situations.

Restoring Nature and Farms Together

> The discipline of restoration ecology aims to provide a scientifically sound basis for the reconstruction of degraded or destroyed ecosystems, and to produce self-supporting systems that are, to some degree, resilient to subsequent damage.
> —Peter J. Edwards, N. R. Webb, K. M. Urbanska, Pehr H. Enckell, and Krystyna M. Urbanska, eds., *Restoration Ecology and Sustainable Development*, 1997

Those familiar with The Nature Conservancy (TNC) probably know it as a conservation group. Many consider it the best of the breed. But I don't have to look any further than the southeast corner of my adopted home state of Virginia for examples of how important restoration has suddenly become to TNC's strategy.

The Virginia Wetlands Restoration Trust Fund is administered by the Army Corps of Engineers. In 2000, it funded TNC's purchase of a 273-acre tract on the Chickahominy River, containing 41 acres of exhausted farmland that will be restored to its previous incarnation as a vital wetland.

A few months earlier, that same restoration trust fund also enabled TNC to obtain a 133-acre parcel. Its revitalization will combine two restorative modalities: habitat reconnection and habitat restoration. The property links Virginia's Great Dismal Swamp with North Carolina's Albemarle Sound, allowing migration between the two ecosystems. The wildlife using this corridor ranges from the black bear to the threatened canebrake rattlesnake (a favorite of mine, as I raised a captive-born canebrake in my bedroom as a teenager; a fact you would've probably preferred I'd kept to myself . . .).

This 133-acre swamp tract had been farmed, ditched, and drained for over a century, so restoring its ecosystems also has meant restoring its hydrology. For that task, TNC, in another smart move, hired a local farmer to fill in the ditches, allowing the land to once again retain water while increasing community involvement. This new acquisition abuts an existing 31-acre TNC restoration project, enhancing the ecological value of both investments.

That same year, TNC, again tapping the Virginia Wetlands Restoration Trust Fund, bought an 18-acre farm that used to be a wetland and will soon be again. Eighteen acres isn't much, but this parcel is strategically located to help remove water pollution from nearby industrial agriculture before it hits Nawney Creek. Thus, TNC will also be restoring Back Bay, into which Nawney Creek drains. After the restoration work begins, TNC will turn management of this site over to the U.S. Fish and Wildlife Service, which already runs the Back Bay National Wildlife Refuge.

Species Reintroduction Considerations

The above description of TNC's southeastern Virginia projects focuses on habitat restoration and habitat reconnection. No mention has yet been made of species reintroduction, a rather more delicate subject. Species reintroduction efforts are faced with far more complex challenges than might be expected, such as the recent discovery that—once a species has left an ecosystem—the "doors" of that biological community can shut on it. This is due to adaptive alterations in the system caused by that species' absence, which often eliminate a vital source of food or shelter.

A related hindrance is that the loss of a single species sometimes triggers a cascade of extinctions, as dependency relationships are severed. For example, Middlesex Park, an isolated 650-acre woodland in Massachusetts, was inventoried in 1993 and found to have lost 40 percent of its species in the previous 99 years. Successive extinctions can drastically change a system in just a few years. This is just one reason why conservation, when possible, is always preferable to restoration.

Yet another challenge for species reintroduction efforts are Allee effects, which describe the essential role of crowding on some species' survival. Allee effects are behind the tendency of some species to suddenly go extinct despite seemingly large populations, because the species requires a certain minimum population density. Drop below that level, and the species becomes overly vulnerable to predation, or it becomes too hard for individuals to find each other for breeding. This should be a caution to extractive industries, such as cod fishing, that are expecting passive restoration to rescue them from overharvesting and mismanagement.

The good news is that reestablishing a *locally* extinct species doesn't have to involve huge numbers of captive-bred animals, especially if one is aware of Allee effects and uses some imagination. In Australia, for example, biologists initially attempted to re-introduce a rare marsupial, the bush-tailed phascogale *(Phascogale tapoatafa)*, by releasing the males and females simultaneously. But the animals dispersed to the point where they couldn't find each other by the time breeding season came around. On the next try, the females were released first, which allowed them to establish and mark their territories so the males could find them when they were introduced later.

The Australians were fortunate: some species, such as flamingos and penguins, simply can't "be themselves" except in a crowd. In small numbers, they probably won't breed, no matter how much we restore their habitat.

Ecosystem restoration is found in some unlikely places, including the middle of the desert. The Azraq oasis in the eastern desert of Jordan has been overexploited for decades, the result of a booming population. Now, it's an example of ecological recovery. "Many of the birds for which the oasis was renowned are coming back," said Chris Johnson in an October 8, 2001, article from the Environmental News Service. He is director of development of the Royal Society for the Conservation of Nature, a non-governmental organization dedicated to the protection and restoration of Jordan's natural systems.

A new variety of species reintroduction project—and a tragic commentary on our times—is referred to as "resurrection ecology." This emerging discipline takes an extinct (not just locally extinct, but *really* extinct) species and brings it "back to life." This is accomplished not via Jurassic Park-style bioengineering, but—in theory—by interbreeding closely related subspecies to produce a combination of traits that closely resembles the lost species.

This isn't done just for the sake of the species itself. Many times, that "restored" species will be critical to the restoration of other animals or plants that depended on the original. A butterfly restoration project in California is the foremost U.S. example of resurrection ecology that I've yet encountered. The amount of time, money, and intellectual energy necessary to accomplish the resurrection of a species will, no doubt, be astronomically out of proportion to the effort and expense it would have taken land developers and our elected leaders to prevent the extinction in the first place.

Resurrection ecology is related to another emerging trend in conservation known as "hospice ecology," whereby park and sanctuary managers simply do what they can to slow the death of an ecosystem (or species) that is clearly doomed. Hospice ecology is most often practiced on islands, where the boundaries, dynamics, and likely outcomes are so much easier to perceive, but many conservation managers across the planet practice it unknowingly. To the best of my knowledge, the term was invented by biologists in Hawaii, who were struggling in a paradise (for humans only) that has the planet's highest rate of endemic species extinction.

Basic Principles

> The park's restoration would accomplish two things. It would serve as a
> memorial to [*famed nineteenth-century landscape architect Beatrix Jones*] Farrand;
> and it would redeem the National Park Service's period of neglect.
> —From Olmstead Center for Landscape Preservation's million-dollar-plus restoration
> plan for Dumbarton Oaks Park (Washington, D.C.), for the U.S. National Park Service

Space will not permit us to review a full representative sample of the ecosystem types and restoration techniques comprising this industry; instead, let's review some broad principles and organizing factors.

The search for universal design principles could probably do no better than the research into complex adaptive systems conducted by University of Michigan professor (and Santa Fe Institute faculty member) John Holland. In his landmark 1995 Book "Hidden Order: How Adaptation Builds Complexity," he identified four characteristics of all healthy complex systems: flow, diversity, nonlinearity, and aggregation. Restoration ecologists would do well to design and monitor projects with these characteristics in mind.

Within the industry and science of ecological restoration, several efforts have been made to establish a theoretical framework for its processes, and to create an overall taxonomy for the discipline. Here are three recent attempts of note:

1. Four categories of ecological restoration were described in a 1996 paper by Hobbs and Norton   Their first category is rehabilitation of ecological disaster areas, which includes such projects as restoring biological activity to the sites of mining activity, decontaminating ecosystems downstream of industrial sites (overlapping the brownfields industry), and others. The second focuses on increasing the production capacity of depleted lands (overlapping the farming industry of restoration). A third category improves the quality of existing wildlife reserves and other protected landscapes.

Finally, Hobbs and Norton describe a category that enhances the ecological quality of seminatural production and/or cultural landscapes, which could include historic battlefield sites, parks, low-intensity ranches, and other sites.

2. A three-tier taxonomy was offered in the June 2001 issue of *Restoration Ecology* by the team of van Diggelen, Grootjans, and Harris[1]   The team starts with reclamation, which is defined as attempts to increase biodiversity on highly disturbed sites. A more ambitious target is rehabilitation, described as the reintroduction of certain ecosystem functions, which may or may not increase biodiversity. In this taxonomy, the highest level is true restoration, described as the reconstruction of a prior ecosystem.

3. Four phases of ecological restoration were suggested by J. H. Willems, also in the June 2001 issue of *Restoration Ecology*[2]   Willems identifies the pre-restoration phase, during which clear goals are defined, based on the site's land-use history and other research. The second phase is initial restoration, focused on undoing the effects of previous land use to create conditions favorable to the reintroduction of desired species. Third is a consolidation phase, which introduces an ongoing management system. This is supplemented by the final phase, a long-term conservation strategy, designed to address such factors as outside disturbances and genetic erosion.

We are at far too early a stage in the development of the science of ecological restoration to make assumptions, even regarding basic goals. Goal definition is actually a fundamental area of disagreement. Some practitioners (the "product" school) feel the goal should be the re-creation of a reference (historical) ecosystem. The "product" school of thought says the goal of ecosystem restoration should be the creation of self-sustaining systems that requires little or no ongoing intervention.

Other restorationists (the "process" school) prefer a focus on restoration of key ecosystem functions, allowing the end results to emerge as they may in response to current conditions. The "process" people say the product approach is unrealistic, for two primary reasons:

1. There is no such thing as a static state in healthy ecosystems, which are always progressing through phases and successions. Any ecosystem state is, by nature, transitory, so any reference state will be purely arbitrary. What's more, each state is the product of a series of unique series of events and conditions. Thus, a historical reference condition might be impossible to achieve, and maybe even irrelevant to modern times.

[1] R. van Diggelen, A. P. Grootjans, and J. A. Harris, "Ecological Restoration: State of the Art or State of the Science?" *Restoration Ecology* 9, June 2001.
[2] J. H. Willems, "Problems, Approaches and Results in Restoration of Dutch Calcareous Grassland During the Last 30 Years, *Restoration Ecology* 9, June 2001.

2. The global nature of threats, such as invasive species and climate change, means that most ecosystem restorations—especially small, isolated ones—will require significant monitoring, defense, and manipulation for an extended period of time . . . at least for decades, and possibly forever.

Compromises are often necessary when restoring natural systems back to a given historical reference state. Many times, the surrounding environment (chemical, biological, meteorological, agricultural, etc.) has changed to a startling degree. Attempting to restore an ecosystem to what it was 300 years ago might mean jettisoning centuries of recent adaptations that are now necessary for its survival.

ISSUES AND INSIGHTS

> Not everyone is happy with the concept of ecological restoration, however. Some have criticized it as an unethical and immoral attempt to substitute "fake" natural systems for nature. Philosopher Eric Katz, for instance, deplores ecological restoration as an unwarranted intervention in natural systems and a form of human domination. He further argues that ecological restoration based on functional attributes destroys the ontological identity of the area being restored. Philosopher Robert Elliot has even condemned perfect restoration as a morally wrong process that replaces "real" nature with a "fake." These critics propose leaving nature to develop as it chooses rather than as humans choose. . . . The debate is ongoing and is unlikely to be settled anytime soon.
>
> —John Cairns Jr., Distinguished Prof. of Environmental Biology Emeritus,
> Virginia Polytechnic Institute, "Life Support,"
> *Forum for Applied Research & Public Policy*, Spring 2001

Each of the eight industries of restorative development will end with an "Issues and Insights" section. I don't mean to diminish readers' enthusiasm, but it's important that those who are new to these subjects—especially our political leaders, since much restoration is publicly funded—not rush around blindly, funding and supporting anything labeled "restoration."

Restorative development is much like medicine: there are basically two kinds. There's palliative (allopathic), "western-style" medicine, which masks signs and symptoms with drugs. It also cuts out vital organs because they've "gone bad," which may be viewed as repunishing the body for succumbing to pathogens or our lifestyle excesses.

There's also holistic, "eastern-style" medicine, which is based on prevention and on strengthening the body's self-healing abilities. When disease does arise, diagnosis and treatment protocol entails looking for the root, systemic cause, rather than focusing on elimination of the signs and symptoms. This often results in recommendations that patients change their lifestyle, which is why so many of us choose drugs and surgery instead (at least, until that approach hits a dead end, which is why eastern doctors tend to get patients in critical condition, often after the "regular" doctor has told them to update their last will and testament).

Classical Eastern medical disciplines, such as Chinese and Indian, have an underlying theoretical framework focused on processes, so they can explain cause and effect. Western doctors function more like plumbers and electrical technicians—reconnecting, removing, and unclogging things with knives, pliers, reamers, and harsh chemicals—and not caring much for theory. As a former military medic, I know that drugs and surgery are wonderful when dealing with bullet holes and other gross trauma, but they really have very little to do with health.

> In our age . . . men seem more than ever prone to confuse wisdom with knowledge, and knowledge with information, and to try to solve problems of life in terms of engineering.
> —T. S. Eliot, *On Poetry and Poets*, 1957

This lengthy digression provides a perfect metaphor for restorative development, especially when we're restoring living systems such as cities or wetlands. You'll see the dynamics of western and eastern medicine at work in the following list of issues. Probably no form of restoration is as rife with opportunities for missteps and outright tragedies as is ecological restoration. Here's a brief sampling of some specific problems:

1. Too much engineering influence Engineers (in many flavors) are probably the key professionals of the Restoration Economy, in all eight industries of restoration (in varying degrees). However, leadership of the Restoration Economy is likely to come only from that minority of engineers open-minded and humble enough to seek out scientists, architects, NGOs, and stakeholders of all kinds during initial project design; to engage them in meaningful dialogue; and to keep them involved throughout project execution and ongoing management.

By far the most common source of ecosystem restoration horror stories derives from projects run exclusively by civil engineers, with minimal—if any—input from the broad range of sciences and community stakeholders that should be involved. Scathing comments concerning engineers are rife at ecological restoration conferences, many of them coming from the mouths of engineers, with phrases like "arrogant ignorance," "childishly simplistic," "lifelessly mechanistic," and "ham-handed" predominating.

Most restoration scientists value engineers' ability to "fix stuff," move large amounts of earth, and generally make big things happen quickly. However, they lament engineers' frequent inability to appreciate the importance of subtler, big-picture issues like cycles, diversity, flows, and natural succession. There's also engineers' tendency to panic and overreact in the presence of surprises, which are normal and to be expected when dealing with complex living systems.

Engineers tend to overvalue—almost worship—linearity and predictability. A perfect example was their horror at how sloppily and unevenly student volunteers were spreading powdered lime (to lower the acidity of the soil) at the restoration of a former coal mining site in Canada. The resulting (accidental) patchwork of high, medium, and low pH turned out to be of crucial value in reestablishing biological diversity, because a wide variety of plant species took root according to their own preferred pH.

Engineers are hardly alone, however, in ignoring "nonexpert" stakeholders, such as the cultural concerns and ecosystem insights of indigenous peoples, archaeologists, local communities, and private property owners who know the land intimately.

> To many people, especially civil engineers, the reclamation of derelict land is really nothing grandly scientific. It is a simple technical problem, a matter of finding permanent economical ways of achieving a few simple objectives: (1) stabilization of land surfaces, (2) pollution control, (3) visual improvement, and (4) general amenity, in order to preserve the structures in which they are interested and to prevent the land from being unpleasant to the people that use it. Also, since the land itself has value for what it can produce, we can add (5) productivity as a possible extra objective. Finally we can take on the more ambitious task of actually restoring the ecological communities that were present originally. This means adding (6) diversity, (7) species composition, and (8) ecosystem function.
>
> In any particular situation only one or two of these objectives may have to be met. Highway engineers, for instance, are looking only for stabilization and visual improvement, but Australian mineral sand miners are looking not only for these but also for everything else, because they are required to put back exactly what was there previously and ensure that it functions properly. All of these examples constitute land reclamation, but only the latter can be considered as full restoration.
>
> —A. D. Bradshaw, from William R. Jordan, Michael E. Gilpin, and John D. Aber, eds., "The Reclamation of Derelict Land and the Ecology of Ecosystems," *Restoration Ecology: A Synthetic Approach to Ecological Research*, Cambridge University Press, 1987

2. Underestimating human ignorance   Ecosystem restoration is an unforgiving crucible of our knowledge, or our lack thereof. By committing to measurable outcomes by a certain date, restoration ecology lays bare our ignorance of what life is, how it emerges, how it organizes, how it heals and renews itself, and other issues. Restoring ecosystems requires constant feedback; continual reevaluation and learning; and tremendous willingness to modify plans, to improvise solutions, to balance theory with "field smarts," and to integrate the rigor of science with the insight of the artist.

Timing is often a crucial factor, as in this simple example: Northern land that has been stripped bare by clear-cutting and resulting erosion is subject to frost heaves that eject seedlings from the soil, ruining days or weeks of work in an hour or two. Planting fast-growing ground cover early in the season changes the soil dynamics, eliminating the heaves and allowing slower-growing plants (such as trees) to take hold. Of course, the choice of "groundbreaking" species is critical, because many fast-growing plants exclude other species, either mechanically or chemically.

Such trial-and-error lessons already fill volumes, and most wouldn't have been learned in the absence of restorative work. Presently, most of these lessons are highly applied, stemming from "dirty-hands" restoration work, but we need far more research, both pure and applied. In summary, the most successful projects usually integrate engineering, science, business, culture, patience, creativity, compassion, and humility.

3. Political cronyism   Another characteristic of the better ecological restoration projects is that they are often run by broad coalitions of NGOs, government agencies, schools, communities, and industry. Unfortunately, these tend to be the smaller projects. In the United States, multimillion- and billion-dollar government-funded projects often go to huge, politically connected firms. In the earliest, bad old days, these were often defense contractors. (In fact, they were often the same firms that caused the problem. Rather than being fined, they were paid huge amounts of taxpayer money to clean up their mess.) Their costly restoration blunders caused a shift from defense contractors to large architectural/ engineering/contracting (AEC) firms in the '90s.

The Army Corps of Engineers has been a major player all along, often designing and coordinating the projects. Larger projects, which are often the most complex, usually suffer worst from the problems described in items 1 and 2 above. Many fear this will be the case with the Corps of Engineers-led effort to restore the Florida Everglades. This fear was heightened when Secretary of the Interior Gale Norton was caught secretly attempting to put control of the $7.8 billion Everglades restoration project under Florida governor Jeb Bush. She even closed down the on-site offices of her own Interior Department biologists: they apparently couldn't be trusted to make politically expeditious decisions, such as determining the ratio of Everglades water that goes to wildlife versus to industry. The good news is that—on June 26, 2002—a House of Representatives subcommittee handed down a decision that effectively forced Norton to do her job. They reasserted the Department of Interior's equal role (with the Corps) in the Everglades project, a move that special interests related to new development decried (as stated in a *Washington Post* article) as an "effort to skew a delicately balanced plan towards nature" (horrors!).[3]

Politically driven projects often result in the worst "reclamations," such as, in the United States, Midwest strip mine "restorations" that were turned into unnatural grasslands in a slap-dash attempt to "paint them green." A few inches below the surface of these sites, mine tailings will be polluting the aquifer—and thus farms, communities, and ecosystems hundreds of miles away—with acid (and worse) for centuries, even millennia to come. Hasty reclamations are often politicians' attempts to hide damage done by their corporate sponsors.

4. Poor follow-through (whether from poor planning or insufficient funding)   As restorationist Dennis Martinez said at a Society for Ecological Restoration workshop in 2001, "Most ecosystem restoration projects are islands in a vast sea of degradation, so we can seldom walk away and say 'our job is done.' " All forms of restoration require some level of ongoing monitoring and management, especially those dealing with living communities (both human and wildlife). But in no form of restorative development is follow-through needed more than in ecosystem restoration.

5. Use of nonnative species in restoration   The use of exotics can be valid, when, for example, they are needed temporarily to aid natural species succession, and when no native species have survived to provide a critical ecosystem function. For instance, on Bermuda's Nonsuch Island (see Chapter 15), native land crabs became a problem because they were no longer being eaten by an extinct heron. A close relative of that heron was introduced to restore this needed function. What some would decry as "compromising ecological integrity" probably saved many plant species, as well as several animal species that depended on those plants.

More often, though, exotic species are misused, especially when short-term economic agendas dominate. In a Copperbasin, Tennessee, reclamation project, native trees were already in place, but they were uprooted and replaced with fast-growing nonnative pines to provide

[3] Michael Grunwald, "Panel Boosts Interior's Role in Everglades Restoration, *Washington Post,* June 27, 2002.

quick bucks. The use of exotics can cause many long-lasting problems, such as introducing and harboring diseases and exotic insects. These can afflict the native species for decades, even after the original carrier has been removed.

6. Insufficient integration of restoration and livelihood Two small towns—one in Queenstown, Tasmania, and the other in Sudbury, Canada—are the sites of horrendous former strip mines, which left them with hauntingly stark, desolate hills of waste materials. Perversely, both towns receive significant economic benefits from busloads of tourists who find these rolling vistas of biological holocaust fascinating. When restorationists unilaterally decided to restore these sites, locals uprooted the trees for fear that restoring the natural beauty would ruin their ghoulish tourist trade. Ecological restoration projects that eschew input from nearby human communities are often doomed to failure.

Process Blindness

Let's quickly review a systemic problem you'll find discussed throughout this book. Our cultural and professional tendency to ignore processes means that we often miss out on "free" (natural) restoration opportunities. Instead of processes, we tend to focus on things, throwing money at problems by buying stuff (e.g., herbicides, algicides).

One of the wonderful changes being stimulated by restorative activities is an increased focus on process. This change is similar to the way urban revitalization projects are switching from needs-based to asset-based strategies: Instead of focusing on what ghetto communities don't have, and then mechanically plugging-in that missing item, project planners focus instead on what they do have, and on what works. The resulting plan strengthens and uses those assets (which aren't just buildings: they can also be community spirit, volunteer groups, and knowledge).

In both the city and the countryside, assets can also take the form of green slime. The algae growing in eutrophic (meaning, polluted with excess nutrients) ponds and lakes are an asset as well as a liability, but we tend to only see the problematic aspect. In thousands of ponds and lakes around the world, park managers complain about algae blooms. In fact, what's happening is that nature is turning the damaging pollution into healthy algal tissue, thus removing it from the water.

Rather than perceiving these dynamics from a functional point of view—whereby the algae are the solution to the pollution—we talk about having two problems: algae and pollution. So, we either wage war on the algae with poisons or we watch helplessly as they suffocate fish (note: algae produce oxygen by day, but consume it at night, which is when the fish die if there's too much algae competing for the oxygen). In fact, what we actually have is a problem *and* a solution: all we have to do is harvest the algae—thus removing the pollution it has captured—and feed it to chickens or cattle, or compost it into fertilizer.

Here's an example of harnessing a very simple natural process to facilitate restoration. At a 2,470-acre former cattle ranch in Guanacaste, Costa Rica, active and passive restoration sit in contrast to each other. Various tracts of land cleared for the cattle sat undisturbed for 20 to 30 years. When a species inventory was made to measure the extent of passive restoration taking place, it was found that the species taking hold were representative of much drier climes to the west, probably because of the change in the local microclimate, due to the deforestation. (Similarly, a study by Stuart K. Allison in the March 2002 *Ecological Restoration* compared remnant Illinois tallgrass prairies with restored ones.[4] Researchers found the hands-off conserved prairies full of weedy, invasive species. The long-term restored prairies—thanks to active planting and control of exotic species—had better species diversity and far fewer invasives.)

Because the passive restoration seemed to be heading in the "wrong" direction, restorationists stepped in to both speed it and redirect it towards the pre-ranch ecosystem. They used one simple strategy: planting three species of native fig trees. The fruit on the trees attracted birds, whose defecation produced a rich "seed rain" from fruits and seeds they'd eaten nearby.

Thousands of birds are thus being recruited as restoration workers to harvest and "plant" indigenous plant species. This is one of nature's most basic processes for spreading DNA. Putting birds to work for this restoration was just a matter of keen observation, combined with a lack of process blindness.

As with many dichotomies, a blend of the "product" and "process" approaches will likely end up being appropriate for many projects. Although the argument is presented in black-and-white terms here, most restorationists in both schools accept—or at least understand—the arguments of the other school, and the dialogue remains open.

CLOSING THOUGHTS

None of the problems discussed above is insurmountable, and many are already being addressed. Take "Issues and Insights" item 1 (above), for

---

[4]Stuart K. Allison, "When Is a Restoration Successful? Results from a 45-Year-Old Tallgrass Prairie Restoration," *Ecological Restoration* 20 (1), March 2002.

instance. Engineers aren't unaware of their limitations in dealing with complex adaptive living systems. At a recent restoration conference I attended, at the headquarters of the American Society of Civil Engineers, one of the invited speakers, a former American Rivers executive, good-naturedly excoriated the audience, (which included many Army Corps of Engineers employees) with stories of absurd, almost farcical engineering blunders on river restoration projects. Even the engineers couldn't help laughing at the mechanical simple-mindedness the stories demonstrated. I don't know if this conference changed anything. I do know that, by importing such a speaker and giving him free rein, ASCE displayed the kind of courage that organizations will require, as they adapt to the alterations in the socio-economic landscape created by the steamroller of restorative development.

A recent "threat" to species restoration efforts (in the Americas) comes from the increasing evidence that Native American populations were probably far larger than originally thought, and that they actively managed most American ecosystems to maximize game animal populations. Some ecologists thus consider Native Americans to have been the "keystone species" of their ecosystems, and claim that the great American prairies and the Amazon Basin are largely human artifacts. Some conservationists and restorationists worry that, if proven, such knowledge will pull the rug out from under their efforts. Why? Because the goal of American conservation traditionally has been to restore pre-Columbian conditions, which were assumed to be raw wilderness, "untrammeled by man."

> According to Peter Stahl, an anthropologist at the State University of New York at Binghamton, "lots" of botanists believe that "what the eco-imagery would like to picture as a pristine, untouched Urwelt [primeval world] in fact has been managed by people for millennia." The phrase "built environment," [Clark] Erickson [University of Pennsylvania archaeologist] says, "applies to most, if not all, Neotropical landscapes." . . . [I]f the new view is correct and the work of humankind is pervasive, where does that leave efforts to restore nature?
> —**Charles C. Mann**, "1491," *The Atlantic Monthly,* March 2002

Research into the degree of human intervention in "wild" ecosystems, past and present, is very important. However, I consider it totally unwarranted to worry that our discovery of strong, long-standing human influences on ecosystems will undermine conservation and ecological restoration.

The critical factor is that American ecosystems were far healthier, more productive, and more diverse in pre-Columbian times than they are today. Let's just restore, to whatever degree we can, the processes and diversity that produced that health and let the philosophers and historians worry about how they got that way. If the restoration requires more active management than we envisioned, then we'll just have to learn more about how the Native Americans did it. Some of that knowledge will be applicable, such as judicious use of fire, while some will not be, such as driving herds of bison over cliffs.

We know almost nothing about what might have existed prior to the rise of the First Nations, so we have no reference ecosystems to guide us there. If it turns out that there's no such thing as an ecosystem unaffected by humans, then that should help us feel more a part of nature. This realization should, in turn, make us feel less comfortable with fouling our home. Either way, delaying the restoration of our natural environment until we can prove how it evolved would be ludicrous.

Now, let's move from this chapter's grab bag of ecosystems to a specific category of macroecosystem—watersheds—upon which all of our lives depend . . . to a much greater degree than most of us realize.

A SMALL SAMPLING OF OPPORTUNITIES

Business and investment
Restorative development of recreational real estate is an obvious opportunity. This buy-low-sell-high investment strategy needn't be long-term. Once a firm has established a track record (or has reduced buyer risk in other ways, such as warranties), properties can be sold—with ongoing restoration management contracts—soon after ecological restoration has begun. Commercial and residential buyers of these tracts can enjoy watching—maybe helping—them come back to life.

NGOs and other nonprofits
Conservation NGOs are finding many new opportunities to partner with developers. For example, an NGO can purchase a small, healthy, endangered ecosystem, and divide the cost of adjacent damaged property with the developer. Part of the degraded land would be restored to expand the ecosystem, and part would be redeveloped for residence or clean industry. The beauty of the enlarged natural area significantly increases the salability of the developers' portion.

Community and government
As with brownfields remediation (Chapter 9), ecological restoration can be an excellent way to restore a community's tax base. It's one of the best ways to create "green space" in poorly planned communities that have lost this vital asset.

Restoring Our Watersheds:
Aquifers, Forests, Rivers, and Streams

[New York City's decision to restore its watershed rather than build a new filtration plant] was a milestone in a world in which Nature's labor has too long been taken for granted. A major government body had acted as if an ecosystem— the watershed—were worth protecting in its natural state for the economic benefits it gives society. And it had invested in its restoration as if it were in fact a precious piece of infrastructure.

—**Gretchen Daily** and **Katherine Ellison,** *The New Economy of Nature,* 2002

New York City is probably the last city you would expect to not filter its drinking water, but that is in fact the case. What's more, the city has long been envied for having some of the best water of any major U.S. city. Although the water is a bit spoiled with small amounts of chlorine and fluoride, mostly for reasons of conformity and legal liability, the credit for this tremendous resource goes to the city's watershed.

The Catskill/Delaware watershed comprises 2,000 square miles of farms, forests, streams, and rivers, and, for most of the nineteenth and twentieth centuries, it produced some 1.8 billion gallons of pure water daily for New York City (90 percent of its supply) and surrounding communities. In the 1880s, 95 percent of that watershed was native forest. In the 1980s, not one acre of virgin forest remained. Even the nonvirgin forest was shrinking fast, due primarily to new residential development and agriculture. As a result, the Catskill watershed's water purification functions were starting to break down.

By 1989, New Yorkers had to make a choice: either spend between $6 and $8 billion building a conventional water filtration facility (plus up to half a billion annually running and maintaining it), or spend $1.5 billion restoring the watershed. The forces of new development fought a fierce battle to protect their right to destroy the watershed for short-term gain, but the forces of restorative development (and common sense)—led in part by Robert F. Kennedy, Jr.—won out.

The plan has stimulated numerous fringe benefits. One is farm restoration, such as the Holley Hill Farm, whose dairy operation was rehabilitated with watershed restoration funds, in return for the owner's fencing-off his cows from the creek, which they had been polluting. This was no small battle, as the new development realm was firmly in charge. Witness the fact that the maximum fine for polluting the watershed was $25, and no one had been fined even that much in four decades, despite widespread lack of control over human, industrial, and farm wastes (which the watershed was purifying at a heroic rate).

In Chapter 1, we discussed the common belief that the primary value of ecosystems was in the products (such as lumber) that they produce, rather than their far more valuable services, like purifying our air and water. New Yorkers are rejecting that myth, and the rest of the United States—and much of the world—is joining them.

Across the Americas, from Quito, Ecuador, to Curitiba, Brazil, not to mention almost 150 U.S. metropolitan areas, cities are now researching and replanning the future of their water, New York City-style. They are taking a fresh look at the old new-development approach of continually building more and larger treatment plants (and throwing away the water after one use). Almost universally, the old way is found to be out of sync with present and future realities, and integrated watershed restoration and management is on the rise.

In 2001, the European Union integrated watershed protection and restoration into the water strategies for its member countries. In Costa Rica, after inspecting the New York City watershed restoration project and liking what they saw, officials added a few cents worth of watershed restoration tax to the water bills of consumers around their capital, San Jose.

Those tax revenues are paid directly to the people who own the property comprising the watershed San Jose relies on, as compensation for the revenue "lost" by not cutting them and selling the timber. I put "lost" in quotes, because it's really only deferred revenue. The trees are continuing to grow and become more valuable; this makes selective logging at some future point an attractive alternative to clear-cutting, which would cause owners to lose the watershed payments. The payments aren't just to conserve watersheds, though: they also reward landowners for reforesting their land and restoring lost or degraded watersheds. What's more, Costa Rica has a very successful fossil-fuel usage tax (dating back to 1996) which also funds restoration; a rare instance of applying the oh-so-obvious wisdom that we should only tax what we want less of.

(Note: More information on the New York City and Costa Rican stories is available in *The New Economy of Nature* (Island Press, 2002). Detailed case studies of both projects, along with seven other integrated watershed projects, are available at www.forest-trends.org/resources/pdf/casesWSofF.pdf).

THE SCOPE OF THE WATERSHED RESTORATION INDUSTRY

> **watershed:** 2. The whole region or area contributing to the supply of a river or lake; drainage area.
> —*Webster's New Collegiate Dictionary*

> **aquifer:** A water-saturated rock with sufficient porosity and permeability to be a usable source of water for wells.
> —J. I. Drever, *The Geochemistry of Natural Waters,* 1988

The watershed restoration industry, as defined here, renews forests (temperate forests, tropical forests, rainforests, etc.), rivers, and streams. It less directly includes the aquifers fed by watersheds. This industry focuses primarily on water quantity and quality; water distribution and treatment are covered in the infrastructure restoration industry.

River and stream restorations are crucially important to health of watersheds, and to the health and economies of communities within them. In an example of the many synergies among these restorative industries, watershed restoration can also be crucial to ocean fishery restoration. The river runs of anadromous fish (the best-known are salmon) are essential to the reproduction of these species. Breaching dams on rivers used by these freshwater-to-saltwater-to-freshwater fish species opens new habitat and spawning areas, dramatically improving both coastal and open ocean fishing.

Who are the players in this industry? American Rivers is the national river restoration NGO in the United States, but most watershed restoration organizations tend to be regional coalitions, rather than national or international. (An exception is the huge Danube River restoration project, involving over a dozen countries.)

The U.S. Army Corps of Engineers—traditionally the greatest killer of rivers the planet has ever seen—is now one of the leading restorers of rivers. The Corps' old-guard leadership (and Congressional supporters, who love its traditional big-bucks, pork-barrel, new-development projects) is divided as to its role in the Restoration Economy. On the other hand, many of its employees feel the Corps' vast expertise positions it perfectly as *the* leading agency of (U.S.) ecological and infrastructure restoration in the new millennium.

Demonstrating the rapidly increasing integration of restoration industries, public and private metropolitan water utilities—while currently minority players—are coming on strong as watershed restorationists. Also strongly involved in the restoration of both ecosystems and watersheds in the United States is the network of some 3,000 "Soil and Water Conservation Districts." The districts sometimes go by other names, such as "natural resource districts," "resource conservation districts," or "land conservation committees." Almost all are involved in restoration programs, usually as partners in projects owned or conceived by other private or public organizations.

One definition of watershed is "land with at least an eight-degree slope." By that definition, about half the land mass of Asia is watershed. Yet much of Asia's territory no longer functions properly as watershed, what with farm terraces capturing the water, and nonterraced farms (and deforested areas) flooding rivers with topsoil. This clearly demonstrates the need for integrated restoration. Besides farms, watersheds overlap with the restoration needs of farms, ecosystems, fisheries, and infrastructure—in fact, with all seven other restoration industries to some degree.

PROBLEMS AND SOLUTIONS

How important is it to restore our watersheds and the aquifers they feed? Consider that less than three percent of the water on the planet is fresh. Only three-tenths of one percent of *that* three percent is free-flowing (the rest being frozen in glaciers and deep polar ice caps), and the vast majority of that free-flowing portion is polluted.

Many droughts are caused by deforestation, and almost all are exacerbated by deforestation. This is because deep-rooted trees are the ultimate cloud-makers. Their ability to extract water from aquifers and evaporate it provides the linchpin of many weather cycles. Most plants only cough up surface moisture—water that would have evaporated anyway and which isn't available during drought. Without the deep water provided by slow-growing tree species (not the shallow-rooted "weed trees" usually planted on tree farms), droughts will lock into ever-drier feedback loops.

Designed to coincide with the 25th anniversary of the Clean Water Act, the Clinton White House asked many federal agencies to design and execute a plan to revitalize the country's commitment to the quality and quantity of our water supply. The result of this interagency project, which included TVA, EPA, USDA, Dept. of Defense, HUD, Dept. of Interior, and FEMA, was the Clean Water Action Plan. One goal of the plan was to ". . . showcase the application of stream corridor restoration technology in 12 demonstration project areas for water quality improvement."

Twelve model sites won the competition based on their application of stream corridor restoration technology, and for their projects' contribution to the local communities, to the environment, and to water quality. Run by a variety of local, tribal, and state organizations, the sites partner public and private lands to create stream corridor restoration. The USEPA website (www.epa.gov/owow/showcase/about.html) says it "celebrates these successful projects as examples of accomplishments through restoration."

The winning showcase watershed restoration projects were Duck Creek, Ark.; Big Nance Creek Watershed, Ala.; Gila River Corridor Recovery Project, Ariz./N. Mex.; Suwanee River Watershed, Ga./Fla.; Bear Creek Watershed, Iowa; Sun River Basin, Mont.; Blackfoot Watershed, Mont.; Carson River Watershed, Nev.; McCoy Creek Watershed, Oreg. (a project of the Confederated Tribes of the Umatilla Indian Reservation); Lititz Run Watershed Alliance, Pa.; White River Partnership Watershed Restoration Project, Vt.; and Duwamish-Green River Watershed, Wash.

If you don't see a winner near you, don't worry: there's probably a watershed restoration within 100 miles of your home. The list on the next page is by no means a complete inventory of U.S. projects; these are only the better ones that were submitted—but *not* chosen as winners—in the "Showcase" competition.

SELECTED U.S. WATERSHED RESTORATION PROJECTS

AK	North Fork Bradfield River Watershed Restoration, Tongass National Forest
AL	Choccolocoo Creek Watershed
AZ	Upper Verde River Adaptive Management Project, Prescott National Forest
CA	Pine Creek Watershed Restoration, Lassen National Forest
CA	Deer Creek Watershed Stewardship Program, Lassen National Forest
CA	Big Flat Meadow Restoration, Plumas National Forest
CA	Lower Tuolumne
CA	Indian Creek
CO	Bonanza Mining Area CERCLA Project, San Juan/Rio Grande National Forests
CO	Alamosa River Watershed Project
CT	Norwalk River Watershed Initiative, Fairfield County
CT, NY	Norwalk River Watershed Initiative
GA	Soque River Restoration Project, Habersham County
IA	Chichauqua Bottoms Greenbelt
IA	Iowa River Corridor
ID	O'Hara Creek Watershed Restoration, Nez Perce National Forest
ID	Salmon River at Challis
ID	Squaw Creek Road Decommissioning and Watershed Restoration, Clearwater National Forest
IL	Illinois River Basin
MO	McKenzie Creek Watershed
MT	Big Spring Creek
NC	Mitchell River Watershed Coalition
NC	Little Tennessee River
ND	Pembina River Floodplain Restoration
NE	South Table Creek, Otoe County
NM	Bluewater Creek Watershed, Cibola National Forest
NM	Comanche Creek Watershed, Carson National Forest
NM	Santa Fe Watershed, Santa Fe National Forest
NV	Carson River
OH	Loramie Valley Alliance Watershed Project
OR	Big Marsh Restoration Project, Deschutes National Forest
OR	Soda Creek Stream Restoration, Deschutes National Forest
OR	Williams Prairie / North Fork Crooked River Channel Restoration Project, Ochoco National Forest
SD	Jennings/Smith Restoration Project

(continued)

TN	Coker Creek Project
UT	Upper Provo River Restoration, Wasatch-Cache National Forest
VA	Kingstowne Stream Restoration
WA	Asotin Creek
WA	Tolt River Basin, King County
WA	Tucannon River
WI	Whitewater River Watershed
WI	Plum Creek EQIP Watershed
WV	Knapp Creek Watershed
WY	Jackson Hole, Wyoming Environmental Restoration Project, Teton County

"The restoration of the Carson River is a great achievement for our state," said Sen. Richard Bryan, D-Nev.[1] The Carson River project was one of those designated as a National Restoration Demonstration Watershed. As he bathed in restoration's heady glow, Bryan explained that the project won because of its use of innovative stream restoration technologies.

The quantity (and quality) of freshwater produced by the planet has declined in the past century, while per capita usage skyrocketed and the human population tripled. Here's a pop quiz for investment-oriented readers: what happens when supply of something decreases, the amount each customer uses dramatically increases, and the number of customers increases by four billion?

The Dam Breaks

> Our country is at a critical crossroads. We are entering a new era of restoration; we must learn from the mistakes of the past and act now to restore the life that should be teeming in our rivers.
>
> Every study has shown that dam removal is the best—and probably only—way to restore the salmon. Dam removal is far less costly than other salmon recovery alternatives such as severe new restrictions on logging, farming and fishing.
>
> —**Rebecca Wodder**, President of American Rivers, April 2000

[1] "Carson River Wins Designation," *The Record-Courier,* July 10, 1999.

"It was really just amazing," said Betsy Ham in a May 29, 2001, Associated Press article.[2] She was among anglers, town folk, and restorationists in a frantic bucket brigade of fish. "If you walked in to scoop them up, you were slipping and sliding on alewives. We were just scooping and scooping and handing them over as fast as we could."

It was the kind of scene that makes a lasting impression: crowds of adults and children standing knee-deep in hundreds of thousands of silvery, foot-long, one-and-a-half-pound fish. They were lifting them from the Sebasticook River as quickly as possible with nets and buckets to transport the fish past the Fort Halifax Dam, which was blocking their migration. Manually lifting them past the Fort Halifax dam gives the alewives access to many more miles of river before the fish hit the next dam.

This scene was even more dramatic for long-time residents. They knew that just one year earlier, these same waters had been largely devoid of fish in general, and alewives in particular. The difference was the removal of the Edwards Dam, some 20 miles downstream, which had stood for 160 years. It was no coincidence that this was also the first time in 160 years that more than a handful of alewives had migrated this far upriver.

The Edwards Dam had been 24 feet high and 900 feet wide. It was built in 1837 to power a textile mill, and, at the time of its demise, was producing just one-tenth of one percent of Maine's hydroelectric power. Its July 2000 removal didn't just benefit "the poor man's salmon," as the alewives are called; alewives are key food items for ospreys, bald eagles, and larger game fish. The numbers of highly prized rockfish (striped bass) immediately surged so dramatically that fly fishers were going crazy, and fishing tour guides were doing a record business.

The renewed availability of this 17-mile stretch of river also restored important habitat for nine other "sea-run" fish species, such as Atlantic salmon and Atlantic sturgeon (both on the verge of extinction), blueback herring, American shad, American eel, rainbow smelt, the endangered shortnose sturgeon, tomcod, and sea lampreys. Although few people would cry over the loss of the parasitic lampreys, their decomposing bodies transfer vital nutrients to watershed soils (as do salmon) when they die after spawning in remote streams. Such restorative effects on forests many miles from the Edwards Dam is just one of many "invisible" benefits of dam breaching.

[2] Glenn Adams, "Alewives Return to Sebasticook," *Bangor Daily News,* May 29, 2001.

An Historic Event

The above river renaissance took place in Augusta, Maine; similar tales are being told in dozens of U.S. communities from the Atlantic to the Pacific. The story of the Edwards Dam is important for its legal and political precedent. The dam was the first *operational* hydroelectric dam closed by the Federal Energy Regulatory Commission (FERC) *against its owners' will.*

The FERC refused to renew its operating license in 1997 when an objective study (an exceedingly rare thing in the energy business) showed that the benefits of restoring the river clearly outweighed the value of the electricity produced by the dam. "Essentially the whole nation is watching," said Matt O'Donnell, who heads the Maine Marine Resources Department's effort to restore alewives and shad to their historical habitat in the Kennebec River basin, in that same May 29, 2001, *Bangor Daily News* article.

Because even the breaching of useless, obsolete dams, not to mention the thousands of make-work dams that never had a legitimate purpose, is usually a contentious process, this decommissioning of a still-functioning power-generating dam signaled a turning point for this restorative industry. It wouldn't have been possible if the Edwards' enemies hadn't been able to point to the sensational results of many earlier dam removals. In the first 15 years of the new millennium, over 250 U.S. hydroelectric dams will be up for relicensing. Power utilities see the handwriting on the wall and are starting the bargaining process early to determine which ones will go.

"Edwards is a historic tremor, but there are dozens of aftershocks rippling out across the country," said U.S. Interior Secretary Bruce Babbitt. "With 75,000 aging dams nationwide, local communities from Bangor [Maine] on one coast to Ventura County on the other are making tough new decisions over what they value from their rivers. Each dam leads to lively debates and consensus-building solutions like these. When it comes to native wild fish and river restoration, states like Maine are the cutting edge 'laboratories of democracy.' "[3]

Adding to the acclaim, the world's largest circulation (1.5 million) science and technology publication, *Popular Science,* awarded the Edwards Dam removal project its "Best of What's New for 1999" designation.

---

[3] Environmental News Network, June 30, 1999.

Even government agencies traditionally associated with habitat degradation are getting into the act. The U.S. Forest Service and the Bureau of Land Management are spending $75 million annually to restore rivers and streams that run through federal land. Besides removing barriers to fish passage, they also restore streamside vegetation and install fences to keep cattle out of the water.

One fact is often lost on those who oppose the decommissioning of dams: no dam is permanent. All have a limited life, and many will have to be taken down—often due to the buildup of sediment—long before their structural lifespan ends. We lose $8 billion worth of reservoir capacity worldwide every year due to silt buildup, making an already bad economic equation far worse.

For example, an 80-year-old dam on Oregon's Rogue River—39 feet high and 460 feet wide—has long served agricultural irrigation purposes. But it also blocked runs of salmon and steelhead trout. The dam served no other purpose—such as electricity, drinking water storage, or flood control—and Oregon's fisheries bureau had condemned it as the Rogue's "biggest killer" of salmon and steelhead. Now, it is being dismantled and replaced with a pumping station.

Quoted in a Reuters article of October 17, 2001, by Bruce Olsen, Oregon governor John Kitzhaber said in a news conference, "The Rogue is one of Oregon's most spectacular natural treasures, a waterway that is legendary for its scenic beauty, fish and wildlife, and amazing whitewater. . . . [The dam's destruction will] restore and protect this incredible river while still allowing farmers to meet their water needs." Olsen went on to quote a Bureau of Reclamation official as saying the restored fish populations would provide about $5 million annually to the area. Maybe more telling was the fact that 63 percent of the farmers who used the irrigation water from the dam voted for its demolition (a $23 million project for some lucky contractor).

On March 14, 2000, a global celebration took place at 65 dams in 20 countries. Its visionary theme for the next 100 years was "A Century of River Restoration." One of those rallies took place at the much-hated Glen Canyon Dam, which created "Lake" Powell and which has been strangling the Colorado River since 1963. The Glen Canyon Action Network (the principal community organization for restoration of the Colorado River) is appropriately headquartered in an old, restored ice cream shop, now named the Restoration Creamery. Visitors purchase cones and root beer floats, with profits going toward the cause. The network's slogan is "Draining Lake Powell: One scoop at a time."

Who Could Possibly Resist Watershed Restoration?

The Army Corps of Engineers' internecine strife regarding its inevitable transition from new to restorative development was perfectly illustrated when the Little Rock, Arkansas, office of the Corps recently rejected an ill-conceived plan for a new dam on Bear Creek, a tributary to the Buffalo National River watershed. Scientific research overwhelmingly condemned the damage the dam would do to 135 miles of the river.

Arkansas governor Mike Huckabee strenuously objected to the loss of millions of dollars in one-time revenues the dam-building project would have brought to a few firms in his state. The Corps buckled, and the Little Rock office's decision was reversed at the Corps' division office in Dallas. "I don't think the information changed when it went to Dallas, only the politics did," said Don Barger, a spokesperson for the National Parks Conservation Association, in an October 26, 2001, Associated Press article by Brian Skoloff. "I can see no reason, other than political, for Dallas' reversal of the documented and well-made decisions by the Little Rock district."

That decision was even made in the face of objections by another federal agency, the U.S. National Park Service. (The USNPS, in contrast to the Corps, has apparently made the transition to restorative development on a wholesale basis, as we'll see in Chapter 11.) The decision resulted in a lawsuit brought by seven national environmental NGOs. Meanwhile, the Association of California Water Agencies (ACWA) defended the proposed dam, warning that if the next drought is as bad as that of 1987–1992, many farmers will be completely without water for up to three years. Unfortunately, ACWA largely ignored the underlying causes—poor watershed management, water wastage, etc.—and instead blamed the problems on an endangered fish species that selfishly required some of the water.

Restoring watersheds is a complex job, whereas restoring rivers and streams is sometimes as simple as knocking down a dam. As usual, though, "simple" does not necessarily equate with easy. The United States alone has literally tens of thousands of obsolete dams, but even obsolete ones often have vehement defenders. Sometimes these defenders are local homeowners with water views on the artificial lake the dam created. Others prefer bass fishing in lakes to trout fishing in streams. Still others are preservationists who see older dams as part of a community's heritage. And then there are folks who simply hate change (or who hate the people proposing the change). And that's just the "useless" dams. Imagine how the intensity of the fight escalates when individuals or corporations have a large vested financial interest in a working hydro-electric dam.

Watershed Desperation and Restoration Around the World

According to the European Commission, two-thirds of Europe's trees are sick or dying. This is due to a complex, interrelated mix of soil exhaustion, global climate change, acid rain (and other forms of air pollution), and poor management (German "forests" were kept as tidy—and near-lifeless—as museums). Borneo's park commission, and its equivalents in many Southeast Asian countries, says that its rainforests have reached the point of no return: no seedlings have taken root in over eight years.

Deforested Pakistan is getting so thirsty that the country floated a plan to melt glaciers with nuclear energy. Despite the vital role the glaciers play in the weather and ecosystems that support their farmers, some Pakistani leaders want to liquidate their future for temporary relief now. Fortunately, a few Pakistani officials joined the international outcry against the nuclear "solution." But as soon as that idea died, glacier-melting reappeared on the agenda; this time, the idea is to spray the glaciers with charcoal. Charcoal, of course, is made from trees, creating more deforestation, and thus more drought. . . .

Environmental groups and science publications are not the only ones on the watershed restoration bandwagon, fortunately. For example, the November/December issue of *Foreign Affairs*, that intellectual flagship of what outsiders call "the Establishment," carried an article titled "Restoring the Forests." It was written by David G. Victor of the powerful Council on Foreign Relations, and Jesse H. Ausubel of Rockefeller University. Not exactly the Alice's Restaurant crowd.

They said, "Fortunately, the 20th Century witnessed the start of a 'Great Restoration' of the world's forests. . . . Geographers have observed a transition from deforestation to reforestation in countries as distant as France and New Zealand. . . . But the Great Restoration is far from complete. . . . The focus is on 2050. That might seem distant, but trees grow slowly, and capital-intensive logging firms change their practices gradually. . . . [F]ive decades work, with steady guidance, will make the restoration of the forests truly great. . . . Such a Great Restoration is truly a worthy goal for the landscape of the new millennium." Longtime readers of *Foreign Affairs* know that such lofty, near-evangelical language is far from the norm. Restorative development seems to inspire all who so much as catch a glimpse of it.

The importance of the *Foreign Affairs* article isn't the content, which didn't really plow any new ground. In fact, it contained some glaring errors, such as calling non-native tree farms of eucalyptus and pine in Brazil "forest planting." The article's importance is its venue. As Marshall MacLuhan taught us, the medium is the message, and this message was, "Restorative development is becoming the new establishment."

The article went beyond lip service, addressing leading-edge issues like the integration of forest restoration with farm restoration, and the integration of forest restoration with the restoration of indigenous communities' socioeconomic health. The authors also called for the certifying bodies of sustainable forestry to raise their standards "with the path to long-term restoration in mind."

ISSUES AND INSIGHTS

> The purpose of the engineer is to put certainty into the constructed environment.
> —**Kyle Schilling,** Former Water Resources Director, U.S. Army Corps of Engineers

The same cautions that applied to the previous chapter obviously apply to watersheds (and to the following chapter on fisheries), because all are ecosystem-based. With that in mind, here are a few problems that seem especially common in the industry of watershed restoration.

1. Over-engineering   Let's pick on our engineer buddies again. It's said that the U.S. Army Corps of Engineers never met a river or stream that didn't need a dam.

Kyle Schilling's quote, above, wouldn't be a problem if we were just talking about structural engineers, mechanical engineers, and so forth: I'm a big fan of bridges and buildings that don't collapse. The problem arises when civil engineers apply this quest for certainty to the natural environment—turning it into "the constructed environment"—such as when a river is converted into a canal, or a pond into a reservoir. This approach turns the natural environment into the built environment, with the concomitant loss of living functions one would expect from such a transformation.

Among many other factors, restoration of streams and rivers involves natural channel designs, a complex subject that we are only now beginning to understand. Although they play a vital role in most large-scale restoration efforts, civil engineers' desire to control must be balanced with "chaotic agendas," such as allowing seasonal fluctuations, serving the needs of wildlife, and allowing streams to reshape themselves.

In other words, engineers must seek a variety of scientific inputs, and even artistic insights: Biohabitats, Inc., one of the top stream restoration companies, often hires an artist to sketch a local area's natural streams, especially the rock formations and the little rapids. The firm has found that artists do a better job (than do photographs) of capturing the essence of the stream's flows and personality. The drawings guide engineers' re-creation of ugly, abused, eroded streams that have "lost their way."

2. Ecosystem utilitarianism   We often look at watersheds and wet-lands as watermaking and watercleaning machines. We task them with cleansing municipal stormwater and with performing tertiary treatment of sewage, often without considering the impacts of this added burden. This is especially true of those wetlands we create: forgetting that we're only replacing what we destroyed, we take a proprietary attitude, basi-cally telling these new ecosystems they have to work for a living.

Of course, ecosystems already work hard for a living. Dale Lead-beater, of the 100-person Canadian environmental engineering company Gartner Lee Limited, says her firm learned the importance of integrating biological and engineering observations. Invoking John F. Kennedy, she advised attendees at the 2001 annual conference of the Society for Eco-logical Restoration, "Ask not what your wetlands can do for you. Ask what you can do for your wetlands."

3. The mitigation trap   Mitigation allows companies and communi-ties to destroy habitat in return for building or conserving similar habitat elsewhere. It's driven primarily by federal laws, such as those (increas-ingly politically undercut) mandates for "no net loss of wetlands."

Mitigation was an aspect of the Edwards Dam removal, and not all environmentalists were pleased. Maine's Native Forest Network (NFN) was angry that fish ladders on seven other dams would be delayed so long (16 years) as part of the deal, and that prime shortnosed sturgeon habitat was being sacrificed for the Bath Iron Works expansion (in return for restoration funds from the firm).

NFN claimed that even though the dam removal officially used no public funds, (thanks in part to $2.5 million from Bath Iron Works), the state was subsidizing Bath's shipyard construction with taxpayer dol-lars to the tune of some $190 million, so Maine citizens were really just getting a 1.3 percent "restoration refund from Bath." Few would say the Edwards project was perfect, but most will say it was as good a river restoration trendsetter as we could have asked for, even with the mitigation.

4. Water privatization   Private investments are flooding towards water these days, as former (and current) oil speculators begin to take seriously the decades-old prediction that "water will be the oil of the twenty-first century." Las Vegas, for example, is projected to run out of water by 2006.

Oilman T. Boone Pickens' water investments were mentioned in Chapter 4: he now owns a 26,000-acre ranch on top of the largest ground-water reserve in Texas. Fellow Texans Ed and Lee Bass scored a $250,000,000 paycheck from a private water utility for rights to 45,000 acres in southern California.

Disgraced former energy darling Enron tried its hand at water specu-lation with its Azurix division, and took a bath. Although the strategic vision was basically good, the company made two mistakes: (1) bad tim-ing (five years too soon, according to *Forbes* magazine), and (2) poor execution (expensive lawsuits over who owns what water with public entities like Madera County, California). Dan Noble of Resource Trends (a water industry consultant) was quoted in *Environmental Business Journal* (Vol. XIII, No. 9/10, 2001) observing: "Azurix was an attempt to get rich quick in water/wastewater privatization in one market that didn't want it that quickly, the United States, and in the global arena where Azurix was too small and inexperienced to compete with the Vivendis of the world."

I am not against privatization of water in principle: My major caution concerns the transference of "oil ethics" to this field. Throughout the twentieth century, no force undermined democracy or instigated warfare more often than did the oil industry, and it persists in doing so. Coinci-dental with the meeting of the Second World Water Forum in 2000—attended by representatives of 115 countries—Italian newspapers reported that their politicians had been offered bribes totaling 200 billion lire to approve a private water supply project. In Africa, a dozen multi-national firms were caught bribing officials to secure Lesotho Highlands Water Project contracts. Such oil industry-style lack of transparency leads to projects that are hyperprofitable for the contractors in the short run, and disastrous for the client countries in the long run.

Referring to the growth of web-based water rights intermediaries, Roger Fillion's article in *Business 2.0* said, "By supplying news and infor-mation, [water rights web-] site operators also hope to inject a heaping dose of glasnost into a market legendary for hush-hush wheeling and dealing."[4]

---

[4] Roger Fillion, "Water, Water, Everywhere," *Business 2.0*, July 2000.

Privatization isn't intrinsically bad. Given the political danger of raising taxes and utility rates (thus the reticence of elected officials to do what's necessary), privatization might be the only way to bring appropriate pricing to water. But it's certainly an area rife with danger.

5. Restoring watersheds is not the only factor in aquifer health Expanding and revitalizing our watersheds will do wonders for both the quantity and quality of water in our aquifers, but those who get their drinking water from wells might still be drinking poison, even after watershed restoration. Many other restorative industries—such as brownfields remediation—have to expand before aquifers will be safe. Unrestored brownfields and leaking underground storage tanks (USTs) are sending continuous plumes of toxins into aquifers worldwide.

What's more, some cities and industries use "deep well injection" to sweep their sewage and hazardous wastes (including nuclear) under the carpet—about 4500 feet deep. There are about 172 of these sites in the United States. One obvious problem with the deep well approach is that the toxic material doesn't go away: Other than anaerobic bacteria, there's no ecosystem down there to purify the waste. Much of it will remain toxic for millennia, but it's not just our grandchildren's problem.

Many of these wells spring leaks within just a few years of use. (They've also been implicated in triggering earthquakes.) Rural dwellers hundreds of miles away are sinking Artesian wells, expecting the earth to offer up pure drinking water, and they are getting sewage (or worse) instead. Due to the inaccessibility of the waste, each injection site is creating, with each passing day, a truly difficult future restoration project.

CLOSING THOUGHTS

> W. K. Dickson & Co., Inc. (WKD) is pleased to announce a major expansion of its wetlands and watershed environmental restoration and mitigation services.
> —from an April 5, 2002, press release by a consulting engineering firm, founded in 1929 and employing 200+ engineers. Quoted here as a typical Restoration Economy announcement. In the four years of researching this book, the author doesn't recall the closing or retrenchment of a "real" restoration firm (as opposed to the now-bankrupt defense contractors that did "fake" restoration work in the '80s)

American Rivers publishes an annual list of "America's Most Endangered Rivers." The 2001 list included (in descending order of criticality) the Missouri, the Canning, the Eel, the Hudson, the Powder, the Mississippi (and tributaries), the Big Sandy, the Snoqualmie, the Animas, the East Fork Lewis, the Paine Run, the Hackensack, and the Catawba. Every threatened river spawns a host of champions. Here's bestselling historian Stephen Ambrose on his favorite: "Though few rivers have been subjected to human influence as much as the Missouri, no river possesses more potential for revitalization."[5]

Again, watershed restoration isn't "just" a matter of unchoking rivers by removing dams. There are many other contributors to watershed degradation, such as clear-cutting, tilling of farms, fire suppression, and acid rain. Some of these will be covered in later chapters.

> Our number one water quality problem in the National Forests is roads.
> —Jim Lyons, U.S. Undersecretary of Agriculture, 2000

Sometimes an entire watershed can be contaminated. The EPA has begun a $359 million restoration of the Coeur D'Alene River watershed, which extends from near the Montana–Idaho border into Washington state. The agency is removing soil (polluted by mining operations) from some 900 residences; the project entails taking about 1.3 million cubic yards of toxic sediment out of 33 streams, and capping contaminated sediments at several parts of the Spokane River. This watershed restoration is just part of an overall environmental restoration of the area, which is projected to cost up to $1.3 billion.

The techniques of active watershed restoration—beyond removing problematic infrastructure and activities—can take many forms, including reforestation, restorative farming, "green housing developments," and restoring natural flows and dynamics to "tamed" rivers and streams. There's not a human community on Earth that doesn't depend, directly or indirectly, on a watershed for its survival.

The dam-breaching stories in this chapter (such as the fish-in-a-bucket brigade in Augusta, Maine) probably sound more like fishery restoration than watershed restoration. The alewives' return was described in detail because it was a sign—an indicator—of a partial river restoration. The complete river restoration will require restoration of the streams that feed the river, and of the forests that feed water to the streams. In other words, watershed restoration. Projects linked to watershed restoration will also be discussed in Chapters 7, 8, and 10, so you may explore this complex and crucially important subject in more detail.

---

[5] Dick Russell, "America's Troubled Waters: Can They Be Saved?" *E Magazine.*

Watershed restoration is often vital to fisheries, so they are the next macro-ecosystem we'll deal with. Shutting off our supply of fish might not throw us into crisis as quickly as shutting off our supply of fresh-water, but most Americans are surprised when they learn just how much of the world economy is dependent on fish. But for the citizens of Japan, Norway, Portugal, Ecuador—and literally dozens of other countries around the world whose economies depend strongly on fisheries—it's no surprise at all.

A SMALL SAMPLING OF OPPORTUNITIES

Business and investment

- The Army Corps of Engineers (and similar governmental agencies in other countries) won't retain its near-monopoly on heavy-duty watershed restoration jobs, such as dam removal, forever. This opening of the market will translate into expanded opportunities for private companies.
- Irrigation and drinking water needs are growing, and many of these systems are currently centered around dams. Firms that combine civil engineering, biological science, and agricultural engineering to create integrated dam removal strategies that successfully address these conflicting constraints will be in great demand.
- While removing the tens of thousands of unnecessary dams is key to restoring many watersheds—not to mention freshwater fisheries, urban waterfronts, etc.—it's not the only tactic: Others include removing ill-placed roads (which cause erosion and facilitate illegal logging), replanting stream banks, reforesting hillsides, and removing hundreds of thousands of unauthorized dikes, erected by farmers to push floodwaters onto other farmers' lands (it's not their intention, but it's certainly the effect). All can be profitable contracts for properly-prepared firms.
- Dot-com companies are finding rich opportunities in the trading of water rights. This growth industry is also providing revenue diversification opportunities for many ranchers and other landowners, who can now easily sell their water on sites such as waterbank.com, waterrightsmarket.com, and waterinvestments.com. $2 to 3 billion worth of water deals are made annually just in the western United States, so this isn't an industry to sneeze at.
- The *real* leading edge (yet to emerge) of this industry's investment opportunities will likely be speculating on the *future* water rights of nonproductive watersheds that will be restored.

(continued)

NGOs and other nonprofits

- There is no national (U.S.) watershed association, restorative or otherwise. Nor is there an international watershed association. Given the vital importance of watersheds and their associated aquifers, this seems a great opportunity for a not-for-profit entrepreneur or for an existing water-related group to expand (or tighten) its focus.
- Conservation NGOs and community revitalization groups can tap tremendous new sources of government funding by integrating their projects with the extremely fast-growing watershed restoration and urban stream revitalization trends.
- As the valuation of ecosystem services becomes more established, conservation groups that would like to purchase important wildlife habitat—but can't afford it—should take a lesson from the water, oil, and natural gas industries. They will often find it possible to purchase the water rights instead. They could then sell the water to communities—or to other restoration projects, such as fisheries or wetlands—and the income would replace that from clear-cutting the forest (which would destroy its water production).

Community and government

For communities and nations whose water supply is already approaching crisis conditions, watershed restoration offers a far more cost-effective long-term solution than legal wrangling—or warfare—over water rights with other states and countries. The fringe benefits alone are usually worth the cost: increased recreational areas and wildlife, less susceptibility to droughts, fewer or less disastrous floods and mudslides, etc.

Restoring Our Fisheries:
Estuaries, Reefs, and Oceans

Let the waters bring forth swarms of living creatures.
—Genesis 1 (restored), Cox, based on Revised Standard Version

We Americans, and the citizens of most other nations, desperately need examples of governmental progress and enlightenment. For that reason, let's begin with examples of the burgeoning government support of fisheries restoration, rather than with the project story that begins the other restoration industry chapters.

On June 13, 2001, the U.S. House of Representatives approved H.R. 1157, a bill authorizing $600 million over three years to First Nation tribes and Western states for Pacific salmon restoration. "Many of these towns have been devastated by the collapse of salmon populations. If we restore salmon populations, future generations—like their ancestors—can enjoy [the salmon] and prosper," said the bills' author, Rep. Mike Thompson, D-Calif., in an Associated Press article, by Katherine Pfleger.[1]

These funds will be matched by the states, further expanding the pot, and are in addition to the tens of millions of restoration funds already in the budgets of the National Marine Fisheries Service and the U.S. Army Corps of Engineers. Most of these projects are related to the "salmon

---

[1] Katherine Pfleger, Environmental News Network, June 14, 2001.

treaty" between Canada and the United States, designed to rescue the 26 endangered anadromous species (those that cycle between fresh- and salt-water) of Pacific salmon and trout.

As with so much restoration legislation, this bill had broad bipartisan support, passing on a vote of 418 to 6, with 66 Republicans and Democrats cosponsoring it. Maybe more importantly, it had strong industry support. Glen Spain, Northwest regional director of the Pacific Coast Federation of Fishermen's Associations was quoted in that same article by Katherine Pfleger: "This is an important investment in the restoration of tens of thousands of salmon industry jobs in economically depressed coastal communities. The broad support for the bill shows that we are getting serious about salmon restoration."

The National Marine Fisheries Service (NMFS) is an agency that has long caught flak (occasionally well deserved) from all sides: Congress, environmentalists, the fishing industry, and communities that depend on fisheries. Now, newly armed (since 2001) by Congress with quadruple its normal funds for habitat restoration, the agency is actively seeking restorative partnerships with all of these parties. Its Community Based Restoration Program is directly restoring fish habitat, while indirectly restoring communities and the many industries related to fishing (boat building/maintenance, net repair, tourism/sport fishing, seafood processing/distribution, etc.). The NMFS estimates that some $35 million of additional restoration funds (or in-kind services) will be aggregated through these partnerships.

Started in 1996, the Community Based Restoration Program has built community partnerships across the United States. Now, the NMFS Restoration Center is expanding its partnerships to include national and regional NGOs that have resources and expertise in the restoration of marine, estuary, and freshwater habitats.

In an Environmental News Service (ENS) article of February 13, 2001, entitled "$8 Million Available for Fish Habitat Restoration," acting NMFS Director Bill Hogarth said, "Public private partnerships are essential to our mission, and the organizations and communities that get behind them are some of our most important allies in restoring and preserving marine habitats. They will help us achieve meaningful habitat restoration. . . ."

In that same article, Scott Gudes, acting Undersecretary of Commerce for Oceans and Atmosphere said, "I have participated in several grassroots community-based restoration projects around the nation and I can personally attest that they work. This year, with the strong support of Congress, we have an additional $6 million in federal funds to add to the $2 million we had planned for restoration activities."

THE SCOPE OF THE FISHERIES RESTORATION INDUSTRY

A fishery can be defined as a system of interactions and interdependencies among fish, their habitats, and humans (primarily the fishing industry). The fisheries restoration industry encompasses the renewal of those parts of the natural environment that are considered commercial fisheries, or that are directly and critically linked to commercial fisheries (such as nursery habitat.) This includes open ocean (pelagic) fishing grounds, coral reefs, and estuaries (plus other areas where freshwater mixes with salt, such as bays, deltas, sounds, gulfs, lagoons, harbors, and inlets).

Not included here are rivers (even though they often serve as breeding grounds for anadromous species, such as salmonids) and lakes. Rivers are addressed in the watershed restoration chapter; lakes are discussed in the ecosystem chapter. The fishing of lakes is generally recreational, rather than commercial, the major exception being the Great Lakes of North America. (The Great Lakes used to be important commercial fisheries, before the catches became too small and too toxic to be worth the trouble.)

As with most of the eight restorative industries, there are many national organizations devoted solely to particular sectors of it. Add in the regional, national, and international NGOs and government agencies focused more broadly on ocean fisheries, and the number of organizations in this restoration industry totals in the hundreds; their projects in the thousands. And then there are the scientists, engineering firms, and contractors who get paid to actually do the restorative work.

PROBLEMS AND SOLUTIONS

> . . . for a moment he pauses to take in the sight of hundreds of prehistoric-looking creatures filling the sky. "It feels like you've gone back 100 million years," [wildlife biologist Dave Brinker] said, marveling that even after centuries of abuse, the great blue herons have survived. Moreover, they're returning to nest this spring throughout the Maryland and Virginia portions of the bay in greater numbers and in more places than scientists have seen before. It's a testament, they say, to the endurance of this iconic bird . . . as much as the efforts to restore the estuary.
> —**Anita Huslin,** "Herons Wing Their Way Back Around Chesapeake,"
> *Washington Post*, May 4, 2001

One might think fisheries would be one of the simpler restoration industries to restore. All we need to do is curb excessive fishing and they'll bounce back, right? This is by no means the case. For instance, many animal species (not just fish) require a certain population density in order to find mates or resist overkill by predators: Simply because there are still a few left doesn't mean they will survive and breed. Such crowding-dependent dynamics are known as "Allee effects," mentioned earlier in Chapter 5.

The passenger pigeon is often used as an example of Allee effects. The passing flocks of these birds once darkened the skies for three days at a time. Daniel Boone spoke of catching supper merely by standing on a hilltop and swinging his rifle into the flying masses. They numbered between 3 and 5 billion in the early eighteenth century. By 1890, most of the remaining individuals were in zoos, where they refused to breed. The last one, named Martha, died at 1:00 P.M., September 1, 1914. Deforestation and (to a much lesser extent) hunting brought their numbers down to "only" a few hundred thousand, which wasn't sustainable.

Allee effects often account for the failure of species restoration programs that are based on the release of captive-bred individuals: there simply aren't enough of them to reach "critical mass." In Chapter 5, we saw how clever management can circumvent such problems, but here's a good example of how much we still have to learn about our ecosystems and how they came to be: the passenger pigeon is now losing favor (in some circles) as an example of Allee effects. It's now suspected that those vast flocks might have been an anomaly, resulting from the sudden European-disease-related disappearance of 90 percent of the Native American population between 1497 and 1550. Without those millions of humans burning forests to maintain prairies (for hunting game), the passenger pigeon's tree habitat expanded greatly in the following two centuries, leading to a population explosion just prior to the U.S. pioneering era.

No such confusion exists as to the relationship of Allee effects to many commercial fisheries, though. There's been a fishing ban (passive restoration) on North Atlantic herring for over a quarter of a century, yet they still haven't recovered. The Peruvian anchovy used to be hauled in at a rate of 11 million tons annually, in the late '60s. They now account for less than 100,000 tons. Many fisheries experts are now expressing pessimism that Atlantic cod, once the most economically important fish in the world, will *ever* recover, no matter how much protection it belatedly receives. When Allee effects are involved, innovative new forms of active restoration may become the only hope of getting populations back to sustainable levels.

Multiple Cures for Multiple Ills

In areas lacking pressures other than fishing, simple fishing bans and limitations can work wonderfully. During a dive in 2000, I witnessed a dramatic increase (compared to areas just a few miles away) in breeding-size fish within the Hol Chan Marine Reserve in Belize. In Honduras, commercially important locally threatened species, including queen conch and spiny lobster, in the Cayos Cochinos Marine Reserve have rebounded nicely. Passive restoration—such as putting areas off-limits to fishing—can be a valid restoration technique all by itself: many fish species respond to that one factor with dramatic population explosions.

But integrated approaches can greatly magnify the results, and are often vital to getting any increase at all. In the case of Cayos Conchos, the Panama-based Smithsonian Tropical Research Institute (STRI) oversees the reserve and is now tackling a multifaceted strategy. Institute members educate the local Garifuna people about marine species, and have shown them how to make charcoal from coconut shell waste, which allows passive restoration of damaged island forests. STRI is also installing photovoltaic power, rainwater cisterns, and sewage treatment plants to help ensure that pressures on local reefs from new development don't worsen.

The norm, however, is for fisheries to be under multiple pressures. Restoring most fisheries is far more complex a job than "simply" reducing fishing pressure. Water pollution, together with the destruction of reef breeding areas and coastal nurseries, are taking huge tolls. Bringing back the world fish harvest involves all the people and industries living and working around estuaries, rivers, reefs, islands, and shorelines—which is some 80 percent of the world's population. The loss of fisheries affects all those people more acutely than they probably realize. Around the world, fisheries are collapsing, with devastating economic impact.

Indonesia, for instance, contains an eighth of all the coral reefs on the planet, and 70 percent of them are dead or dying. The estimated loss to the country's economy is between $500,000 to $800,000 annually, per square mile of dead reef. Worldwide, half a billion people will be out of work if coral reefs continue their decline, and that's just from the loss of fishing jobs. Add in diving-related tourism and sport fishing (saltwater anglers land over 300 million fish annually, just in U.S. waters), and reefs alone account for an estimated $400 billion annually. The United States is the fifth largest fishing nation and the third largest seafood exporter (over $2.3 billion in 1998). In 1998, U.S. commercial fisheries pulled $3.1 billion worth of seafood—about 10 billion pounds—onto our docks.

Directly causing the collapse of major commercial species such as cod, bluefin tuna, and swordfish are so-called "perverse subsidies" from a variety of national governments. These handouts total about $15 billion per year, which equals about 20 percent of the total value of the worldwide catch. This welfare system insulates the industry from both market forces and biological realities, so fishing operations don't feel enough economic pain to make intelligent decisions. Subsidies ensure enough hooks, nets, and boats to land twice as many fish as are available to be caught, with the predictable result of overfishing, leading to industry collapse. Not just fish, either. For instance, in Kodiak, Alaska, the king crab harvest ended in 1982, when the floor fell out from under this population. King crabs still haven't recovered, despite there having been no significant harvesting.

In recent years, there's been a number of articles, and even a book or two, implying that the fisheries problem has been exaggerated. These are often triggered by reports of a particular fishery that had experienced a countertrend growth spurt. Sometimes these recoveries were the result of population dynamics not yet understood, and sometimes they were the result of conservation or restoration efforts.

Recently, such writers were embarrassed by the revelation (in 2002) that Chinese officials had been grossly inflating their numbers. It turns out that the careers of fisheries officials in China are often contingent on their meeting certain harvest goals. Out of self-preservation, they simply gave their superiors whatever numbers were requested. Like most governments, the Chinese officials are convinced that increasing one's catches is simply a matter of throwing more boats—and better technologies—at the fish. But we've been doing that for the last 30 years, and catches have been on a steady downward slide. Sudden collapses are almost inevitable, as the fast growth of these high-tech fleets collides with the shrinking fisheries.

Not everyone in the industry is optimistic that better technology will enable them to catch more of the fish that aren't there. A fisherman in Newfoundland, unwilling to wait for Atlantic fisheries to recover, has switched his livelihood from the global fish shortage to the global freshwater shortage. His Iceberg Corporation of America "fishes" for icebergs, and melts them into delicious (really!) drinking water that is ultra-pure (being rain and snow frozen thousands of years ago).

Trying to cover global fishery problems and restoration efforts in a few pages would result in only a list, with no insight. To get more depth, let's focus on one example: the Chesapeake Bay. The issues here, and even many of the restoration techniques, are broadly applicable around the globe, despite the Chesapeake's uniqueness.

The (Impending) Comeback of the Chesapeake

> Regrettably, we have ample places to examine the slow degradation of an ecosystem, but very few where we can witness and study the reverse—the rebirth of the environment from decades of mistreatment.
> —**Dr. Kennedy Paynter,** professor, Univ. of Maryland Chesapeake Biological Lab

Chesapeake Bay is the largest and most commercially valuable estuary in the world. It's home to some 3,600 species of plants and animals, according to John Wolflin, supervisor of the Chesapeake Bay Office for the U.S. Fish and Wildlife Service, including many threatened and endangered species. As of 1997, over 15 million people were living in the 64,000-square-mile Chesapeake watershed—an increase of 28 percent from 1970—which includes parts of Virginia, Delaware, Maryland, New York, Pennsylvania, and West Virginia, plus the entire District of Columbia.

Chesapeake Bay is now in the global spotlight as a pioneer of integrated fishery and watershed restoration. An article entitled "Act Would Make Bay a Conservation Lab" by Anita Huslin in the October 3, 2001, *Washington Post* discussed the $170 billion Farm Security Act, which had $19 billion earmarked for programs that would restore the Cheasapeake. Huslin said, "At the heart of the proposal is a plan to make the Chesapeake Bay region a test laboratory for the nation . . . [and] transform the Chesapeake Bay cleanup into a national model. . . . Farmers would receive 'green payments' for preserving lands from development, restoring wetlands and planting buffer strips of vegetation around fields to stem the flow of pollution into area waterways."

> Spending on Chesapeake Bay restoration has reached tens of millions per year and is growing . . . [but] "there is no Silicon Valley" in the field of ecosystem restoration.
> —**Raymond McCaffrey,** quoting **Dennis King,** economist at the
> University of Maryland, in "Restoring, Documenting Revival of River Habitat,"
> *Washington Post,* August 13, 2001

If the Chesapeake Bay were a corporation—and if it were in the condition it was in 200 years ago— it would probably be the wealthiest company on the planet (assuming honest accounting). The Chesapeake once accounted for half of the entire planet's commercial oyster harvest. Over 50 years ago, warnings were already being sounded that it was in danger.

Chesapeake Biological Laboratory founder Dr. Reginald Truitt was one of those prescient few; he was branded an irresponsible alarmist for his troubles. In the 1940s, he predicted that, without wise management, oysters would largely disappear from Chesapeake waters within 50 years.

His prediction turned out to be right on schedule. Oysters were at two percent of historical levels in the '90s, and oysters weren't alone in their predicament. In September 2000, scientists and economists reported that blue crab harvests were also at an all-time low. Meanwhile, the number of crab boats and other harvesters was at an all-time high, a surefire recipe for total collapse (known in economic circles as "the tragedy of the commons").

As recently as 1954, the Chesapeake oyster harvest was 38 million pounds annually, but by 1993, it was down to about one million pounds. Pollution kills oysters in a variety of ways, one of the most devastating being the one-two punch of introducing new diseases while simultaneously weakening oysters' immune systems.

> Scientists hope reintroduction of the sea grass will help the waters in many ways. First, the plant life should help stabilize the river bottom, which should result in clearer water, which in turn should promote the growth of more sea grass. Eventually, oysters will be reintroduced to the area. 'When you put grass out there, fish will come.'—lab biologist Bob Stankelis.
> —**Raymond McCaffrey**, "Restoring, Documenting Revival of River Habitat,"
> *Washington Post*, August 13, 2001

Oysters aren't being restored just for the sake of biodiversity, or even just for commercial harvests. Oysters filter vast quantities of water, creating a powerful feedback loop: the more oysters are in the bay, the cleaner the water will be, which encourages more oysters. In 1988, Roger Newell at the University of Maryland's Horn Point Laboratory estimated that the Bay's oyster populations in the late 1880s were capable of filtering the entire volume of the Chesapeake in under six days. He and his colleagues further estimated that the 1980s population would require over 300 days for the same job (and that's assuming a static volume of water, with no ongoing addition of pollutants).

The major bay grass decreases began in the '60s and '70s, as urban growth and increasing agriculture flushed growing amounts of topsoil, sewage, polluted storm runoff, and fertilizers into the bay. These excessive nutrients allowed epiphytes to grow on the sea grasses, preventing sunlight from reaching their food-making photosynthetic cells. This created a triple whammy: the pollution load was increasing, the wetland filters (which are supposed to keep the pollution from the bay) were decreasing, and this killed the grasses and oysters that would have removed the pollutants that did enter the bay.

Oyster-cleansed water encourages more submerged aquatic vegetation (SAV), such as bay grasses, which further cleans the water, encouraging more oysters, which cleanse the water even more, reducing the epiphytes that retard SAV, and so on. "Both seagrasses and oyster beds function as the 'kidneys' of the Bay, cleansing the water of impurities [and allowing] the rest of the ecosystem to function normally," says Professor Walter Boynton of the Chesapeake Biological Laboratory.[2] The intentional creation and optimization of such natural feedback loops is going to be just one of many new disciplines that will be in great demand in the Restoration Economy.

The University of Maryland is far from alone in the effort to restore the Chesapeake. There's the private nonprofit Save The Bay, as well as the Chesapeake Bay Program (a joint effort of Maryland, Pennsylvania, the District of Columbia, and the EPA). Restoring bay grasses is a top priority of the latter: the program signed an updated Chesapeake Bay Agreement in 2000 to increase total acreage of bay grasses to 114,000. If that project is successful, the Chesapeake will still be far short of the 600,000 acres that existed at the beginning of the twentieth century, but it's a great start. In November 2001, oysters got another boost when Congress decided to supplement Maryland's and Virginia's efforts by giving an additional $5 million to the cause: $3 million to the Army Corps of Engineers and $2 million to NOAA to restore oyster reefs.

> . . . we still have a long way to go in restoring the Chesapeake [but] recent findings show some positive trends. The bay grass beds in the Gunpowder River are of particular interest because this area held less than 100 acres in 1989. Now the area holds 24 times as much grass and is home to a great diversity of native species—both benefits of a forested watershed. This area clearly shows the connections between watersheds, water quality and living resources, and is a model for conditions we'd like to see elsewhere.
>   —**Dr. Robert Magnien,** director of tidewater ecosystem assessment at the Maryland department of Natural Resources, in an Environmental News Network article, "Underwater Grasses Growing Again in Chesapeake Bay," May 30, 2001

The year 2000 saw total Chesapeake SAV acreage increase by 7 percent over the previous year. SAV is one of the most important indicators of bay health and provides critical nurseries to blue crabs and many fish

---

[2] Merrill Leffler, "Improving Bay Water Quality," *Maryland AquaFarmer Online,* Winter 2001.

species. This addition of 4,635 acres was the result of both restoration efforts and favorable weather.

Bay grasses are essential in other ways, as well: They reduce shoreline erosion by absorbing wave energy, they oxygenate the water, and they provide both food and habitat for aquatic and marine animals. They also trap sediments, thus clarifying the water. Even high-level predators such as ospreys (fish hawks) are returning; rarely sighted in the '70s, they are now quite common.

Estuaries Are Often the Key

The fact that estuary restoration increases both water quality and nursery habitat for ocean fisheries—and because they are (were) important fisheries themselves—makes them triply important. As a result, the Chesapeake is far from the only U.S. estuary targeted for restoration: the National Marine Fisheries Service has partnered with a private conservation group, Restore America's Estuaries (RAE), in a three-year initiative to restore marine estuaries. RAE is an alliance of 11 coastal, community-based, regional environmental organizations, with a combined membership of more than a quarter-million citizens.

RAE championed The Estuary Restoration Act of 2000 (S. 835), which was signed into law by President Clinton on November 7, 2000, with strong bipartisan support. Sponsored by Senator Lincoln D. Chafee (R-R.I.) and Rep. Wayne Gilchrest (R-Md.), the Act takes an integrated approach. It authorized $275 million over 5 years, and shares RAE's goal of restoring one million acres of U.S. estuary habitat by 2010.

It includes the Chesapeake, as well as the Gulf of Maine, Long Island Sound, the Albermarle and Pamlico Sounds, Narragansett Bay, the Hudson–Raritan Estuary, the Mississippi Delta of Louisiana, Texas' Galveston Bay, San Francisco Bay, Puget Sound, and Tampa Bay.

The Act's $3,400,000-per-year funding comprises the largest single-year award ever made by the Restoration Center of the National Oceanic and Atmospheric Administration (NOAA) through its Community Based Restoration Program. Restoration activities include cleaning up creeks, removing exotic plants, rebuilding marshes, revegetating and reconstructing barrier islands, re-creating forest buffers for streams, and stabilizing shorelines. "With this strategic alliance we further our critical journey to restore the health of our estuaries, the nation's coastal sanctuaries where we live intertwined with the natural world," RAE president Mark Wolf-Armstrong told the Environmental News Service in July 2001.

"Besides rebuilding essential habitat, this partnership will empower communities and engage thousands of volunteers toward our national goal of restoring one million acres by 2010."[3]

Not all estuaries are large, but all are important. Cape Cod alone has 13 estuaries for which restoration plans are being drawn up by The Estuary Project and by the Southeastern Massachusetts Embayment Restoration. The initiatives of just these two organizations involve 89 Massachusetts estuaries. They have $12.5 million in start-up funding from the state and from the University of Massachusetts at Dartmouth.

> When Edward Baker first came to the tip of Mashpee Neck Road in 1967, the Mashpee River was a virtual seafood store. Now it is not. " . . . [Y]ou could get blue crabs this big," Baker said, holding his hands 8 inches apart. "I could get my legal limit of steamers, 1 peck, in 45 minutes. Flounder? My wife, daughter and I would fill a 5-gallon bucket in an hour." The flounder are gone. There are plenty of clams, but you can't eat them anymore. A neat, hand-painted sign, complete with skull and crossbones, explains why: 'Contaminated Waters.' [Brian Howes, a scientist at the School of Marine Technology at UMass Dartmouth, said,] "We are at a crossroads, where we can restore them or allow their continued degradation and accept an erosion of what most in the region consider a critical part of their quality of life."
> —**John Leaning,** "From Pollution to Solution," *Cape Cod Times,* December 10, 2001

As illustrated in the above quote, we're so used to seeing dead waters that we're often surprised to learn just how recently our estuaries were healthy and productive.

ISSUES AND INSIGHTS

A central assumption of new development has been that the oceans are the ultimate toilet and garbage dump, with infinite ability to shield us from our slovenly behavior. That lie has now been put to bed, but we are still in danger of making equally sweeping assumptions about the process of undoing the damage it caused.

Again, the "Issues and Insights" in the previous two chapters also apply to fisheries, and most of the following apply to watersheds and ecosystems.

1. Conservation of the natural environment sometimes equals passive restoration   Maybe more than in any other restoration industry, passive

[3] "$3.4 Million Program Targets Estuary Restoration," Environmental News Service, 2001.

restoration ("stop hurting it and it will recover") of fisheries plays as large a role as active restoration. Politically sensitive measures such as fishing bans and subsidies to allow fishing communities to survive during these bans will remain important tools, so we shouldn't abandon them in our infatuation with active restoration.

In 1999, Reef Check reported that one-third of the world's reefs made a partial recovery, due to a combination of protection efforts and a dip in ocean temperatures. The previous year had seen 15 percent of reefs around the globe die from the opposite: high water temperatures and overfishing. Although we're not likely to make rapid progress on global climate change given current political realities, even our small efforts often pay off.

Rising water temperatures bleached so much of the Maldives reefs in 1998 that most people considered them a lost cause. By 2002, however, they had made a stunning comeback, with fish populations better than people had seen in decades. Why? Most scientists believe it was because the area is relatively pristine; there was enough biodiversity and overall health to give the system the recuperative powers it needed.

2. Hatchery-reared fish—especially genetically engineered varieties—can drive wild fish into extinction Captive-raised fish, often used to restore wild populations, are usually a poor substitute for fish bred in the wild. In fact, they often do great harm to wild populations by introducing diseases, and by competing with them for food. Danger also comes from the use of both exotic and bioengineered species, which escape in large numbers every year. They outbreed (or interbreed) with native species, disrupting ecosystems and damaging biodiversity (by contaminating the gene pool).

Hatchery fish often don't recognize natural predators and/or haven't learned effective avoidance, so their survival rate is extremely low, often around five percent. "Hatchery-reared fish are much more vulnerable than wild fish," says Culum Brown at the University of Edinburgh.[4] Teamed with Kevin Laland of Cambridge University, they are developing training courses—including videos, if you can believe that—for these ignorant fish.

Fishery restoration took a huge step backwards in 2001 when an aquaculture industry-influenced judge—apparently emboldened by the Bush administration's war on environmental regulations—ruled that

[4] *New Scientist,* September 2001.

hatchery fish were legally identical to wild fish. This meant they could be used to meet the requirements of the Endangered Species Act, removing the legal imperative to protect habitat. In effect, the judge's ruling says that ability to breed a species means it's no longer endangered, even if the species is nearly extinct in the wild. Restoration might be the coming thing, but that doesn't mean it's immune to ignorance, incompetence, or corruption.

3. Open-system aquaculture pollutes Many hope aquaculture and mariculture (the saltwater version) will relieve fishing pressure on wild stocks. However, most of these operations are tremendously polluting and are often built right in crucial wild nurseries.

Open-system aquaculture takes clean water from rivers or coasts, runs it through breeding tanks, and dumps it, along with waste and diseases, into the habitat of wild fish. Closed systems endlessly recycle the same water, only adding new water to replace that lost to evaporation. The future is in closed-system aquaculture/mariculture. This is a sphere of tremendous opportunities for farmers, ranchers, and equipment manufacturers.

4. Demanding revenue before restoration is complete The tremendous economic value of fisheries can sometimes encourage compromises in the scientific integrity of restorations for short-term gain. The different approaches to Chesapeake oyster restoration taken by Maryland and Virginia provide a perfect example.

Maryland integrates commercial and ecological goals by restoring native oyster species. Maryland governor Parris Glendening (D) pledged $25 million over a ten-year period for restoration of native oysters. In summer 2001, Maryland planted over 3,100,000 bushels of oyster shells on 22 distressed oyster bars to improve oyster habitat. Over a million oyster larvae ("spat") per acre will be seeded onto these shell beds, where they will attach themselves to old shells to obtain a stable base for growth.

Virginia's government, on the other hand, caved in to fishing industry pressure and forced restorationists to introduce exotic Asian species of oysters that show a greater tolerance for pollution. This, despite good evidence (documented by the Virginia Institute of Marine Science) that it was the introduction of Pacific oysters *(Crassostrea gigas)* into the Chesapeake that imported the MSX virus, which wiped out a huge swath of the native oyster population. Virginia's former governor James Gilmore (R), whose focus on instant gratification drove the state into fiscal crisis, liked this "quick and dirty" approach: it (seemed to) reduce the need for politically painful pollution controls.

5. Declaring success too early   This issue applies to any restoration dealing with living systems, but fisheries react to restorative efforts and lapses faster than most.

It took us centuries to degrade these fisheries (although the past 40 years did the majority of the damage); we need to measure their restoration in decades, not years. After four straight years of improving health, the Chesapeake Bay Foundation's 2001 State of the Bay Report revealed that its ecological health had declined over the previous year.

The foundation uses 13 indicators, each scoring up to 100 points, to compile an average numerical score in which 0 means total destruction, and 100 equals pre-Columbian condition. A score of 70 could be a successful recovery, and the Chesapeake needs to hit 40 to be delisted from the EPA's list of "impaired waters." The low point was in the early '80s when the Chesapeake scored 23. It then climbed to 28, before dropping back to 27 in 2001. While a few indicators, such as shad, improved, others declined significantly. The worst decline was in the blue crab population (the most economically valuable species), which scored 6. Regarding the Chesapeake restoration's regression in 2001, Chesapeake Bay Foundation President William C. Baker said:

> I see a little bit of resting on our laurels, a sense that the bay was just going to get better and better and that it would take care of itself. The most alarming trend in this year's report is not what has changed but what hasn't . . . pollution—primarily from excess nitrogen and phosphorus—has mired the bay's health in the 20 percent range. We need to cut this pollution in half before underwater grasses, crabs, oysters, and other life will thrive and restore the bay system.
> —**Anita Huslin,** "Bay's Progress Seen Slipping Away," *Washington Post,* October 24, 2001

Reducing that pollution will require at least $8.5 billion over the next ten years, spread primarily over five restorative industries: watershed, agricultural, fishery, brownfields, and infrastructure.

CLOSING THOUGHTS

Of the hundreds of fishery restoration programs worldwide, the Black Sea—which is bordered by Turkey, Russia, Georgia, Ukraine, Bulgaria, and Romania—provides maybe the best closing example. It's one of the most endangered inland seas in the world, reeling from the simultaneous insults of overfishing, dredging, invasive species, destructive fishing techniques (such as bottom trawling), coastal erosion (from loss of wetland),

and monstrous levels of pollution. The rivers and watersheds feeding it are in horrible condition, as are the native wildlife populations. The Black Sea fishery is in precipitous decline, with catches falling by a third in the past 20 years alone. Of the 26 commercial species fished in 1960, only six remain in economically significant quantities.

The human communities of the Black Sea are collapsing, too, both from the economic impact of the dying fishery, and from the pollutants' direct effect on their citizens. Industrial toxins abound, but much of the filth is their own bodily waste coming back to them, because the cities dump raw sewage into the sea. The extent of this challenge is vast: The watersheds polluting the Black Sea extend to an additional five countries: Hungary, the Czech Republic, Slovenia, Germany, and Poland.

But restorative development is reaching even here. The six nations on the shores of the Black Sea formed a Black Sea Convention in 1994, in an attempt to avert its complete death. Along with the Global International Waters Assessment (GIWA)—an initiative of the United Nations Environment Programme (UNEP)—the nations are launching a $100 million Black Sea restoration program, timed to coincide with the results of some 66 active research projects.

Coincidentally, the world's largest river restoration is already underway: that of the Danube River (mentioned in Chapter 1). Its restoration will help restore the Black Sea, the Danube's terminus. A new restoration partnership is forming, called the Black Sea Basin Strategic Partnership; it comprises the World Bank, the European Union, UNEP, and UNDP (United Nations Development Programme). With sound management, those funds should create many local jobs over the next few decades: restoring the Black Sea might eventually become as large an employer as destroying it used to be.

Futurists have long envisioned a time when hunger would be eliminated by "farming the oceans." That vision turned out to be a little off, because they didn't take into account the effect of decades of high-tech ocean "strip-mining" by factory trawlers, not to mention massive pollution, and other problems. When the discussion concerns the restoration of a system generating hundreds of billions of dollars per year, businesses large and small will be found nearby. Firms that actively help restore the fisheries on which they depend will likely be exempt from the sudden, often clumsily imposed, fishing bans, which are proliferating as fishing nations finally react to the crises they have caused. That's just one of many significant competitive advantages they'll enjoy.

As vital as our fisheries are to the world economy, land-based food production is even more so. In the same way that our fish catches are decreasing, despite the presence of far more boats and greatly improved technologies, so too is most farmland suffering decreasing yields, despite heavy chemical stimulation, genetically modified plants, and efficient new machinery. So let's look now at restorative agriculture.

A SMALL SAMPLING OF OPPORTUNITIES

Business and investment

- Closed-system aquaculture and mariculture, both for food, and to restore threatened species.
- Some of the most profitable and effective opportunities will likely be public–private partnerships that integrate the restoration of fisheries with sustainable harvesting by those same companies, thus avoiding the "tragedy of the commons" dynamic.

NGOs and other nonprofits

A recent trend in fisheries restoration and management is the ecosystem approach. Fisheries have long been defined in a very limited manner, mostly focused on the areas where fish are caught, and where they breed. A more integrative approach is required, a natural role for NGOs. The American Fisheries Society (a scientific group more than 130 years old) is moving in this direction, but numerous opportunities for industry and application-oriented NGOs are emerging. The best will facilitate integrated restoration. For example: Many coastal reefs suffer from cloudy water, which robs them of light. Restoring them requires cleaner water. That means restoring sewage infrastructure, restoring watersheds, restoring farmland, restoring mangroves & wetlands, etc. With good integration, the economic value of fisheries spills over to ecosystem projects that have more trouble getting funded.

Community and government

Ocean fisheries are more dependent on international cooperation than any other restoration industry. A unique opportunity thus exists for struggling regional economic development entities (Caracom, Mercosur, etc.). Creating a regional fishery restoration strategy—such as for the Caribbean or the South Pacific—could result in increasing stocks when everyone else's are declining. Regional approaches are traditionally undercut by countries with large fishing fleets (like Japan, Norway, and Russia) who "buy" the votes of small (often island) nations.

Restoring Our Farms
and Rural Economies

Almost lost among the more than 7,000 islands of the Philippines is the little 150,000-acre island of Guimaras, with its 130,000 residents. The Azgar family farm sits on a hill in the village of Sebaste, overlooking the tranquil turquoise waters of the Guimaras Strait. The Azgars are among the pioneers of restorative agriculture, which is revolutionizing ranches and farms of all sizes around the globe, already accounting for billions of dollars.

As recently as the early '90s, the Azgar farm, despite a location that has all the usual ingredients of paradise, was a site of devastation. It was surrounded by dry, barren land—the legacy of slash-and-burn clear-cutting of the once-lush forest. Now, thanks to a project funded and managed by the U.S.-based charity, Save the Children, the Azgars are in paradise again. Since 1992, the Azgars' farming practices have been a contributing factor in restoring the forest and watershed, restoring the health of their farm, restoring the health of nearby fisheries, all while restoring the finances of their family and community. Though they currently refer to their style of farming as "agro-forestry," it's more accurately called restorative agriculture, since not all agro-forestry starts with debilitated land and brings it back to life.

By restoring the watershed, the Azgars are reducing the silt that washes off the hills and kills nearby reefs and mangroves, which are critically important nurseries for sea life. The Philippines had 1,125,000 acres of mangroves at the beginning of the twentieth century, and just 375,000 acres at the end of the century. The Azgars are thereby contributing to the restoration of local fisheries for their nonfarming neighbors, most of whom use small sailing or paddled boats, and thus can't go far afield.

> "My husband and I knew a long time ago that rice would not provide us with enough money to send our children to school," says Merle Azgar. "We were introduced to a farmer who was raising trees—bringing the jungle back to life—and making money. Now we are doing it too, and sending our children to school." The Azgars worked with Save the Children and began to restore the land, embarking on a sustainable agriculture project that not only provides for their family, but has restored the environment as well. The rough terrain proved hospitable to native mahogany trees and they planted over 1,400 trees on their land. The trees prevent soil erosion, protect the watershed, and provide compost that they sell to other local farmers to fertilize their own fruit trees and vegetables. In addition, the shade of these tall trees provides the perfect cover necessary to raise pineapple and forage crops for their goats. They are also raising mahogany seedlings and selling them to their neighbors.
>
> "The Philippines" [cited June 10, 2002]. Available from
> www.familyplanet.org/featuredproj6.php

Of more immediate importance to the Azgars, their assets have swelled from 5,000 pesos (U.S.$100) to about a million pesos. They've leveraged these newfound assets as collateral for loans that enabled them to diversify, such as by purchasing beehives to pollinate crops and trees while producing honey. The mahogany trees they planted will be harvestable around 2006, when they thin out the crop and add yet another revenue stream.

At over 75 million citizens, the Philippines has the fourteenth largest population in the world, and is doubling its numbers every 30 years, because the country also has the highest fertility rate in Asia. This population explosion has already surpassed the capacity of Philippine fisheries. Former fishermen are desperately invading the jungles in search of food and livelihoods, with disastrous results for wildlife, rivers, and farmers (without forests, cloud creation is crippled, causing local droughts).

The Azgar farm is thus the essential model for a nation that already went from 75 percent forest to 25 percent forest last century, and where the pace of destruction quickens every year as hunger increases. The restorative agriculture model is, quite literally, the key to the Philippines' future as a viable country. Globally, it's hardly a unique situation.

THE SCOPE OF THE AGRICULTURAL RESTORATION INDUSTRY

Rural economic revitalization is mostly about farm restoration, which includes a number of restorative aspects, such as rebuilding soil quality, increasing economic viability, and integrating with the natural environment.

This restoration industry also extends to rural redevelopment and integration of rural lifestyles and economies with encroaching suburban-urban lifestyles, and with the effects of globalization. As with all of the restoration industries, there is significant overlap with other industries, such as watersheds and ecosystems.

I identify three basic forms of restorative agriculture:

1. Integrating conventional farming or ranching with other aspects of restoring the natural environment (ecosystems, watersheds, or fisheries). An example is fencing streams to keep cattle out, thus allowing passive restoration of the stream, or actively restoring the stream by planting the bank with native shrubs and trees.

2. Integrating conventional farming or ranching with restoration of the built environment (brownfields, infrastructure, heritage, and disaster/war). An example would be remediating the contamination of leaking underground storage tanks (USTs), using a portion of the property to create a wetland for revenue-generating tertiary sewage treatment.

3. Converting existing farms or ranches from unsustainable usage to modes that remove contamination (herbicides, pesticides, etc.) from the soil, increase soil flora and fauna, rebuild depleted topsoil, restore the biodiversity of the property, and/or contribute to the restoration of surrounding ecosystems. Switching a conventional farm to organic techniques is restorative agriculture.

PROBLEMS AND SOLUTIONS

> Nor rural sights alone, but rural sounds,
> Exhilarate the spirit, and restore
> The tone of languid nature.
> —**William Cowper** (1731–1800), from John Bartlett, *Familiar Quotations*, 10th ed., 1919

According to a May 2000 report by the International Food Policy Research Institute (IFPRI),[1] almost 40 percent of agricultural land worldwide is seriously degraded, casting doubts on its food production capacity for the future. Soil depletion has already drastically reduced productivity on 16 percent of farms around the globe.

The depletion is not evenly spread, however: nearly 75 percent of agricultural land in Central America is heavily degraded, as revealed by IFPRI's innovative maps (based on satellite and other data). The causes are also varied: The Central American problem mostly stems from erosion due to the widespread modern practice of tilling, which allows the soil to blow or wash away. In Asia, the main problem is salinization due to irrigation. In Africa, the soil lacks nutrients, due to a combination of overuse, lack of access to fertilizers, and interruption of the natural systems that replenish the soil.

As a result of projected population increases, we'll need to increase grain production by 40 percent in the next 20 years, so the prospect of *decreased* production makes the outlook especially grim. According to Ismail Seragldin, World Bank vice president and chairman of a consortium of international agricultural research centers (of which IFPRI is a member), "The results of this innovative mapping raise all kinds of red flags about the world's ability to feed itself in the future."[2]

But the news wasn't all bad: "It's not necessarily irreversible. Careful land management can restore soil health," said Phil Pardy, senior researcher on the IFPRI project, in a Reuters article.[3]

Modern farmers suffer from (and cause) a wide variety of problems, many of which are reaching crisis proportions. In some cases, these challenges are converging to make farming all but impossible. A short list of challenges includes:

- Overdependence on near-monopolistic agricultural product distribution firms that control prices Soviet-style. This discourages innovations by masking the financial pain of irresponsible practices. The immense political power of these firms has—with token exceptions—shielded them (so far) from federal antitrust action.
- Federal subsidies that encourage unsustainable farming practices (inappropriate crops, overly intensive land use, etc.).

---

[1] "40 Percent of Food Land Degraded, Study Finds," *The Toronto Star*, Business Section, May 22, 2000.
[2] Ibid.
[3] Ibid.

- Increasing dependence on nonlocal, undependable, expensive water supplies, due to watershed destruction.
- Loss of topsoil due to the antiquated practice of tilling, combined with other forms of poorly designed, energy-intensive land management.
- Overdependence on expensive pesticides and artificial fertilizers.
- Overdependence on a few plant and animals species with insufficient genetic diversity to withstand disease and climate change. Humans used to farm or collect over 10,000 plant species; now, 120 species provide 90 percent of our food.

The War Between Agriculture and Conservation

> Alley cropping can increase yields of staple crops by more than 50% over unsustainable systems. With multistory cropping, participants grow . . . shade coffee and cacao (the primary ingredient in chocolate) under the shade of rainforest trees planted by participants. The 750,000 trees planted . . . will restore degraded lands and reverse more than half a century of destruction.
> —from the donor literature of Sustainable Harvest International, an NGO founded in 1997 that works with some 500 subsistence farmers in Central America

For decades, farming and ranching have been among the primary enemies of wildlife, though not necessarily by intention. Poorly designed environmental initiatives have unnecessarily positioned conservationists as the natural enemies of agriculture. The fact is that, despite their barbed wire, their damming of streams, their campaigns to exterminate wolves, bears, coyotes, prairie dogs, and so on, most farmers and ranchers are much greater lovers of nature than are many city-based environmentalists.

On May 8, 2001, the World Conservation Union (IUCN) and Future Harvest, the Washington, D.C. based agriculture organization, released a study showing that almost half of the 17,000 major nature reserves worldwide are actually under heavy agricultural use. To anyone who has visited the much-touted high-biodiversity conservation areas of the developing world, the report came as no surprise, but it was subduing nonetheless.

Some observers viewed that IUCN report as another nail in the coffin of the "hot spots" strategy for conserving biodiversity, and it probably would be, if not for the rise of restorative agriculture and "wild farms." Trying to find a workable approach despite the miniscule funding and political support available to conservation, British ecologist

Norman Myers devised the idea of focusing conservation efforts on the 25 "hot spot" areas of the world that contain the highest levels of biodiversity. This "would go far to stem the mass extinction of species," he told *Nature* in 2000.[4]

Unfortunately, it turns out that over a sixth of the world's population—in excess of a billion people—lives in these hot spots. These people also tend to be among the most impoverished, meaning that wildlife conservation is seldom a factor, much less a priority, in their decisions. "There's no hope of conserving biodiversity that way," said Jeff McNeely, the World Conservation Union's chief scientist. "Hot spots are where people live, too."[5] And the IUCN report concurs: "Endangered species, essential farmlands, and desperately poor humans often occupy the same ground. It is unrealistic to expect isolated protected areas to carry the full responsibility for conserving biodiversity."

The Beginning of the End of the War

The IUCN report went on to recommend a combined farm/ecosystem restoration approach unfortunately labeled "ecoagriculture" (the "eco" label is the kiss of death to many projects and concepts: "restorative" agriculture garners far more support from political leaders and farming communities). Restorative agriculture is turning these "problem farmers" into part of a strategy for actually *expanding* these hot spots. In border areas of the Sahara (a biodiversity hot spot in pun only, though the region does have many unique species), it's already been documented that small farmers are responsible for pushing back the expanding desert through their replanting of native trees.

In Costa Rica, ecoagriculture (also called "agroecology") has already been proven: it restores farmers' incomes, restores their soil, and restores populations of endangered species (including native pollinators), in one fell swoop. Integrating such projects with other forms of restorative development—such as government initiatives to restore watersheds, to decentralize/defossilize/reconstruct power grids, and/or to revitalize fisheries—would expand these restorative agriculture pilot projects from isolated learning experiences, to high-profile international models.

[4] Norman Myers, "Biodiversity Hotspots for Conservation Priorities," *Nature*, February 24, 2000.
[5] "People vs. Nature," *New Scientist*, February 26, 2000.

Combined with the related, nascent "wild farms" movement, which uses the restoration of surrounding wildlife habitat to restore the productivity of agricultural activities, the next step is obvious: a formal recognition of—and commitment to—restorative agriculture on the part of independent farmers, agribusiness, academia, government agencies, and NGOs.

When not excessive, and when sufficient recovery time is allowed between burnings, even slash-and-burn agriculture can actually increase species diversity, by creating a greater variety of microhabitats. For instance, seedlings of the endangered, commercially valuable big-leafed mahogany require a cleared, sunny area within the jungle canopy. The clearing enables them to reach a sufficient height before having to compete for sunlight with faster-growing trees. Similarly, many animals depend on plants that grow primarily in disturbed areas: witness how often we see deer, rabbits, and woodchucks on the edges of roads and farms.

One method of increasing farm productivity (by reducing water-logging and erosion from flooding) *and* the health of our ecosystems and waterways is by converting key portions of farmland back to wetlands. The current, antiquated method of engineered flood control, the levee system, only channels excess water to downstream communities (flooding them instead), and spreads tons of gravel and sand over towns and farms when the levees break. Wetlands adjacent to farms actually solve the problem, because a single acre of wetlands can absorb up to 1,660,000 gallons of floodwaters. These revived wetlands have many fringe benefits for agriculture, such as encouraging native insect, mammal, and bird species that prey on pests.

The cost of this kind of farmland-to-wetland restoration is about $1,000 an acre. Restoring 13 million acres—the amount of wetlands needed to naturally *and permanently* control flooding on the entire Mississippi—would thus be $13 billion. That's just two-thirds the value of the damage done by a *single* flood in 1993.

The United States does have such a program, but it needs better funding. Although 150,000 acres were restored to wetlands under the program in 2000, the U.S. House of Representatives cut the program back to 15,000 acres for 2001. As a result of the reduced funding, over half a million acres of former wetlands are backlogged in the program, awaiting restoration to their natural state. Many more acres would be backlogged, but farmers know the funds are limited, so many don't bother registering. When you consider that Congress has spent over $30 billion paying farmers *not* to grow crops, cutting back on this program seems especially ludicrous.

Now that ecological restorationists are showing how restorative agriculture can save family farms and provide vital connectors and buffers for wilderness areas, the formula for the future health of agriculture is clear: restorative agriculture, integrated with restoration of the rest of the built and natural environments.

Restorative Agriculture (Nonintegrated)

> . . . this sort of growth—sustained at a steady 20 percent a year for more than a decade—has attracted the attention of the very agribusiness corporations to which the organic movement once presented a radical alternative and an often scalding critique. . . . [N]ow that organic food has established itself as a viable alternative food chain, agribusiness has decided that the best way to deal with the alternative is to own it. [referring to General Mills' purchase of organic pioneer Cascadian Farm]
> —**Michael Pollan,** "The Organic Industrial Complex" *The New York Times,* May 13, 2001

In a moment, we'll examine the manifold opportunities restorative agriculture has for integration with other restorative industries. But even without such expansion of the concept, restorative agriculture is well under way, often under the guise of organic farming (and ranching, such as organically raised cattle and bison).

The $7.7 billion organic food industry is the fastest-growing category of supermarket products and is a subset of the $20 billion U.S. natural food industry. Organic foods increased their annual growth rate to 24 percent in the most recent eight years and are projected to continue or

ORGANIC FARMING IS NOT NECESSARILY RESTORATIVE AGRICULTURE

Turning a forest or wetland into an organic farm is not restorative agriculture; it's just a greener form of new development. Organic farming only qualifies as restorative when a conventional farm with toxic and/or debilitated soils is converted to organic production. Conventional farms can also qualify as restorative, when, for example, they integrate their lands with ecosystem restoration. In all forms of restoration, there are degrees of "restorativity": Thus, a conventional farm that converts to organic *and* integrates with ecosystem restoration would rate higher than a farm using either practice alone.

increase that rate of growth (stimulated by disasters like Mad Cow Disease) for at least two more decades. Organic farming restores soil that has been depleted and poisoned by tilling, herbicides, pesticides, fungicides, and harsh artificial growth stimulants like ammonia.

What's more, organic crops and meat sell for higher prices and often cost less to produce (especially in developing countries, where poisons and stimulants are often unaffordable). And organic crops are often sold locally to individuals, restaurants, and health food stores, which boosts margins further. These end-user sales frequently lead to even more revenue opportunities, such as for processed foods (jams, cider, etc.), services (B&Bs, corporate retreats, etc.), and specialty items (mushrooms, herbs, handicrafts, etc.).

Even land grant colleges—notorious laggards regarding agricultural innovation—have finally smelled the compost and are teaching organic techniques, led by trailblazers like North Carolina's Center for Experimental Farming Systems. Some 7,800 farms in the United States are now certified organic, and many more are pursuing certification.

Restorative Agriculture (Integrated)

As farmers and ranchers grow more desperate to earn a living, and as they see their quality of life diminish, several restorative development industries are converging with the farming and ranching industries. This convergence is spawning a trend towards rural economic revitalization and farm/ranch restoration, which is currently distributed very unevenly around the United States (and even more unevenly around the world).

Here are five of the more common examples I've encountered of restorative industries that are converging with the trend towards restorative agriculture (and with other types of rural land use).

1. Restorative agricultural plus ecosystem restoration   Several projects, most of them mislabeled "conservation," are involving farmers and ranchers in mutually beneficial prairie, wetland, and endangered species restoration efforts:

- Beef ranchers in Arizona and New Mexico teamed up with Defenders of Wildlife in the Wild Country Beef project, designed to encourage the highly endangered Mexican (White) Wolf to recolonize the area.
- The Predator Friendly Wool certification program in Montana and Idaho rewards ranchers for raising sheep in a way that allows the restoration of coyote, mountain lion, wolf, and bear populations.

- On the shores of fabled Lake Titicaca in Bolivia, the Aymara people are restoring *tortora* reed beds. These will restore the lake's water quality, restore breeding grounds for the lake's fish, and provide food for their cattle.
- The reversion of coffee plantations in many parts of Latin America from the use of ecologically disastrous shadeless coffee plants back to shade-dependent coffee is a form of restorative agriculture. [Shadeless coffee was forced on developing countries by well-meaning development banks that, as usual, forgot to think through the collateral effects of their policies.]
- The Wildlands Project (www.twp.org) envisions farms and ranches as "green corridors" that restore wildlife by allowing migration. A restored 500-acre valley farm might have little ecological value by itself, but it can ignite a resurgence of wildlife on 500,000 mountain acres by connecting two 250,000-acre forests, or by connecting both to a river.
- The Community Baboon Sanctuary in Belize is a well-established attraction. It shows how mutual benefits can accrue when farms are integrated into the surrounding ecosystems. Belizeans voluntarily set aside or restored riverside trees and vegetation, thus allowing black howler monkeys to forage from forest to river. The income from tourists wanting to view the monkeys up close has become an important supplement to these Belizeans' agricultural incomes.

2. Restorative agriculture plus watershed restoration   Watershed restoration benefits farmers and ranchers in a variety of ways. The most obvious is that it helps ensure reliable water supplies; it also reduces flooding, encourages native insects that are predators on crop pests, beautifies the area to enhance quality of life, buffers damaging winds, and increases wildlife for better hunting and fishing.

An Audubon–California project helped ranchers restore native species of grasses. This restoration was ostensibly done for the sake of biodiversity, but the native species do a better job of retaining water and soil, and also, it turns out, provide livestock feed that is more dependable and nutritious. Native perennial grasses tend to have deep roots that bring up subsurface water to form clouds (via transpiration) during dry times, thus benefiting farmers throughout the area with more rainfall.

3. Restorative agriculture plus public infrastructure restoration   Smaller farming and ranching operations are increasingly looking to revenue diversification—something other than taking a job in a local factory—as a strategy for retaining their land and restoring their shrinking incomes.

One of fastest growing and most restorative of these diversification strategies is energy-related. Power utilities, responding to increased public demand for (and legislation demanding) "green" energy, are leasing agricultural land. Often, these land parcels are depleted tracts that desperately needed a break from agriculture to restore their topsoil and soil ecosystems (worms, fungi, bacteria, etc.). Placing wind turbines and/or solar arrays on the land allows the soil this restorative vacation, and generates more reliable revenue than farming or ranching.

According to a report from the Environmental and Energy Study Institute (EESI) in Washington, D.C., entitled "The 2002 Farm Bill: Revitalizing the Farm Economy Through Renewable Energy Development," "developing our nation's on-farm renewable energy resources has the potential to boost farmer income, create jobs in rural communities, diversify our nation's energy market, and protect our environment." The report suggested that Congressional reauthorization of the Farm Bill should encourage farm-and ranch-derived bioenergy (such as methane and ethanol), as well as wind, solar, and geothermal energy.[6]

Energy isn't the only aspect of infrastructure restoration that can be integrated with restorative agriculture, though. As we saw in Chapter 6, water utilities are increasingly incorporating watershed restoration and management into their traditional realm of municipal infrastructure (water mains, sewers, treatment plants, etc.).

4. Restorative agriculture plus fisheries restoration   This combination can benefit farmers directly and indirectly. The collapse of ocean and river fish stocks is stimulating the fast-growing aquaculture industry, providing dramatic revenue diversification opportunities for "regular" (soil-based) farmers and ranchers.

Fishery restoration can also benefit farmers in less direct ways. Oregon's Salmon Safe program, for instance, trains farmers in how to reduce agricultural runoff to rivers, a major element in salmon restoration efforts (and an element that overlaps with watershed restoration). The practices, such as planting cover crops and restoring natural buffer strips along streams, also revitalize soil quality, enhance wildlife, and restore the natural aesthetics (and value) of the land. The program certifies farms, enabling them to put the Salmon Safe label on their products to attract ecologically conscious consumers.

---

[6] "The 2002 Farm Bill: Revitalizing the Farm Economy Through Renewable Energy Development," [Report] Environmental and Energy Study Institute, Washington, D.C.

5. Restorative agriculture plus heritage restoration   The past two decades have seen the rapid growth of three forms of tourism: eco-tourism, heritage tourism, and agritourism (B&Bs on working farms and ranches). Organic farms and those integrated with ecosystem, watershed, and/or fisheries restoration are often able to offer the double-barreled attraction of eco-agritourism.

Other rural properties are able to do even better. If the land is the site of an historic battle or other important event, or if an old or architecturally significant house, barn, silo, etc. is on site, and the landowners restore these assets, they can combine agritourism with heritage tourism, and maybe with ecotourism as well. For farmers and ranchers who find the hospitality industry an attractive form of revenue diversification, such triple-barrelled restoration can add powerful competitive advantages.

Restorative Agriculture Comes of Age

> For many farmers, converting unused farmland back to wetlands makes good environmental and economic sense . . . One such farmer is Steve Querin-Schultz, a Wisconsin grower of corn, soybeans and alfalfa, who is due to have 96 acres of his land restored this year. He said that some years he is unable to farm several acres of his land because it floods two or three times during the summer.
>
> "Wetland restoration helped keep my family in farming, clean the water, and reduce flood risks for downstream residents," said Steve Querin-Schultz, Cottage Grove farmer and Wetland Reserve Program (WRP) participant.
>
> —"Restoring Wetlands the Key to Lower Floodwater," Sierra Club,
> www.sierraclub.org/wetlands/news/jun12_00.asp

The 2002 Farm Bill mentioned earlier funded many forms of farm restoration (along with copious quantities of wasteful, non-ecologically-sound subsidies). Much of it focused on conservation of both wildlife habitat and farmland (protecting it from development), but restorative activities were the focus of at least five key sections: the Wildlife Habitat Incentives Program, the P.L. 566 watershed program, the Grassland Reserve Program, the Conservation Security Program, and the Forestry Programs. Properly implemented, the bill's impact could be tremendous, because agricultural land accounts for about half of all land use in the United States: some 907 million acres of watershed.

In a lovely convergence of ecosystem restoration and restorative agriculture, there's a fast-growing interest in restoring native pollinators.

Over 90 percent of the world's food crops depend on pollination by insects, bats, and birds. Habitat destruction and pesticides have wiped out many native pollinators, making us dependent on commercial hives of European honeybees. But 75 percent of these hives have been lost to those same pesticides, as well as to parasites like ear mites, other forms of pollution, and "killer bee" invasions. Restoration of native pollinator species has become crucial to the future of world food production, and nothing will accomplish this faster than restoration of wetlands, forests, and other native ecosystems bordering our farmlands. Recent research is finding that some native bee species are even more efficient pollinators than European honeybees, and that butterflies are second only to bees in this capacity.

Restoration ecologists are working with farmers and ranchers worldwide to reestablish wildlife habitat along creeks, re-create ponds, and restore native ground cover. A plethora of for-profit suppliers support them, from native plant nurseries to specialized equipment rental firms. Some fast growing firms have invented ecological restoration technologies, such as the Truax Company, which manufacturers a special drill for installing native trees, wildflowers, and grasses without tilling.

> [W]e learned that to do habitat restoration in California, we needed farmers.
> —**Dan Taylor,** Executive Director of Audubon–California, from Jane Braxton Little,
> "Sowing New Wildlife Habitat Seed by Seed," *Audubon,* January/February 2001

The list of farm-related restoration professions, needs, and solutions can and does fill many books. Broadly-focused supportive organizations like the Bioneers are being joined by farm-focused newcomers. Meanwhile, restorative farmers like Joel Salatin in Virginia's Shenandoah Valley keep innovating: he claims his system of rotational grazing restores up to an inch of topsoil every year.

Issues and Insights

> Feed the soil, not the plant.
> —organic farming axiom

1. Genetically engineered crops   The danger here is not genetic engineering itself, but the fact that (mainly) U.S. and British government agencies have allowed politically connected firms to rush untested products into production. The level of research into the possible negative effects on human and wildlife health of these crops barely qualifies as rudimentary, even though everyone acknowledges that recapturing errant genes would be next to impossible.

We're so impressed with our relatively simple mapping of genomes that we've forgotten that the complexity of gene interactions is an area of ignorance thousands of times greater. It's like naming the animals and plants in a wetland, and claiming that as a result of this list of labels, we now understand the chemical triggers, community dynamics, succession cycles, and species relationships that comprise a swamp.

2. Agriculture's resistance to change   "New ideas don't win, really. What happens is that the old scientists die and new ones come along with new ideas." Max Planck's hoary wisdom certainly applies to agricultural engineering.

Long since no-till agriculture (planting without plowing) was shown to be more efficient in most situations, many U.S. agricultural colleges are still telling students to plow. Likewise, organic agriculture has been con-clusively proven to be more cost-effective than conventional techniques in many developing countries (as mentioned earlier), but you'd never know that from looking at today's agricultural college curricula.

Every time an agricultural college graduates someone from a lesser-developed region (many aspiring farmers come to the United States for training), that college inflicts topsoil loss, muddy rivers, dead reefs, and fossil fuel use on an already-struggling country for three decades or more. The prestige of a U.S. diploma makes it difficult for local people champi-oning more enlightened practices to challenge the diploma's holder.

CLOSING THOUGHTS

> I feel we've gone from an era of ranching to an era of restoration.
> —**Kate Faulkner,** chief of resource management for the Channel Islands National Park
> (California), quoted in Chuck Graham, "Pig-Free in the Channel Islands,"
> *E Magazine,* March/April 2001

According to *The 2002 Farm Bill: Revitalizing the Farm Economy Through Renewable Energy Development* referred to earlier, renewable energy gener-ation can be a major factor in the restoration of private farm profitability, help restore planetary health, and boost U.S. national security via diversi-fied energy sourcing. The report pointed to the 2002 Farm Bill as the best opportunity to link agriculture and sustainable energy production.

This is one of the most natural weddings that could take place, as farmers have the solar real estate, the wind, and sometimes the geothermal assets to eliminate dependence on foreign oil, with proper development. They also have tremendous amounts of waste biomass, in the form of crop residues such as corn, rice straw, and sugar cane, plus animal waste. Besides energy, these materials can produce many chemicals currently created from petroleum.

Farmers aren't waiting for the legislation, though. In Iowa, for instance, 115 farmers and ranchers are already paid $2000 per wind turbine per year to lease a quarter-acre of their land. The wind energy projects are already generating $2 million in tax dollars per year for these hard-hit agricultural counties, along with over 40 new jobs.

These days, trucks are running around farm country emblazoned with business names of a type never before seen, such as "Creative Habitat Corporation," "Ecological Restoration, Inc.," "Marshland Transplant Aquatic Nursery," "Bitterroot Restoration," "Applied Ecological Services," "Prairie Restorations, Inc.," and "Spence Restoration Nursery" (its slogan: "Creating Hope for the Future"). As we've seen, these are by no means the only professionals whose financial futures are deeply embedded in the restoration of rural economies.

The theoretical underpinnings of restorative agriculture have yet to be fomulated. A step in the right direction is a new mathematical model for conservation forecasting, developed jointly by researchers at Texas A&M and the Department of Wildlife and Fisheries Sciences. The model purports to predict which conservation and restoration policies are likely to have the best success. The research team included members from a restorative agriculture project in Costa Rica that was funded largely by McDonald's (and run by Conservation International), known as The Amisconde Initiative, which blends sustainable agriculture and restoration of degraded lands. Such new tools have only recently started emerging, though, so restorative agriculture remains a nascent industry.

We've now surveyed four restoration industries, which comprise most of what we consider the *natural* environment: ecosystems in general, watersheds, fisheries, and agricultural lands. We've seen that the soil of farms using large amounts of pesticides, herbicides, and petroleum-based fertilizers has become toxic and largely lifeless. In other words, many of our farms could be considered *brownfields:* contaminated properties.

By shocking coincidence, brownfields restoration just happens to be where we'll begin our exploration of the other major frontier of the Restoration Economy: restorative development of the *built* environment.

A SMALL SAMPLING OF OPPORTUNITIES

Business and investment

There is a vast inventory of exhausted, eroded, and/or salinated farmland on the market. The fire-sale prices these often unattractive properties fetch provides a treasure trove of opportunity for those who wish to get into restorative farming. It's also an opportunity for restorative real estate development, which can be combined with restorative agriculture, especially when the property is close to a population center, beach, or other economic magnet.

NGOs and other nonprofits

Probably no other restorative industry has more potential for improving the success of ecological restoration projects than does restorative farming. The opportunities for conservation NGOs to grow into this area—and to tap the vast public funding available for agriculture-enhancing projects—are tremendous. A whole new realm of resources and synergetic projects can thus become available, ranging from land donations/trusts and wildlife corridors to tax breaks, water rights tie-ins, and access to well-funded government and university research facilities.

Community and government

For lesser-developed countries (and their rural communities) that have a "wealth" of ravaged land and poorly educated citizens, along with a dearth of economic alternatives in a high-tech world, restorative agriculture offers dramatic development potential. It's the only strategy that can actually increase a country's inventory of arable land.

Part Three

The Four Growth Industries Restoring Our Built Environment: Brownfields, Infrastructure, Heritage, and Misfortunes

The built environment is where we find the most visible elements of the Restoration Economy. While new development's destruction of the natural environment has gotten the most attention in recent decades, public ire is increasingly focused on our deteriorating *built* environment.

The realm of new development has become the Frustration Economy: our existing frustration with new development's degradation of the natural environment is being compounded by our growing frustration with our leaders' new-development-only approach to the built environment. It seems everyone is frustrated with new development (and with its often poor-performing related investments) these days.

The sprawl, the pollution, the unsustainable resource usage, the way new development always seems to destroy something we would rather not lose . . . all lead to liability lawsuits, hidden expenses, bad press, and regulatory hassles. Once people take off their new-development blinders and become aware of the colossal surge of startups and investments in restorative development, the floodgates will really open.

The brownfields restoration industry launches our discussion of the built environment because most brownfields contain substantial natural and built components. Some contaminated properties have no structures on them at all, but they have some characteristics of built environment. Although these properties are not "built" in the sense of a highway or a courthouse, they can be seen as "built environments" on two counts: (1) they are made by humans, and (2) they are (mostly) dead. At their worst, brownfields are as visually unappealing as a sewage treatment facility and sometimes smell worse.

Many projects that restore the built environment involve renewing old and decrepit structures. This dynamic applies far less to restorative development in the natural environment, due to the self-renewing capacity of ecosystems. The defining principle applies to both natural and built, though: properly designed and executed, restorative development adds value without reducing value elsewhere.

As unlikely as it sounds, farmers, conservationists, and urban planners are now joining forces politically, because metropolitan sprawl has become their common enemy. There are now a number of organizations designed to conserve land for agricultural use, preventing it from becoming built environment. Some of them focus specifically on conserving family farms (which are most likely to embrace restorative agriculture).

Large property owners, especially farmers, who traditionally use the land in ways that are highly polluting, will find a growing number of opportunities to benefit financially from deals with public infrastructure, such as water and power utilities (and with associated governments). Benefits can include everything from tax breaks, to subsidies for decreased production, to the long-term leasing of land parcels to the city or district (which are then restored to wetlands, forests, etc.), all the way to public–private partnership businesses. Most times, these partnerships are envisioned and driven from the private side, but the realm of restorative development also seems to generate many examples of enlightened (and successful) leadership from the public sector.

The brownfields restoration industry described in Chapter 9 might be the best example of a truly emergent, new form of restorative industry. This industry does business via diverse partnerships—true partnerships, not just paper alliances—of banks, communities, developers, and environmentalists.

Restoring Our Brownfields: Industrial Sites, Ports, and Military Bases

Brownfields have emerged as the preeminent economic development issue of the 1990s. Communities all across the country have had to address the legacy of their past in the context of contamination, complexity, and uncertainty. . . . [A]s important as these initial successes are, the potential exists for even greater activity.
—**Charles Bartsch,** "Coping with Contamination" in H. J. Rafson and R. N. Rafson, eds., *Brownfields: Redeveloping Environmentally Distressed Properties,* 1999

What was once a lovely green expanse of rolling hills in Woburn, Massachusetts has been used, since 1853, as an industrial site for the production of pesticides, leather, chemicals, and munitions. So it comes as no surprise that the site, known in recent times as Industri-plex, became a hellhole of contamination, and that it had the honor of becoming one of the first Superfund projects in 1983. It also had its moment of fame as the subject of the excellent book *A Civil Action,* and the dumbed-down, whitewashed movie based on the book.

In terms of danger to the public, Industri-plex ranked fifth out of some 1,400 worthy competitors nationwide. The surrounding residential area had virulently venomous groundwater and became one of the world's worst childhood leukemia clusters. Six-term Woburn mayor John Rabbitt once described Industri-plex as "the albatross of the Woburn

(River)." The site has been now been renamed in honor of Jimmy Anderson, one of the many local children who died of leukemia. The families who suffered horribly—leukemia was just one of the many toxin-related diseases that afflicted them—said the pollutants in the water were bad enough to detect with the nose.

"I've replaced the faucets in the house three times in 15 years; the seats were eaten away," Jimmy's father complained in the May 1, 1980, Woburn edition of *The Daily Times*. "The dishwasher door was just eaten away." The companies that caused the pollution—those sued included Grace, Beatrice Foods, and Unifirst—were certainly to blame, but so was the city, which sank drinking water wells in an area of known pollution, against the advice of the consultant they hired in 1958.

The largest annual national brownfields conference is organized by the Engineers' Society of Western Pennsylvania and is sponsored by over 100 companies. Since 1997, exemplary and recently completed brownfields projects—usually one from each of the ten USEPA regions—receive the Phoenix Award. The awards are a national program—created by the Pennsylvania Department of Environmental Protection—to recognize "innovative yet practical remediation projects." Industri-plex was a winner in 2000.

> Industri-plex today is the result of unprecedented collaboration and cooperation between the public and private sectors and all three levels of government, a success story [based on] the commitment, competence, perseverance and hope of many individuals and organizations that dared to dream the impossible and then worked together for more than a decade to make that dream a reality. Instead of a toxic wasteland, good planning and hard work . . . has produced a vital area that will forever be a testament of man's commitment to right the wrongs done unto nature. [The redevelopment] is projected by the City of Woburn to create up to 12,000 new jobs by 2010 and contribute $3–4 million annually in tax revenue. [The project has attracted] millions of dollars in private sector investment . . . and . . . will help heal a community [and] overcome the stigma of Woburn's past . . . by providing an environmentally safe and vital place to live and work.
>
> —from the Industri-plex Phoenic Award presentation at the Brownfields 2000 conference in Atlantic City, N.J., October 13, 2000

During the Phoenix Award ceremony, Woburn city leaders were quoted as saying that Industri-plex now "represents this community's economic future," and it has "become a vital source of pride, renewal, and hope." I attended the Brownfields 2000 conference and must admit that, despite their being straightforward and devoid of pomp, the Phoenix Awards ceremony made quite an impression on me. After all, how often does one get to witness for-profit companies being recognized for turning some of the worst places on Earth into sources of "pride, renewal, and hope"?

THE SCOPE OF THE BROWNFIELDS RESTORATION INDUSTRY

> Brownfield: A property whose potential is hindered by contamination due primarily to former industrial or waste disposal practices.
> —**Lawrence F. Jacobs**, "Urban Brownfields," *Urban Land*, February 2000

Despite that opening story, this chapter isn't about large, federally funded cleanup efforts, known in the United States as Superfund sites. It's mostly about smaller, locally funded and managed public–private redevelopment programs. These "brownfields projects" are transforming tens of thousands of less-polluted abandoned tracts back into valuable properties for industry, commerce, recreation, housing, and even farming.

Specifically, this chapter deals with the restoration of old industrial sites, the redevelopment of closed military bases (which usually have areas of significant contamination), the reuse of defunct landfills, and the remediation of other forms of polluted properties. Brownfields can take a broad variety of types, sizes, and locations. Until we recently standardized (somewhat) on "brownfields redevelopment," their restoration went by many names, such as "voluntary cleanup programs," "industrial infill," "land recycling programs," and "urban reindustrialization."

The U.S. brownfields inventory, currently estimated by the USEPA at between 500,000 and a million sites, has been growing quickly and steadily, partly because we're actually looking for them now, and partly due to the decline of our manufacturing sector, which has put more properties on the market. But our inventory growth was nowhere near as spectacular as that of Germany's after reunification: the former East Germany is basically one huge brownfield.

Not even the Antarctic lacks contaminated sites (off-whitefields?), depressingly enough, and that can be blamed on scientists, not industry. The Australian government has taken on the job of removing 330,693 tons of waste, much of it highly toxic (e.g., mercury from thermometers, lead and cadmium from batteries, etc.) from Antarctica, using a French company as the contractor. France and South Africa have already begun cleanups of their own research bases.

Tribal lands aren't exempt, either: Besides having long been used as industrial dumping grounds by new development-based agencies that took advantage of native Americans' economic desperation, the lands also have "normal" brownfields. The Puyallup Tribe of the Tacoma, Washington area, for example, received a $100,000 grant from USEPA to launch a Regional Brownfields Assessment Pilot program.

Lest you're envisioning bison and wolves, let me specify that this project is for the redevelopment of an industrial port and waterfront area in urban Tacoma. Besides the usual contamination cleanup, the project includes wetlands mitigation, integrated with their adjacent properties. It also involves students at their Tribal College, which should prepare the students nicely for careers in restorative development.

The Genesis of Brownfields Redevelopment

> Brownfield: Abandoned, idled, or underused industrial and commercial
> sites where expansion or redevelopment is complicated by real or perceived
> environmental contamination that can add cost, time and uncertainty to a
> redevelopment project.
> —U.S. Environmental Protection Agency (USEPA), Region 5,
> "Basic Brownfield Fact Sheet," 1996

Brownfields redevelopment, as an industry, is barely more than a decade old, and its roots reach only a decade before that. It's only now beginning to mature out of its formative period. The USEPA's Brownfields initiative emerged in 1993 to clean up abandoned, lightly contaminated sites and restore them to productive community use.

Brownfields initiatives should not be confused with the Superfund program, which was designed to clean up the largest and most highly contaminated sites, such as the infamous Love Canal in New York. Since its creation, the Brownfields initiative has awarded over 500 grants to communities nationwide, totaling over $140 million. These grants resulted in the creation of nearly 7,000 new jobs and leveraged over $2.3 billion in private investment. For every dollar invested by federal, state, and local governments, almost $2.50 of private investment was harnessed. All this was accomplished without the need for a single new law or regulation.

The industries of new development have long followed a three-step formula for success: (1) gain cheap or free access to publicly owned natural resources, (2) turn them into profits and pollution, and (3) close down (or sell) the company when the resources run out or when the environmental cleanup bill comes due. In this way, new-development firms' material, waste disposal and liability costs are heavily subsidized by tax-payers, but the profits accrue solely to the companies. (Interestingly, the Soviet Union used the same model during its frenzy of new develop-ment. The Soviet Union is dead [as are many of its ecosystems], but the model, although definitely on the decline, is still well-entrenched in the United States.) This model adds the insult of unemployment to the injury of contamination, entire communities can go down the drain.

> There is as yet no ethic dealing with man's relation to the land and to the animals and plants which grow upon it. Land . . . is still property. The land relation is still strictly economic, entailing privileges but not obligations.
> —**Aldo Leopold**, *A Sand County Almanac*, 1949

The business of redeveloping industrial sites actually got started in the '60s and '70s, but was virtually halted as an unintended result of the 1980 Comprehensive Environmental Response, Compensation and Lia-bility Act (CERCLA), more popularly known as the Superfund Law.

CERCLA was an attempt to gain a little justice, in its effort to go after those companies and recover some of the cost of remediating their for-mer sites. In a further attempt to make sure these polluters didn't make additional profits by selling the spoiled property for more than it was worth, CERCLA made *buyers* responsible for cleanup, even if they had had nothing to do with contaminating the land.

Although there was certainly a basis in justice for pursuing corporate deep pockets to help taxpayers with the cleanup costs, the simplistic, blunt approach of pursuing buyers was the wrong approach. CERCLA should have gone the more tangled root of recovering funds from the original polluters, by attaching the divisions and assets they sold to other firms (doing business with despoilers *should* be dangerous), by raiding the often-huge estates of their former executives, and by other means. But CERCLA didn't, and the net result of punishing often innocent buy-ers was to kill the market for contaminated properties: the legal liabilities and costs of cleanup were not measurable enough for buyers to make sound business decisions.

What's more, the definition of "present owner" included whomever held the title—often a bank or other financial services company—so even when a sufficiently adventurous developer came along, financing was usually unavailable. At this point, we had the "brown vs. green" stand-off typical of new development-based economies, and cleanup was lim-ited to sites with heavy enough contamination to qualify for Superfund.

Tens of thousands of nicely situated chunks of real estate went to waste, "forcing" growing cities and companies to sprawl, and allowing millions of tons of poison to continue seeping into our rivers, wells, and oceans.

Some innovative thinkers at the USEPA saw a solution.

To launch the brownfields program nationwide with minimal funds, the USEPA cleverly established over 228 grants of up to $200,000 each—a total of over $42 million—for "Brownfields Assessment Pilots." The outcomes and/or progress of these pilots can be found on the USEPA's website (www.epa.gov). This pilot program had four goals:

1. To increase participation of all interested parties in designing the process of cleaning and productively reusing contaminated sites
2. To stimulate a national investigation of "best practices" among the states and communities
3. To aggregate federal, state, and community entities into a single body dedicated to learning from each other's innovations
4. To help ensure that the brownfields remediation process maximized its contribution to environmental justice, since lower-income (often minority) communities were disproportionately affected by brownfields.

Recent Industry Developments

National statistics about brownfield development are notoriously difficult to come by because definitions vary and there is little uniformity among state reporting systems. Nevertheless, the National Brownfields Association, a trade organization, has reported that, based on environmental insurance policies purchased, the total spending for goods and services by companies cleaning up brownfields totals $1 billion to $1.5 billion a year and is growing at a rate of 15 to 20 percent annually. However, *this does not account for the value of the properties involved* [emphasis added]. "No one defines a brownfield and no one wants their property on a list of brownfields, so hard data is hard to find," said Robert V. Colangelo, publisher of *Brownfield News*.
—**John Holusha,** "For Developers, Brownfields Look Less Risky,"
The New York Times, April 21, 2002

At the beginning of the 1990s, virtually no one had ever heard the term *brownfields*. Now it's in *Webster's*. The past decade has seen a phenomenal increase in brownfields investment and associated cleanup, mostly due to modifications to CERCLA that stopped it from scaring away buyers. Add other factors, such as a plethora of municipal and state laws and incentives, plus the rise of related insurance products, and we find that risks have now been rendered at least manageable, sometimes even negligible.

In Europe, the Network for Industrially Contaminated Land in Europe (NICOLE), has emerged as the primary forum for brownfields issues (including those larger, highly toxic sites that would qualify for Superfund status if they were in the United States). NICOLE's purpose is to bring together researchers, contaminated site owners, and reme-diation contractors throughout Europe. They help identify research needs, gather and disseminate best practices, collaborate with other international brownfields networks, and generally build a functional community from the various stakeholders, which also includes land developers, local and regional authorities, and the insurance and finan-cial industries.

The NICOLE website (www.nicole.org) states: "The problem of land and groundwater contaminated by industrial activity is a significant one that affects all industrialised societies. Whilst businesses and authorities are striving to identify and manage such problems responsibly and cost-effectively, they are often doing so without a clear understanding of the complexities or the scientific and technological aspects of the problem."

In the April/May 2002 issue of *New Urban News,* an article entitled "New Urbanism Makes Inroads in Germany" said, "In the 1980s and 1990s the discussion about [German] cities has focused more on reusing abandoned industrial areas and dealing with the threat from suburban shopping centers. It quoted Harald Kegler, head of the Laboratory for Regional Planning in Wittenberg, as saying, "So, in Germany, much more than in the US, you can find a big collection of practical experiences with renewing historical cities and brownfields."

In the early days, cleanup projects in the United States suffered from a "study it to death" sickness, which meant that most funds went into consulting, site assessment, and cleanup methodology research. Now that the industry is maturing, the construction and redevelopment side of the business is growing quickly.

Another positive recent development is the exit of most defense and nuclear power contractors from the business. Many of these exits are the result of lawsuits and protests from states over inefficient projects that were often dangerous to the public. For example, when nuclear power company BNFL tried to burn radioactive waste from a contaminated site in an incinerator, thus dumping it into the air, citizens' activist groups, *not* public health agencies, quashed the attempt.

When Superfund monies were flowing fast and furious, defense and nuclear power firms used their immense power on Capital Hill to capture a major chunk of the business, even though (with a few exceptions, such as consulting firm SAIC) their expertise was in manufacturing, not in civil engineering or the sciences.

The present shift to civil engineering firms has greatly cut down on the Pentagon-style cost overruns and sloppy work that typified early Superfund projects. Federal remediation work is improving in other ways, too: performance contracting, thanks to sophisticated new metrics and monitoring, is becoming the norm, causing firms to pay strict attention to the quality of their work in order to ensure full compensation (not to mention contract retention and renewals).

Many would argue that the 1990s pendulum initially swung a bit too far in the direction of accommodating the developers. This was probably an understandable overreaction to CERCLA's early '80s draconian approach, which nearly killed the cleanup industry (in part by making it totally dependent on government, rather than business, initiative). For this restoration industry to remain healthy—both for practitioners and the public—industry and government will need to allow the pendulum to oscillate a bit closer to the mid-point. Such moderation would better balance the need to contain costs and liabilities for lenders and developers with the health of people and wildlife.

Unlike most environmental programs, brownfields redevelopment (like all restorative development) has strong bipartisan support. Thus, no slowdown was projected to occur after George W. Bush was elected. Passage of the historic Brownfields Revitalization and Environmental Restoration Act on April 25, 2001 further solidified this new industry.

This Brownfields Act was the first bill to achieve a unanimous 99 to 0 "yes" vote in the Senate during the new Bush administration. It authorized an additional $1 billion per year to be spent on brownfields between 2001 and 2006, mostly in the form of state programs that leverage many times that amount in private funds. The House version (HR 2941) also passed unanimously, in June of 2002. As a result, growth in the U.S. brownfields remediation industry is expected for some time to come.

Superfund reauthorization has been stymied in Congress for a decade, due primarily to pressure from the mining and manufacturing lobbies. Legislators also worry that the program spent over $30 billion between 1981 and 1996, yet only 97 out of the 1300 priority sites were removed from the list (successfully remediated). Although it's true that the program could have been far better designed and administered, Congress needs to wake up to the real size (and true long-term costs) of the problem and realize that $30 billion was a token amount.

After a fast start in the early '90s, the U.S. remediation industry had three down years from 1996 to 1998, caused primarily by a lack of new cleanup regulations and by a slowdown in government cleanup programs. But 1999 and 2000 saw renewed activity. Total U.S. remediation revenues in 2000 were $6.28 billion. The fact that Superfund accounted for only 11 percent of that figure proves this industry has been successfully weaned from public funds, with a corresponding growth in business opportunities.

For such a young industry, brownfields has shown amazing stability, despite the federal government's having been such a large player. Small and minority-owned firms reportedly grew their share of the market from five to ten percent in the mid-'90s to 15–20 percent in 2000, according to the *Environmental Business Journal,* Vol. 13, No. 5/6, 2001.

PROBLEMS AND SOLUTIONS

> [Earlier] reluctance to rehabilitate brownfield properties has resulted in increased development of suburban greenfield areas, urban sprawl, and continuing economic and environmental blight in former industrial and commercial urban areas. . . . Despite the potential environmental risks, the development of brownfields has certain advantages over other properties. . . . [M]ost of these sites have a useful infrastructure already in place, including access to markets for labor, materials, and final output; access to transportation facilities; access to existing roads, water, sewer, and electric power; and the presence of existing structures. Further, site preparation costs of a brownfields redevelopment project are significantly lower than costs associated with developing raw land.
>
> —**Mark S. Dennison,** *Brownfields Redevelopment: Programs and Strategies for Rehabilitating Contaminated Real Estate,* 1998

Discussion of remediation strategies and technologies, which focus on *how* toxins are removed, fills many volumes, and is far beyond this book's scope. What we *can* review here are some decision-making issues related to the choice of remediation methods. There are usually three basic considerations: time, cost, and effectiveness. Obviously, there are no either/or decisions here: the solution that balances all three factors best, given the unique priorities of each project, is usually the one chosen.

Some communities and companies add a fourth (optional!) criterion when choosing a remediation method (the basic three being time, cost, and effectiveness): environmental sustainability and/or social responsibility. The most environmentally sound and socially responsible—as well as the least costly—decontamination methods are often *in situ* biological methods, such as phytoremediation (use of plants and/or algae to take up and/or break down toxins).

Unfortunately, time is often the most critical of the three priorities for businesses (and lenders). It's much quicker to incinerate on-site, or just cart the problem away to dump somewhere else. Although biological techniques have the lowest out-of-pocket cost, their time cost is usually the highest.

That fourth "optional" criterion—environmental and social responsibility—will probably need to become mandatory before biological approaches achieve their rightful dominance. However, if measured in terms of the rate of R&D—rather than the level of current use— biological remediation may already be the dominant category. One increasingly popular option is *ex situ* (off-site) bioremediation: this combines the speed of hauling the problem away (which allows redevelopment to start immediately) with the low-energy, low-pollution, low-cost advantages of biologically based decontamination.

A recent Houston cleanup required the removal of 440,000 cubic yards of dirt, entailing 1,300 trucks a day being sent through the city throughout the project's duration, a huge consumption of fossil fuels, and no small amount of noise pollution. The MetroNorth Corporate Park project (a Phoenix Award winner) in Arizona instead used a nonbiological *on-site* remediation method: an ultraviolet facility that removed peroxide contamination from the groundwater. Now, if the ultraviolet lights were powered by wind or solar electricity. . . .

Five Common Misconceptions About Brownfields

It shouldn't be surprising that such a newly birthed industry would be poorly understood. Here are five of the most popular mistaken assumptions about brownfields.

Misconception #1: The primary purpose of the brownfields remediation industry is to clean the environment   It's vitally important that we realize, and openly acknowledge, that the principal driver of brownfields cleanup and redevelopment is economic, not environmental. Within the brownfields industry, this economic agenda is out in the open; it's outsiders who make bad assumptions about a project's purpose.

Unlike the Superfund program, which was created to protect the public, the primary motivation behind brownfields cleanup is making a profit. Understanding this will help communities maintain vigilance over local projects. Such community vigilance, in turn, will help the entire brownfields industry avoid what might be its greatest threat: a public backlash against sloppy projects that threaten human and ecosystem health due to overly aggressive cost-cutting.

The chief priority of virtually all brownfields programs is to expedite the return of sites to a useful condition. Along with the speed of cleanup, the depth of legal protection (from environmental lawsuits) for developers and investors is another top goal. Other concerns—such as research, environmental justice, ongoing monitoring, or impact on local ecosystems—often lag far behind in priority.

Misconception #2: Brownfields contamination just involves the ground and groundwater   We've probably been misled a bit by the term brown*field*. It's not just the land that's "brown": buildings themselves are usually extremely toxic structures. Tearing down or renovating older buildings means dealing with challenges such as lead paint, asbestos insulation, PCBs (in electrical transformers), and mercury (such as in most vapor lights), not to mention whatever substances were used in the line of work the buildings housed.

Removing toxic building materials, plus normal rehab tasks such as demolishing masonry, ripping out plumbing, etc., are all considered "hard costs" (as opposed to "soft costs" like insurance and legal). Hard costs also include cleanup of the surrounding soils, which is where we find VOCs (volatile organic compounds) such as fuels and solvents; SVOCs (semivolatile organic compounds) such as lubricating (and some fuel) oils; pesticides and PCBs; plus heavy metals like cadmium, zinc, lead, and mercury.

Misconception #3: Most brownfields are heavily contaminated (basically just small Superfund projects)   In fact, many have fairly minimal levels of contamination. In many instances, abandoned industrial sites sit idle for decades because they are *assumed* to be contaminated (such is our abysmally low level of expectation regarding the ethics of new-development industries). But nice surprises do occur, which is why a complete assessment of each country's brownfields is so important. The ultimate pot of gold for adventurous communities and private developers is buying a cheap site that's assumed to be contaminated, only to find it clean.

Misconception #4: Most brownfields are abandoned If we expand the definition of "brownfields" to include all contaminated sites (not just abandoned), those that are still in use—and which are often still being polluted—would actually be the largest category. Unfortunately, they aren't even being inventoried, to the best of my knowledge.

The relationship between the growth of our brownfields inventory and our industrial decline is quite direct. For example, Lynn, Massachusetts lost 15,000 manufacturing jobs during approximately the same period that its catalog of available commercial properties was flooded with brownfields; about 80 percent, in fact. Between 1986 and 1997, 30 percent of the industrial acreage in Hartford, Connecticut was abandoned. Much of it was contaminated, and all of it was suspected of being so. Over 750 empty buildings stood unguarded, left to get vandalized, to turn into drug emporiums, or to deteriorate catastrophically from water damage due to leaky roofs and broken windows.

As reuse of abandoned property becomes the basic strategy of metropolitan economic development, cities are becoming better at quickly allocating funds to have someone "stabilize" abandoned sites, in order to maintain whatever value the sites have while awaiting revitalization.

The U.S. General Accounting Office estimates some half-million brownfields in the United States, but most observers feel this number is extremely conservative, even when limited to abandoned sites. Waiting until polluting companies fold (and their property sold) before assessing the contamination might not be the best strategy for public health.

Misconception #5: Brownfields are large industrial sites in urban locations The truth is that brownfields can also be small and rural. In fact, rural sites might outnumber urban brownfields. Probably the most common are rural gas stations—both abandoned and operational—with leaky underground storage tanks. *In 27 U.S. states, the EPA does not have the power to prevent a company from putting fuel or chemicals into an underground storage tank (UST) that is known to be leaking.*

If you live in one of those states, and you see a tanker truck at a gas station, a portion of that delivery might be going straight into your local aquifer; maybe into your drinking water, or that of someone in the neighboring county. Unfortunately, federal funding for UST cleanups has been meager in recent years. It's getting an especially hostile reception from the Bush administration, which seems to take criticism of petrochemical industries very personally. Mark this category of brownfields as a colossal—and still ballooning—backlog of future restoration.

Our Militaries Don't Just Kill Our Enemies

Remember that $6.28 billion in U.S. remediation revenues in 2000? The Department of Defense (DOD) paid only 14 percent of that, despite the fact that military bases often make industrial sites look like Martha Stewart's backyard by comparison. The Pentagon's small monetary contribution shows their continued resistance to cleanup. Cleanup of military bases is a job that will take decades, and is another lucrative backlog of work contractors can anticipate.

The brownfields challenge posed by the military forces of the world probably amounts to a multitrillion-dollar backlog, all by itself. The EPA estimates the backlog of military base cleanups to be $350 billion, a figure most experienced remediators consider extremely conservative. The General Accounting Office (GAO) was even more conservative—putting the number at $100 billion—and the Pentagon itself provided comic relief with an estimate of $14 billion. These figures, by the way, are only for cleanup of contamination at bases in the United States (we have about 1,700 installations worldwide). They do not include warfare-related cleanup, or the restoration of military buildings, heritage sites, ships, infrastructure, ecosystems, etc.

The U.S. military is among the most irresponsible (contamination-wise) among highly developed nations. In fact, the DOD is one of the few U.S. agencies that is actually resisting restorative development on some—not all—fronts. However, the armed forces of China, Russia, and dozens of other less-developed countries (those largely lacking environmental protections) are even worse.

The DOD is generally very enthusiastic about restorative development of its built environment, but its anti-green sentiments come to light when base redevelopers encounter contamination. This bias was recently illustrated by the "tentative legislation" the Pentagon floated in April 2002, designed to exempt the military from many environmental regulations. The attorney general of Massachusetts, Thomas Reilly, immediately sued the Pentagon. He was apparently unwilling to let the

Pentagon escalate what many see as chemical warfare on the American people by their own protectors.

During the Clinton administration, the Pentagon spent just $3.5 billion annually remediating contaminated bases, but most of that went to assessment (a legitimate need), not to actual cleanup. In 1998, the Defense Science Review Board, a federal advisory committee, reported that the Pentagon had no clear brownfields cleanup goals, policies, or program (despite its having an Office of Environmental Cleanup).

A Defense Environmental Restoration Program was created, but George W. Bush—normally a fan of restorative development—allowed his anti-green agenda to override his pro-restoration agenda. Even while pushing to increase the overall Pentagon budget by $14.2 billion, his administration is trying, at the time of this writing, to reduce the military's remediation program by over 7.5 percent.

"Brownfields remediation" is a phrase that covers a lot of ground, ranging from posting a sign saying "Contaminated area: Keep out," to deed restrictions forbidding residential use, to actual cleanup. That first example, "sign-based remediation," is a favorite of the U.S. military. Budget restrictions are usually cited as the reason. Even when the military does an actual cleanup, it's usually to "industrial use" standards for the same reason; "residential use" standards are simply too expensive.

Asbestos and lead abatement, as well as PCBs and gasoline/jet fuel/diesel/motor oil contamination, are found in *all* closed U.S. bases: they are givens. Many of the plumes of groundwater pollution are so extensive that people write books about them. In fact, the toxic plume from Otis Air National Guard Base on Cape Cod, Massachusetts, inspired two books (both by Seth Rolbein), *The Enemy Within: The Struggle to Clean Up Cape Cod's Military Superfund Site,* and *About Face: Cleanup, Conflict, and New Directions on Cape Cod,* published by and available from the Association for the Preservation of Cape Cod, Barnstable, Mass.

With military bases, the threats left behind aren't always as subtle as PCBs: many sites also include munitions contamination and unexploded ordinance (UXO). Buried bombs (and land mines) can ruin someone's day just as thoroughly as PCBs, and much more quickly. The Army readily admits it doesn't know how to handle UXO, especially when it's not U.S. citizens who are at risk, as in Panama.

In 2001, Ray Clark, Principal Deputy Assistant Secretary of the Army at the Pentagon, told me we could spend $10 billion removing munitions on U.S. bases, and that would only achieve 95 percent of the job. It's rumored that the U.S. Army Corps of Engineers is going to add UXO cleanup to its mission in a big way; that's a job that will keep many organizations busy throughout the twenty-first century.

The cleanup job we did when pulling out of Panama didn't come close to that level. Even if it had, who but the most desperate would live or farm on top of a five percent residual rate of unexploded munitions? As with all brownfields issues, there are many unknowns: the Army estimated the cleanup of one former U.S. base in Panama, Ft. Sheridan, at between $35 million and $750 million. That's a heck of a range, due mostly to insufficient assessment, along with not knowing which remediation technologies will be used (difficult to ascertain prior to assessment).

Redeveloping military bases became a significant growth industry with the collapse of the Soviet Union. When planned and executed in a transparent, collaborative manner with all stakeholders—and when the contaminated land or UXO is properly remediated—the redevelopment of closed military bases has been a godsend for many communities in the past decade. Such outcomes usually take people by surprise, because most towns panic and assume their economic life is over when a nearby base closure is announced.

What actually happens is that large new green spaces (such as for parks) suddenly become available, and a large amount of taxable real estate (such as industrial parks, residential developments, etc.) is added to the town's assets. California has about a third of all the military bases that have closed in the past decade or two, and many of these sites have large expanses of green space—even important wildlife habitat. As a result, communities that foolishly developed all of their green space are getting a second chance. Many of these former bases are right in the path of development and sprawl, giving California an opportunity to once again be on the leading edge of a major national (and world) trend.

ISSUES AND INSIGHTS

> Brownfield: An environmentally contaminated property that, with government approval, is put back into service without a complete cleanup or removal of contamination.
>> —**Noah Shlaes,** CRE, former director, Corporate Real Estate Consulting, Arthur Andersen, from his "Appraisal of Brownfields Properties," section in *Brownfields: Redeveloping Enviromentally Distressed Properties,* H. J. Rafson and R. N. Rafson, 1999

This discussion of the brownfields industry is more heavily loaded with cautions than that of the other restoration industries, so readers may come away from the following section with the mistaken impression that

I'm not very excited by the brownfields restoration industry. Not true, but anytime we're dealing with contamination, we're on dangerous ground, so it's sensible to be especially cautious.

We've already covered several sensitive issues in the body of this chapter; here are four additional considerations:

1. Brownfields redevelopment is inherently restorative, but the processes are not   Each acre of redeveloped urban brownfields is an acre of greenfields saved, right? Well, not necessarily. As exciting as this field is, it is very much in its infancy. It's in desperate need of workable standards set by organizations whose primary concern is human and environmental health.

What if those hundreds of truckloads of clean topsoil that now cover the remediated site came from healthy farmland or prairies? On one recent project, eight million cubic yards of topsoil were taken from greenfields and farmland to cover a slag heap slated for residential development. On the flip side, what if contaminated soils are dumped out in rural or tribal lands? What if vast quantities of fossil fuels are used to oxidize pollutants, thus contributing to global climate change, air pollution, etc.? All of these practices are common.

Some methods of removing toxins from dirt use solvents that leave their own toxic residuals. This is a classic case of following a prescriptive specification ("remove compound XYZ") rather than a performance specification ("return the soil to preindustrial levels of purity as established by standard ABC").

2. Increased involvement of local stakeholders is needed   The USEPA has made great efforts to encourage public participation in brownfields projects, but yet more progress is needed. "Community involvement" is too often synonymous with "public relations." The challenge with both environmental and social agendas, of course, is to achieve them within the bounds of time and money that will keep the project attractive to those taking the financial and legal risks.

3. Prevention of new brownfields must be better addressed   One aspect of the industry that is grossly underdeveloped is brownfields prevention programs. There's a ton of money to be made in cleaning and redeveloping properties, but many industries treat contaminating them in the first place as an affordable expense. Any fines that result are merely a predictable "cost of doing business" to be budgeted for. Worse, many industries continue to assume that the public will pay these expenses for them.

Some municipalities are on the ball, though: a major task of the brownfields pilot program of the West Central Municipal Conference of

Illinois was "to identify ongoing industrial activities that pose a risk of creating new brownfields."

4. Moving into the next growth phase will require more standardization Currently each state—even each major metropolis—has developed or modified rules, regulations, and redevelopment approaches based on its local needs, philosophies, and history. Thus, the formative period for the brownfields industry has been both rich in innovation and expeditious in deployment.

The brownfields industry is past the initial decade that comprised its birth, and growth has slowed. Maturing into its major growth phase will require increased national and international standards, not the least of which concerns public responsibility. Such standardization will include liability issues, regulations, financing models, research support, and quality standards. At the Huxley College of Environmental Studies of Western Washington University, faculty member Alan Lloyd grades the states on such factors. In 2001, only nine of the 50 got an A, with 11 Bs, 12 Cs, 5 Ds, and 13 Fs.

Restoring Chicago

> Developing a parcel of property will undoubtedly bring new scrutiny to the environmental condition of the property. Many industrial parcels have a long manufacturing history, and the owners are convinced, even in the absence of any confirmatory evidence, that if you test you will find contamination of some sort. Therefore, many owners would rather not know what is below the surface of a plant.
> —**Gary W. Ballesteros,** assistant general counsel, Rockwell International Corp., from his chapter on "The Industrial Company" in *Brownfields: Redeveloping Environmentally Distressed Properties*, H. J. Rafson and R. N. Rafson, 1999

A good example of how brownfields redevelopment revitalizes cities (and prevents further erosion of their economic base) is the story of Madison Equipment, Inc.'s aborted exodus from Chicago. This 70-employee firm needed to expand and was about to move to greenfields outside the city. But Chicago caught "brownfield religion" earlier than most cities and convinced Madison to consider expanding into a brownfield site which had a useful preexisting building, and which was adjacent to its current property. Madison Equipment and the city moved forward together, and the site assessment revealed only minimal contamination; it was effectively clean. So, for the price of a little research, the city kept a growing employer, and the company dispensed with an expensive and traumatic relocation.

Chicago is probably the leading U.S. metropolis in terms of integrating brownfields restoration into its redevelopment plans. Mayor Richard M. Daley couldn't have made the importance of brownfields any clearer than when he reportedly said: "Industrial development in Chicago *is* brownfields redevelopment."

The U.S. Army Corps of Engineers has so far identified 711 potential brownfields in Chicago alone (other surveys put the number over 2,000). Chicago is within the broad swath of the United States called the "rust belt," so attracting the private resources necessary for revitalization required aggressive efforts, not just to stimulate opportunities, but to overcome that death-spiral image. It's important to recall that cities possess great (though often underutilized) problem-solving powers, such as the ability to negate tax delinquencies, the ability to offer future tax incentives and/or low-cost loans, the right of eminent domain, etc.

Following Chicago's Example

> Benderson views brownfields as the last frontier on which to make money.
> —attorney for Benderson Development Company, quoted by Charles Bartsch,
> "National Lessons and Trends," in H. J. Rafson and R. N. Rafson, *Brownfields:*
> *Redeveloping Environmentally Distressed Properties*, 1999

The general public doesn't yet call it restorative development, but people know an improvement in their world when they see one. The next step will be when the public stops being pleasantly surprised by brownfields-based redevelopment projects and starts expecting them . . . even demanding them.

How common is it for metropolitan (and state) planners to recognize brownfields as being core to their city revitalization efforts? Here are some excerpts from the plans of cities and states around the United States, (quoted in Mark Dennison, *Brownfields Redevelopment: Programs and Strategies for Rehabilitating Contaminated Real Estate*, 1998):

A SAMPLING OF U.S. CITIES
ON THE BROWNFIELDS REDEVELOPMENT TRACK

"Jacksonville's objectives are to establish a redevelopment process with defined policies, procedures, and mechanisms that will restore brownfields sites into economically productive properties, create new jobs, and increase quality of life for nearby inner-city neighborhoods."

(continued)

A SAMPLING OF U.S. CITIES
ON THE BROWNFIELDS REDEVELOPMENT TRACK *(continued)*

"**Maine's** goal is to use redevelopment of brownfields as a catalyst for revitalizing many communities. . . . [B]rownfields redevelopment is a key strategy for channeling development to these growth areas, many of which support historically significant buildings or water frontage."

"**New Bedford's** goal is to convert area brownfields into productive aquaculture sites [in response to the collapse of its fisheries]."

"The goals of the **St. Paul** Port Authority are to optimize the reuse of abandoned and underused industrial sites, . . . create increased employment opportunities for local residents, and generate sufficient tax revenues to provide services needed for long-term, ecologically sound, industrial growth."

"**Perth Amboy's** goal is to provide technical expertise, public/private support, and vision [for the] remediation and revitalization of the redevelopment area. The city aims to delineate contamination; . . . innovative technologies and site cleanup protocols; improve public accessibility to brownfields and risk information; and develop sustainable insurance coverage programs."

The city [of **Fayetteville**, N.C.] has developed numerous partnerships, including Cumberland County, Ft. Bragg [home of the Green Berets and the 82nd Airborne], and Fayetteville State U., to identify redevelopment opportunities, including brownfields, that will help to restore over 3,000 downtown acres to residential, recreational, educational, business, and industrial use."

"**Lima's** [Ohio] brownfields program will complement the river corridor redevelopment project, enhance water quality of the Ottawa River, and provide adjoining greenspace."

"The brownfields inhibit the city's ability to generate property tax revenue, create jobs, . . . mitigate environmental health risks, and abate crime and drug abuse. **New Haven's** goals include remediating contaminated sites. . . ."

"**Atlanta's** goals are to inventory brownfields within the Empowerment Zone, encourage industry involvement in brownfields redevelopment, provide environmental justice planning, and develop sustainable communities."

"**Kalamazoo** intends to create a systematic approach for redeveloping underused and potentially contaminated properties in the city."

"**Concord's** [N.H.] overall brownfields goals are to identify contamination in a 440-acre industrial corridor, [and] develop a comprehensive remediation and redevelopment plan; . . . [besides] new [tax] revenue . . . the employment potential exceeds 2,500 jobs, or eight percent of the city's total employment."

"**Tulsa's** goal is to restore abandoned, idled, or underused industrial and commercial sites to productive use and create jobs."

Gets a little repetitious, doesn't it? That's a good thing. But we've focused far too heavily on U.S. communities in relation to brownfields, so let's pick a less obvious city for our final story. How about Istanbul?

A CLOSING STORY

As many U.S. cities have found, it's hard to revitalize a city's waterfront when the water is foul, and its stench ruins couples' romantic *al fresco* dining experiences.

Such was the case with the area of Istanbul bordering the Golden Horn, the 4½ miles of waterway leading to the Bosporus Strait. This is the famed site where visitors can stand at the European end of the Bosporus Bridge (one of the longest suspension bridges in the world) and look at Asia at the other end. Sultans once rode the beautiful blue waters of the Golden Horn in their royal boats, but Istanbul went through its own new development-based economy. During most of the twentieth century, citizens walking or driving anywhere near the water would cover their noses in an attempt to keep out its foul odors, and avert their eyes from its depressing blackness.

Now, Istanbul is embracing restorative development with both arms, having already spent $500 million dollars restoring the Golden Horn area. Locals are even starting to swim and wade in it (not yet a safe activity), something that would have been unthinkably disgusting a decade ago. A profusion of aquatic vegetation is returning, and the city has removed 6,500,000 cubic yards of toxic mud, piping it into an abandoned stone quarry outside the city (an example of adaptive reuse?).

An Associated Press article was published by the *Environmental News Network* on November 27, 2001, titled "Turkey's Bay of the Ottoman Sultans Recovers from Industrial Filth." In it, writer Selcan Hacaoglu says, "Authorities have razed some 600 factories and a city-owned slaughterhouse that spewed filth into this fabled waterway. . . . [It] was once described by the Ottoman poets as 'Sadabad' or 'place of bliss.' [Resident] Ali Kaplan said the waterway 'was like a cesspool.' But it is getting better each day. . . . Fish are returning—though not yet enough to entice fishermen. Former Mayor Bedrettin Dalan, who first launched the cleanup in 1984, promised: 'The color of the Golden Horn waters will be as blue as my eyes.' "

Brownfields redevelopment still retains some peril for practitioners— although much more peril exists for society and wildlife. But society and wildlife are already at risk if redevelopment *doesn't* happen. We've removed much of the danger to redevelopment companies and banks. Now, we need to make sure community and ecological health are equally protected. If practiced sloppily, unethically, without sufficient assessment, and/or without sufficient integration with the other restoration industries, brownfields remediation risks becoming the equivalent of warding-off nuclear holocaust by painting "smiley faces" on bombs and missiles.

You've now gained a familiarity with a very sizeable industry that many people haven't heard of, and that others consider very exotic and specialized. Let's move on to a sector that almost everyone has heard of, and upon which we depend every day of our lives, but which few can even define properly, much less describe in any detail: public infrastructure.

A SMALL SAMPLING OF OPPORTUNITIES

Business and investment

- No restoration industry offers as many technological opportunities as does this one. Demand for safer and more efficient tools, reagents, and processes related to assessment, decontamination, and monitoring will grow explosively for decades to come. *Ex situ* bioremediation will be one of the hottest areas of growth for researchers and contractors.
- There's an enormous need for consultants who can guide projects through the rapidly evolving maze of incentives, codes, laws, and insurance products, which differ substantially among cities, states, and countries.
- While expert consultants (above) can help maximize access to funds—and minimize exposure to risk—for actual projects, there's a related opportunity to help investors and developers at a much earlier point in the process. Web-based (due to the daily announcements of new programs) services are needed, to help developers compare and evaluate cities and countries as to their friendliness to brownfields restoration and other forms of restorative development. A point-based system would greatly facilitate the initial stage of strategic planning. Such services would also help economic development planners compare their cities and countries to others competing for those investors, and see where improvement is needed.

NGOs and other nonprofits

This restoration industry is probably the one with the fewest not-for-profit entities. Whether due to the intimidating level of technical expertise required, or simply to the youth of the industry, the field is wide open.

(continued)

A SMALL SAMPLING OF OPPORTUNITIES *(continued)*

There's a great need for professional associations and activist groups that can better integrate the many professionals involved in brownfields, set codes and standards, identify potential projects, raise funds, and share best practices.

Community and government

For decades, contaminated industrial sites and closed military bases have been synonymous with dying communities. In just over a decade, these "problems" have morphed into windfalls. Communities searching for dramatic economic growth opportunities need only look to these nonrevenue-generating former military properties to see their future.

Restoring Our Infrastructure: Transportation, Power, Solid Waste, and Water

In 1996, a "report card" prepared by the city's former U.S. Army Corps of Engineers chief gave New York City's infrastructure failing grades, particularly for its aging water mains and solid waste treatment system, which dumps raw sewage into city harbors during storms.
    —**Shelly Barnes**, "New York City: An Island Ecology," *E Magazine,* Sept./Oct. 2000

Santo Domingo, on the southern coast of the Dominican Republic, is one of my favorite large Caribbean cities (though I love the rural villages and underwater life of the Dominican Republic even more). But from overhead, Santo Domingo looks like a toilet. A monster plume of pure, unadulterated, raw sewage gushes down the river that flows through the city, forming a huge brown plume in the otherwise turquoise Caribbean. Street children swim and fish in and near the plume. Locals with a car or bus fare travel miles down the coast to find clean water for recreation. Tourists go to the northern and eastern coasts.

Santo Domingo residents tell me they are ashamed of the "Rio de Caca." So why this barbaric flood of feces, which is impeding the Dominican Republic's goal of becoming a major U.S. tourist destination? This is the largest metropolis in the Dominican Republic—and its capital: Doesn't it have the money for a modern sewage treatment plant?

Sure it does. The country has tremendous natural resources, along with industrious people. The Dominican Republic has a strong trade relationship with nearby Puerto Rico, which—along with the millions of Dominicans living in the United States—gives it access to U.S. markets. The Dominican Republic shares the Greater Antilles island of Hispaniola with Haiti. Unlike its neighbor, the Dominican Republic hasn't yet destroyed all its forests and watersheds; such destruction led to Haiti's grinding poverty and political instability, so typical of ecologically ravaged nations. (Of course, the Dominican Republic isn't the only Caribbean "paradise" to be wallowing in its own filth; the bays of Point Lisas in Trinidad & Tobago, Bahia de Pozuelos in Venezuela, and Bluefields in Nicaragua are other examples.)

So again, why the open sewer? You're probably expecting me to say it's due to antiquated infrastructure that needs to be restored, but it's actually due to a *lack* of infrastructure. Incomplete, anyway; the country does have aging sewers, but someone forgot to build the treatment plant, and that's more of a political problem.

Fortunately, a greater sense of responsibility seems to be evolving, exemplified by the government-supported work (aided by The Nature Conservancy) of biologist Francisco Nuñez and his staff to preserve and restore the vitally important Madre de Las Aguas watershed. In 2001, the country raised half a billion dollars for revamping its infrastructure. We can only hope it will be spent as wisely as were the watershed restoration funds.

For now, let's leave the Dominican Republic and review the infrastructure restoration industry as a whole. We'll return to Santo Domingo toward the end of the chapter, by way of introducing the concept of "restorative technologies".

THE SCOPE OF THE INFRASTRUCTURE RESTORATION INDUSTRY

> The biggest economic boom in history is bearing down on us. . . . There's just one problem: It might not happen. . . . America's infrastructure on land, water, and air is not only unprepared for such a vast economic breakout, it is already in crisis. . . . Harbors are silting up [river restoration is needed to stop that], bridges are crumbling, landfills are being topped off with last year's PCs. Even the water, which must be purer for making semiconductors than for washing human organs during surgery, is running dry. The great economic boom of the 1990s, the largest and most sustained in U.S. history, was built on the foundation of America's investment in infrastructure in the 1950s and 1960s. But that infrastructure is now either used up, worn out, or incomplete. . . . And we are running out of time.
> —**Michael S. Malone,** "Rebooting America: Getting Real and Getting It Right,"
> *Forbes,* September 10, 2001

Originally a French word, "infrastructure" was limited to describing military installations, and it carried this meaning when the English adopted the word in the 1920s. After crossing into English, the word quickly started encompassing all other aspects of public works beyond those of the military. The "infra" portion is Latin, meaning "underneath," so "infrastructure" literally means "below our structures."

According to Webster's New World Dictionary; "infrastructure" is "the substructure or underlying foundation, especially the basic installations and facilities on which the continuance and growth of a community or state depends." My definition of infrastructure: "fabrications that facilitate flows among folks and facilities" (sorry: I'm a Monty Python fan). Those flows include cars, trains, water, sewage, electricity, natural gas, communications, etc. Infrastructure keeps us fed, watered, mobile, and in touch, but we seldom notice it or think about it.

For simplicity's sake, I've divided public infrastructure into transportation, power, solid waste, and water. Telecommunications is also infrastructure—and the system has certainly undergone a major technological rehabilitation from copper wire to wireless and fiber optic—but it's privately owned for the most part, so we won't include it in this discussion of public infrastructure.

Public buildings and schools are also considered infrastructure in many circles, and many of the older ones also qualify as heritage. We won't discuss them here, though, except to point out the monstrous backlog of rehabilitation needed by the 80,000 public schools in the United States. According to the National Education Association (NEA), that backlog amounted to $322 billion in 2000. That's a frightening figure (or exciting, if you're in the restoration business) to be sure, but even scarier is its rate of growth. The NEA's 1998 report had put the figure at "only" $112 billion, so a rather dramatic increase occurred in two years.

PUBLIC TRANSPORTATION INFRASTRUCTURE

The United States has over 6.3 million kilometers of roads (by way of comparison, Brazil has over 1.6 million, Canada 912,000, and Mexico about 323,000) and we spent about $54.5 billion maintaining our roads in 2000, a historic high, thanks to the flush economy of the '90s. But the Federal Highway Administration says even that level of spending wasn't enough to maintain roads in their current "fair" condition; an additional $40 billion was needed just to bring their average condition up to "good." "Very good" or "excellent"? Forget about it.

In Chapter 1, we mentioned the "Report Card on America's Infrastructure" issued in 1998 by the American Society of Civil Engineers (ASCE). This was the first overall accounting of the $1.3 *trillion* backlog of rehabilitation needed by U.S. public infrastructure. Other reports have since stated that 50 percent of U.S. infrastructure needs to be replaced by 2005.

Chapter 1 also mentioned the Transportation Equity Act (TEA-21), and the TEA-21 Restoration Act. They poured $218 billion of federal funds into rebuilding the U.S. transportation infrastructure over a six-year span ($177 billion for highways plus $41 billion for mass transit) and states will add billions to this amount.

Only 20 percent of those funds are for "new starts," and about 25 percent are officially designated for restorative projects. But almost the entire remaining 55 percent are allowed to be spent on restoration (as opposed to maintenance, e.g., patching potholes), and most of it *will* be, according to my conversations with officials from the Departments of Transportation (DOT) of several states. This means that some three-quarters of transportation funds now goes to restorative development. (In an overlap between the infrastructure and heritage restoration industries, TEA-21 allocated $50 million to "rehabilitation of historic covered bridges," according to the January 2000 issue of *Civil Engineering*.)

What Chapter 1 didn't say was that, despite this 70 percent increase in highway spending, the backlog of needed upgrades and restoration to the nation's infrastructure remained at $1.3 trillion in ASCE's updated 2001 Infrastructure Report Card. The good news is that the nation's overall score improved from D– to D+, thanks to the transportation sector. That's certainly no reason to drop our guard; witness the headline in the April 2001 *ASCE News:* "ASCE's Infrastructure Report Card Paints Dismal Picture."

The article quoted ASCE President Robert W. Bein as saying, "When you've got rolling blackouts in California, bridges crumbling in Milwaukee, and kids in Kansas City attending class in a former boys' rest room, something is desperately wrong. . . . With a projected budget surplus of $5.6 trillion dollars, our leaders in Congress have the funds needed to restore our ailing infrastructure." (We've managed to make that nasty federal budget surplus go away, but the point is valid nonetheless.)

Impacts of the Backlog

Infrastructure projects (both new and restorative) frequently go over budget (just ask anyone from Boston about the "Big Dig"). One of the major reasons is that our infrastructure has not undergone a comprehensive national assessment: only when we start working on it do we find out just how rotten it is.

For instance, when planning the rebuilding of Virginia's I-95 Springfield Interchange (the "Mixing Bowl" mentioned in this book's Introduction) and the replacement of the nearby Woodrow Wilson Bridge, engineers bidding on the project didn't know they would have to rebuild ten existing bridges. Nor did they realize they'd have to dredge the Potomac, which was constipated by silt from unrestored watersheds and nonrestorative agriculture, as well as by dams. Underestimating the restoration challenge—primarily the "Corrosion Crisis" elements—added a cool $1 billion to the combined tab, with the Mixing Bowl price tag alone ballooning from $220,000,000 to almost $700,000,000 in eight years.

Fortunately, preventive maintenance is now the fastest-growing trend in highway maintenance. At the 2000 annual convention of the American Public Works Association (APWA), Richard Herlich of VMS, Inc., a national road maintenance firm based in Richmond, Virginia, told me that state DOTs were finally awakening to preventive maintenance. He said Virginia was an early leader of this movement, but that many states are still stuck in the mode of funding primarily new development and rehabilitation, with just token amounts for maintenance.

This leaves states with a nasty combination of near-perfect roads (either new or recently restored) plus dangerously decrepit roads, with little in between. Traditionally, roads have had to reach an acute condition before getting funding; fortunately, this mindset is fading. Some states, such as Wisconsin, Michigan, New Mexico, Ohio, Illinois, Indiana, and Utah are now using long-term warranties (from road builders) to get a handle on costs, and to give contractors increased incentives to build roads that last.

Exiting the Highway

> . . . [T]he New York-Washington line is badly in need of a multibillion-dollar overhaul. . . . [Amtrak's January 2000] report estimates that $12 billion will be needed over 25 years[;] . . . the $12 billion estimate is almost certainly an understatement. . . . The long, slow, leaking tunnels into Baltimore were dug shortly after the Civil War. . . . Most of the basic infrastructure, including many major bridges, dates from the Pennsylvania Railroad's total rebuilding in the late 1920s and early 1930s . . . the railroad equivalent of the Pyramids.
> —**Don Phillips**, "Arriving: Amtrack's Hopes for a High-Speed Future," *Washington Post*, September 17, 2000

There's a lot more to transportation than roads, of course. Many airports are in sad shape. It's not just the buildings and runways: virtually the entire world's aviation radar network must be replaced. In the infrastructure restoration industry, the word "billion" is exceedingly common—consider, for example, the $3.2 billion renovation needed at Chicago's O'Hare airport, and the $3.4 billion renovation plan for Virginia's Washington Dulles airport.

America's love affair with automobiles brought our passenger rail system to the brink of death. General Motors and Ford reportedly bought up metropolitan trolley systems and dismantled them in the first half of the twentieth century in order to expand the market for cars. The combined pressure from consumers and industry left us with a public transportation gap that the airlines eventually filled, but only for the longer distances with any efficiency.

What with airport congestion, remote airport locations, and poor connections from airports to local public transportation (Washington, D.C.'s restored National Airport being a happy exception), flying has become a stressful, unproductive experience; more Americans have rediscovered the joys of being able to read and write on trains. (September 11, 2001, added another factor: we gained a new appreciation for the difficulty of hijacking trains and crashing them into buildings.)

The above circumstances, combined with the shocking condition of U.S. rails and rail bridges (not just compared to Europe and Japan, but even compared to many lesser-developed countries) should lead to a massive rail restoration in the United States. Because we have so little decent rail infrastructure in place, such a restoration even offers the opportunity to leapfrog several technological generations. The current state of the art in high-speed rail is the nearly silent maglev (magnetically levitated) train, powered by hydrogen fuel cells. Some of these trains can achieve 528 kilometers (330 miles) per hour.

Shanghai is installing a German maglev to connect its downtown to Pudong International Airport, 33 kilometers away. The U.S. Department of Transportation has committed $950 million to putting a maglev in one of two places by 2004; either between Baltimore and Washington, or between downtown Pittsburgh and its airport. These aren't fuel cell projects, but they should be (they can be converted later, since maglevs run on electricity.)

Given the use of fuel cells in cars; public transport; mission-critical institutional installations; plus remote, off-grid communities and homes, their appearance in urban and suburban homes won't be far behind. Let us now, therefore, consider the reconstruction of our public power infrastructure.

PUBLIC POWER INFRASTRUCTURE

> The people that spread thousand-megawatt power plants across the planet now see the future in small generators, each little more than a millionth as powerful, in basements and backyards round the world. One of the biggest enthusiasts is Karl Yeager, who heads the U.S. industry-funded Electric Power Research Institute in Palo Alto, California. By 2050 he thinks that most of our electricity will come from millions of microturbines, solar panels, and, most importantly, hydrogen-powered fuel cells. "Within five years I'll be able to go down to Wal-Mart and pick a microgenerator off the shelf to power my house," says Yeager. "I will take it home and connect it to the gas pipe. It will generate power as well as heating my house and producing hot water. And it will be much cheaper than using the power grid."
>
> —Fred Pearce, "People Power," *New Scientist*, November 18, 2000

The reconstruction of our energy infrastructure, as suggested in the above quote, is shifting the seat of power from public and semi-public entities to private companies, and an entirely new type of power grid is emerging. There will be at least three key differences between our old power infrastructure and this new one:

1. Power production will be largely decentralized, with most energy being produced where it is used.
2. Utility companies (assuming the oil companies drop the ball on creating a hydrogen infrastructure) will switch from being primarily energy producers to being energy distributors, both for the electricity itself and for hydrogen. Remaining fossil-fueled power plants will become the grids' backup generators, but that function rapidly will become unnecessary.
3. Power utilities (at least, the more innovative ones) will assume other new roles, too. These include trading energy and pollution credits, partnering on technology R&D, and integrating the power with other forms of public infrastructure. Probably the leading example in the United States is the Electric Power Research Institute [EPRI], a think tank in Silicon Valley funded by leading power companies to help their industry make this

historic shift in roles, technologies, and values. Their EPRIsolu-
tions division is especially interesting in this regard. They have
Adam Davis working full-time to find ways to market "Eco-
Assets," such as the services provided by watersheds and other
ecosystems.

It has been said that the U.S. power grid is the largest machine ever
built by humans. Most countries already have extensive national grids
that can be adaptively reused into a kind of "energy internet," with each
residence and business uploading and downloading power as needed.
While existing grids have value, countries lacking such infrastructure can
leapfrog past the need for all those wires and cables.

Most of us just want to save money on our energy bills. Some of us
also consider it important not to contribute to air pollution, or to our
country's dependence on foreign oil (or domestic oil, for that matter). The
rush towards "green" energy—whether motivated by dependability, cost
savings, environmental concern, or national security—is picking up
tremendous momentum, and this will automatically result in adaptively
reusing our grid into a decentralized energy generation system.

For the past decade, wind power has been the fastest-growing
energy source in the world, with a steady 20 percent annual rate of
increase. Denmark already gets over 10 percent of its power from wind,
and the state of Navarra in Spain is 20 percent wind-powered. Germany
has installed 1.6 gigawatts of wind power in recent years.

More recently, solar hit the 20–25 percent annual growth mark. Wind
will continue to grow nicely, especially for use in large installations and
for the production of hydrogen. This hydrogen is for fuel cells, which will
be a key technology of this decentralized power system. Stationary (non-
vehicular) fuel cells are already a $40 million market, and the most con-
servative projections expect it to hit $10 billion by 2010.

Fuel cells enable everyone to have local power without the noise,
smell, air pollution, and unreliability of diesel and gasoline generators.
But fuel cells have been—until now—too expensive, except for high-tech,
medical, and other mission-critical businesses that require completely
dependable, blackout-proof power. Now, the number of companies
switching to fuel cell power is skyrocketing. Many switches have been
precipitated by the Internet revolution: large electronic commerce companies, banks, and other types of firms can lose enough money in one
minute of blackout to pay the entire cost of these one hundred percent-
reliable fuel cell systems.

The major driver of fuel cell affordability in the future will be the automobile industry. Every year, it produces enough engines to equal half of all the generating plants in the world. Replacing engines with fuel cells, which will happen sooner than the public realizes, will cause the price of cells to plummet. And because fuel cells will be in widespread use in buildings by that time, much of the hydrogen refueling infrastructure will already be in place. Because large-scale fuel cell generators are merely aggregations of small fuel cells, prices will come down for everyone.

> The problem is that the existing network of high-power transmission lines, the interconnected web of electricity that keeps the continent charged . . . was built in the middle of last century and was never meant to handle the complexity and congestion of today's ever growing energy demands and changing markets.
>
> —Peter Fairley, "A Smarter Power Grid," *Technology Review*, July/August 2001

It's important to remember that the key to this rehabilitation of our world power system isn't just in the nature of the energy source, but the location of the energy source. Using renewable sources is a great step in the right direction, but it would be a shame to waste half of it by using the old centralized systems of distribution.

Centralized power generation is hugely wasteful. We wouldn't tolerate a gasoline tanker that spilled half of its load, but that's what those massive high-tension transmission lines are doing. Only about half the energy in coal, oil, or nuclear actually becomes electricity, by the time you figure in heat loss. The loss of another 50 percent in transmission makes for a horribly inefficient system. Add in the energy used to mine, refine, and distribute uranium, coal, and oil, and the net delivery comes down to five percent, sometimes dropping to a net loss. Most appliances, such as incandescent lights, waste 75 percent of the power they consume, so the bottom-line numbers are truly appalling.

Centralized power is also highly fragile. Most of southern Brazil—11 of the most populous and industrialized of its 26 states—discovered this on January 21, 2002. A single broken transmission cable (that's the official story, anyway) left millions of people (not to mention businesses large and small) in total blackout for two hours. Three years earlier, the region had been in the dark for four hours after lightning struck a substation in São Paolo. Part of the design problem of "modern" systems is that the failure of a large dam or a nuclear plant can be so disastrous that they automatically shut down whenever the power grid becomes unstable.

Those shutdowns make the system even more unstable, and so the ripple becomes a tsunami.

Using fuel cells and (to a lesser extent) microturbines to power buildings gives the buildings more reliable energy than does today's grid, and a distributed "embedded generation" network of millions of fuel cells and microturbines would be almost completely blackout-proof. The backup system (the grid) would actually be less reliable than the building's primary system, since ice storms, hurricanes, etc., can knock down power lines.

Grid Restoration Is Powered from Within and Without

Only immense political influence, combined with purposely misleading cost-accounting systems, keeps the world's most wasteful "business" (electric power generation and distribution) operating. But this is changing. San Francisco's citizens recently voted to switch all of the city's public offices to clean, efficient energy sources. Santa Barbara, Calif., did nearly as well, voting to go 80 percent green power. Every major government office in Britain is now supplied by renewable energy sources. Where demand appears, supply will follow.

Britain's energy regulation agency, the Office of Gas & Electricity Markets, is studying how to remove the regulatory barriers that block small generating facilities from connecting to the power grid. That office envisions getting at least 10 percent of the United Kingdom's power through embedded facilities such as windfarms, rooftop solar, and cogeneration (a combination of the heating and powering processes). As in the United States, this will offer tremendous economic revitalization opportunities to the struggling farm economy, which has vast capabilities to generate energy from wind, solar, and farm wastes (biogas).

Turning farm waste and landfill gases into energy is actively restorative: it takes existing contaminants from circulation. What appears to be an energy production industry from one angle, looks more like a pollution remediation and waste cleanup industry from another.

PUBLIC SOLID WASTE INFRASTRUCTURE

The difference [regarding Europe's faster adoption of anaerobic waste digester facilities; 70 by the end of 2002] with the United States is that the landfill crisis in Europe is real. We are so densely populated, especially in areas like Belgium and Holland, that there is not any space left to site a landfill in the next town or the next state. There is much opposition to

landfills, and landfilling cost is about $60 to $80/ton. That is very expensive, and also many countries have a landfill tax—as much as $40/ton. All this really changes the playing field and drives opportunities for anaerobic digestion. There is also strong opposition to incineration; which must meet high air emission standards and costs between $80–$100/ton. All this means that in Europe, composting, digestion and biological treatment can compete. (In contrast, in the U.S., there are still landfills charging as little as $10/ton.)
—**Luc de Baere** of Organic Waste Systems of Gent, Belgium, quoted in Jerome Goldstein, "Power from Recycled Organics," *In Business,* Nov/Dec 2001

In Amsterdam, the highest point of elevation is a so-called "Dutch Mountain" of trash. After closing a decades-old landfill, the Dutch capped this "peak of poison"—comprising everything from heavy metals to cyanide—with a layer of relatively non-toxic rubble (sand, peat, and plastic), and layered that with a little topsoil and grass. It's now becoming a popular hiking and strolling destination for local citizens in search of a little altitude. (At 98 feet, it's not exactly Alpine: they climb it "because it's there.") There's debate, of course, over whether throwing a pretty park over an ugly landfill qualifies as restoration. Visually, sure. Environmentally? Hmmm . . .

ASCE's "Report Card on America's Infrastructure" gave our hazardous waste infrastructure a D–, and our solid waste infrastructure a C–. The solid waste portion of our infrastructure is almost as decrepit as our water infrastructure; design-wise, it's even worse. Rather than cleaning solid waste poorly and recycling it (as we do with water), we just bury our garbage (or sometimes we incinerate it, which is just a way of "burying" it in our air).

Reducing waste production is the obvious solution in the long term, and there has also been significant growth in recycling businesses. Manufacturers are making inroads into reducing their waste. Because a quarter of the average landfill's volume comprises construction waste, more communities are requiring that condemned buildings be deconstructed (allowing valuable, often no-longer-available materials to be recovered), rather than demolished.

One positive, waste-reducing trend that combines the two is "servicizing." This is where a firm leases the use of the product, rather than purchasing the product, such as elevators, chemical solvents, carpets, etc. The manufacturer thus retains ownership of the product, taking it back for recycling or restoration and resale at the end of its useful life. But these are all matters of sustainability, not restoration.

These are all trends that will slow the growth of landfills and thus retard the further despoilment of our world, so they contribute to passive restoration—but none of them remove the toxins and wastes that have already been released into the environment. That would be actively restorative.

A more active form of restoration, for instance, would be sealing an old landfill to stop the groundwater contamination, landscaping it to use as an industrial park, and then tapping the methane from rotting garbage to heat or cool the buildings, thus cutting fossil fuel use and preventing the methane from leaking out to destroy the ozone layer. The most restorative approach, which will require some significant technological breakthroughs, will remove all the waste in these old landfills and reprocess it into raw materials for remanufacturing. Such a process, of course, would need to be powered by clean energy and would not release toxins or new forms of unusable waste.

Interim efforts to restore old landfills to a more productive and aesthetically pleasing state were worth a mention, but we're not going to spend any more time on solid waste. Eliminating waste production is the real solution, and that will require a rehabilitation and reconstruction of our economy—maybe even our society. Readers are directed to many excellent books on the industrial ecology for more on this topic.

PUBLIC WATER INFRASTRUCTURE

> As more sources of surface water have become off-limits . . . industry has had to turn to once-unthinkable alternatives such as inferior ground water and even recycled waste water. . . . One rapidly growing example . . . is the use of municipal secondary sewage effluent as cooling tower makeup. Large power stations find this an excellent way to conserve fresh water and eliminate discharge problems. . . . The trend toward having to "do more with less" is expected to continue.
> —**Arthur J. Freedman,** Ph.D., "The Changing Face of Water Management: A Look to the Future," *Materials Performance,* July 2001

ASCE's Report Card gave U.S. water infrastructure the lowest marks of all public infrastructure, with wastewater getting a D+, and drinking water a D. Part of the problem is the sheer age of the facilities, and part is their antiquated processes.

In 2001, a bipartisan coalition of U.S. senators sent a letter to their leadership asking for up to $5 billion for the purpose of "upgrading this critical, but aging and failing, infrastructure." The letter continued, "Although Americans take clean, safe water for granted, our drinking and wastewater infrastructure is in disrepair throughout the nation, with literally billions of dollars in documented critical needs."

Wastewater

U.S. wastewater infrastructure already went through one extended—though relatively superficial—national rehabilitation. It started in 1948 with the passage of the Clean Water Act. The act has been amended nine times since then, with each amendment pushing the restoration further. The most significant change was in 1972, when the federal government took over as the primary enforcer (through the USEPA, which was only two years old at the time). What had really helped catalyze action was when Ohio's Cuyahoga River caught fire in June 1969 (capturing our attention requires good visuals).

In 1992, three major changes to the act occurred:

1. It became illegal to pollute—defined by the EPA as discharging any type of industrial, municipal, or agricultural waste (including heat) into water—without a permit.
2. The use of better pollution control technologies was encouraged.
3. Billions of dollars were provided for the construction of new sewage treatment facilities.

The Clean Water Act—bitterly opposed by the industries of new development at its passage—is widely acknowledged to be one of the most successful U.S. federal legislations ever, and it did make a significant difference in the quality of our waterways and coasts. So, why did I call the Clean Water Act a "superficial" rehabilitation? Because it only addressed sewage treatment plants. Our water infrastructure also includes sewers, water mains, drinking water treatment plants, and watersheds (sometimes referred to as part of our "green infrastructure").

For example, our aging, leaking, under-capacity sewers went largely untouched by the Clean Water Act. What's more, while the quantity and quality of sewage treatment plants improved, the basic processes and underlying paradigms remained the same. All were based on outdated technologies. (The Act also didn't address drinking water treatment facilities for the most part, nor their mostly ancient, rupture-prone systems of mains and pipes for collection and distribution, which we'll discuss next.)

In other words, the Clean Water Act partially addressed the Contamination Crisis portion of our water problem, but focused even less on the

Constraint Crisis, and almost completely ignored the Corrosion Crisis. Even in 1948, many U.S. cities had century-old water mains and sewers. The act also ignored some of the big picture issues, such as the ethical assumptions underlying a system that solves local problems by sending partially treated effluent to an endless chain of anonymous downstream communities.

Drinking Water

The drinking water domain comprises two components, water treatment plants and the distribution system for that water. These systems were designed in the early twentieth century to treat water polluted primarily by biological pathogens. They don't even monitor, much less remove, hundreds of dangerous industrial compounds now lurking in aquifers and surface water.

The water mains that distribute "clean" water in the United States average over 50 years old, with most older U.S. cities relying on mains over 150 years old. The *Washington Post* regularly features photos of local broken mains geysering fifty feet or more into the air. Less dramatically, many are clogged with calcium deposits, and most leak a substantial portion of their contents. Some are even made of creosote-treated wood, now known to be carcinogenic. All are restoration opportunities.

Drinking water treatment plants tend to be in better shape than their distribution network. This is due in part to the Clean Water Act, and also because renovating them doesn't involve tearing up the whole city. But many plants are quite decrepit, and most are grossly undersized, due to population growth.

A bigger problem is that their design is based on getting rid of pathogens by poisoning the water with chlorine. Chlorinated water is obviously better than water carrying cholera. But, if it weren't for those deadly diseases, would we for even a moment think of adding something as nasty as chlorine to our drinking water? Not if we knew anything about it, or its breakdown products. We need to get away from the chemical manufacturers' doctrine that the only way to make water safe is to poison it. Nature knows a better way: it improves the healthfulness of water without destroying health elsewhere—in other words, it uses a restorative process.

Most of us are also aware that we have been poisoning wildlife with the carcinogenic breakdown compounds of chlorine for decades (we've mostly switched to chloramines, which don't break down, so now we're chlorinating our rivers and oceans). But only recently has anyone bothered measuring—and telling us about—the degree to which our rivers and bays are loaded with hundreds of excreted prescription drugs (not to mention caffeine: billions of fish drink secondhand Starbucks on a 24/7 basis).

Scientists in Britain are investigating possible links between the large amounts of estrogen excreted by women taking birth control pills, and the fish (in the North American and U.K. rivers receiving that estrogen) whose males are turning female by the millions. These same rivers supply our drinking water, but treatment plants not only don't remove estrogen (or the other drugs and industrial compounds); they don't even attempt to detect it.

Many of these drugs, such as those from birth control pills, are hormones that have powerful but largely unknown effects on humans and wildlife. Because most cities get their drinking water from rivers, we are drinking the drugs of upstream cities. Public health authorities only test our drinking water for a handful of toxins or pathogens (just three, in many cases) despite the presence of well over a thousand harmful pollutants in the average river. Our primary "warning system" seems to be the tracking down of unusual cancer (and other disease) clusters years— even decades—after the fact. So, buy a filter or be a filter.

It's not just pharmaceuticals that are rife in our drinking water: One of the not-commonly-acknowledged facts about public health is that the vast majority of household products that end up in our water— shampoos, sunscreens, toilet cleaners, etc.—are not tested for their effect on humans or wildlife when ingested. The labels say "do not ingest," and that's considered good enough. But it isn't good enough, because we ingest them every day in our drinking water.

Restorative Technologies

What did the opening story of Santo Domingo's missing sewage treatment plant have to do with restorative development? It sounds more like they need some old-fashioned *new* development, right? But Santo Domingo does, in fact, have a sewage treatment "system" that needs to be replaced: it has a network of sewers linked to the ocean, and the city uses the Caribbean to purify its wastes.

Adding any kind of sewage treatment plant would be restorative for the river and the ocean, but that would still be new development. There are such things as "restorative technologies," and building them from scratch will be part of the "restoration of new development". Again, new development isn't going away, so there are plenty of opportunities to take it beyond the current goal of "greener," all the way to restorative.

> Even manufacturing can become a restorative act.
> —**William McDonough,** professor and architect, University of Virginia, quoted in
> Florence Williams, "Prophet of Bloom," *Wired* magazine, February 2002

What would a restorative sewage plant look like? Let's define "restorative technologies" first. From a waste or toxicity perspective, these are technologies that aren't just less polluting, or even nonpolluting (a feature most "sustainable" technologies strive to achieve): They actually reduce existing environmental pollution, in addition to not adding any of their own.

A restorative sewage plant, then, wouldn't just remove the waste that has been flushed into the already-polluted drinking water: it would discharge water that is cleaner than it was before that waste was added to it. For instance, most cities use river water for residential use. Some is used for drinking, but most either becomes greywater (from the kitchen, bathtub, etc.) or blackwater (from the toilets). A restorative sewage plant wouldn't just remove the fecal material, soaps, drain cleaners, and whatnot added by this household use. It would remove the pesticides, fertilizers, and sewage from upstream farms and cities that were in the water when it arrived at the plant (and which were passed on to consumers). A restorative sewage plant, ideally, should discharge spring-quality water: water that's ready for drinking.

Spring water is (usually) the result of (1) solar-driven plant and algal purification (and oxygenation) at the surface, (2) anaerobic bacterial action (which breaks down complex compounds) in the muck, and (3) mechanical filtration through porous rocks and earth. The good news is that Santo Domingo's lack of water treatment infrastructure frees the Domican Republic to leapfrog past several generations of sewage treatment technology, going straight to the state of the art, which is restorative.

From the Caribbean to Canada

With this in mind, let's hop from the Dominican Republic up to Nova Scotia. One of the major tourist attractions of Bear River, Nova Scotia, is its sewage treatment plant, the $400,000 Bear River Solar Aquatic Facility, which attracts some 2,000 visitors annually (hey, this is a tiny town, not on a major tourist route!). Located in the middle of its tourist district, the solar-powered, 4,200-square-foot, 80,000-gallon plant emits no odors. The water that reenters the river is literally fit to drink, with not a single chemical having been used in the process (except those produced by the plants, bacteria, snails, and algae and other organisms that actually do the cleansing work).

The plant, built by Environmental Engineering Associates of Massachusetts, also produces high-quality compost from the solids. It costs about the same to operate as a traditional plant, but takes up far less room. This was important, because the town had no land available for the normal space-hogging technology. (In a perfect example of my earlier warnings concerning "engineering think," someone informed me (as this book was going to press) that an engineer without any background in such systems had been recently hired to manage it. He reportedly reengineered it in a way that "mechanized" it and destroyed most of the vital flows and processes. The same source told me that the town is currently trying to restore the original system.)

Why would tourists want to view Bear River's sewage? It's not just the pretty green plants floating on the water of these ecosystem-based treatment facilities: this facility is (was?) a microcosm of restoration. The filth of civilization enters at one end, and pure, oxygenated water is discharged at the other. It's more like a greenhouse than anything else, and revitalizing oxygen emitted from the plants floods the air. People are mesmerized, and being there makes them feel really good.

These ecosystem-based sewerage systems—like the Living Machines long pioneered by Dr. John Todd—actually have an advantage over nature, at least in terms of edutainment value. In the great outdoors, it's difficult to perceive the complete cycle of cause and effect. But when a miniature ecosystem takes sewage in at one end and dispenses drinking water from the other, and when each portion of the process is visible, peoples' perception of sewage treatment goes from disgust to wonderment. No school field trip in the wild could teach as much about the invisible processes of nature as does this machine/ecosystem hybrid technology. In fact, our planet's interrelated built and natural environments might be considered such a hybrid.

Integrated Water Management:
The Path to Restoring Water Quantity and Quality

> The integrated approach is definitely what's happening. We have to look at
> any kind of water as a water resource—wastewater, stormwater, groundwater,
> imported water, seawater. [Los Angeles] for the first time ever is looking at

the integration of all its water sources. [The Orange County Groundwater
Replenishment System is] the largest project of its nature on the planet.
—**Kellene Burn Roy,** Senior V.P. for Camp Dresser & McKee's (CDM) western U.S.
operations, quoted in *Environmental Business Journal,* Vol. XIII, No. 9/10, 2001
[CDM is leading a team of 20 companies in this project's $352 million first phase.]

The only sound method of creating economical sewage plants that produce high-quality drinking water is to use systems that combine the same
organisms that have been purifying the earth's water for millions of years:
plants, algae, and bacteria. Besides restoring public health, a wholesale
restoration of our sewage and drinking water treatment plants using such
technologies would be the single greatest thing we could do to restore our
rivers, estuaries, and oceans, and thus our fisheries. Take those collateral
benefits into account, and the cost-effectiveness of such systems drops far
below the full cost of current systems.

Despite the efforts of a few dozen forward-thinking communities like
Bear River, Nova Scotia, ecosystem-based sewage treatment is a restorative technology that has disappointingly little momentum. What does
have momentum—counterintuitively—is something even more grand:
The integration of wastewater, drinking water, and stormwater systems
with watershed and wetlands restoration.

Ideally, our drinking water and sewage treatment systems should be
one and the same. This kind of integrated, closed-loop water management will actually be the core dynamic of the water infrastructure rehabilitation and reconstruction of the next few decades. Closed-loop design
is the real test of a system's integrity. Our current systems are horribly
primitive, mostly based on dumping huge quantities of chemicals into
the water to precipitate dissolved solids. Anaerobic bacteria are briefly
used to break down a few of the compounds, but the flow-through is far
too great for this bacterial decontamination to be in any way thorough.

It's always amazing how quickly we can come to accept the most
abhorrent behavior as normal. The infamous Nut Island wastewater
treatment plant fouled the waters of Boston Harbor horrendously for
three decades. Before it was built in 1952, Boston dumped its raw sewage
directly into the harbor, a startling reminder of how recently the realm of
new development started developing a conscience (or watchdogs).

The March 2001 *Harvard Business Review* published a shocking study of
the dismal state of affairs at Nut Island, specifically the city's state of denial
about the plant's barely functional condition, and its resistance to change.[1]

---

[1]Paul F. Levy, "The Nut Island Effect: When Good Teams Go Wrong," *Harvard Business Review,* March 2001.

The article told the following story: "It seems that one day, James W. Connell, Nut Island superintendent in the 1960s, went to Boston to ask the MDC [Metropolitan District Commission] for funds to perform long-deferred maintenance on essential equipment. The commissioner's only response: 'Get rid of the dandelions.' Startled, the superintendent asked the commissioner to repeat himself. 'You heard me. I want you guys to take some money and get the dandelions off the lawn. The place looks terrible.' " The Nut Island facility was recently rehabilitated with "modern" equipment, which has contributed much to that harbor's restoration, but it's still based on an antiquated paradigm.

There are three primary sources of wastewater: residential, industrial, and storm. One might think storm water runoff wouldn't be much of a problem, since it's nice clean rainwater, but it is, in fact, a major challenge, for two reasons. The first is that, in between each rain, our city streets become coated with vehicle exhaust deposits and tire "rubber" (mostly a petrochemical product), not to mention oil drippings, dog doo, pigeon droppings, detergent from neighborhood car washings, fertilizer and pesticide runoff from lawns, etc. By the time it hits the sewer system, rainwater is anything but pure.

The second problem is related to quantity, rather than quality. Our sewage treatment plants are designed to handle fairly linear inputs, and their capacity has been outstripped by population growth. Storms thus cause them to overflow, spewing raw sewage into the river or bay to which they are connected. This is a major threat to the restoration of rivers and estuaries, so the restoration of our wastewater infrastructure must be integrated with those projects.

> Maryland, Virginia, the District [of Columbia], and Pennsylvania will announce the first major restoration effort since . . . July 2000 to correct. . . pollution and sediment problems in the Chesapeake and its tributaries by 2010.
>   . . . In one year, rain pouring off streets, roofs, and parking lots washes more than 442,000 tons of sand, mud and grit, nearly 3 million pounds of phosphorous and 28.2 million pounds of nitrogen into the watershed . . . [and is] responsible for fouling nearly 1600 miles of streams and destroying thousands of acres of habitat for crabs, fish, and other aquatic life.
>   . . . Redeveloping older properties . . . poses an even bigger challenge because of the cost associated with retrofitting storm drainage systems in urban areas. . . . So state officials have allowed builders other options. [Maryland official Brian Clevenger said,] ". . . it could be in-kind contributions, like stream restorations, that will still help them meet these goals."
>
> —**Anita Huslin**, *Washington Post*, December 3, 2001

Ten or twenty years from now, we will begin a massive overhaul of the primitive technologies and designs causing the "point source pollution" described in the above quote, that is, pollution entering a body of water from an identifiable source where it can be measured. Waterless composting toilets and residential gray water (showers, sinks, etc.) treatment units are being incorporated into homes on an increasing basis. This portion of infrastructure restoration—as with many concepts that wreak fundamental changes on industry and society—will likely be stimulated by a successful model operating in some smaller country, island nation, or sovereign indigenous territory. For now, let's return to the present, and look at the infrastructure restoration that's already going on, and at what's planned for the near future.

The funding, and maybe even the paradigm shift, might come from the "Water 21" initiative being advanced by a number of associations, such as the Water Environment Federation (WEF), the American Public Works Association (APWA), the Association of Metropolitan Sewerage Agencies (AMSA), and others. Designed after the TEA-21 and AIR-21 legislation, which provided major new funds for the rehabilitation of the nation's roads and highways, Water 21 aims to get Congress to take the renovation of our water infrastructure equally seriously. These organizations have documented an *annual* shortfall of some $22 billion in water infrastructure construction and maintenance in the United States alone, so the restoration backlog is continuing to grow at an alarming rate.

Water 21 is supported by the Water Infrastructure Caucus, a bipartisan coalition of legislators led by the chairman and ranking members of the House Water Resources, Health, and Environment Subcommittees. WEF and AMSA announced in 2002 their joint goal to "build and maintain sustainable wastewater and water supply infrastructure." If they take the word "sustainable" seriously enough, this project will catalyze the wholesale abandonment of current water system designs: nothing less than such a tabula rasa approach to this sector of the Restoration Economy is needed.

> The staggering cost of maintaining, operating, rehabilitating, and replacing our aging water infrastructure requires a new partnership between federal, state, and local government.
> —**Dennis Archer,** Detroit mayor in a February 13, 2001, press release from the Water Infrastructure Network (WIN), announcing their new report, "Water Infrastructure Now"

The Water Infrastructure Network, a broad-based coalition of governments, engineers, and environmentalists, has asked the Bush administration for $57 billion to be spent on water infrastructure over five years. The backlog includes replacement, enhancement, complete restoration, and ordinary maintenance. In many cases, the dollar amounts categorized as "overdue maintenance" have morphed into restoration, due to the deterioration that took place during the period of delayed maintenance.

> About four years ago, we identified integrated water resources planning as one of our focus areas. . . . [It involves] wastewater collection and treatment, stormwater management, and watershed management, which is emerging as one of the big drivers. EPA and the states are now looking holistically at watersheds and planning at that level. . . . We're seeing that as a growth area. Governments are embracing it, and industries are beginning to do so.
> —John Shearer, Executive V.P., PBS&J [an environmental engineering consultancy, with major projects nationwide, including participation in the Everglades restoration], quoted *in Environmental Business Journal*, Vol. XIII, No. 9/10, 2001

Integrated restoration strategies will greatly improve water infrastructure and its impact on the natural environment. Such strategies will help prevent project failures, such as when oysters are reintroduced into a bay before the sewage plants have been rehabilitated, causing the new oysters to die off for the same reasons their predecessors died off.

Most of our sewer systems are as old as our drinking water systems, and those of many European cities make the century-old sewer infrastructure of U.S. metropolises look sparkling new. Thus, sewage treatment plants have two serious problems: age and design. We need both drinking water treatment systems and sewage treatment systems that remove everything undesired from the water, while adding desirable oxygen to the water: only plant-algae-bacterial systems do this. But closed-system biological designs like Dr. John Todd's Living Machines— which use enclosed ecosystems in tanks to break down and take up pollutants, using only sunlight for power—aren't the only way to accomplish this, or necessarily the best.

Increased funding is a step in the right direction, but the real growth phase in the restoration of the world's water infrastructure will involve a third element (in addition to the current two, restoring drinking water treatment plants/distribution and restoring sewage treatment plants/collection): integrated watershed management (IWM). IWM is coming on fast as planners belatedly realize that drinking water and sewage issues cannot be separated from regional watershed issues.

We've mostly discussed public infrastructure here, but it should now be obvious that the future of energy, water, and solid waste infrastructure will be an internet-like grid, linking public and private infrastructure. Private residences and commercial buildings will become part of the system, rather than just the endpoint of the flow. On private property, more energy will be generated, more water will be collected, treated, and recycled, and more solid waste will be composted or burned as fuel.

ISSUES AND INSIGHTS

> Executives concur that water reclamation/reuse/recycling is the leading growth market within the [$87 billion per year (U.S.)] water industry . . . The evolution from the *process* of managing water to the *business* of managing water is still occurring as private interests and government clarify their roles—and increasingly compete. . . . [M]ajor trends are reshaping the water industry like never before. Some of the more prominent trends include:
>
> * *closing the loop* via onsite recycling and system-wide water reclamation;
> * *real pricing* based on all costs, magnifying a host of economic drivers;
> * *privatization* . . . with an emphasis on public/private partnerships;
> * *new contract mechanisms* . . . commissioning, construction and management;
> * *convergence of water and energy industries.* . . ;
> * *globalization* of foreign competition and *consolidation* of the industry.
>
>   —*Environmental Business Journal*, Volume XIII, Number 9/10, 2001 [Note: The name of
>   this journal refers more to environmental engineering than to tree-hugging.]

1. **Perversion of restorative technologies by dying new development industries** Fuel cell technology offers a good example. Although the cells aren't actively restorative, they do eliminate new pollution, allowing passive restoration. But some people want to make fuel cells produce pollution.

Let's back up a moment. Hydrogen-powered fuel cells get their energy by putting hydrogen and oxygen back together into water. The amount of energy this produces is exactly the same as the energy it takes to split water apart at the hydrogen production plant. Splitting it "stores" that energy until the fuel cell allows the two elements to merge again, so there are zero byproducts.

But oil and gas companies are trying to force us to use fossil fuels in fuel cells, such as natural gas, instead of hydrogen. (They can do this quite easily, simply by blocking the establishment of a hydrogen refueling infrastructure.) Fuel cells do burn natural gas more thoroughly than do reciprocating internal combustion engines, but the net effect would be an incremental improvement, rather than a paradigm shift to a non-polluting energy infrastructure.

What's more, fuel cells burning these dirty fuels don't last anywhere near as long as those burning hydrogen. It would help tremendously if the federal government were to ban the burning of anything but hydrogen in fuel cells for 20 years or so, just to give the industry a clean start, but that would probably require replacing 80 percent of U.S. Congressional incumbents (political restoration).

Part of the oil firms' disinformation campaign tells us that hydrogen won't work, because you have to burn so much fossil fuel to create it. They "forget" to mention that it can be (and is already) produced from clean energy sources. When the hydrolysis creating the hydrogen fuel is powered by electricity from nonpolluting energy sources—such as geothermal, solar, wind, methane (from waste), etc.—the use of fuel cells will be almost completely non-polluting, except for aspects such as the initial manufacturing and distribution of the fuel cells.

In fact, Iceland plans to base its entire economy on hydrogen produced from geothermal, hydroelectric, and wind in the near future. That country will use only hydrogen domestically, and as other countries adopt fuel cells, hydrogen will quickly become its major export.

2. Other forms of infrastructure restoration can also be compromised by retaining old designs and investments   While rebuilding our roads and bridges is a good thing, taking advantage of their decrepit condition to direct the money towards replacing some of them with public transportation would be better. Rehabilitating inefficient water filtration and sewage plants, as we've just discussed, is also a good thing, but getting rid of them in favor of an integrated watershed/water infrastructure system is even better. Somewhere along the way, we need to make bold decisions as to when we cut ourselves loose from dysfunctional designs: when to replace, rather than rehabilitate.

Such decisions will be easier when the restoration of all aspects of our built and natural environments is integrated. Presently, the fact that a city's rehabilitated sewage plant will help restore an estuary 200 miles downriver is an "oh, that's nice," rather than a factor entered directly into its cost-benefit analysis, or into its repayment scheme.

CLOSING THOUGHTS

> Most of the communities across the United States are facing unprecedented
> challenges in restoring their infrastructure systems. Maintenance of roads,
> bridges, and utilities demands ever-increasing operating budgets and capital
> investment for municipalities. Nationwide, most sewer systems suffer from
> chronic overflows and bypasses . . .
> —**Yuseff, Czek,** and **Tittlebaum,** "A benefit analysis model for sanitary sewer
> rehabilitation," *Public Works Management & Policy,* July 2001

Some readers might be wondering if these hundreds of billion of dollars
put into infrastructure restoration wouldn't be better spent on something
more urgent and irretrievable, like endangered species. Are the needs
of pipes, roads, and buildings really as critically important as saving
whales? I wouldn't argue with them, except to point out that rotting
infrastructure leads to huge waste, which leads to environmental damage, which threatens species.

Some of that waste is obvious, such as the millions of gallons of gasoline burned daily in traffic jams. Some of it is more subtle, such as wasted
educational efforts due to uncomfortable students in dilapidated schools.
Either way, the quality and efficiency of the built environment is directly
connected to the health of the natural environment.

One problem encountered by water recycling projects is the public
perception that recycled water is inferior to "fresh" water. This can only
be attributed to a failure of our public school system: how can students
graduate from high school not knowing that every drop of water they've
ever put in their mouth has already been recycled through kidneys,
colons, and swamps millions of times? On the plus side, this means people obviously trust nature's water treatment system more than those
based on concrete and industrial chemicals. This makes systems that integrate watersheds and water infrastructure—such as New York City's—
that much more marketable.

No one needs to tell public works directors that they've got an infrastructure restoration crisis. They've been waiting for the rest of us to
wake up to it. One hurdle is that city and state budgets are not formatted
in a trimodal manner, making it difficult to properly budget for new
capacity, maintenance, and restoration. Once they start using the right
terminology, politicians will find that restoration is a far easier "sell" to
the public when bond issuance time rolls around.

This chapter has been intentionally U.S.-focused: I wanted to show
how bad things are (infrastructure-wise) in the country that many
assume has world-class infrastructure. Countries whose infrastructure

was built even earlier than ours can be assumed to have even greater restoration challenges/opportunities.

If we want to restore the world, we must restore the built and the natural together, or we'll restore neither. This isn't a pipe dream (no pun intended), as demonstrated by New York City's success. Until our cities (and eventually our buildings) are on closed water systems, ensuring both quality *and* quantity means integrating infrastructure restoration with watershed and agricultural restoration, and this will lead to ecosystem and fishery restoration.

Unless you're a civil engineer, you probably found infrastructure to be the "coldest" and least interesting of the restoration industries so far. Let's change pace, moving to one of the most human and subjective of the restoration industries: heritage.

A SMALL SAMPLING OF OPPORTUNITIES

Business and investment

- Private companies are increasingly purchasing, restoring, and operating aged public infrastructure (often due to shortfalls in public funding). This includes transportation, power, water, and solid waste, plus public assets not mentioned here, such as prisons.
- The recent enterprise-level software/hardware trend towards "grid"—also called "utility"—computing (systems that dynamically reallocate resources) will likely find many applications in the public–private world of infrastructure, especially transportation, water, and power.
- The privatization of water is producing a growing number of stock market investment opportunities. French mega-firm Vivendi—originally a stuffy utility, now an entertainment giant (via acquisitions)—had a very successful IPO on the Paris stock exchange for its Vivendi Environment division in July 2000. In 2001, it got listed on the New York Stock Exchange (symbol: VE) in preparation for U.S. trading. The parent firm's current accounting woes don't negate the intelligence of moving into addressing "real" problems like water.

NGOs and other nonprofits

Infrastructure (as well as brownfields) is a restoration industry in sore need of more not-for-profit activity. Smart growth groups are currently the main citizen players, but many niches remain. Among the most obvious are those that would integrate infrastructure with other industries of restoration, e.g. water infrastructure with watershed and fisheries restoration. This would leverage the current government trend towards integrated water management.

(continued)

Community and government

- Once again, integrated approaches are the future of public utilities, but this might go much further than "simply" integrating public drinking and wastewater with watershed and wetlands restoration (à la New York City). Eventually, all infrastructure, public and private, will likely achieve web-like integration: transportation, energy, solid waste, and water.

- Bulk water transfers aren't limited to the state and municipal level, as is common in the western United States. National governments shouldn't miss the trend towards international swapping of water. As of this writing, China had just completed its first large-scale water exchange, Iran and Kuwait had just done a deal, South Africa and Lesotho are in the process of doing their first transfer, and the U.K. is moving in that direction. As water increasingly becomes a tradable, strategic international commodity, restoration of infrastructure and watersheds becomes ever more urgent to national security and economic welfare.

Restoring Our Heritage:
Historic Sites and Structures

We came across a large, low-income housing complex, La Hacienda de Ybor. The nondescript, concrete-block apartments with occasional splashes of terra-cotta represented one of the few promises the government had kept. José Vega Díaz greeted us, his sprightly gait disguising his ninety-four years. He explained how bureaucrats had forced him and his wife, Blanca, from their nearby home. Blanca wailed in grief on eviction day, "I can't. I can't!" She was dead by sunset. The couple had survived the rigors of immigration, revolution, radical politics, and union strife, but they could not endure the wrecking ball.

—**Gary R. Mormino** and **George E. Pozzetta,** *The Immigrant World of Ybor City: Italians and Their Latin Neighbors in Tampa, 1885–1985,* 1987

In their wonderfully written and lovingly researched 1987 biography of Ybor City (a section of Tampa, Florida) authors Mormino and Pozzetta cite many examples of what they refer to as "the horrors of urban renewal," illustrated by the above excerpt.

Ybor City was, until World War II, a colorful, cohesive, dynamic, creative, vibrant community; a national model of ethnic diversity, cooperation, and peaceful coexistence. It had once been the economic heart of Florida, enabling Tampa to account for some two-thirds of the entire state's revenues at the dawn of the twentieth century. Although its cigar factories had mostly closed, robbing it of much economic strength, Ybor was still a healthy community until the 1960s, when it was murdered by urban renewal and buried under the concrete of new highway development.

Today, Ybor City is making a strong comeback, albeit with a very different personality. It's now Tampa's center of nightlife and weekend public celebrations. Its sexy new image is now attracting many "normal" businesses, as well as high-rent residents, who used to be scared off by the nearby '60s-era public housing project (also recently renovated). This renaissance is almost entirely attributable to the restoration and adaptive reuse of its many historic buildings. Old cigar factories now house microbreweries, shopping malls, offices, and self-serve storage centers.

Ironically, a 3.2 mile section of the interstate highway that destroyed a major part of Ybor City in the early '70s is itself about to be restored (via replacement), to the tune of a hundred million dollars. At the same time, a portion of the adjacent Port of Tampa has been cleaned-up and renovated, gaining a cruise ship terminal and beautiful aquarium.

This time around, some lessons have been learned. The Florida Department of Transportation is moving and restoring 32 old buildings that otherwise would have been demolished to make room for the widening of the highway. What's more, the City of Tampa is moving and restoring several other nearby buildings, and is offering, free of charge, additional old buildings to private citizens, even paying for the cost of relocating them. In just a few decades, we've come a long way from the style of urban renewal that tortured José Vega Díaz and killed Blanca.

THE SCOPE OF THE HERITAGE RESTORATION INDUSTRY

> . . . [T]he historic preservation [restoration] movement . . . swept seemingly out of nowhere in the 1970s and 1980s to reverse everything that had been done to the built environment in the 1950s and 1960s. Modernist architecture, urban renewal, go-go real estate—all were suddenly treated as the enemies of civilization and beaten back. How did such a profound change come about? Why wasn't it noticed in the media?
>
> Preservation [restoration] was one of the swiftest, most complete cultural revolutions ever, yet because it happened everywhere at once, without controversy or charismatic leadership, it never got the headlines of its sibling, the environmental movement. Also its payback cycle was much quicker, and therefore quieter, than environmentalists could count on.
> —**Stewart Brand,** *How Buildings Learn,* 1994

Heritage is a very subjective thing: it's as consciously and subconsciously selective as is our perception of the present. What we choose to restore, and to be proud of, says as much about who we are now—and how we choose to see ourselves—as it does about our ancestors.

In the most generic sense, a community's physical heritage simply comprises those parts of the built environment that lasted long enough for us to get attached to, or where something happened that we consider intrinsic to our sense of identity. Heritage restoration is thus much subtler than, say, infrastructure restoration. One person's historic building is another person's obsolete eyesore, and one person's sacred battlefield is another person's wasted space. But one person's broken water main is another person's broken water main.

Almost anything that is authentically from our past can qualify as heritage. Archaeologists find bliss rooting through ancient trash piles. Go to Scranton, Pennsylvania's remarkable Steamtown, USA, and you'll find that heritage can turn formerly ugly, noisy, smelly places—in this case a railroad switching yard—into a must-see spot for family vacations. The transition from utility to heritage (in the absence of some historic event's happening on the site) is often just a matter of time.

> We are convinced by things that show internal complexity, that show the traces of an interesting evolution. Those signs tell us that we might be rewarded if we accord it our trust. . . . This is what makes old buildings interesting to me. I think that humans have a taste for things that not only show that they have been through a process of evolution, but which also show they are still part of one. They are not dead yet.
> —**Brian Eno,** artist and musician, as quoted in Stewart Brand's *How Buildings Learn*, 1994

Bottom line: Heritage is what we want it to be, so this restorative industry spills into all of the other restoration industries, both natural and built. In Nantucket, fisheries are heritage. Farms are heritage in the Amish countryside of Blue Ball, Pennsylvania, while in nearby Gettysburg, heritage comprises open fields seeded with lead balls. In Concord, Massachusetts, infrastructure (a small bridge) is heritage. In San Antonio, Texas, war—in the form of a bullet-riddled old convent—is heritage. In Galveston, Texas, a natural disaster is heritage. In Dallas, Texas, a relatively young public building, the Texas School Book Depository, became heritage overnight when Lee Harvey Oswald is said to have shot John F. Kennedy from one of the building's windows.

There are also intangible heritage assets—skills, languages, crafts, etc.—that have been experiencing opposing dynamics of wholesale destruction and passionate restoration in the past two or three decades. In the United States, the nonprofit Cultural Survival (www.cs.org) has been the leading champion for revitalizing indigenous languages, not to mention restoring the crafts, lands, and human rights of threatened indigenous cultures. For this book, though, we're going to keep it simple, dividing heritage restoration into natural and built.

NATURAL HERITAGE

> We've come here from California to help restore the Highlands' wild forest, but . . . hacking heather suddenly feels less like ecological atonement than petty vandalism. After all, I once thought the Highlands were just fine the way they are. Most tourists and many Scots still do. . . . The Highlands seem primal, pristine. They are nothing of the kind. As I slip another tree into the ground, I remind myself that we have joined volunteers from the Scottish group Trees for Life to right some wrongs, many of them ancient. The Highlands were once covered by what the Romans called the Caledonian Forest, a vast mosaic of pine, birch, willow, alder, elm, ash, and oak. Within that forest lived a Celtic people with a reverence for trees. They taught their children the alphabet using the names of trees. They built their homes, their boats, their lives from trees. But since those days, Scotland has been stripped of 99 percent of its wildwood (as they call it here) and most of the attendant flora and fauna.
> —**Guy Hand**, "Planting on Barren Ground," *Audubon,* January–February 2000
> [Trees for Life can be contacted at www.treesforlife.org.uk]

Trees for Life was founded by Alan Watson Featherstone, who, in 1985, visited India and was inspired by the long-term ecological and farm restoration project at Auroville, in India's south. Auroville citizens had planted some 2 million trees in an area that had been an unproductive, near-desert wasteland. It's now a vast expanse of lush forest and fertile farms.

Trees for Life is doing for Scotland what the Wildlands Project has been trying to do for North America. The organization provides the large-scale vision needed to coordinate the disparate ecological restoration projects being performed by groups and government agencies such as the Scottish Wildlife Trust, the Forestry Commission (which, like its counterpart in the States, the U.S. Forest Service, takes an agricultural, nonecological approach to forests), and the Nature Conservancy Council for Scotland.

The goal is to connect both conserved and restored ecosystems and restore the aggregate "Scottish ecosystem" that existed when they were all just components of a higher-level system, rather than isolated biological communities. The initial goal, though, was more modest: Trees for

Life started with the hope of restoring 1,500 square kilometers in the north-central Highlands.

When the Ghost of "Heritage Lost" Becomes Our Heritage

Just as most Americans admire the green expanses of tree farms we call National Forests, not knowing that we're gazing at sites of corporate theft and ecological annihilation, so do Scots love their heather, even though most of it is the "scar tissue" formed over the much earlier theft of their forest heritage. Besides their grand shoreline, heather-covered hillsides are just about the only natural heritage modern Scots have known. (On the plus side, heather is a Scottish native . . . it just wasn't meant to be the *only* Scottish native.)

Once up to 80 percent forested, Scotland now has only eight percent tree cover, and just a tiny percentage of that is real forest; most consists of sterile tree farms of foreign species. Gone are the Scots' pine, birch, rowan, aspen, willow, and alder. In their place: North American sitka spruce, and, well, North American sitka spruce.

This is obviously a loss of ecosystem function and wildlife genetic resources, but it's a loss of heritage, too. However, the heather-covered Highlands are supremely beautiful, in their own haunting way, so it's highly unlikely that the Scots would allow the heather to be restored out of existence. Therefore, restorationists should probably ignore those heather expanses that are most visible to tourists, such as Glen Coe (which even I would hate to see restored, so breathtakingly majestic is its blend of biological devastation and geological grandeur). No worries, though: This would still leave centuries of restorative work to be done.

The ecorestoration challenge goes far beyond planting trees, of course. Scotland suffers from a plague of deer, caused by managing protected areas for the benefit of hunters, rather than for nature. The over-populated deer devastate native plants (and the smaller animal species that depend on these plants), just as they do in the United States, and for much the same reason.

The few remnant native forests are mostly in hospice care. All the trees are old: new growth is nowhere to be found on the site of the former Caledonian forest. A student at Edinburgh University inventoried an area that contained 100,000 pines. Because they averaged less than 4 inches tall, he assumed they were seedlings. On closer examination, he discovered that they were all a decade old, but deer browsing kept them to grasslike levels.

Using a fence, he excluded the deer; the pine, birch, and rowan seedlings within the area are now growing to maturity—the first ones in that part of the country to do so in over a century and a half. In fact, a large part of what Trees for Life does, by way of restoration, is "merely" build fences, allowing Scottish forests to do what they haven't been able to do for hundreds of years.

The Scots, who recently restored their self-rule, are increasingly looking at their land and culture, and trying to figure out what is truly Scottish, and what has been imposed by centuries of invasion by other cultures. Since it was once between 70 and 80 percent woodland, you would assume that forest restoration is one of Scotland's top heritage restoration priorities, right? Wrong.

And what about the denizens of those forests—the wolves, brown bears, wild boars, lynx, European beaver, and moose—that have such profound influences on native culture? All are extinct in Scotland now (though not elsewhere): surely the return of those definers of the Scottish soul must be in demand, right? Not necessarily. Restorationists are often confronted by angry landowners, much of whose income has long come from allowing others to hunt deer, with easy shots in wide-open fields of heather. These landowners see the return of the Caledonian forest as a loss of their heritage, not as the return of it.

There probably was never a time when the residents of the Highlands weren't being invaded by someone. The famous Highland warrior clans encountered by the Romans and English were originally the successful Irish conquerors of the indigenous Picts. But Ireland itself was probably inhabited originally from Scotland and Norway. Given such histories, delaying restoration until "true heritage" has been defined would freeze us into inaction. Heritage restoration often involves a tremendous degree of selecting what we like about our past, to the exclusion of what we are ashamed of, or what we find too painful. Witness how few cities make wartime shrines out of bombed-out building hulks, even when they were the winners.

From Scotland to the World

In 1991, Trees for Life was named the United Kingdom's "Conservation Project of the Year" in the annual Ford Conservation Awards Competition, which brings a check equalling about $15,000, plus extensive media coverage. The project's success has inspired others in the U.K., such as the Carrifan Project, designed to restore the native forests of the Southern Uplands, an area that reportedly has lost even more of its forests than the

Highlands (if that's possible). Likewise, the Moor Trees project is attempting to restore native forests to the Dartmoor region in the south of England. Trees for Life has even inspired at least one initiative in the Americas, where the Matatu project is trying to bring back the near-extinct Araucaria trees of Brazil's Atlantic Forest.

Featherstone has more recently organized an effort to have the United Nations declare the twenty-first century as "The Century of Restoring the Earth." This designation would coincide nicely with the U.N.-backed effort to establish The Earth Charter, a guideline for sustainable development, which includes such principles as "Protect and restore the integrity of Earth's ecological systems, with special concern for biological diversity and the natural processes that sustain life," and "Protect and restore outstanding places of cultural and spiritual significance."

On May 14, 2002, U.N. Secretary General Kofi Annan departed from his long-standing calls for sustainable development and joined the Restoration Economy when he declared, "We must rehabilitate our one and only planet . . . water, energy, health, agriculture, and biodiversity." He missed a couple of the eight restorative industries, but who's counting?

A Heady Pint of Heritage

As long as we're already in Scotland, let's not waste any fossil fuels moving elsewhere. Here's a story that neatly integrates the restoration of cultural heritage, ecological heritage, and a heritage building, and so provides a perfect segue from natural heritage to built heritage. All this is being accomplished by a small, for-profit firm, Historic Ales of Scotland—a true (if unlikely) Restoration Economy company.

In the town of Strathaven in Lanarkshire, close to Glasgow, Bruce Williams has been reviving a delicious realm of Scottish heritage: He brews "extinct" ancient ales based on indigenous botanicals. Scotland once had dozens of homegrown ales that used the leaves, flowers, and fruit of local trees, bushes, and forbs.

On the Isle of Rhum, for instance, archaeologists have discovered the remains of a brewing site dating back over 4,000 years. (Note: Ale is what most Scots drink. Scotch whiskey, better known than Scottish ale outside Scotland, is mostly for export, and "only" dates back about 400 years.) It contained traces of the ingredients for heather ale. Long the national drink of Scotland, the making of heather ale—along with ales made from (or flavored with) gooseberries, elderberries, Scotch Pine needles, and even seaweed—was forbidden by English invaders.

Scots were instead required by law to make only "industrialized beer," using standardized ingredients like barley malt and hops. (Of course, even this formula is far superior to the corn-based chemical soup that comes from the major U.S. industrial brewers, many of whom add plastics to form a longer-lasting head.) This was done to raise taxes from sales of malt, as well as to increase sales of hops, because the House of Lords owned all the hop farms. After disappearing for a couple of centuries, these tasty brews have now been brought back to life by Bruce Williams, who, the son of a brewer, has been making beers and ales since he was thirteen.

Originally produced in such small quantities that six local pubs consumed it all, William's *Fraoch* Heather Ale (its ingredients also include wild bog myrtle) is now distributed throughout the United States and many other countries. The concoction has won countless awards, including two World Gold Medals in 1996 and 1997. (It was reportedly the only beer that Mel Gibson allowed on the set during the shooting of *Braveheart*.)

Historic Ales of Scotland (www.heatherale.co.uk) now also produces seasonal supplies of *Grozet* gooseberry ale, *Ebulum* elderberry black ale, and *Kelpie* seaweed ale. The *Alba* Scots Pine ale is another favorite. *Alba's* comeback restores both Scottish and Norwegian heritage, since it was originally brought to Scotland by Viking invaders. It quickly became popular with other sailors, including Captain Cook. He never set sail without Scots Pine ale, prizing its ability to travel well, and its value as a scurvy preventative and tonic for his crews. Now, thanks to Williams, I can easily find it here in Virginia.

What's more, Historic Ales of Scotland operates out of an early eighteenth-century mill, restored under the supervision of the national nonprofit organization, Scottish Heritage. When Williams first encountered Craigmill—located on the banks of the River Avon (which supplied its power)—the picturesque river was eating the foundation out from under the waterwheel, and the mill was, quite literally, a pigsty. The restoration and adaptive reuse of the old mill began around 1987, with the shoveling out of a few tons of "pig heritage."

Several years were spent rebuilding the waterwheel, which involved restoring and reforesting the river banks. The owner of the mill, Andrew MacGregor (now a minority stockholder in, as well as the landlord of, Historic Ales of Scotland), then applied to Scottish Heritage for a restoration grant. Grant in hand, work recommenced in 1992, and was completed around the turn of the millennium.

You'd think that would be about as many different kinds of restorative activities as could be packed into one modest little business, but wait . . . there's more. In Maybole, just 18 miles from Strathaven, is a square mile of peat-and-heather-based ecosystem known as the flat moss. This entire area came close to being turned into a monoculture tree farm, thanks to the government incentives being handed out. The tennant, Ian Campbell, would have gone for the conversion, except for one factor: Historic Ales of Scotland harvests heather for its *Fraoch* ale from the flat moss, and pays him for it.

Although not enough to equal what Campbell would eventually earn from a tree farm, that income is close enough to make it affordable for him to conserve the property. It's not ecological restoration, granted, but it's certainly conservation resulting from restoration (of ales). A slightly more restorative effect occurred at the farm where Historic Ales gets gooseberries. The farm was overgrown and not especially productive, because there's not much of a market for gooseberries (and that's a real shame: I love 'em). At the prodding of the Historic Ales folks, the farm was cleaned up (though there's still lots of room for wildlife) and is now more efficient: a minor form of agricultural restoration.

One last restorative tie-in: A Scottish (and Irish) method of fertilizing fields, which dates back at least 400 years, uses seaweed. But seaweed use was dying out in Scotland, except along the Argyll Coast, where it gives the vegetables and grains a unique (and prized) color and flavor.

Then, Historic Ales began producing *Kelpie,* which adds bladderwrack seaweed to the mash tun with the barley. The barley itself is organically grown on a farm that has revived the ancient practice of fertilizing with seaweed. This was at Bruce Williams's request, so that *Kelpie* would be as authentic as possible. *Kelpie* (a malevolent water creature of Gaelic myth, such as the Loch Ness Monster) is a delightful black ale (much like a rich, dry porter) and is a World Beer Championships Gold Medal winner.

BUILT HERITAGE

St. Augustine founded it. Becket died for it. Chaucer wrote about it.
Cromwell shot at it. Hitler bombed it. Time is destroying it. Will you save it?
—from an advertisement for the Canterbury Cathedral restoration fund

The U.S. Park Service's restoration of the home of Jack and Rachel Clark strikes many as a strange choice, because nothing happened there. At least, not by the usual standards of historic places. The Clarks weren't famous, nor were they the parents of anyone famous. The Clarks were the black sharecroppers that former President Jimmy Carter called his "second parents." "Except in my own room in my own house, this is where I felt most at home," he wrote.

Embarrassing Heritage

Sometimes, historic buildings convey a heritage that not everyone wants to be reminded of. The motivation behind the Clark house restoration comes from the Park Service's desire to broaden and deepen its concept (and the public's perception) of what's culturally important. It's quite possible that the Clarks' influence on young Jimmy contributed to his becoming president. But the Park Service didn't just restore the house because the Clarks knew an important white man. Rather, it's part of the Park Service's agenda to restore our memory of all aspects of our past. Poor sharecroppers are as much a part of who we are as are generals, inventors, and business tycoons.

Some think we should forget this portion of our past, so as to not damage the self-image of young blacks today. Others say that being kidnapped and forced into slavery—and then surviving to help form a powerful new culture—is nothing to be ashamed of: If anyone is going to be discomforted by such a restoration, it should be those whose ancestors perpetrated the crime, and whose current fortunes may have been built on it.

The Manassas Museum in historic Manassas, Virginia, conveys this ugly piece of heritage both powerfully and tastefully. One example is the museum's reproduction of a "Wanted" poster concerning an escaped slave: the language, which describes the escapee in terms one would normally use for livestock, makes almost every reader cringe and squirm.

A similar dynamic—discomfort with one's history—is at work in China. Many southern Chinese cities, such as Shanghai, Xiamen, and others have been dramatically revitalized in recent decades. Most observers focus almost exclusively on the economic aspect of this renewal. Shanghai, for instance, was until recently a coastal city on the skids, but is now the most powerful city in China, usurping much of Beijing's guiding role. It's not just financial power, either: Shanghai—maybe because it's so far from the seat of government—is a hotbed of cultural experimentation and business innovation.

The city's economic and political revitalization is largely due to this freer business environment. Another factor though, is its heritage: Many people enjoy living and working in Shanghai because, despite its plethora of recent high-rises (many of which destroyed priceless heritage), the city still boasts many buildings of tremendous historical and architectural value. They are especially rare, due to that mass erasure of China's past, the Cultural Revolution, and to continued "urban renewal."

Toxic Heritage

Brownfields can be considered the heritage of our new development-based manufacturing sector. It might be the only form of built heritage that literally nobody wants, and it's the only restorative industry that is based on eradication. Even the creators of this "heritage" want no part of it, except to cleanse it from the earth and build anew.

The heritage restoration industry frequently (and unfortunately) overlaps with the brownfields restoration industry. Due to the new development realm's dirty habits, many historic properties are contaminated. Contaminated historic sites often get overlooked for restoration and redevelopment, because adding cleanup to the costs of the building restoration puts it out of reach, budget-wise.

Not all historic buildings can or should be saved. Consider the demolition (by the USEPA) of the Independent Leather Manufacturing Co. in Gloversville, New York, in August 2001. The company was, in the 1800s and early 1900s, one of the region's biggest employers. The leather glove trade's collapse in the 1960s left a hugely toxic legacy, now being remedied with $1.3 million from SuperFund. An article from the Environmental News Network on August 14, 2001, stated, "For more than a century, a large number of tanneries in the area discharged their wastewater into creeks and streams. Tannery operations included processes that required the use of solvents, acids, lime, chromium compounds, and dyes and pigments that contaminated soil, sediments, groundwater and surface water on and nearby the facilities."[1]

This demolition decision was easy, because the building was both contaminated and structurally unsound. Once cleared and detoxified, the site will be redeveloped for commercial use, as part of the brownfields program of the state of New York. It's hoped that the project will help revitalize this economically depressed region of upstate New York. "This site has a lot of potential. It's in an idyllic location and the contamination at the site is relatively easy to address. Once we remove the contamination, this site could be put to use—so this cleanup is a real boost to both

[1]Environmental News Network, "Officials Demolish Toxic Remains of Gloversville, NY, Glove Industry," www.enn.com.

the environment and the local economy," said the EPA's Paul Kahn in that same article.

But some brownfield sites are designated historic and opened to the public without remediation, such as Gas Works Park in Seattle. This unique recreational area retained the rusting hulks of previous industry as a sort of hybrid between manufacturing heritage and decorative metal sculpture. Although some remediation was attempted, it's reported that the city dealt with the brownfields issue primarily by posting signs warning of the soil contamination.

While not doing much for the wildlife or the groundwater, the ongoing toxic threat does give the park a sort of perverse integrity, making it truly representative of the new development heritage it commemorates. The warning signs also have educational value, reminding us of the side effects of our shortsightedness (it feels like the set of an apocalyptic *Mad Max* movie, its ubiquitous radioactive contamination signs). One might consider this a partial restoration: like Amsterdam's green mountain of garbage, the park restored some value and functionality to an eyesore, but restoration certainly could have gone further.

Adaptive Reuse

> Adaptive reuse of a building or structure on land means the modification of the building or structure and its curtilage to suit an existing or proposed use, and that use of the building or structure, but only if:
>
> (a) the modification and use is carried out in a sustainable manner, and
>
> (b) the modification and use are not inconsistent with the conservation of the natural and cultural values of the land, and
>
> (c) in the case of a building or structure of cultural significance, the modification is compatible with the retention of the cultural significance of the building or structure.
>
> —(U.S.) National Park and Wildlife Amendment Bill, 2001 [modified definition]

Adaptive reuse (often called "adaptive use" in the United States) is hardly new, though its recent surge in popularity may lead some to think so. Adaptively reusing existing structures has been a style of human development ever since the first troglodytes evicted (or ate) the original tenants of a bear cave, and moved their families into the rainproof dwelling. Adaptive reuse wasn't invented by loft dwellers in SoHo or Georgetown.

Now it's time for the adaptive reuse of buildings (and redevelopment of brownfields) to assume its rightful place as the first choice of developers, with greenfield development being the option of last resort. Americans have been especially slow to see the advantages of adaptive reuse, possibly because the United States is the prototypical start-up nation. Our economy began (quite recently) with almost pure new development, since most of the thousand-or-so conquered Native North American nations and cultures—even the nonnomadic ones—created little reusable built environment.

(Exceptions to the lack of Native American built heritage include the Maya, Inca, and Aztec civilizations. Upon first beholding Tenochtitlan (later Mexico City), Spanish priests wondered if they had stumbled into heaven. The Aztecs had many gorgeous permanent structures, but the Spaniards' agenda called for erasing existing cultures and religions, so they recycled the stone blocks of buildings and pyramids into cathedrals and forts, rather than adaptively reusing the structures. They didn't even retain and maintain the infrastructure—the aqueducts and sanitation systems— of the wonderfully clean Aztec cities, coming as they did from cities where human waste was simply dumped out of windows into public streets.)

> Guinness Storehouse is located in what had been an old abandoned
> fermentation plant within the main Guinness brewing complex in a gritty,
> industrial part of Dublin. The building's design is like a candy with a
> chocolate shell and a creamy filling: It has tradition on the outside,
> tomorrow on the inside.
> —**Scott Kirsner,** "Brand Marketing: Guinness," *Fast Company* magazine, May 2002
> [the article illustrates that a structure—such as this 1904 factory—doesn't need to
> change hands to be adaptively reused. It's now a visitor and training center, hosting
> some 570,000 tourists and 45,000 trainees annually. The old visitor center—
> the Hopstore—*did* change hands: It was sold to, and adaptively reused, by the
> MIT Media Lab as a research center.]

Adaptive reuse has finally caught on big in the United States and elsewhere. I'm writing these words in the Homewood Suites (owned by Hilton) in San Antonio, Texas. Located on San Antonio's famous Riverwalk (actually a nicely landscaped storm drain full of filthy water, but that's another restoration story), the hotel is an adaptive use of the San Antonio Drug Company building, erected in 1919. In the boardroom is a plaque donated by retired drug company employees, thanking Hilton for saving their old workplace, and for being good stewards of their memories.

Restored Heritage as a Revitalizing Force

> It used to be that old buildings were universally understood to be less
> valuable than new. Now it is almost universally understood that old
> buildings are more valuable than new.
> —**Stewart Brand,** *How Buildings Learn,* 1994

Government buildings (courthouses, schools, etc.) have a tendency to become heritage more quickly than residences and commercial structures. In Washington, D.C., the 66-year-old U.S. Supreme Court is due for its first major restoration, which will take five years and $110 million ($60 million less than was asked for). We mentioned the $3 billion Pentagon restoration in the Introduction, and the list goes on: the just-completed $33.5 million restoration of the U.S. Botanic Garden, the new National Archives project, and dozens more D.C. monument/institution restorations.

Since the 1976 U.S. federal program of tax credits for historic restoration was implemented, some 28,000 U.S. historic properties have been rehabilitated and reused, accounting for over $20 billion of private investment as of 2000. The original 25 percent tax credit was reduced to 20 percent in the 1986 tax reform, and many tax shelter programs were discontinued.

> In addition to the financial considerations of the historic-rehab tax shelters, "all of our investors enjoy the touchy-feely experience of seeing their dollars going to historic rehabilitation," says Spokane developer Ron Wells.
> —**Ben Brown,** "Taking Credits," *Preservation* [the National Trust for Historic Preservation's magazine], July/August 2000

This led to a temporary drop in activity, to less than $1 billion in 1988, but historic restoration boomed again when states (45 as of 2002, up from just 16 in 1998) started piling their own incentives on top of the federal ones. Private investment hit $2.3 billion in 1999. The commercial side is larger than the residential, but housing is no slouch: Over 85 percent of the homes sold annually in the United States are existing—not new—and over 550,000 of the existing homes in the United States are considered historic (over 50 years of age).

Heritage restoration is hot, huge, and global. How hot? U.S. contractors reported that restoration and reconstruction projects increased 42 percent in the year 2000 alone. All this talk of how good heritage restoration is for communities shouldn't lead the reader to forget that this is a *very* attractive growth business.

Consider this: Heritage is in such demand that we're starting to build new abandoned factories. In 2002, the largest new multi-housing development in Washington, D.C.'s increasingly chic Bohemian neighborhood of Adams Morgan was designed to resemble a defunct industrial building that had been converted for residential use. In just two decades, some communities seem to have moved from a plague of forsaken factories to a shortage. What's more, the units—priced from $179,000 to almost $1 million—sold out almost immediately. Is this a good thing? To the degree to which it contributes to infill (thus saving greenfields) and enhances the desired feel of the neighborhood, sure. But it can't really be considered heritage restoration. Some find this approach a bit Disneyesque. *Washington Post* staff writer Benjamin Forgey, for one, seems to prefer the real thing. In an article entitled "In Adams Morgan, Lofty Ambitions for a Manufactured Factory" (July 6, 2002), he said, "Despite these virtues, the . . . projects . . . smack a bit of architectural theming."

Almost everyone has heritage to restore, even beach resorts that are often considered chintzy. A major part of Miami Beach's attractiveness comes from the restoration of its distinctive art deco buildings. Meanwhile, Atlantic City is spending $72 million to renovate the classic Atlantic City Convention Hall, where the Miss America Pageant takes place. Local citizens are raising another $3 million to restore the Convention Hall's 1932 pipe organ, the world's largest.

The restoration of many cities' heritage has usually taken place in piecemeal ways such as these, as opposed to grand citywide plans. With formal recognition of restorative development now becoming common, however, this approach is changing.

Many states and cities encourage heritage restoration via tax credits; incentives such as tax forgiveness; transferable development rights; low-interest loans; expedited writing of "smart" (building) codes; elimination of "dumb" codes; and the creation of historic districts that add extra value to the properties within them via higher rents, increased tourist traffic, etc. The value of the last point is underscored by the fact that in many European countries, architectural heritage is the single largest tourism asset.

Worldwide, there are literally tens of thousands of historic buildings and other sites under restoration at this very moment. Each has its own interesting story, but the process of organization and executing the projects is often very similar, as are the effects these projects have on their communities.

- Bologna, Italy (home of the Ducati motorcycle factory, a bit of world heritage cherished by this author), tops public opinion polls as Italians' favorite city. This is largely traceable to their vigorous restoration of heritage buildings.
- Melbourne, Australia has long suffered by being seen as running a distant second to Sydney, because it lacked the latter's skyscrapers. But recently, Melbourne leveraged this calmer, more genteel heritage by restoring large numbers of older buildings that had grown shabby. Many now call it "the hippest city in the Southern Hemisphere."

- Copenhagen, Denmark has, for decades, suffered the deterioration that accompanies urban flight to the suburbs. Many neighborhoods, such as Vesterbro, had become crime-filled, drug-infested hellholes. City leaders finally fought back with an enlightened form of urban renewal centered on restoration, targeting Vesterbro in particular for revitalization. To preserve the feel and consciousness of neighborhoods, they even went so far as to rehabilitate old tenement buildings, when tearing them down and building anew would have saved money.
- Glasgow, Scotland long represented the worst of that country's new development-based economy. Scotland is often considered the home of the industrial revolution, having contributed many of the key technologies and economic concepts that made it possible. Glasgow had a concentration of the dirtiest of those industries, along with eminently Dickensian working conditions. The built environment thus created kept the city dark and depressed long after more enlightened labor practices had evolved, and long after many of the older industries had died. Few new industries took their place, because no one wanted to move to Glasgow. But a concerted, long-term revitalization campaign, centered on restoration of the city's built (and cultural) environment, led to Glasgow's being crowned the "European City of Culture" in 1990, and the European "City of Architecture" in 1999.

I could have literally filled this book with such vignettes of village, metropolitan, and even national revitalization via restorative development, but we're out of room, so let's look at some of the broader issues.

Lessons Learned from the Urban Renewal Debacle

> Sixty percent of German buildings survived the Second World War. Only less than 15 percent of these survived the industrial plans of the last thirty years.
> —Leon Krier, "Houses, Places, Cities," *A.D. Profile 54*, 1984

Anyone with a sense of recent history and culture knows just how far we've come, especially if he or she lived in a major Western Hemisphere city during the 1960s and 1970s. Thousands of architectural treasures, from courthouses to baseball stadiums, were blithely demolished in a frenzy of "modernization," and replaced by sterile eyesores that are now themselves being demolished. This architectural holocaust was aided and abetted by "dumb" building codes and even tax incentives. Accompanying the profusion of short-lived, hideous office buildings were the dysfunctional, penitentiary-style public housing developments that many blame (at least in part) for the sudden proliferation of gangs, violence, and drugs in formerly peaceful low-income neighborhoods. Many of these housing projects are also being demolished, long before the expiration of their intended life span.

A 1999 trip to Tampa was illustrative. I arrived by Amtrak at Tampa's Union Station, built in 1912 for $250,000, which was undergoing a $3,000,000 restoration. Sitting on the balcony of my hotel room, I gazed across the Hillsborough River at the recently restored silver minarets of the University of Tampa (UT). This picturesque campus started life in 1891 as the Tampa Bay Hotel, constructed by someone who knew all about the profits to be had from restoration: Henry Plant, who made a fortune rebuilding the South after the Civil War. In 1931, the hotel was restored and adaptively reused as the UT campus.

Such restoration efforts have played a significant part in putting Tampa back on the national economic map. Had the founders of UT chosen to build from scratch, or had they not funded continued restoration work, it's unlikely that the campus would be what it is today: Tampa's most treasured and widely recognized feature, the icon of Tampa's personality (though many locals would put the restored Tampa Theatre at the top of their list of favorite places.).

Tampa's planners addressed the restoration of Ybor City's heritage, infrastructure, brownfields, low-income communities, economy, and recreation. Unfortunately, that restoration focused almost exclusively on the built environment, neglecting ecosystems and waterways. Nonetheless, Ybor City demonstrates that we're beginning to recognize the complex demands of multifaceted, simultaneous, *integrated* restoration. This approach revitalizes *everything* that adds (or could add) value to an area, rather than focusing on an isolated outcome at the expense of all else.

Ybor City's 1960s experience also demonstrates that, without an integrated approach, some forms of renewal can be as disruptive and unhealthy as new development. In fact, they *are* new development. Even when it's benign, nonintegrated restoration wastes profits and other value-adds that would have been "free" bonuses with a bit more thought, planning, sensitivity, and/or research.

The Upside of Down Times

Economic distress during the '60s and '70s turned out to be a blessing for many communities—such as Charleston, South Carolina—that are today experiencing a renaissance. Economic distress meant Charleston couldn't afford urban renewal. As a result, its heritage largely escaped the planners' bulldozers and has now become the key to the city's revitalization.

Tampa wasn't so blessed with poverty in those days. As we've seen, they fell victim to the urban renewal craze, when architectural classics were torn down by the thousands nationwide, simply because they were old. Senior residents still mourn the wanton destruction of the distinctive, Moroccan-styled Tampa Courthouse Building. This was probably Tampa's single most costly and culturally tragic error. The city has been struggling ever since, at a cost of many millions of dollars, to woo people to its downtown, which is mostly deserted on weekends and after six o'clock on weekdays.

Vital, prosperous downtowns always have a physical "heart": Tampa ripped its out. Fortunately, the three key restorations—the classic Tampa Theatre, the UT campus, and nearby Ybor City—are mitigating that loss to some degree. The less interesting Florida cities—those too young to have "heritage," or those that took a wrecking ball to their history—are struggling to develop a diversified economic base. Orlando has been trying for decades to convince theme park tourists to drive a few miles to visit its expanse of shopping malls, office buildings, and residential areas, all of recent vintage.

Until you read the opening story, "urban renewal" probably had a positive connotation for you. It certainly *sounds* like a legitimate, desirable component of restorative development, right? Not without integration with our heritage, it isn't, as the Ybor City story illustrated. One of the keys to truly holistic urban (or building) renewal is—as Stewart Brand, president of the Long Now Foundation, would say—to view "the whole" as not just whole in space but whole in time as well. Now that we're learning that urban renewal is supposed to renew and retain, not just replace, metropolitan revitalization plans are proliferating, and heritage restoration is often at their core.

ISSUES AND INSIGHTS

1. Historic restoration can be defined in many ways   One such definitional clash concerns whether to restore sites to an arbitrary "original condition," or to recognize that buildings "live and evolve," and that this evolution is itself genuine and historic. A good example comes from the Nelson House, a National Park Service (NPS) project. Built in Yorktown, Virginia, in 1735, the Nelson House was named by *National Geographic Magazine* "Virginia's Most Famous Revolutionary Home." Its restoration was a nightmare for the descendants of the original owner.

Nelson House was purchased and restored in 1914 by George Preston Blow. It remained in the Blow family until 1969, when it was sold to the NPS, which spent $10 million (in 2000 dollars) restoring it to its original condition, which meant removing many eighteenth- and nineteenth-century modifications of historic value. In doing so, "they obliterated almost 300 years of history" says John Blow, Captain Blow's grandson and one of four brothers who sold the house to the NPS. Here's how Blow describes the project on his website:

> Ballast-brick walls were bulldozed, English boxwood trees possibly—probably—planted in the eighteenth century . . . reduced to kindling while two Charles F. Gillette-designed gardens were plowed under and one left to rot. The NPS ignored a whole lot of Civil War history and Colonial Revival input in its rush to rejuvenate.
>
> They had too much money and had to spend it (they could have restored two additional historic Yorktown houses for the same budget). Today the Nelson House stands looking garish and naked like an old lady found wandering without her clothes. The town, once alive and prosperous, is half the size it was in the 1960s as the Park Service condemns and destroys any house, church or business without an eighteenth-century pedigree. Almost every business has fled. The entire town has the ambience of an eighteenth-century Levittown.
>
> On October 7, 1977, perhaps in an attempt to prevent another rape of historic property, the Park Service issued "The Secretary of the Interior's Standards," [which] included the following paragraph: "4. Most properties change over time; those changes that have acquired historical significance in their own right shall be retained and preserved."
> —http://members.telocity.com/blowstandard/N1snHsPage.html (1998)

Despite this story, please bear in mind that the NPS is one of "the good guys," a great champion of heritage restoration. The NPS has had little difficulty transitioning from new development to restoration (its only major area of unresolved internal contention being the restorative burning of park lands). The NPS is active in at least four restorative industries: ecosystem, watershed, infrastructure, and heritage. It is actually a leading force in heritage restoration, facilitating the flow of private investments totaling over $2.5 billion annually into the thousand or more restoration projects it has going on at any given moment. Between 1994 and 2000, there was a 47 percent increase in the volume of federal tax credits NPS approved for restoration projects.

Making the decision as to what part of a building's accumulated renovations and expansions qualify as heritage is a thankless task, guaranteed to anger someone. Witness the hot debate over restoration of James

Madison's home, Montpelier. This $40 million project must decide whether to keep the expansions—which also qualify as heritage in the eyes of many people—added by the DuPont family a century after Madison's death.

2. Few performance specifications exist for historic restorations, so the definition of authenticity varies widely The restoration of the ancient Cambodian city of Angkor (its regional ecosystem collapses and restorations were described in Chapter 2) provides a perfect example. As soon as Cambodia's long civil war ended in 1991, many nations rushed in to restore Angkor, as described in a January 15, 1998, Associated Press article. In it, John Sanday, who oversees work at Angkor's Preah Khan monastic complex for the World Monuments Fund, said:

> They're healing the scars of time on the wondrous temples of Angkor—and bickering in a babel of languages about how it should be done. . . . [The] Japanese think the French are using too much concrete. The Americans question whether the Japanese have enough expertise in stone work. And everyone criticizes the Indians for apparently having used corrosive chemicals. Angkor ranks among mankind's greatest artistic creations . . . [but] UNESCO-sponsored master plan for Angkor has been quietly shelved and Cambodia admits it doesn't have the know-how or resources to direct a harmonious rehabilitation. There are at least five different groups using five different approaches.
> —**Denis D. Gray,** "Nations' Trials Meant to Prevent Errors during Restoration of Angkor," *Seattle Post-Intelligencer,* January 15, 1998

Later reports claimed that the Japanese take an "aggressive approach" to restoration, stressing beautification and filling-in of missing elements, rather than authenticity. Other major players in what will be at least a 20-year, $100 million effort are Japan, Indonesia, Germany, Italy, Hungary, UNESCO, the European Union, France, and China. "There isn't one globally accepted way of restoring a monument. It is important that there is debate and that it continues," said Ang Choulean of APSARA, the Cambodian agency overseeing Angkor's restoration, in the same article quoted above. "It's simply a dream to think that we can have one way of restoring Angkor. But we must avoid any damage."

3. Historic preservationists can sometimes go a bit overboard Local heritage groups sometimes go beyond restoring old buildings to demanding that all new buildings match the style of the period deemed desirable. This can have a stifling effect on architectural creativity and innovation. It can also impede other important agendas, such as the use of environmentally efficient designs and technologies. "Green" (planted) roofs are a no-no, for instance, even when they would be invisible from the ground.

Such all-out authenticity agendas are often of value when creating entire historic districts. However, they sometimes can reduce the charm and uniqueness of the older buildings, by surrounding them with too much sameness. Such an approach makes it harder for people to tell real heritage from fake.

4. Context is too often undervalued   It's surprising how often heritage conservation and restoration projects focus on the visual aspects of the project, ignoring all other senses, such as sounds and smells. For instance, at George Washington's lovingly restored Mt. Vernon property, security personnel patrol the otherwise pastoral scene in a huge, noisy, smelly diesel pickup truck. Why not horses? Or a horse-drawn carriage, to protect guards from the elements?

5. Nonstandardized terminology   In Chapter 4, we mentioned the somewhat esoteric problem of terms having mutually exclusive meanings in different restorative industries: Here's an example of how it affects business. National Public Radio recently told the story of a master roof repairer who was fined $10,000—mercifully reduced from the standard fine of $25,000—by the German Economic Criminal Police. He was restoring a church, and had to replace the rotten, 300-year-old wooden beams. The fact that he replaced the beams, rather than fixing them, officially crossed the line into roof construction, as opposed to restoration. Construction is a different guild, upon whose turf he had unknowingly trespassed. That's an expensive bit of terminological confusion for an independent craftsperson.

Restoration can legitimately be considered one of the tools of preservation, and using the two terms interchangably wouldn't be a problem if the world consisted only of inanimate objects. But restorative development addresses more than the built environment: it encompasses the living systems of the natural and the socioeconomic environments, as well. "Preservation" is what one does to dead things. We would greatly serve the cause of integrated restoration if we standardized our language a bit. (Given the evolutionary perspective of buildings offered by Stewart Brand in his landmark book *How Buildings Learn*, it's probably quite appropriate to speak of buildings as if they were alive, too.)

A Closing Story

> Old places, as in Europe, gather memories and associations. Thousands of
> lives write them as if they were a big historical novel, thousands of feet and
> hands wear them smooth, remake them. But most of America's old places
> decay and are discarded, or are replaced and restored to a false and sparkly
> new use, all suffering and ambiguity erased, renovated out of existence.
> —**Howard Mansfield,** *The Same Ax, Twice: Restoration and Renewal*
> *in a Throwaway Age,* 2000

I wrote much of this chapter in one of my favorite refuges in the world,
the lovely Hotel Britânia in Lisbon, Portugal. Lisbon is a city embodying
a cornucopia of heritage, even by the very high standards of Europe. Popular legend names Ulysses as the city's founder, though most historians
credit the Phoenecians with the deed some 3,000 years ago. The Greeks
took it from the Phoenecians, who were displaced by the Carthaginians.
The Romans had their day, of course, from 205 B.C. to the fifth century A.D.

The Hotel Britânia is part of an expanding group of restored hotels
owned by a partnership of the Sousa and Fernandes families in Lisbon.
The hotels are marketed together as Heritage Hotels Lisboa (Lisboa is the
actual name of the city we call Lisbon) at the website www.heritage.pt.
This 30-room haven of civilized tranquility is a love affair of the charming gentleman responsible for its revival, Luis Alves de Sousa.

His lovely wife, Ana Maria de Mendonça T. S. Alves de Sousa,
authored the romantic short story, "Hotel Britânia: The Magic of Places,"
and did the historical research related to the restoration. She also discovered and restored many of the murals that had been painted over. Built
in 1944, the Britânia is very young by European standards, but it's rich
with heritage nonetheless. Designed in the art deco style by famed Portuguese modernist architect Cassiano Branco, the Britânia's history is rife
with intrigue. It was constructed during the height of WWII, when Lisbon was known to the world as "the city of spies," thanks to its international crossroads location and to Portuguese neutrality.

Sousa is a perfect example of a Restoration Economy leader, someone
who is earning his living entirely from restoration, and who is expanding
those activities as quickly as possible. He is currently bidding on a 1912
building just down the street; his partners recently purchased a small
building on the grounds of the castle overlooking Lisbon and created
14 guest rooms within the ancient structure.

Sousa seems to have arrived accidentally at restorative development.
He purchased the Britânia in 1976, intending to fix it up a bit and resell it
at a profit. But with each improvement, he fell more deeply in love with

the building. He finally committed to a thorough restoration in the mid-1990s, recreating much of the original charm, while enhancing it with the most uniformly excellent hotel staff I've encountered. (Thank you, Pedro, Elisabete, Rui, and Eugénia!) All are multilingual, not to mention phenomenally attentive and caring. In the interests of accurate restoration and guest comfort, Sousa kept the spacious, high-ceilinged room layout, even though he could have had more rooms by shrinking them.

> It is better to preserve than to repair, better to repair than to restore, better to restore than to reconstruct.
> —**A. N. Didron,** archaeologist, *Bulletin Archeologique,* Volume 1, 1839

"I'm a happy man," Sousa told me as we lounged in the bar, with its absolutely stunning parquet floor, in December of 2001. "I love being in this building. I love our employees. . . . I love our guests: They share my sensibilities. The kinds of people who seek out a place like this are different from the 'consumers' who stay in new hotels. Restored hotels have soul . . . are living structures with a history and personality. Restoration work is too difficult to undertake unless one has a passion for it; unless one derives deep personal rewards from it. But how can one not be enriched, on all levels, by restoring one's heritage, and having the privilege of earning one's living doing so?" he said.

What's truly exciting is that, these days, you're likely to find someone with a story similar to Luis Alves de Sousa's in almost every city of significant size worldwide.

You've probably found this chapter on heritage restoration "warmer" than the preceding hypertechnical subjects of brownfields and infrastructure. But for sheer depth of emotion, no industry of restorative development can touch the one that ends this survey of the built environment: disaster and war restoration.

A SMALL SAMPLING OF OPPORTUNITIES

Business and investment

Heritage strikes many as a nontechnological restoration industry, but a wealth of opportunities awaits inventors. The sudden growth of most restoration industries, including heritage, is so new that most of the progress has been in knowledge: technological advances are the next stage. A vast array of older museum, education, residential, office, and government projects awaits.

(continued)

A SMALL SAMPLING OF OPPORTUNITIES *(continued)*

NGOs and other nonprofits

As mentioned earlier, heritage tourism has been one of the fastest-growing aspects of the travel industry for over a decade, and shows every sign of continuing its growth. The natural synergy between heritage restoration, community revitalization, travel, and cultural education is spawning many not-for-profit opportunities for new and established organizations.

Community and government

Both metropolitan and national governments are in the unique position of being able to greatly reduce costs and enhance results by integrating the restoration of natural and built heritage with the restoration of brownfields, infrastructure, watersheds, etc. Regions offering tourists nature, picturesque family farms, heritage, efficient infrastructure, good fishing, water sports in clean rivers, etc. will have a *powerful* advantage over competing areas that rely on just one attraction.

Restoring Our Misfortunes: Natural Disasters, Human-made Disasters, and Wars

From where will a renewal come to us, to us who have devastated the whole earthy globe?

—**Simone Weil,** French philosopher (1909–1943)

Let's not leave Lisbon just yet: the city also has a great disaster restoration story to tell. In fact, I'd like to nominate one of Lisbon's most beloved historical figures as "The Patron Saint of Restoring the Built Environment": the Marquês de Pombal.

Poet Luis de Camões called Lisbon "the princess of the world . . . before whom even the ocean bows." It was built on the trading empire created by arguably the three greatest ocean explorers in recorded history, Ferdinand Magellan, Vasco de Gama, and Prince Henry the Navigator. All were Portuguese (although Magellan was snubbed by the Portuguese king, and ended up sailing mostly under the Spanish flag).

WHY ISN'T COLUMBUS ON THAT LIST OF "THE THREE GREATEST NAVIGATORS"?

Columbus wasn't on the list because he only sailed west to India out of ignorance: the Portuguese, who kept their maps a closely guarded state secret, knew that the eastern route was far shorter. It was only the dumb luck of bumping into the Americas (combined with his courage and management skills, which prevented mutiny) that saved Columbus from disaster. Chinese explorer Zheng He might deserve inclusion, but his accomplishments aren't well documented.

A HORRIFYING HALLOWEEN

In 1755, Lisbon was the most prosperous city in Europe. But on All Saints' Eve of that year, as the majority of citizens celebrated High Mass in their many magnificent cathedrals, three major earthquakes struck in quick succession, followed by a 45-foot tsunami. Thirteen thousand people died in Lisbon (60,000 overall) and much of the city lay in ruins.

As chief minister of Portugal, Pombal heroically rose to the occasion. He organized a massive relief effort for the survivors, had the dead quickly buried to prevent disease, and immediately laid plans for the city's restoration. But others had their own vision of how Lisbon should rebuild, and many of those plans were of the tabula rasa variety: tear everything down and create the city anew. It was our hero, the Marquês de Pombal, who was the voice of reason.

He envisioned a grand, revolutionarily new style of city plan, but he argued strenuously and successfully for retaining many of the city's surviving heritage buildings. Fortunately, he had the political authority to pull it off (not in a democratic process, thankfully, as few of his peers thought old buildings were worth saving).

One of Pombal's design goals was to create a feeling of openness and calm. He designed Lisbon's first public garden, called *Passeio Público* (Public Walk) and all of Lisbon's high society liked to stroll in its shade and romantic ambience. In the late nineteenth century, the *Passeio Público* became the key to Lisbon's northward expansion when it was converted to the wonderfully wide, pedestrian-friendly *Avenida da Liberdade*. (Previously, Lisbon had only grown "sideways," along the banks of the Tagus River, a shape that became rather dysfunctional.) The *Avenida* retains that value as a path to balanced growth today. In fact, most of Pombal's plan still works wonderfully, and the buildings he saved and restored almost three centuries ago are a visual feast.

Lisbon is uniquely positioned for Restoration Economy leadership. It retains, of course, the strategic location that once helped make it Europe's greatest city. Building on that natural asset, Lisbon today boasts a large amount of restorative development. What's more, "restoration" is constantly on its citizens' lips. The largest of Lisbon's many city squares is the Plaza of the Restorationists *(Praça dos Restauradores)* (honoring a political, not physical restoration), which has restaurants, hotels, bus stops, and metro stops, all with *Restauradores* in their name. A huge adjacent plaza, *Praça Dom Pedro IV* (known familiarly as "Rossio"), is composed entirely of restored buildings.

The Marquês de Pombal has his own plaza and statue, of course, and owning a restored preearthquake house in Lisbon bears a significant cachet of distinction. Thus, Lisbon is a city with a very deep and conscious connection to restoration. This could serve it well as the Restoration Economy continues to assert its growing dominance.

All this is not to say that Lisbon's love of restoration rendered it immune to fads. Lisbon went through an "urban renewal" frenzy like the one that afflicted the United States in the '60s and '70s, but Lisbon's was a bit later, doing its widespread damage to the city's heritage and appearance mostly from 1975 through 1995. It was at that point that a restoration-sensitive mayor, João Soares, took office.

During his tenure, Lisbon built Expo '98 on a brownfields site, which involved cleaning up heavy oil and industrial contamination. The property is now a pleasant residential area with a huge pavilion for public events. Many sensitively restored buildings now grace the old districts of Alfama and Chiado, and adaptive reuse of old buildings is rampant.

Under Soares, Lisbon put a lot of money into transportation infrastructure, expanding and rehabilitating roads, highways, and bridges. Lisbon now has excellent public transport: an efficient mix of buses, light rail, and charming old restored electric trolleys (the real thing, not the loud, foul-smelling diesel trucks with trolley bodies used by many American cities in an attempt to purchase an instant veneer of heritage).

João Soares was indeed the first restoration-oriented modern mayor of Lisboa. The present mayor, Pedro Santana Lopes, is very interested in following the same logic and even in increasing this activity. He is determined to bring young people to the center of the city. He is restoring not only the so-called historic quarters such as Chiad, Baixa, Bairro Alto,

Alfama and Madragoa, but also the nineteenth-century Lisboa. This is the
so-called "Avenidas Novas" that had been forgotten for decades. So, we
believe that the future of our city is linked to restoration, a promising
business that will increase enormously.
     —**Luis Alves de Sousa,** principal, Heritage Hotels Lisboa, email with author, January 2002

Of course, Lisbon's continued revival will require much more than
adaptive reuse of old buildings, restoring heritage structures, and rehabilitating public transportation. The city's water infrastructure is in need
of reconstruction, and the highly polluted Tagus River is in desperate
need of restoration, to name just two challenges.

Bear in mind, also, that I'm discussing Lisbon here, not Portugal.
Although the country as a whole has recently invested significantly in
refurbishing its transportation infrastructure, Portugal's energy grid is a
wasteful antique. Rather than using the opportunity to leapfrog, the
country is pursuing an early twentieth-century style of energy development, such as damming the beautiful Guadiana River. This current project will flood priceless archaeological treasures and tourist sites (and
entire towns) in an ill-conceived hydroelectric scheme.

Ecologically, the country is an utter disaster area, almost completely
agricultural. Water-hungry, often illegal, nonnative eucalyptus plantations are replacing Portugal's pitifully few remaining natural forests at a
horrendous rate. Meanwhile, toothless government agencies stand by
helplessly, in a country with significant drought problems.

Maybe Portugal will get a clue from the Balearic Islands of neighboring Spain, which get 10 million visitors annually. In May 2002, they
started charging tourists a restoration tax to fund (1) the rehabilitation of
areas damaged by tourism, (2) the demolition of decrepit hotels and
restoration of the sites to a natural state, and (3) the restoration of monuments. (It's demonstrative of how restoration hasn't yet entered the public dialogue that they misnamed this an "ecotourist" tax.)

With its enlightened local leadership going against the national
tide, though, Lisbon *could* become the model for the rest of Portugal,
and maybe the world. Most models are small-scale, so making the
entire capital a model for the country would be truly revolutionary.
Then again, Portugal is a country that knows revolutions (once going
through 16 governments in three years). I, for one, am rooting for the
Marquês de Pombal's city to become a Restoration Economy front-
runner.

AN EXAMPLE OF HOW THE RESTORATION ECONOMY IS CHANGING OUR WORLD

Imagine that the 9/11 disaster had occurred in 1970, when "urban renewal" was at a fever pitch. Rebuilding lower Manhattan would likely have meant demolishing almost anything old. Compare that with today's reality, where the New York City Infrastructure Task Force has been formed. It's a coalition of private-sector organizations, tasked with the job of developing a vision for rebuilding the damaged area (which includes 67 city landmarks). The Marquês de Pombal had to fight to save his historic buildings. This task force includes five heritage restoration associations: the National Trust for Historic Preservation, the World Monuments Fund, the Preservation League of New York State, the New York Landmarks Conservancy, and the Municipal Arts Society. That's a lot of societal evolution in just three decades.

THE SCOPE OF THE DISASTER/WAR RESTORATION INDUSTRY

> The restoration of normal conditions in France is only a matter of time and is a problem which France herself is capable of solving independently. However, the more rapidly this restoration can be accomplished the greater the advantage to America and to the world as a whole. . . . The problems of reconstruction which faced the French Nation at the close of hostilities were far greater than those which confronted England and the United States. One of the first needs of the invaded areas was the restoration of the means of transportation, [all statistics to follow are as of September 1, 1919, only one year from war's end] . . . 90% of the double track [rail] road and 93% of the single track road had been permanently restored . . . of the railways serving the mining districts 114 miles out of 143 miles have been rebuilt. . . . 6,950 square miles of tillable lands were devastated by military operations. 1,540 square miles, an area larger than the state of Rhode Island, had been made fit for cultivation. Much of this work has been performed under handicap of barbed wire, trenches and the constant danger of unexploded shells. . . . The Republic has already expended more than ten billion francs in restoring the devastated regions.
> —*France: The Reconstruction 1919*, 1919

Three categories of disasters comprise this restoration industry.

- **War** This category includes world wars, civil wars, police actions, terrorism, and drug wars. This includes recent new forms of "warfare," such as the long-standing U.S. spraying of Colombia's farms and ecosystems with Agent Orange-like herbicides. As of 2002, Columbia had *increased* coca production by 20 percent (similar to the results of our other misguided drug wars), while significantly *decreasing* both the health of the local farmers and the biodiversity of one of the richest ecological treasures on the planet. The restorative follow-ups to modern wars are far more extensive and multifaceted than ever before.

- **Human-made (anthropogenic) disasters**   This category includes both nonnatural anthropogenic disasters, such as oil spills, industrial explosions, nuclear power accidents, etc., and anthropogenic natural disasters. The latter subcategory includes mud slides and floods due to deforestation, river straightening, dikes, levees, and dams. It also includes many forest fires, as well as climate change, global-related storms and droughts.

- **Natural disasters**   This category includes natural flooding (usually not a problem if people don't build or farm in floodplains), natural forest fires, volcanic eruptions, earthquakes, tsunamis, and non-climate change-induced (not presently distinguishable from anthropogenic) hurricanes, tornadoes, etc.

PROBLEMS AND SOLUTIONS

Restoring a city or country from civil war, invasion, earthquake, or flood usually involves both the built and natural environments. It also involves creating entirely new built structures when the old ones are obliterated or beyond repair. Thus, this restoration industry often involves the same techniques and players as new development, because it doesn't matter to the designer or constructor what caused a piece of property to be made available.

Integrated restoration is the future, but it's not entirely a new concept. We've seen that Lisbon discovered, centuries ago, that heritage restoration and disaster restoration must be integrated for a city's rebuilding to be maximally successful in the long run. As in nature, disasters can have the healthful effect of stimulating new growth, and of removing unwanted but hard-to-get-rid-of features. Some of our most treasured buildings and neighborhoods arose after disasters cleared space for them.

The more we treasure a structure, the more restoration will become a normal part of its life cycle. Almost a century after San Francisco's destruction, many of the best buildings that were part of its restoration are themselves being restored. For example, the architecturally gorgeous

Mark Hopkins Hotel, long a favorite of royalty and celebrities, commands a magnificent view of San Francisco and the bay from atop Nob Hill. It was built in 1926 on the site of a 40-room mansion (owned by the widow of Mark Hopkins, cofounder of the Pacific Railroad), which was destroyed in the 1906 earthquake and fire. A three-year, $12 million restoration was completed in 1982; a major renovation took place in 1988; the hotel's famous Peacock Court was restored in 1995; its legendary "Top of the Mark" sky lounge was restored in 1996 for $1.5 million; and in 2000, the Mark completed yet another multimillion-dollar renovation. "Essentially, we have a new hotel within our historic walls," said general manager Sandor J. Stangl at the reopening. (In 1998, the Mark became the first luxury hotel in San Francisco to offer an electric car recharging station—yet another reason it's my favorite accommodation in that lovely city.)

New development-oriented firms entering the disaster restoration industry, despite the construction process similarities mentioned above, will find themselves working in a very different milieu with many unique rules, expectations, rhythms, players, and processes. For instance, funds often come from disaster relief agencies and wealthy donors, rather than from investors. What's more, hurricanes and earthquakes (not to mention wars) often spill large quantities of fuels, chemicals, and raw sewage, so working conditions are often abnormal—even dangerous—and a variety of urgent restoration priorities might be executed simultaneously.

In the case of damaged (rather than destroyed) buildings, or of destroyed buildings containing valuable artifacts (such as museums), such firms need to work with restorationists from a wide variety of disciplines. As with everyone else in times of disaster, restorationists and new developers must work hand in hand for the public good.

Depending on the extent of the disaster, the term "restoration" might apply more to the larger process—restoring the damaged entity (city, nation, etc.),—than to many of its components, which would be rebuilt from scratch. But replacement, whether due to old age or disaster, is still a legitimate form of restoration, even when all the materials are new. This is because replacement adds value without consuming more space (that is, the structure itself is new but is regarded as restorative development because it reuses and restores value to the same property, rather than contributing to sprawl).

Unlike new development, replacement must integrate desired new functionality with the preexisting needs that were served before the tragedy. There are, of course, significant differences between rebuilding a community after a disaster or war, and creating or expanding a community in normal times. Here are just four of them:

1. Disaster/war reconstruction timetables are far more urgent, and the psychological environment is very different   If the destruction of an older community is extensive, and the leaders use its "rebirth" as an opportunity to give the city a new plan, they will have very little time to think it through. If the precipitating event was a natural disaster, leaders might even want to rethink the community's location or orientation before rebuilding (as Valdez, Alaska, did after its 1964 earthquake). They also might need time to research new technologies, such as seismic building and infrastructure designs.

2. Disasters bring out the best and the worst in people. Restorationists must often deal with political interference that's different from the usual graft   Unpopular politicians throughout history have capitalized on disaster recovery situations to advance private agendas while the citizenry is distracted, vulnerable, and desperate for leadership of any sort. They wrap venal schemes in recovery language (or the national flag), taking advantage of the unity that disasters inspire among voters.

They can make themselves into heroes while violating the victims, because the public's desire to pull together stifles dissent, with criticism of leaders in times of emergency often perceived as inappropriate, even unpatriotic. Forming large, diverse, transparent coalitions to plan disaster and war restoration helps resist such machinations.

3. Rebuilding the community must compete with other urgent agendas for attention and funds   Surviving citizens have been displaced and often require immediate access to food, clean water, shelter, and medical aid. In the case of war, it's not just the natural and built environments that need to be restored. A new government, new currency, and new constitution might be required, and a healing process begun.

> . . . [H]ow do we repair societies rent by inhumanity? . . . [T]he practical concerns of rebuilding after intrasocietal violence are inextricably bound up in these considerations of moral economy. Since the Nuremberg trials, the global community has accepted that justice is a precondition for restoring the social viability of nations . . . civil wars require restorative justice at least as much as retributive justice . . . What remedy exists [referring to Sierra Leone] when you recognize a fellow churchgoer as the attacker who cut off your brother's hands? Can the society rehabilitate, or should it punish, the legions of children—many of them kidnapped and forced into combat—who committed atrocities? . . . To be truly restorative, the processes must be just, mirroring the society they seek to create.
> —**Alice Chasan**, "After Horror, Healing," *World Press Review,* January 2001

Such activities might include a new "bill of rights," war crimes tri-
bunals, restoring (or invalidating) prewar property titles, etc. This
renewal sometimes even requires the destruction of certain forms of heritage, such as statues of disgraced political and military figures. Many
activities comprise the postdisaster response—restoring law, order,
peace, homes, infrastructure, trade, removing land mines and contamination, etc.—but many are not currently recognized as restoration.

**4. Activities (and funding) in this restorative industry are far more auto-
matic than in the other seven restorative industries** Restoring heritage,
fisheries, and other sectors often requires government, citizen, industry,
or NGO activism to raise funds and stimulate public support, but this is
seldom the case with wars and disasters. (Activism *is* sometimes needed
to properly fund the rebuilding of poverty-stricken Southern Hemisphere nations, though.)

Because war and disaster reconstruction is the oldest, best-established,
and most familiar of the eight restorative industries, this chapter differs
from the other "industry chapters" in two ways: (1) There are fewer examples of restorative projects than in the other restoration industries. More
time is spent defining the broad spectrum of disasters that produce the
related industries, and (2) many of the projects that *are* featured come from
the past, in order to give the book more historical context. This wasn't possible with the more recently emerged restorative industries.

WAR RESTORATION

> The water system, communication lines, electricity lines, gas works and
> pipes all had to be painstakingly restored so that life could commence again.
> . . . [T]he biggest task of all is the reconstruction of the city itself on the
> basis of a carefully worked out plan. This task is staggering to contemplate.
> An entire city must be rebuilt where once a proud city gave to the world
> Chopin, the genius of Madame Curie and the matchless gallantry of
> hundreds of thousands of unnamed citizens who were the first to take up
> arms for the liberty of Europe in World War II. . . . Reconstruction will take
> time; even the minimum restoration of the city will take time; and time is a
> precious commodity because an already starved and weary population must
> nurse itself back to health and life under conditions which would try the
> strength of a far healthier people.
> —*Rebirth of a City: The Reconstruction of Warsaw*, 1946 [a booklet distributed by the
> Polish Supply and Reconstruction Mission in North America]

Lisbon was an extreme example of restoration following natural disaster,
but Warsaw is an even more extreme example of postwar rebuilding.

World War II

The damage to Warsaw's built environment resulting from World War II was even more extensive than Lisbon's, leaving precious few heritage structures to restore. With or without surviving cultural assets, though, Warsaw's functions needed immediate restoration, as they had almost completely ceased.

The scope of the restoration crossed the entire spectrum of the built environment: housing, infrastructure, schools, industry, heritage, government, and contamination. In addition to being Poland's capital, Warsaw had, for some three-and-a-half centuries, been the country's economic, political, and cultural heart, so razing this city erased much of what the nation held precious.

And erase it the Nazis did, as a way of demoralizing resisters. They didn't just eliminate physical assets and treasures, either: the human carnage was so extensive as to beg the label "extermination." Nearly half the entire population was killed: 600,000 out of 1,300,000. In 1943, the Jewish ghetto was thoroughly "cleansed," following a weeks-long resistance supported by the Polish resistance movement.

In 2002 dollars, over $14 billion worth of structures was destroyed. Libraries, museums, or colleges that survived the bombing were looted and burned. General Eisenhower surveyed the city on September 21, 1945. Having witnessed horrors all over Europe, he said: "Warsaw is far more tragic than anything I have seen." The loss of life, livelihood, and assets made even Lisbon's eighteenth-century earthquakes look minor.

The litany of destruction was amazing: 59 of the 82 churches and synagogues, 24 of the 31 libraries, 36 of the 47 professional schools, 146 of the 232 hospitals, 25 of the 33 museums, 335 of the 438 schools, and 20 of the 21 theatres. Of those buildings and institutions listed as surviving, not even one escaped undamaged.

Industry was completely paralyzed, so, armed with a meager supply of hand tools and virtually no powered tools or construction equipment, each private citizen started rebuilding, focusing first on infrastructure. The streets were cleared, the dead were buried, and by December 1945(!), city transit lines were moving five million passengers. Thus began one of the most heroic city restoration efforts of all time.

By the end of 1946, 12 million cubic feet of debris had been cleared and 86 million cubic feet of buildings had been repaired, but this amounted to only one percent of the structures damaged. Forty-two million cubic feet of those buildings left standing were damaged beyond repair, constantly threatening to collapse on the laborers. Housing was worst hit, with only 15 percent of prewar dwellings remaining. Workers returned from their daily restoration labor to "homes" lacking windows, doors, heat, light, and water.

Exactly how does one go about restoring a completely devastated city in a hurry? In Warsaw's case, the restoration's "carefully worked out plan" (mentioned in the quote that opens this chapter's "War Restoration" section) involved the confiscation of all land in the city by the municipal government. This gave planners the design freedom they needed to plot the rebuilding of some 779 million cubic feet of buildings, and it sped the process tremendously.

Former owners had the choice of receiving some compensation for their property from the city, or taking out a long-term lease at token cost. The terms of the lease required that they redevelop the land in accordance to the city's master reconstruction plan. In *Rebirth of a City* (quoted earlier), here's how one goal of the plan was worded: "[While we will] maintain the character of a thriving metropolis, gone will be the crowding and haphazard layout which had resulted from Warsaw's rapid economic growth in the 19th Century."

One resource of immense value surfaced in a country village: an extensive collection of photos and architectural drawings of Warsaw's historic structures. This allowed planners to accurately rebuild the city in a way that would retain some of its old personality. Integrating heritage into the reconstruction turned out to be a stroke of genius.

In contrast, many other cities devastated during WWII were rebuilt without thought to their culture. The result was a sterile collection of drab, utilitarian buildings and layouts, rather than vibrant, interesting communities. Rotterdam and Dresden are two examples. The latter had been known worldwide as the most beautiful city in Europe. That was prior to the massive British and U.S. firebombing of this undefended city—probably intended to demoralize the Germans—which contained no significant military targets and was packed with civilian refugees (over 50,000 civilians burned to death).

The recreation of Warsaw's historic buildings wasn't just done quickly: it was of such painstaking quality that Warsaw's restorers found themselves in great demand throughout Europe as each country launched its own decades-long postwar restoration. These new restoration professions—which often became lifelong careers—were a Godsend for a country in desperate need of foreign currency (their own having been rendered nearly worthless).

More recently, Warsaw has undergone a restoration of a subtler sort. The collapse of the Soviet Union allowed Warsaw to restore its long-stifled entrepreneurial zeal for enterprise—and its place in the world economy—which had been stifled during the postwar decades of communist "supervision." Those of us presently performing war and disaster restoration would do well to remember Warsaw's story anytime we feel helpless or overwhelmed, or are overcome with self-pity.

The U.S. efforts after WWII to rebuild former enemies Germany and Japan might rank as the two most successful postwar economic restorations of all time. In fact, we focused far more on rebuilding our enemies than on rebuilding their victims: we revitalized Germany and Japan into two of our largest trading partners.

The Cold War

> The quick processes provide originality and challenge, the slow provide continuity and constraint. Buildings steady us, which we can probably use. But if we let our buildings come to a full stop, they stop us. It happened in command economies such as Eastern Europe's in the period 1945–1990. Since all buildings were state-owned, they were never maintained or altered by the tenants, who had no stake in them, and culture and the economy were paralyzed for decades.
>
> —**Stewart Brand,** *How Buildings Learn*, 1994

Let's move forward a few years and touch briefly on the Cold War.

I accidentally discovered the German dimensions of post-Cold War restoration while researching one of Scotland's most interesting examples of heritage restoration, the nineteenth-century experimental utopian/industrial village of New Lanark. (Many of the twentieth-century's more enlightened business practices were pioneered by its founder, Robert Owen.)

In the bar of a wonderful hotel occupying one of New Lanark's restored old mills, I met Rudi Nasshan, a lovely German gentleman who had recently retired from teaching. Sipping Lagavulin that September of 2000, we discussed this book-in-progress.

Here's an excerpt from an email he later sent me on December 25, 2000, in response to my request for German examples of Cold War-related restorative development:

> Restoration is a major factor in the German economy. Some years ago, after the collapse of the Soviet system, most of the American (and French) troops left Germany. Rhineland-Palatinate in the south-west of Germany (where I

live) was particularly hard hit. There were quite a few negative consequences of the withdrawal of the 'Allied' troops, such as growing unemployment or loss of purchasing power.

But there was also one major positive result: All of a sudden, hundreds of buildings and facilities (e.g. former barracks) and thousands of acres of mostly woodland . . . were given back to the German government. And then began what we call "Konversion": the restoration of land and buildings. Hundreds of millions of D-mark have been pumped into "Konversionsprojekte" with remarkable results. There's lots of new, modern housing, very often for families with children, especially families that are not so well off. There's much reforestation, but also development of new industrial estates on these old bases.

I find this all very interesting, and doing this research for you is very rewarding for me. It is an important aspect of the part of Germany I live in. I see the results and advantages of Konversion every day, and yet this is the first time that I have probed into this topic. It also enlightens me on a political basis, as I am involved in local politics. I am the "whip" or the "leader" of the 5 Social Democrats in our local "parliament", and we sometimes must decide on topics of conversion.

Few bombs were dropped in anger during the Cold War, but there is a surprising amount of rebuilding and cleanup associated with it. Some of the worst—and most ignored—Cold War damage is underwater, where the U.S. Navy and the Atomic Energy Commission (now called the Department of Energy) dumped thousands of drums of toxic—often radioactive—waste. The Soviet Union did likewise. Many of these nuclear and chemical dump sites—according to David Helvarg, in his excellent 2001 book, *Blue Frontier: Saving America's Living Seas*—are in areas that have now become marine sanctuaries. Worse, the dump sites weren't recorded for the most part, so there's no map to the danger areas in need of remediation.

Many of these containers are already leaking, and most will soon be, so maybe a new form of international underwater "Superfund" will need to emerge to remove them before they corrode and rupture. Or, if a method is found to accomplish this using free enterprise, maybe a "bluefields" industry will emerge to join the land-based brownfields industry.

Modern Long-Lasting "Brown" Wars

As mentioned earlier, most war (and disaster) restoration is obvious and straightforward—rebuilding buildings and infrastructure—so let's focus on two new wrinkles in war restoration.[1]

---

[1] For our purposes, the initial humanitarian emergency response is not considered part of the restoration response.

The World Bank recently completed a study of 52 conflicts that began since 1960, and discovered a disturbing recent trend: Starting around 1980, conflicts started lasting three times as long as the average conflict prior to the most recent two decades. Since wars usually metastasize with time, ever-larger numbers of countries are now likely to become involved, directly or indirectly, in present and future conflicts.

Modern wars have also become more persistent in another, even more damaging manner: their long-lasting toxicity. Wars have always left various forms of contamination in their wake, but the quantity, toxicity, and longevity of war-related contaminants have all mushroomed in recent decades. A century ago, the only lasting battle pollutant would usually have been lead. In the twentieth century, petrochemicals from motor pools, blown-up vehicles, and bombed fuel depots became the primary source of "brown" battlefields.

Now, we're adding radioactive contamination to the mix, as U.S. armor-piercing bullets and artillery shells frequently use depleted uranium. Over 270 tons of depleted uranium were used by U.S. troops in the Balkans and in the Gulf War from 1991 to 2001. Most is still in the soils of these countries, but a fair portion of it is now found worldwide, spread by rivers, oceans, and windblown dust. This means that most wars using U.S. munitions will now add to the background radiation of every country and ocean, even without the deployment of tactical or strategic nuclear devices. The Royal Society (London) issued a report in 2002 documenting kidney failure in soldiers exposed to depleted uranium.

A United Nations report on the aftermath of the Kosovo conflict in Yugoslavia was issued in March 2002.[2] The Environmental News Network (www.enn.com) published a related March 28, 2002, Associated Press article by Naomi Koppel, which quoted the study's team leader, Pekka Haavisto, as saying, "The team was surprised to find DU (depleted uranium) particles still in the air two years after the conflict's end. Based on these findings, the authorities should carefully plan how DU-targeted sites are used in the future. Any soil disturbance at these sites could risk releasing DU particles into the air."[3]

In an article by John Einan Sandvand in Oslo, Norway's newspaper *Aftenposten* (January 13, 2001), Dr. Jinan Galeb, a pediatrician and oncologist at Basra Children's Hospital, said, "Our statistics show the rate of malignant cancers among children in 1999 was 242 percent higher than

---

[2] "Depleted Uranium in Serbia and Montenegro," United Nations report, March 2002.
[3] Naomi Koppel, "Yugoslavia Still Contaminated by Depleted Uranium Three Years After NATO Bombing," Associated Press, March 28, 2002.

the level before the [Gulf] war." Leukemia has skyrocketed in villages close to the battlefields, shepherds have reported far higher rates of birth defects in their lambs, and one small village reported that 40 percent of families have at least one member with cancer.

Dr. Melissa McDiarmid, professor of medicine at the University of Maryland in Baltimore, has been studying the effects of exposure to depleted uranium, and has personally cared for some of the 60 U.S. combatants who were victims of "friendly fire," which exposed them to the toxic side effects of our own weapons. In an article by Steve Conner, "The Uranium Minefield," in London's *The Independent*, she said: "This is a surreal situation. We are being asked, 'What are the health risks of something that's supposed to blow you up?' "[4]

The use of depleted uranium in munitions is an enormously profitable application of used nuclear power plant fuel. It's also a very natural one, because most companies in the nuclear energy industry are also major military contractors. In a perversion of green business practices, the nuclear power industry has accomplished what every environmentally conscious manufacturer dreams of: selling its toxic waste for big bucks.

HUMAN-MADE (ANTHROPOGENIC) DISASTER RESTORATION

> The waters were rising again. The sandbaggers were sandbagging again. The politicians were declaring disaster areas again. And the media were recycling clichés about "hardy" Midwesterners battling "swollen" rivers in their "flood-ravaged" communities again. Yes, there was a 100-year flood event on the Mississippi this spring. Again. This was the Mississippi's *fourth* "100-year flood" in the past eight years. . . . The news media usually presents this as an odd coincidence . . . with some hardy Midwesterner noting wearily that 100 years sure ain't what it used to be. But it's a real trend. Floods killed 957 people and caused $45 billion [U.S.] in damage from 1989 to 1998. They're getting worse. . . . They are natural events, but they are mostly man-made disasters. . . . Here's how people created these disasters: First they settled and farmed in floodprone areas. Then they drained wetlands and farmlands that used to sponge up water during floods. Then they built levees and flood walls that imprisoned rivers into tight channels, walling them off from their natural flood plains. And all those artificial barriers—as well as a generous federal flood insurance program—have inspired a false sense of security that encourages even more Americans to build in those flood plains. [Emphasis mine.]
> —**Michael Grunwald,** "Disasters All, But Not As Natural As You Think,"
> *Washington Post,* May 6, 2001

[4] Steve Conner "The Uranium Minefield," *The Independent,* January 26, 2001.

Michael Grunwald went on to say (in the above-referenced article), ". . . that's one reason the tub keeps overflowing: the sides of the tub have moved closer together. But there's another problem: there's more water pouring into the tub. . . . Over half the [Mississippi] basin's wetlands have disappeared, including more than 80 percent in Iowa, Missouri and Illinois. . . . (Who's responsible for protecting those precious wetlands? The Army Corps of Engineers.) . . . The federal government finally learned that lesson after the $12 billion Mississippi flood of 1993.

He continued, "Meanwhile, the federal government has paid farmers to convert about 600,000 acres of farmland back to wetlands. . . . It is not yet clear whether the lesson will stay learned in the Bush administration, [whose] budget plan has prompted harsh criticism from state disaster officials and environmentalists for eliminating flood prevention initiatives, including a $162 million program that pays farmers to restore wetlands." The Bush administration's flood creation agenda eventually failed to pass, and most of the wetlands restoration funds were restored to the 2002 Farm Bill.

For Humans, Unnatural Disasters Come Naturally

> The really big catastrophes are getting larger and will continue to get larger, partly because of things we've done in the past to reduce risk. For example, building a dam or levee may protect a community from the small- and medium-sized floods the structures were designed to handle. But additional development that occurs because of this protection will mean even greater losses during a big flood that causes the dam or levee to fail.
> —**Dennis Mileti** headed a team of 132 experts that did a 5-year, $750,000 study (primarily funded by the National Science Foundation), resulting in the publication (in 1999) of *Disasters by Design: A Reassessment of Natural Hazards in the United States.* Among other insights, the study showed that the United States had averaged $1 billion per week in natural disaster damage since 1989, and that many were made far more expensive by our efforts to control, rather than work with, nature.
> —National Science Foundation website www.nsf.gov/search97cgi/vtopic, May 19, 1999

Anthropogenic disasters aren't new, of course. Boston has long been addicted to molasses-rich Boston-style baked beans (hence its nickname "Beantown"), and this led to one of the city's more memorable anthropogenic disasters (no, I'm not referring to deadly clouds of digestive methane). In 1919, a molasses tank ruptured, and over 2 million gallons washed over Boston's North End. The 8-foot wall of goo drowned 21 people and knocked down a fire station.

Tragic, yes. Toxic, no. Long-lasting damage, none. Today, though, nontoxic industrial accidents are almost unheard of. Most spills, explosions, and fires now involve noxious materials, often with long-lasting health effects. Even worse, many of the ill effects don't strike until years, even decades later, which retards our disuse of inappropriate materials.

On April 7, 2000, the Chalk Point Generating Station of the Potomac Electric Power Company (PEPCO) accidentally dumped over 120,000 gallons of oil into Maryland's Patuxent River. Six hundred people were immediately employed to operate over 50,000 feet of protective booms in an effort to minimize damage to 17 miles of the river's shoreline. Despite this, 76 acres of wetlands and 10 acres of shoreline were oiled.

Daily news bulletins documented the cleanup effort, but—with the exception of an April 21, 2000, *Washington Post* article by Raymond McCaffrey—almost no attention was focused on the suffering and deaths of the wildlife (an estimated 553 ruddy ducks, 376 muskrats, and 122 endangered diamond terrapins died, to name just three high-profile species), or of the long-term effects the residual oil would have on the ecosystem. It's also telling that almost all wildlife rescue efforts were volunteer-based, rather than hired and paid for by the power company.

It was two years before a token $2.7 million ecological restoration plan was announced by a combination of federal and state agencies, designed to make the politically well-connected PEPCO restore the entire area to "pre-spill conditions." It was "token" in relation to the more than $65 million spent on cleaning up the oil, which—while removing the oil—leaves lifeless, detergent-contaminated land in its wake. "Doggone, if you're going to spend seventy to one hundred million to clean it, spend a few more to restore it," said former Maryland senator "Bernie" Fowler, head of the Patuxent River Oil Spill Citizens Advisory Committee, in a May 31, 2002, *Washington Post* article, also by McCaffrey.

Oil spills occur hundreds of times a day around the world. It's become so normal that only truly momentous spills make the evening news anymore (unless they're local). The restoration of oil spills is a hugely profitable and hugely tragic industry that desperately needs to grow a heart. Although mechanical efforts to minimize the spread of oil and to clean up what has already spread can be heroic, inattention to long-term ecosystem effects and rescue of animal victims is rampant.

Disastrous Accounting

New technological monitoring and feedback systems are vital, but so are more integrated and more effective legal and accounting systems, designed to deal with disaster. As with so many of the world's problems, new development-style accounting practices are at the root of many or even most anthropogenic disasters. Fortunately, disasters are having the healthy effect of stimulating a reassessment of these antiquated systems. They are (slowly) evolving into a form that stimulates and supports restorative development.

For example, Lester Brown reports in his book *Eco-Economy* (2001) that the Yangtze River floods of 1998 made China realize that trees were worth three times more standing than logged. But because new development-based accounting systems are unable to factor-in eco-system services, most nations still feel compelled to log.

> Someone told me that more damage has been done by these floods than in 16 years of civil war. . . . Mozambique has been one of the major success stories in Africa in terms of post-war reconstruction and a liberalised economy. It was emerging from destruction and working towards a promising future until this natural disaster occurred and set development back by at least 15 years.
>
> . . . Mozambique has enjoyed one of the fastest growing economies with an annual growth of more than 8 percent for 3 years. Its key sectors, port and rail, agriculture and fisheries, were thriving and expanding. With massive donor investment, from partners such as Canada, Mozambique had rebuilt schools and hospitals. Now that infrastructure will need to be repaired, or even rebuilt. . . . [I]t will take $250 million and many years to rebuild the country.
>
> —**David Kilgour,** The Front Line, "The Floods in Mozambique," *Canadian Social Studies,* 35(1), Fall 2000 (From Canadian Social Studies, Canada's national social studies journal—by permission.)

Just as Mozambique is becoming aware of how expensive it can be to magnify natural floods with deforestation, dams, and inappropriate development, so too has China. China has now realized that in many cases logging (especially clear-cutting) often *inhibits* economic growth, by causing "natural" disasters, by sabotaging farm production (via decreased rain), and by destroying fisheries (via silted rivers).

The Chinese calculations didn't take all factors into consideration—such as how deforestation reduces the useful life of dams via silt buildup—so its factor of three is probably quite conservative. However, it was enough to motivate the $12 billion reforestation program mentioned in Chapter 1.

Despite formidable political barriers, adoption of restorative accounting (full cost accounting applied within the context of the trimodal development perspective) will likely hit the tipping point in several countries this decade. I mention it in this chapter because one of its major catalysts will probably be disasters. More specifically, we need to properly account for anthropogenic disasters, so that our legal and budgetary systems can become a tool for reducing them, can better mitigate their economic disruption, and can properly prepare for the ensuing restoration.

"Creeping Crud," and Other New Trends in Anthropogenic Disasters

> . . . [I]n environmental politics . . . catastrophes are making the world fall apart. . . . Recently I spent well over a year investigating one of those alleged catastrophes—the state of the world's fisheries . . . but I couldn't find such a disaster. . . . I found real trouble in some places . . . but in other places, stocks were recovering. . . . What I saw was less immediate and more alarming than a catastrophe. . . . The most frightening thing I encountered in my research was not the cod crash off Newfoundland but something a skipper told me in Dakar, Senegal: "The fish just get a little smaller each year." Like rain taking a mountain apart grain by grain, the unspectacular change takes the biggest toll.
> —**Michael Parfit,** "Disasters Aren't the Problem: The Real Environmental Catastrophe Is the Slow Creep of Crud," *Washington Post* [editorial] December 17, 1995

The above quote ignores the effects of the nonlinear dynamics—such as Allee effects—that are so common in nature. However, it certainly seems reasonable to assume that lots of little insults tend to create a big problem over time. That's the mechanical view we were taught of the world.

Parfit was probably as surprised as anyone by the recent catastrophic fishery declines that he had searched for in the early '90s. But he was absolutely right that the little things we do each day are more damaging to the world than are the major oil spills and other "official catastrophes" (other than nuclear accidents, due to the damage they do over tens of thousands of years).

Besides "creeping crud," there are many forms of human-caused disasters, currently masquerading as natural, that are only now beginning to get researched (again, because some of them are politically sensitive). For instance, in 1989, nuclear tests in Kazakhstan triggered so many earthquakes and radioactive gas discharges from the earth's crust that local miners went on strike until the underground explosions were stopped.

> . . .[W]hat may well turn out to be the worst of all the threats presented by the Three Gorges Dam [in Chongqing, China]—dam-induced seismic activity. . . . Chongqing lies in a seismically active zone . . . [but] seismic activity often follows the construction of large dams—even in areas where there are no records of any previous seismic activity.
> —**John Prewer,** letter to the editor, *New Scientist*, April 28, 2001

In the thousand years prior to the nuclear tests in neighboring Kazahkstan, Iran had just three major earthquakes. In the 30 years since testing began, Iran suffered 60 damaging earthquakes. Some geologists also suspect that subterranean oil helps lubricate the movement of tectonic plates, and that sucking oil fields (and aquifers) dry has increased the frequency and/or severity of earthquakes.

> . . . [A] change in climate has major implications throughout the world in terms of agriculture, water supply, fishing—and the repair and restoration of damaged ecosystems. . . . [R]estorationists, especially those in academia, [should] conduct long-term experiments that attempt to create plant communities outside their "normal" range. . . . [M]anagers and others should begin immediately to monitor existing natural areas and restoration sites for changes in vegetation, composition, and health. With these data sets in hand, researchers could then begin to tease out answers . . . How does a species or guild react to climate change? How do they reassemble? What role will exotic and invasive species play in the new compositions? Will we have to rescue more and more species as climate reduces their habitat? . . . Should we attempt to play gods in this situation or just trust that a new, sustainable biodiversity will emerge?
> —**Dave Egan,** *Ecological Restoration,* Volume 19, No. 3, 2001

It would be absurd to leave this subject without mentioning global climate change, because it will likely give rise to the largest new category of anthropogenic "natural" disasters. (Global climate change's only potential competitor for this honor is the genetic engineering industry, should pathogenic (to humans, wildlife, livestock, crops, etc.) organisms and/or DNA strands go "feral.") Global climate change is expected to (or might already) include increased (or more severe) floods, fires, droughts, storms, human/crop/livestock plagues, and ecosystem collapses, not to mention the extinction of species that can't adapt or migrate quickly enough.

But "mention" it is all we'll do, for two reasons: (1) global climate change is far too complex to cram into the few pages that are available, and (2) global climate change, at present, is mostly a matter of prevention, not restoration (though this status may change more suddenly than we expect: remember that climate dynamics are nonlinear).

On the other hand, I can't resist taking a moment to ask two (unoriginal) questions of any readers resisting efforts to reduce the emission of carbon dioxide (and other greenhouse gases). You say global climate change hasn't been proven (to your satisfaction) to be anthropogenic, but what's the downside of proceeding on the assumption that it *is* caused by human activity? Are you afraid that the world will become too clean . . . unnecessarily healthful . . . that we'll have too high a quality of life?

> Don't wait until you touch bottom before you start swimming.
> —**Luis Gamez,** advisor to Costa Rica's Ministry of Environment and Energy, quoted by
> Gretchen C. Daily and Katherine Ellison, *The New Economy of Nature,* 2002

Such attitudes make me wonder if one of the greatest values of restorative development is that it's raising our standards. We had become so complacent about pollution that we demanded proof of impending global catastrophe before feeling justified in reducing it. Now, as new development is increasingly seen as the enemy of progress rather than its source, we're finally admitting that our current world is not healthful enough. We're actively cleaning the planet, not "just" reducing the rate at which we despoil it. With luck, restoration will trigger a feedback loop, where each act of restoration will raise our expectations, which—in turn—increases demand for restoration.

Radioactive Disasters

> Rain laden with sand from the Sahara desert, which regularly coats cars and buildings across southern Europe with a layer of yellow dust, is spreading radioactive material from the Chernobyl accident 15 years ago. [discovered "accidentally" by researchers at Aristotle University in Thessaloniki, Greece]
> —**Rob Edwards,** "A Hot Rain's Gonna Fall," *New Scientist,* May 5, 2001

We all know about Chernobyl. Well, we know that it happened: The reporting of its true extent, and its long-term implications, was—and still is—strongly discouraged in most nuclear countries. Governments usually justify this policy to the press under the umbrella excuse of "avoiding public panic." Chernobyl was too big to hide, but most nuclear accidents are easily hidden, especially outside North America and the U.K., because they are silent, invisible, and odorless.

Scientists posit that there's now no human, domestic animal, or wild creature on earth whose body doesn't contain a bit of Chernobyl: we only differ in degree of contamination. Once powdered fissionables get spread by wind and rain, cleanup and restoration seem all but impossible.

After all, few toxins or isotopes are monitored, and none broadly and on a regular basis. Thus, our "monitoring system" for unreported— *and reported*—industrial and military accidents consists mostly of watching for unusual disease clusters. Due to the long time delay between occurrence and awareness, it may seem as if there's nothing we can do to remediate these disasters now. Fortunately, this isn't true.

Cleaning up all this nonlocalized creeping crud is where the combination of restorative technologies (mentioned in Chapter 10) and restorative development comes in. If all of our water treatment systems discharge water that is cleaner than the original source; if all contaminated industrial and war sites are properly remediated; if ongoing contamination is reduced by a worldwide, Internet-based grid of 24/7 toxin monitors (integrated with investigative agencies, dedicated courts, cleanup crews, and restoration firms); then we will see the background levels of radioactivity and other pollution start to come down.

NATURAL DISASTER RESTORATION

> On September 21, 1938 . . . suddenly, just before dark, in the teeth of a
> howling southwest gale which increased momentarily to hurricane
> proportions, a steadily rising tide which in some places rose twenty feet in
> as many minutes, swept . . . across the Shore Line Route of The New Haven
> Railroad . . . carrying on its crest hundreds of boats, ships, cottages,
> buildings and wreckage. Communications by rail, wire, and telephone . . .
> [were] completely cut off. . . . [T]he next morning revealed a grim picture
> of death and desolation . . . Where yesterday fast freights and . . .
> passenger trains . . . sped in rapid succession between New York and New
> England . . . carrying the vital necessities of life . . . now miles of silent
> track hung at crazy angles over yawning chasms. . . . It must be restored
> without delay.
> —The New Haven Railroad, *The Devastation and Restoration of New England's Vital Life
> Line: The New Haven R.R.*, November 30, 1938 [a photographic journal bearing the
> dedication, "As a remembrance of the strenuous days we all experienced following the
> floods, hurricane, and tidal wave of September 21st, 1938, the Trustees (of the New
> Haven Railroad) are presenting each member of the New Haven family with a copy of
> this graphic record of the reconstruction of the New Haven Railroad."]

Thirty-one bridges, two hundred culverts, and 75 miles of track were destroyed, moved, or buried on the September day described above. Thousands of trees were blown across the remaining rails. Over five million feet of telephone and signaling wires lay in a tangled mess. Freight sheds and passenger stations were wiped out or lifted off their foundations and relocated. But restoration began immediately: "Over 5000 men, including engineers, linemen, trackmen, pile drivers, divers, skilled and unskilled laborers, toiled night and day in 3 shifts to restore in record time the vital life-line between New England and points south and west," to continue the essay's narration.

"In 2 days partial passenger service had been restored between Boston and New York, with bus detour around flood-devastated areas. In 6 days through freight service had been restored between New York and important New England points. In 13 days through rail passenger service was restored on the Shore Line between New York and Boston." In the front of the booklet, an open letter "to the officers and employees" from the New Haven Railroad Trustees concluded, "The restoration of the railroad to a condition permitting nearly normal operation in such an unbelievably short time has made it evident that in capacity and morale the railroad organization is able to meet the severest test with a spirit so commendable that it is the admiration of everyone." Here in the twenty-first century, where government bailouts and corporate whining seem to be the norm, we would do well to keep the New Haven Railroad's rapid, self-organized disaster restoration response in mind.

Catastrophe as Status Quo

Such disasters—and heroic responses—are not only nothing new; they are downright normal in some parts of the world. Floods directly affect some 100 million people every year. Take Central America, for instance. The capital of El Salvador, San Salvador, has been destroyed by earthquake no fewer than 10 times in the past four centuries. Not just hit by earthquakes . . . absolutely destroyed. Earthquakes, volcanoes, tsunamis, and hurricanes devastate the half-dozen countries of Central America so frequently that we normally only hear of the ones that do severe damage to multiple countries. The governments of these countries are so inured to injury that they usually don't call the complete destruction of a town a disaster. They save that word for national-level events. The loss of a mere community is just a "tragedy."

As the Constraint Crisis continues to force people into riskier areas, the deadliness of earthquakes and hurricanes will increase, even if their strength and frequency remains the same. According to the U.S. Geological Survey, 1999 and 2001 were normal years in terms of the number of earthquakes, but they were unusually deadly. Earthquakes killed 22,711 people in 1999, and 65 significant earthquakes in 2001 killed 21,436 people. There's nothing linear about earthquake patterns, though, which is why 2000 saw only 231 deaths.

At $25 billion, the most costly natural disaster in U.S. history was 1994's Northridge earthquake in California. The most costly in the world was 1995's earthquake in Kobe, Japan. In 20 seconds, it did over

TOP 24 VOLCANIC ERUPTIONS OF ALL TIME, IN TERMS OF (RECORDED) HUMAN DEATHS

Deaths	Location	Date
92,000	Tambora, Indonesia	1815
36,417	Krakatau, Indonesia	1883
29,025	Mt. Pelee, Martinique	1902
25,000	Ruiz, Colombia	1985
14,300	Unzen, Japan	1792
9,350	Laki, Iceland	1783
5,110	Kelut, Indonesia	1919
4,011	Galunggung, Indonesia	1882
3,500	Vesuvius, Italy	1631
3,360	Vesuvius, Italy	A.D. 79
2,957	Papandayan, Indonesia	1772
2,942	Lamington, Papua New Guinea	1951
2,000	El Chichón, Mexico	1982
1,680	Soufriere, St. Vincent	1902
1,475	Oshima, Japan	1741
1,377	Asama, Japan	1783
1,335	Taal, Philippines	1911
1,200	Mayon, Philippines	1814
1,184	Agung, Indonesia	1963
1,000	Cotopaxi, Ecuador	1877
800	Pinatubo, Philippines	1991
700	Komagatake, Japan	1640
700	Ruiz, Colombia	1845
500	Hibok-Hibok, Philippines	1951

$100 billion dollars worth of damage, left 300,000 people homeless, collapsed 111,123 buildings, severely damaged 137,287 buildings, killed 6,400 people, and injured over 40,000 people.

Both the number of deaths and the amount of damage to assets vary widely, due to socioeconomic factors. Earthquakes are costlier in countries with weak building codes or corrupt enforcement, and they are deadlier, because most victims die in collapsed buildings. On the other hand, the February 28, 2001, 6.8 magnitude earthquake in the Seattle-Tacoma area, which has fairly advanced seismic codes, recorded no deaths (though 400 were injured) but still managed to rack up $1.5 billion worth of restoration work.

Aftermaths of disasters last a lot longer than is apparent from their short shelf life on the evening news. Hurricane Mitch, which hit Honduras the hardest, wasn't just a 1998 disaster: it's still killing people today and will be spawning recovery and restoration activities for some time to come. In fact, the immediate deaths caused by disasters—especially those like Mitch, which destroy infrastructure—aren't always the greatest toll. As of 2002, large numbers of people in Honduras are dying of malnutrition and waterborne diseases directly attributable to Mitch's infrastructure destruction.

Less than a year after Mitch, the world community had rounded up some $9 billion in disaster relief and rebuilding funds. Honduras required over $1 billion for infrastructure restoration alone (out of a $4 billion reconstruction master plan). Just as nature uses storms to cleanse and renew, very few major disasters are without benefits to their human victims. Honduras, for instance, is taking advantage of the Mitch reconstruction to restore and reform its national school system. Honduran children had suffered a horribly dilapidated educational infrastructure for three decades. It didn't work very well, and they had a 30 percent illiteracy rate and a 43 percent graduation rate—and that's for primary school.

In the United States, we've been lucky so far. Few of us realize that we have more active volcanoes than all but two countries: Indonesia and Japan. Our active volcanoes aren't all remote, either; near Washington's Mt. Rainier, tens of thousands of folks in the Seattle-Tacoma area are living on top of the semi-dried mudflows from the last eruption.

ISSUES AND INSIGHTS

1. Missed opportunities to take advantage of ecological disasters   One of the many anthropogenic tragedies to hit the Great Lakes in recent decades has been the invasion of the zebra mussel, introduced via the bilgewater of ships. In addition to displacing native species, these mussels have caused millions of dollars of damage to industry and public infrastructure by clogging water pipes. That much is well known.

An incredible opportunity for restoring the Great Lakes was offered us in 2001, when the waters of Lake Erie were the cleanest they had been in decades. Lake Erie owed its cleanliness to the massive filtering of the water performed by those invasive zebra mussels. In fact, the water became so clean that the mussels started dying off, having proliferated beyond the ability of the Great Lakes to supply them with edible filth (thanks to modern pollution laws).

Therein lay the opportunity. Billions of zebra mussels had been sequestering untold tons of toxic metals, industrial chemicals, and organic waste. If a concerted effort had been made to harvest them before they died and decomposed (releasing all that pollution back into the water), the whole episode would have had a silver lining. Leaving the zebra mussels in place, on the other hand, released all that captured pollution back into the lakes, giving the surviving mussels their food back, leading to their renewed proliferation.

This lost opportunity relates to "process blindness" (mentioned in Chapter 5); our cultural and professional tendency to focus on things, rather than processes.

2. Insufficient focus on environmental restoration following war There's so much human tragedy, loss of precious heritage, and destruction of vital infrastructure in most wars that both contamination cleanup and ecosystem restoration often take a distant back seat to more urgent (though not necessarily more important) needs. Often, the reconstruction money runs out before they are addressed at all.

At the time of this writing, we have a wonderful opportunity brewing in Afghanistan. In a statement issued by the United Nations Environment Programme (UNEP) on December 6, 2001, Klaus Toepfer, UNEP's Executive Director, said, "Armed conflict, which has been waged in Afghanistan for at least 20 years, can lead to environmental degradation in areas such as freshwater, sanitation, forests and soil quality. A healthy environment is a prerequisite for sound and sustainable development. People cannot secure real and sustainable economic development against a background of contaminated water, polluted land, and marginalized natural resources."

While acknowledging that attending to the humanitarian needs of the Afghan people must take priority, Toepfer affirmed that UNEP was ready to assist in the forthcoming rehabilitation and reconstruction phase. This will be vital if the restoration of this tragic nation is to include the natural environment, as well as the built and socioeconomic environments.

3. "Donor fatigue" and quick fixes As with ecological restoration, the restoration of a society and nation takes time. Initial restoration successes must be closely monitored and managed to ensure that a just, open society emerges. Simply rebuilding demolished infrastructure isn't enough—but this phase alone often exhausts donors.

Long-term strategies must restore both the government and the access of local businesses to opportunities and resources. Lacking that, nascent governments are easily subverted by military leaders, organized crime, radical religious fundamentalists, and/or foreign resource extraction megabusinesses. Such situations disenfranchise the poorer elements of the population, who often turn to guerilla warfare and/or terrorism in desperation, to begin the cycle again.

4. Failure to take a regional approach   Long-term civil wars and other extended conflicts can destabilize an entire region. For instance, Afghanistan's triple whammy of Soviet invasion, Taliban suppression, and U.S. invasion has significantly affected the neighboring states of Pakistan, Tajikstan, Uzbekistan, and the Kyrgyz Republic.

Besides aiding nearby nations directly, restoration plans must often involve them in the restoration of the war-torn county. "Rehabilitation and reconstruction will require a long-term approach for all the neighboring countries," said Yoshihiro Iwasaki, a director of the Asian Development Bank (concerning the restoration of Afghanistan), in a February 2002 issue of *World Press Review.*[5]

The Age-Old Disaster and War Restoration Industry

Restoring the world after disaster and war is usually perceived as the most heroic of the restoration industries. This is probably a good thing, because disasters and wars are not in short supply (and probably never have been) and only promise to increase in the twenty-first century.

According to Munich Re, the world's largest reinsurance company, 2000 was a record year for natural disasters, and the company expects global climate change, combined with rising populations, to make coming years even more costly. The number of natural disasters jumped from 750 in 1999 to 850 in 2000, although the death toll was much lower— 75,000 in 1999 vs. 10,000 in 2000—because the disasters tended to strike less-populated areas in 2000.

Material damage was pegged at $30 billion for the year 2000, but only $7.5 billion of that was insured. Storms accounted for 73 percent of insured losses, and floods for 23 percent. The biggest single event of 2000 was in Mozambique, where floods left half a million people homeless. Forest fires did over $1 billion in damage in 2000, just in the United States.

As a direct result of the Constraint Crisis, ever-increasing numbers of people are living in harm's way: near volcanoes, in floodplains, on coastlines, etc. For instance, one out of every twelve people in the world now

---

[5] Nadeen Iqbal, "Mission: Afghanistan—The Monumental Task of Reconstruction," *World Press Review,* February 2002.

lives dangerously close to an active volcano. During the 1980s, more people were killed by volcanic eruptions than in any other decade of the twentieth century since 1902, when three Caribbean eruptions killed some 35,500 people (over 29,000 people died in Mt. Pelee's eruption in Martinique alone).

The characteristics of disaster and war reconstruction funding—its suddenness and uncertainty (concerning the eventual total)—usually scare away all but the largest, best-capitalized firms. This is a shame, because smaller firms could bring much-needed new thinking to the process, and there are good profits to be made.

It's generally considered unseemly to talk about profits related to disaster and war reconstruction, which is another reason the players in this industry tend to be a tight-knit little group. This is rather ironic, since we have so little difficulty talking about the profitability of military contractors, who provided the weapons and machines that created the destruction. . . .

The funding uncertainties are somewhat ameliorated by the previously mentioned "automatic funding" factor, which helps make this restoration industry especially vigorous. Disaster and war restoration is almost never a "yes/no" question; only a "how much" question. The funds are usually available, often very quickly. Of course, the complexion of the victims, as well as the strategic value of their resources, can make a big difference in both the speed and adequacy of that restoration funding, but that's another story. Suffice it to say that this is a more-than-$100 billion growth business that shows few signs of weakening, and many signs of strengthening.

The World Restoration Bank?

Organizational agendas and strategies change regularly, but name changes are far less frequent. Thus, many restorative activities are hidden within organizations whose names, slogans, and mission statements are loaded with references to new development, conservation, etc. For instance, the World Bank has a program called "Alliance for Forest Conservation and Sustainable Use," but here's an excerpt from its website:

> In the context of both WWF [World Wildlife Fund] (and its new Campaign
> targets) and the Alliance's targets, forest restoration is taking on growing
> importance—forest restoration directly tackles the link between people
> (livelihood security) and forests. The Alliance partners attended an
> international workshop on forest restoration held in Spain from 3–5 July,

> under the joint WWF/IUCN forest restoration initiative Forests Reborn.
> Workshop participants included economists, foresters, ecologists,
> development experts, with representatives from the EU [European Union],
> the World Bank, USAID (U.S. Agency for International Development], CIDA
> [Canadian International Development Agency], DFID [Department for
> International Development (U.K.)], and WWF/IUCN regional staff involved
> in forest restoration.

It was hard not to notice that "restoration" was used five times in that passage, whereas "conservation" and "sustainable" weren't used once. Yet both of those latter words are present in the name of the alliance, and "restoration" isn't. The number of such restoration conferences and projects, involving large institutions long associated with new development, has flourished in recent years. But names haven't kept up.

The World Bank is the leading institution in the business of making war and disaster restoration loans. The bank was established, along with the International Monetary Fund (IMF), at the Bretton Woods conference in 1944. The two entities were assigned different but complementary ends. The IMF's goal is to protect the international monetary system. This usually means helping distressed countries overcome balance-of-payments problems. The World Bank is primarily focused on development and redevelopment.

The World Bank has been trying, largely unsuccessfully, since 1995 to execute its projects (mostly infrastructure-related) in ways that don't produce the environmental, economic, political, and social disasters that long typified its efforts. (The bank hired a consultant in the early '90s to determine how it could avoid doing so much damage. The consultant's conclusion was that only dissolving the bank would achieve that aim. Strangely, his contract wasn't renewed.)

In this case, adopting a more restoration-oriented name would simply be a matter of going back to the bank's roots. The World Bank's full name (which it rarely uses) is the International Bank for Reconstruction and Development. It was created primarily to promote postwar reconstruction. Given its atrocious record in new development—and given the current proliferation of conflicts and disasters—the bank might do well to drop the "development" and focus on the "reconstruction."

Even better, in terms of positioning itself within the Restoration Economy, the bank could rename itself the "World Restoration Bank." This would be in line with the likely emergence (in the near future) of Departments of Restorative Development within city, state, and national governments. It would also tie in the bank nicely with the United Nations, should the U.N. be wise enough to approve the aforementioned proposal to designate the twenty-first century "The Century of Restoration."

CLOSING THOUGHTS

Of the myriad forms of catastrophes inflicted daily by nature, by humans, and by nature aided by humans, we've barely scratched the surface. On beaches, for instance, coastal storms are happening at almost every moment, somewhere on the planet. Even nonhurricane-level storms do tremendous damage to beach properties. Many excellent books are already in print on that subject, though, so let's stick to the big picture.

Disasters and wars destroy natural, built, and socioeconomic systems, so it's fitting that it is the last of the eight restoration industries we discuss. It should be obvious that an integrated plan for restoring war and major disaster damage would include many—maybe all—of the other seven restorative industries. But it's the suddenness of the degradation, as well as the urgency of the restoration, that adds very unique characteristics to the disaster/war restoration industry.

Let's end this discussion with a story that elegantly combines natural disaster, global warming, and other anthropogenic influences with the serendipitous opportunity for extensive restoration that major disasters so often offer. On December 26, 1999, winds exceeding 100 miles per hour lashed France, something that had never before happened in recorded history. Called an "act of God," the storm was exactly the sort of freak event that has become normal (kids are throwing snowballs in Venice, Italy, as I write this passage), thanks most likely to global climate change. Besides killing 91 people, denying electricity and phone service to tens of thousands, and devastating 300,000 farms, the gales flattened 1.24 million acres of "forest," some 360 million trees.

I enclose "forests" in quotes because these were actually industrial tree farms, containing miles and miles of near-identical trees of the same age. It was this lack of age diversity and species diversity that made the damage far worse than it would otherwise have been. Large trees protect smaller ones from wind and prevent the domino effect that struck the French tree plantations.

Now, here's the serendipity. Just before the storm struck, the Worldwide Fund for Wildlife-France (WWF-France) had just recruited Daniel Vallauri to head its new Living Forest Campaign. He was just starting to map his strategy when the storm made the path clear, and he renamed the program "Forest Restoration." In a December 13, 2000, Environmental News Network article entitled "France Digs in to Restore Its Forests," Sally Zalewski wrote, "WWF-France has come up with a comprehensive forest restoration plan. Instead of focusing on wood production and agricultural methods of exploitation, the group is pressing for a more global use of the forest, encompassing leisure and sports activities, water and soil protection and stressing the importance of maintaining biodiversity."

We've now explored, very superficially, the current state of restorative development in both the natural and the built environments. It's time to step back a bit and think about all this activity in a larger context. What does restorative development really mean to the future of the world in general?

A SMALL SAMPLING OF OPPORTUNITIES

Business and investment

- The dearth of political will to address global climate change means big opportunities in disaster restoration, but investing in property insurance companies could be extremely risky.
- The growth of toxic disasters and "brown wars" means there's a great deal of technological overlap with the brownfields restoration industry. Some firms already do both, but it's an overlooked expansion market for many firms from each industry.
- The fact that disasters and wars tend to inflict damage on such a wide spectrum of natural and built assets makes this the most logical restoration industry for the first "hyperintegrated" restoration megafirm to emerge. The first company to create divisions for all eight restoration industries— and to integrate them effectively—will find ready customers among cities and countries in need of extensive rebuilding. The expertise thus acquired would position that firm perfectly for less-urgent markets, such as metropolitan areas embarking on a comprehensive, long-term course of cultural, environmental, and economic revitalization.

NGOs and other nonprofits

- How about a public TV channel devoted to restorative development? War and disaster reconstruction could be the "action heroes."
- As comprehensive restoration megafirms (see above) emerge, especially those focused on the disaster/war industry, they will require a multitude of effective partnerships with professional associations, technical societies, citizen-based activist and watchdog groups, etc. The NGOs who are most proactive in forming such partnerships will likely be the big winners.

(continued)

Community and government

The obvious flip side of the spill-related cleanup expenses cited here is that they are revenues for restoration firms. Even a "little" disaster like Pepco's Patuxent River spill has "generated" $60 million so far. But governments are overlooking a related opportunity. Larger cleanup fines—along with more effective prosecution—are needed to provide true deterrent effect. Fully funded disaster-recovery projects have tremendous potential for revitalizing communities, so they should tap the "upside" of disasters (the opportunity they frequently offer for rebirth). Cities must learn to avoid being left holding the bag when companies are folded to avoid retribution, or when corporate PR agencies short-circuit fines via specious arguments like "saving jobs." Fines are a legitimate public revenue source and management tool with many positive side effects, since they both repair and prevent disasters (but only when large enough and certain enough). Such enhanced accountability will result in more comprehensive liability insurance, so this strategy shouldn't damage a community's attractiveness to legitimate businesses.

Part Four

Putting It All Together

In times of drastic change, it is the learners who inherit the future. The learned usually find themselves equipped to live in a world that no longer exists.

—**Eric Hoffer,** *Reflections on the Human Condition,* 1973

In Part One, we saw how development's three modes—new development, maintenance/conservation, and restorative development—apply to both built and natural environments. We saw how awareness of three global crises—Constraint, Corrosion, and Contamination—helps us think more clearly about our restored future. After some historical context, Part One also explained the Restoration Economy's "invisibility."

Part Two divided the business of restoration into four industries restoring the natural environment, and described their characteristics, players, principles, trends, and opportunities. Part Three did the same for the built environment.

Parts Two and Three were a high-level flyover of the realm of restorative development. Here in Part Four, we return to the broader view of Part One, this time to examine where we go from here and to think about three things:

- How restorative development affects conservation of the natural world, and how it affects the organizations and agencies whose mission is conservation.

- How restorative development relates to sustainable development, and how it will affect the organizations and agencies that are championing sustainability.
- How restoration of built and natural environments fits together, forming a path to accelerated economic growth. Towards that end, Chapter 15 offers a national case study.

Part Four thus focuses on that tricky, oh-so-evasive issue of balancing present-day economic growth with environmental health, and with the economic future of our children.

It's easy to point to the new development realm's antienvironment politicians and business leaders as the source of our environmental problems, but our marginal progress also stems from overreliance on conservation and sustainable development as remedies. We've been largely ignoring the third—arguably the most economically vigorous and sustainable—of the three development modes: restorative development.

Conservation and sustainable development are not remedies. Conservation protects something from new development, but that is seldom enough. Combine conservation with ecological restoration, however, and now a pristine ecosystem is not just protected; it is able to *expand* its domain (maybe for the first time in centuries) into the damaged land around it.

> Aldo Leopold called it "a wilderness on its last legs." Now, the North
> Woods of Wisconsin is a comeback site for bears, fishers, and wolves.
> —**John Hildebrand**, "A Winter Wildland," *Audubon*, January–February 2000

Sustainable development also is not a complete remedy, for different reasons. It has tended to focus too heavily on making new development less damaging. This is, no doubt, a truly important mission, but the downside is that sustainable development too often becomes a force for perpetuating new development at the cost of restorative development, which would do far more good. Sustainable development has thus been floundering at the most resistant end of the life cycle. The good news is that there's nothing to stop it from focusing more attention at the restorative end. Even better news is that the best sustainability projects are already doing just that.

Chapter 15 attempts to encapsulate as many of the book's points as possible in an informal case study of the charming little island nation of Bermuda. The Conclusion provides a retrospective (and introspective) cap, plus a big-picture look forward.

Ecological Restoration: Conservation's Ideal Partner

Restoration conferences and fairs proliferate now. Practitioners write essays on restoration as theater, on restoration theory, on restoration aesthetics, politics, ritual. Where once we had just one model—the University of Wisconsin Arboretum and the Leopold farm—now we have models everywhere. . . .

From the beginning there have been preservationists who have argued that restoration is premature. All available resources, they believe, should be devoted first to the preservation of authenticity of wilderness and restoration can wait till later. Later has arrived.

In the history of the environmental movement, the century or two of the Preservation Era will prove to be prologue: an introductory chapter, noble but brief. For the duration of human time on the planet—for whatever piece of eternity we have left here—restoration will be the great task.
—**Kenneth Brower,** "Leopold's Gift," *Sierra Magazine,* Jan./Feb. 2001

The conservation vs. restoration debate was largely worked out during the '90s, but the dialogue wasn't heard beyond the circle of practitioners and insiders. The initial furor has died down, but it's by no means over. It is, however, becoming increasingly moot, as one conservation NGO after another becomes more involved in restoration.

The old, combative approach of environmentalists has resulted in phrases like "this is good for the environment." Such language separates society from the environment, implying that what's good for "the environment" is not good for humans or not good for business, and even suggesting that we are not a part of the environment. Hopefully, that language is being replaced in the Restoration Economy, with less-exclusionary catch phrases, such as "making the world healthier and wealthier."

Although there's no question that we need more conservation, that's not what this book is about. Conservation does not repair the damage already done (unless one is comfortable with geologic timescales), it does not repair the damage still being inflicted, and it does not offer a viable economic alternative to new development. As stated earlier, when our environment is being attacked so relentlessly, equally vigorous countermeasures must be taken. Such countermeasures mean restoration, *plus* conservation. The only defense, in our current situation, is a good offense. Restorative development doesn't improve—or combat—new development: it supplants it as our path forward.

CONSERVATION JUST CAN'T DO THE JOB BY ITSELF: IT'S ACHIEVED SOME GREAT VICTORIES, BUT IT'S LOSING THE WAR

> . . . [S]uccessive bouts of reformist activity—from the patrician preservationism of John Muir to the conservationism of Gifford Pinchot to Rachel Carson's campaign against chemical pollution—permitted us to indulge ourselves in the comforting notion that we were gradually bringing the collateral damage of industrial progress under control.
> —**Chip Ward,** review of *The Greening of Conservative America,*
> by John R. E. Bliese, *Washington Post,* April 22, 2001

Until now, conservation has mostly operated within the context of new development—as its opponent—rather than within the context of the entire life cycle, where maintenance/conservation is a discrete mode of development unto itself, with its own realm of industries and values. This has cast conservation in the role of business's adversary—a role that "can't get no respect."

The conceptual leap that needs to be made is twofold: (1) to stop defining conservation as what it isn't (an absence of new development), and (2) to start defining conservation as what it is, an essential mode of the development cycle that retains resources needed by the other two modes (new development and restorative development). As item 1 implies, the context of new development tends to devalue conservation, whereas the restorative development paradigm revalues it.

Conservation has a vitally important place in the scheme of things, but, to use a medical analogy, relying on it to keep the world's ecosystems vigorous would be like relying only on safety precautions to maintain one's health. Yes, it's important to avoid accidents, but there are plenty of other threats to our health (pathogenic microbes, parasites, bullets, industrial toxins, etc.). What's more, accidents do happen, in spite of precautions, so radical surgery is sometimes our only alternative to death. Saving only what's healthy, while failing to actively restore what's ailing, is not much of a wellness program.

How ineffective have most conservation efforts been? Rain forests and coral reefs have received a huge share of the conservation movement's attention, so you'd think we would have made substantial progress in these areas, right? The sad truth is that, despite decades of hard work and sincere efforts, less than one-tenth of one percent of the world's rain forests is under sustainable management, and 80 percent of the world's coral reefs are dead, dying, or extremely sick.

Despite over two decades of constant international attention focused on Brazil's Amazonian rain forests, deforestation there in the year 2000 was greater than in any of the four preceding years. The mean annual rate of gross deforestation in Brazil was 7,658 square miles (more than twice recent estimates). A year earlier, it had been 6,663 square miles per year. It's been far worse in the forests that didn't "enjoy" the limelight, such as in the Solomon Islands, where Mitsubishi has long been ravaging the homelands of many tribes and undermining the integrity of the national government.

Not even the CMVs (charismatic megavertebrates) that garnered superstar levels of media attention have made much progress; quite the reverse is often true. The plight of elephants has been in the news for a quarter of a century, yet "[m]uch of what has changed has been for the worse," says Steve Osofsky of the World Wide Fund for Nature. Vietnam, for instance, was down to 150 wild elephants in 2000, a tenth of the 1990 population. Everyone's favorite poster-child, the giant panda, is in similar trouble, despite its having been the logo of the largest conservation NGO in the world. Imagine what has been happening to the smaller, less-glamorous species that haven't "benefited" similarly from having so many champions, so much public funding, and so much sympathy.

The Restoration Economy (at least, that part of it dealing with the natural environment) is based on the kind of honesty demonstrated in Osofsky's statement. We must not confuse our love of conservation's goals with a love of tools and methods associated with those goals that have now proved ineffective. For instance, the United States has received much praise for its system of national parks, preserves, and wilderness areas, but the focus has been too much on quantity, and too little on quality and connectivity. A 2001 study by the U.S. Geological Survey documented what biologists had long suspected: the lands set aside for wildlife were generally selected for their lack of interest to developers or resource extraction companies, not for their biodiversity or other ecological value.

Trying harder at the wrong activity isn't going to help much, just as digging a deeper hole in the wrong place won't uncover the treasure. The partnering of conservation with restoration has begun just in time. Of course, it's only "just in time" if you don't mind chalking off as unimportant the 800 or more recently expired mammal, bird, reptile, amphibian, and fish species, and a larger number of plant, insect, and microorganism species. Those are only the known losses (or those intelligently surmised to be lost): species that went extinct before they were discovered and classified probably outnumber the known.

Conservation of the natural environment is obviously essential, because maintenance/conservation is the second basic "mode" of the development life cycle, but we need to stop thinking it's the only tool we have with which to "save Nature." In fact, it's often not even the best tool for rescuing nature, considering the present dire state of affairs.

Conservation is more appropriate *early* in the economic development of a country, when there is plenty to conserve. After widespread damage has been inflicted, conservation must be teamed with restorative development in order to save what's left, and to retrieve some of what should never have been lost. Depending on conservation alone, when the natural world is under attack from all sides, is like an army's relying solely on defensive maneuvers, never taking the offensive, even when the enemy is vulnerable. Expanding conserved areas, by restoring degraded land and water surrounding remnant ecosystems, is the strategy of the twenty-first century.

> You hold in your hands, I sincerely believe, one of the most important documents in conservation history; indeed, one of the most important documents in the last five hundred years. What you have here is a turning back and a going forward. It is a bold attempt to grope our way back to October 1492. . . . What we seek is a path that leads to beauty, abundance, wholeness, and wildness. . . . The centerpiece of this issue is Dr. Reed Noss's detailed model for Wilderness Recovery Plans—core wildernesses surrounded by buffer zones and connected by corridors. . . . [plus] several specific proposals for restoring wilderness.
> —**Dave Foreman,** introducing the Wildlands Project special issue of *Wild Earth,* 1992

Vast expanses of dead land, polluted water, and severely damaged ecosystems await restoration—far in excess of those that are in pristine condition awaiting protection. Conserving many of these ecosystems would be like embalming a corpse: it keeps the smell from getting worse, but it doesn't bring them back to life. When keystone species are missing and macroenvironmental changes have taken place (such as global climate change), remnant ecosystems can do little self-repair, unless one assumes a million-year viewpoint. Such damaged ecosystems have small hope of returning to a state of health, nor can they expand their borders on any practical timeline; at least, not without active assistance.

Some intellectual purists point to our ignorance of natural system function, saying we should trust nature to heal itself. This makes for pretty philosophy, but such a cold, ivory-tower approach ignores the unconscionable suffering of wildlife every moment of every day, as well as the simple, bumper-sticker-obvious fact that extinction is forever. Sure, nature in general will eventually rebuild and create new species, but cavalierly chalking off the chimpanzee, the jabiru stork, or the hawksbill turtle makes me shudder in revulsion.

> If gardening provides a model for a healthy relationship with nature, then restoration is that form of gardening concerned specifically with the gardening, maintenance, and reconstitution of wild nature, and is the key to a healthy relationship with it. . . . Restoration . . . holds out at least the possibility of conserving the system, not by stopping change, but by directing it, and not by ignoring human influences, but by acknowledging and seeking to compensate for them. . . . The criticism that restoration is impossible generally applies only in the strictest sense. One cannot duplicate a natural system root hair for root hair and bird for bird, but there is no reason to try to do this. What is called for, rather, is the assembly of a system that acts like the original. This implies not only complete species lists and the reproduction of crucial aspects of community structure, but also the reproduction of function and dynamics . . . it means not just setting the system up, like a diorama, but actually setting it in motion.
> —**William R. Jordan III,** *"Sunflower Forests": Ecological Restoration as the Basis for a New Environmental Paradigm,* in A. Dwight Baldwin, Judith DeLuce, and Carl Pletsch, eds., *Beyond Preservation: Restoring and Inventing Landscapes,* 1993

I must confess some queasiness about talk that combines gardening concepts with wilderness. Attempting to re-create wildness seems the worst form of hubris: the kind that results from blending arrogance with ignorance. But I travel too much, and spend too much time in what's left of the wild, to indulge in the paralyzing luxury of such sentiments. Massive, immediate intervention is necessary.

Fortunately, much of the philosophical clash is mere semantics: the simple truth is that we *can't* create wildness, any more than we can create a zucchini. Just as the best doctors focus more on empowering the body to heal itself, rather than allowing their egos to convince them that they are doing the healing, so, too, with ecological restoration: all we can do is give nature the ingredients, assistance, and time needed to do the job. The difference between a wilderness area and an area undergoing ecological restoration is often just a matter of how long the component ecosystems have had to develop and express themselves, and to work out their relationships with each other.

I've seen what's possible when open-minded, highly knowledgeable, learning-oriented people work *with* nature to repair what others have destroyed. These restoration ecologists are not just helping nature heal her wounds: they are building the knowledge that future generations will need for survival.

The grandest, most efficient, and most intelligent ecological restoration vision is probably that of The Wildlands Project, the brainchild of Dr. Reed Noss and legendary conservationist Dave Foreman. It dreams of connecting protected areas via a network of strategically located wild farms, restored habitat, parks, and other corridors. It restores North America's ecological functions by restoring its flows.

The necessary connectivity would come primarily from restoring the land between protected areas, thus creating a functional whole of all public and private protected lands. The project's slogan is "reconnect, restore, rewild." "Rewilding" is an emergent property, deriving from the size and roadlessness of a protected area, the presence of top predators (wolves, grizzlies, and pumas), and the age of its restoration.

We are in a most severe ecological crisis. In any crisis, continued reliance on inappropriate solutions is every bit as dangerous as failure to address the causes. The heroes of conservation have done a wonderful job of identifying the causes over the past few decades, but they have been crippled by a dearth of efficacious remedies.

THE DANGERS OF RESTORATION

Reparation of new development's rampage, as well as reconstruction of the world in the wake of disasters and war, are both so profitable that a dark thought has probably occurred to you: Industrial leaders might, after reading this book, simply create "restoration divisions" to complement their "destruction divisions." Less profitable modes (such as conservation or peace) would go by the wayside. Many would say this is *already* the way of the world.

An example is West Virginia, where state policy requires the restoration of streams and mountaintops that have been damaged by coal mining. But that same policy allows companies to mine via the "mountaintop removal" process, which is even worse than strip-mining. As West Virginia Secretary of State Ken Hechler says of the restoration that follows this horrendous damage, "It's like putting lipstick on a corpse." Fortunately, the coal industry's stranglehold on West Virginia's younger politicians is beginning to slip, so such egregious examples of misusing restoration to green-light unnecessary destruction will hopefully disappear.

Restoration-as-a-profitable-substitute-for-conservation is certainly attractive—even irresistible—to leaders in the new development realm. There's nothing theoretical about it, either: witness how so many of the twentieth-century's worst polluters landed 9- and 10-digit SuperFund contracts to clean up their own pollution. Short-circuiting this deadly feedback loop is actually quite simple, though not necessarily easy. The solution comprises three steps, which will be revealed a few pages hence.

As discussed earlier, restorative development is the mirror image of new development. It's every bit as dynamic economically, but it moves in the "opposite direction," increasing rather than decreasing resources, which makes it eminently sustainable. Thus, only restorative development has the power to stand up to new development; conservation gets trampled almost every time. But conservation *plus* restorative development . . . ah, now, there's a marriage made in heaven.

How Ecological Restoration and Conservation Are Tying the Knot

> Preservation still seems like a good idea where it is both feasible and meaningful, but it is inadequate as a comprehensive solution to our worldwide ecological problems. In the best of circumstances, preservation is applicable only to the limited portion of the earth that has not already been tampered with—and even those areas are menaced by people and states that sense far more acutely an immediate need to use the land rather than preserve it. Even traditionally preservationist groups like The Nature Conservancy have had to extend their mission beyond the once-hallowed goal of wilderness preservation. Reclamation and restoration of damaged lands are now common projects for these types of organizations.
> —**A. Dwight Baldwin, Judith de Luce,** and **Carl Pletch,** (eds., Introduction) *Beyond Preservation: Restoring and Inventing Landscapes,* 1993

The landmark (and still very relevant) 1993 book *Beyond Preservation: Restoring and Inventing Landscapes* was the first to directly address the relationship of restoration to preservation, compiling essays from a range of viewpoints. But it only dealt with ecology. The realm of restorative development includes the built environment—along with the socioeconomic environment that emerges from the interaction of the two—so let's address the argument on all of these fronts.

Restoration Resolves Two "Intractable" Conservation Problems

> The smaller the reserve, the higher the rate of extinction. So the logical second stage in a well-designed conservation program is restoration, the enlargement of reserves by encouraging the regrowth of natural habitat outward from the periphery of the core reserve, while reclaiming and restoring developed land close by to create new reserves. The final stage of conservation is the one pioneered by Suriname with the aid of the nongovernmental organizations: to secure or rebuild wilderness by the establishment of large natural corridors that connect existing parks and reserves.
>
> —E. O. Wilson, *The Future of Life,* 2002

Restorative development helps overcome two of conservation's biggest problems: (1) what to do with small but unique pieces of habitat, and (2) how to justify the price of conservation. In nature, size matters . . . a lot. If a tract of property isn't large enough to withstand the encroachment of its borders by suburban or agricultural chemicals, domestic animals, poachers, etc., it is normally sacrificed to development, or allowed to degrade into pretty but biologically barren greenspace. It's hard to get support for a conservation project that has no biological future. (On the other hand, we shouldn't let the general rule about the value of size blind us to the value that some small reserves can have. When the goal is to restore individual species—especially birds, which are so mobile—rather than entire ecosystems, very small patches of strategically placed food-producing and nesting habitat can have an enormous impact.)

These small "islands" of nature, despite being surrounded by development, often contain endemic species that are on the verge of extinction. Or, they might be the last remaining example of what used to be the dominant ecosystem (ecosystems come in "species," too, and can also suffer extinction). Such little ecosystem patches, although of little value or viability as a park or wilderness area, can have untold value as seed stock for restoration projects that seek to bring back such ecosystems. Their small size is thus transformed from a liability to an asset, because it makes them affordable. Combining their bargain price with the "newfound" biological importance they have to restoration, saving these postage-stamp-sized patches of ecological history suddenly becomes far easier (such ecological restoration is discussed more fully in Chapter 8).

Restoration thus increases both the biological and the economic value of conservation projects. Justifying the "cost" of conservation has always been an elusive goal: it might, in fact, be conservationists' single greatest barrier. This is another example of operating according to new development's rules. Conservation actually has no intrinsic cost: What's mistakenly called an expense is actually just a forfeited or delayed new-development opportunity.

The cost of restoring land is real, however, and it's much higher than the "cost" of conserving it. Yet restoration gets funded with comparative ease, because it's more politically saleable: people almost universally get excited at the prospect of restoring something. "Merely" conserving it too frequently elicits yawns. This is especially true in the United States, where we love action (and spending money) above all else.

Restoration can, in fact, be astronomically costly when the standards are high, such as remediating a contaminated site for agricultural or residential use. The lower standards of decontamination involved in turning a brownfield into recreational greenspace, or into a site for new industry, is much cheaper. But even the cheapest restoration projects cost far more than simply protecting the land from pollution or destruction in the first place. The key point is that partnering conservation with restoration allows both to do their jobs more effectively.

Conservation-Restoration Partnership Strategy #1:
True Costing of New Development

Again, restoration is usually far more expensive than conservation, but the costs are generally known. New development, on the other hand, has twisted and manipulated our current accounting systems to hide the costs of pollution, sprawl, and extraction. This Soviet-style system passes the costs to society (or future generations), while the income accrues to the politically connected companies. Most extraction firms—oil, gas, coal, mining, lumber, and nuclear power—are built on this model. But, as with the Soviet Union, this model is on the verge of imploding, and for much the same reason: increased transparency is making its victims aware of their being violated.

True costing (also called "full costing") allows society, and responsible businesses, to make better-informed decisions by reflecting new development's real costs. By doing so, it lowers the comparative cost of both conservation and restoration. In fact, under true costing, restoration funding would already be figured into the life-cycle cost of new development's damage. As a result, many ill-advised new-development projects would never get financed in the first place, and those that did would automatically fund the eventual restoration up front.

The true costs of new development need to appear in the form of higher prices for its products and services, rather than in our tax bills (to support government funded projects like the Everglades restoration, Superfund, etc.). The clandestine manner in which new development firms' costs are currently underwritten by the public constitutes subsidization . . . corporate welfare.

Restorative development's treasure trove of new revenue opportunities offers a migration and evolution path for those who would otherwise lose out in the transition from "New Development Economy" to "Restoration Economy." With true costing doing the pushing, and with restoration opportunities doing the pulling, new development-based firms will be weaned from subsidies and other government welfare, and it will be "restore or starve." The result will be what conservationists always dreamed of: a massive reduction in wasteful, polluting industries, and a great reduction of threats to greenfields.

Conservation-Restoration Partnership Strategy #2: Recognition of Conservation's Essential Role in Restorative Development

Extinct species can't be restored (see Chapter 8 for a partial exception). Ecosystems that no longer exist can't be expanded or replicated. Similarly, in the built environment, historic buildings that are demolished can't be rehabilitated and reused. But, as we saw in post-WWII Warsaw, our built heritage can be rebuilt, provided we have the original plans, materials, and skills. Likewise, conservation of ecosystems, combined with an understanding of restorative processes, provides the components, information, and skills for restoration.

Knowledge deficits are an especially important factor in ecological restoration: We are decades away from a real understanding of the complexities of ecosystem functionality. We have little choice but to let nature do the bulk of the restoration work, while we merely provide the opportunities and reduce the constraints. As already noted, the greatest value of conservation projects might soon be their role as "seed banks" for future restoration projects.

Conservation for the sake of conservation is fine, but conservation for the sake of restoration has far more promise. It's like the difference between perpetually leaving our savings in a bank account, and saving that money for the eventual creation of a business that enhances our income, lifestyle, freedom, and personal satisfaction (and which allows us to put more into our savings account as a result).

The loss of genetic resources in the natural world is mirrored by the loss of cultural assets and knowledge-based resources in the built and socioeconomic environments, and the result is similar: loss of restoration resources and opportunities. The demolition of one-of-a-kind built structures, just as in the extinction of species, therefore goes from being "merely" a loss of cultural and natural assets, to a loss of ability to restore. There is a powerful psychological difference between a restorable and an irrecoverable loss: We humans usually adjust quickly to the loss of our assets, but we rebel at a visceral level to the loss of our potential. It's like the difference between getting an infection, and having one's immune system impaired: One merely makes us sick. The other destroys our ability to regain health.

The penalties for destroying irreplaceable resources must therefore skyrocket. They must reflect the loss of that asset, the theft of our capabilities, *and* our abandonment of hope for the return of those assets in the future.

Conservation-Restoration Partnership Strategy #3: Appropriate Use of Restoration (Recognizing Its Legitimate Roles and Limitations)

> Copies made by chimpanzees entertain us, partly because we are amused by how little the chimp understands of his creation. We should consider seriously how little we know or understand of our own imitations when we propose to restore whole ecosystems.
> —**Orie L. Loucks,** Prof. of Zoology, Miami University, "Art and Insight in Remnant Native Ecosystems," *Beyond Preservation*, 1994

In his response to Professor Loucks' humility-engendering caution above, pioneering ecological restorationist Frederic Turner responded (also in *Beyond Preservation*), "It also rather misses the point to argue, as Orie Loucks does, that there exist ecological 'originals' of which humanly mediated reproductions can only be copies; part of the new paradigm is precisely the reminder that nature is already in the business of reproduction and copying, and thus the linear and dualistic distinction between authentic original and artificial reproduction is profoundly questionable."

Even Loucks, also from his article quoted previously (and immediately after he compared restored landscapes to art forgeries), admitted, "One truth is that the remaining natural systems dispersed across our landscapes show the subtle effects of pesticides, air pollution, exotic species, and the absence of fire. Virtually no site is truly an 'original.' Some level of restoration is a sine qua non for the preservation of natural systems, as it is for great works of art."

The argument over what is "original" also tends to obscure the obvious: the vast majority of restorative processes are actually carried out by the organisms, not by us. The fact that humans might determine when and where a plant should grow doesn't diminish the plant's own power. Its multimillion-year-old DNA, along with its DNA-derived chemicals, mechanisms, and behaviors, still remove nitrates from the water, still perform carbon or heavy metal sequestration, still produce oxygen and biomass, and still perform the other functions vital to a restorative process. Ecological restorationists are installing natural, adaptable beings, not machines.

But Loucks had a good point, nonetheless: we must clearly acknowledge that a restored ecosystem will (when young, anyway) usually be— biologically, economically, and aesthetically—a very poor substitute for a well-conserved, centuries-old one. On the other hand, a failed attempt to restore an ecosystem (when properly documented) is usually a *far* superior learning experience to a failed attempt at conservation, and that knowledge enhances both future restoration and conservation.

For at least the next four decades, restorative development, especially of ecosystems, should thus be treasured as much for the knowledge it generates as for the tangible results it produces. What's more, the value of that learning must be accounted for as an asset in our financial ledgers, and the insights must be codified and taught in our universities. Using restorative development as the ultimate learning experience also helps us avoid that most toxic of compounds, ignorance plus arrogance, which typifies so much of the new development realm's business, science, engineering, and government players.

> Acknowledging our membership in the land communities is the first crucial step toward our reenfranchisement in it. . . . [I]n the long run the best natural areas—the ones most closely resembling their historic

counterparts—will not be those that have simply been protected from human influences (complete protection is impossible) but those that have been in some measure restored through a process that recognizes human influences and then effectively compensates for them.

—**William R. Jordan, III,** *"Sunflower Forests": Ecological Restoration as the Basis for a New Environmental Paradigm,* from *Beyond Preservation: Restoring and Inventing Landscapes,* 1993

One last time: ecological restoration is a lousy substitute for effective conservation. I can't say that too strongly or too frequently. One of the defining characteristics of complex adaptive systems is that they cannot be reversed: too many of a system's current features—whether it be a metropolitan economy or a wetland—are based on phenomena that emerged and disappeared without a trace along the path of its evolution. That said, it must also be reiterated that there are precious few opportunities these days for effective conservation, *sans* restoration. Teaming restoration with conservation can combine the profitability of restorative development with the biological value of conservation.

The Future of Conservation NGOs

Despite this chapter's litany of conservation troubles, there are, of course, bright spots. Some court-based activities do a lot of good, such as those of efficient little groups like the National Resources Defense Council (NRDC) and the Environmental Defense Fund (EDF). Some of the best results have been achieved by habitat purchase programs, the premiere one being The Nature Conservancy (TNC), which, as we've discussed, has become much more restoration-focused.

The Nature Conservancy increasingly finds itself involved in large-scale restoration efforts. . . . [W]e are engaged in large-scale efforts to restore native prairie outside Chicago, to restore natural flow on crucial rivers . . . and [to] replant [. . .] the decimated rain forests of Brazil's Atlantic coast. When we take on habitat restoration, we are often making a commitment beyond ourselves. We are committing our children and those after them to continue the process.

—**Steven J. McCormick,** president of The Nature Conservancy, "President's View," *Nature Conservancy,* July/August 2001

Like most highly successful organizations, TNC must reinvent itself regularly, evolving to keep pace with a changing world. TNC's original strategy was to purchase discrete parcels of important habitat threatened by development and protect them from human intervention, letting nature run its course. This strategy was later modified to allow sustainable resource extraction in cases where this was vital to project financing or community acceptance.

The "prime habitat purchase" element of the strategy worked well only when TNC could afford a huge tract of land. The "walled-off," passive management approach didn't work very well, especially on smaller properties. Many human-caused factors—invasive species, domestic cats, feral pigs, global warming, etc.—ignore fences and require vigorous corrective action. "Hands-off" is largely synonymous with degradation in today's protected areas.

TNC has realized that isolated reserves, no matter how numerous, seldom save species, and never save "wildness": reserves need to be both expanded and connected. The most recent modification to TNC's approach is a combination of restoration and active management. The switch was both rapid and quiet. As a longtime member, I never saw an official proclamation embracing restoration; I just noticed that restoration had become a component of an increasing percentage of new projects. Restoration has become a core practice at TNC. This greatly expanded the inventory of potential sites to purchase.

TNC's effectiveness has been due largely to its talent for partnering with landowners, governments, and local NGOs. Its focus on habitat, rather than on species, is another distinguishing characteristic. Now, TNC's projects are increasingly integrated, its properties are more linked to other protected areas, and its strategy is more restoration-oriented. Taken together, these changes could soon make The Nature Conservancy the leading environmental organization of the Restoration Economy.

Conservation often resembles the Maginot Line; passive, immovable, and easily bypassed. That's not to say that those who fight for conservation are passive: There's nothing passive about the tireless courtroom efforts of groups like NRDC and EDF, nor of the often-heroic, physically dangerous awareness-raising services performed by Greenpeace volunteers. Even the delaying tactics of monkeywrenchers like Earth First can be of tremendous value when the courts move too slowly to prevent the destruction of an irreplaceable treasure.

It's the *mode* of conservation I'm referring to as passive, compared to the other two development modes: new and restorative. Those who work in the conservation field full-time are probably thinking of exceptions to this provocative statement right now, but a closer look at these "exceptions" will probably reveal many of them to actually be either active or passive restoration projects masquerading as conservation.

For those who make their living from wildlife conservation, it's fortunate that most restoration projects involve conservation. Protecting pools and patches of genetic resources is essential to restoration efforts: allowing local wild ecosystems to seed restoration projects is vastly preferable, and far more economically viable, than relying on translocation or captive breeding. Captive breeding is, of course, preferable to extinction, but only if the ultimate goal is repopulation of the wild. Otherwise, it's just torture for the animals, and entertainment/guilt assuagement for us.

The present nascent state of restorative development (compared to where it will be in a decade) means that much, if not most, ecological restoration is carried out under the auspices of conservation groups, since they are already in position to perceive the need and act on it. Many of these groups, like TNC, have apparently joined the "restoration revolution" with no second thoughts. They don't have the definitional (or self-image) problems that plague some conservation NGOs. Their publications are full of restoration projects that are clearly labeled as such.

As the realm of restorative development grows and matures, this situation will reverse, with most conservation being performed by ecological restoration NGOs. Restoration NGOs will have vastly more resources at their command, especially if they specialize in—or have alliances with— organizations that specialize in multidimensional projects that integrate the restoration of the built and natural environments (which we will discuss in the following chapter). Of course, some of these restoration groups will be former conservation groups that successfully made the strategic switch in time.

CLOSING THOUGHTS

Conservation is still mistakenly seen as an expensive sacrifice, but ecological restoration is correcting that, in two ways: (1) the far higher costs of ecological restoration make conservation look like the bargain it is, and (2) by relying on them for seed stock, restoration greatly enhances the biological value of small conservation projects.

I find conserving and restoring our world far more promising and exciting than continuing the losing proposition of a solitary focus on conservation, and it appears I'm not alone. Being on the "side of right" is little consolation for failing to save a million-year-old species. It doesn't much matter whether it was destroyed to benefit a company that probably won't exist in 20 years, or destroyed due to a philosophical conflict among government agencies and conservation NGOs. Expanding and reviving ecosystems is something most corporations, agencies, and NGOs can support . . . and already are.

> Nature bats last.
> —**Yogi Berra**

Destruction-restoration is the most basic and constant mode of nature. Destruction is an integral part of all three modes of the development life cycle. It's obvious that new development often destroys before it builds, but this is also true of much restorative development (dam removal, stream reshaping, etc.). It's even true of maintenance/conservation: Maintenance workers cut grass and remove old wallpaper, and conservation managers burn land and destroy invasive animal and plant species. As Jim Bishop of the Department of Energy said in the January 2002 issue of *Wired* magazine, "There's no such thing as an old plant in the ocean. Each week the biomass changes."[1]

Let's now move on to a closely related subject: sustainable development. Understanding the difference between conservation and sustainable development will be critical to shaping the development and environmental policies of this century—indeed, of the entire millennium.

[1] Jennifer Hillner, "Testing the Waters," *Wired,* January 2002.

Restorative Development:
Sustainable Development's Salvation

As serious scientists, restoration ecologists can gain from having the
strength and the courage to question the theoretical robustness and practical
feasibility of the demands of politicians drunk on the heady rhetoric of
sustainability.
>
> —**Michael J. Clark,** "Ecological Restoration—The Magnitude of the Challenge:
> An Outsider's View," *Restoration Ecology and Sustainable Development,*
> K. M. Urbanska, Nigel R. Webb, and Peter J. Edwards, eds., 1998

Sustainable development is very different from conservation. One of
those differences is the "nailing jello to the wall" nature of its definition.
At "green" conferences over the years, I've heard many definitions of
sustainable development, including (1) a way to live comfortably
within the confines of one's economic, environmental, and social limits;
and (2) thriving in such a way as to allow our children to thrive equally.
Academics offer more rigorous definitions, but not one is yet accepted
as a standard.

Conservation is, in concept, relatively simple (not easy): protecting
irreplaceable natural assets, entities, and functions. Sustainable development, on the other hand, is a complicated dream, an intoxicating brew of
enlightened policies, unpopular lifestyle changes, expensive (in the short
term) process improvements, innovative designs/products/materials,
hazy goals, and splendid values.

The debate over restorative development versus sustainable development has been more harmonious than that between ecological restoration and conservation. Like lovers, the two concepts can "spoon" interchangeably: Champions of sustainable development can comfortably envelop restorative development as a part of their vision, and champions of restorative development see sustainable development as a vital element of their worldview.

MY PERSONAL SUSTAINABILITY CRISIS

A deep love of wildlife has been the common theme throughout this author's life, and I suspect it ranks high on the passion scale with a fair portion of this book's readers. Some readers are, no doubt, colleagues with whom I've been working under the banner of sustainability for many years. Friends, I'm calling it quits.

I spend a number of weeks each year hiking in the shrinking jungles of the world and diving on its dying reefs, and have finally realized it's time to get serious. Do we *really* want to sustain things the way they are now? Is "not letting things get worse" the most inspirational goal we can shoot for? Of course, despite this polemic, the real goal of sustainable development isn't just to sustain the status quo; it's to rehabilitate human society so that it becomes less wasteful and less toxic. This, in theory, will allow planetary ecosystems to restore themselves. So, sustainable development is, in many ways, passive restorative development under a more mundane moniker.

Sustainable development is a noble concept and goal, and it has been the battle cry of many environmentalists for over two decades. However, it's hamstrung by foggy definitions, a paucity of measurement criteria, a boring image, and often unperceivable results. "Thriving in a manner that allows future generations to thrive," one of the many definitions of sustainable development, is a wonderful slogan, but it makes a lousy guide for business and government decision making on a day-to-day basis.

One of the early reviewers of this manuscript, sustainable development writer and editor Sheila Kelly, offers a "cultural" explanation for the unacceptably slow progress of sustainable development. She says that environmentalists who wandered deeply into the world of business were branded traitors by "deep green environmentalists," and business leaders who became passionate about sustainability were branded traitors by their "deep brown" fellows. The already challenging goal of making both conservation and business sustainable was thus aggravated by being shunned by one's peers. Kelly introduced the resolution of this situation thusly: "Enter restorative development, stage left. . . ."

Sustainable development's fuzzy goals and confused definition have greatly hindered it. Its leaders have allowed corporations and government agencies to display many nonsubstantial (even downright cynical) greening "efforts" under the banner of sustainability. Sustainable development is in fact painless for these corporations, because no one can prove that their token, lip-service projects are *not* progress towards sustainability. The dearth of metrics, if not remedied, will be the death of sustainability.

> [The absence of sustainability standards makes sustainable development] a
> vague rhetorical aspiration rather than a real policy goal.
> —Forum for the Future [U.K. think tank], *Estimating Sustainability Gaps for the U.K.*, 2000
> [a report showing that the U.K.'s current sustainability plan would require 126 years]

The few sustainability metrics we do have are so poorly defined that they make most competent, responsible planners highly uncomfortable. Almost any reduction of waste, sprawl, or toxins—no matter how minor—can be called sustainable (or at least movement in that direction).

Sustainable designs often cost more up front, and the compensating long-term savings or increases in productivity are sometimes hard to prove, other than through common sense. Even when the numbers work, communicating them effectively can require politically dangerous (read: more honest) changes in accounting, or in stockholder reporting methods. This isn't to say it shouldn't be attempted, just that it's a far steeper slope to climb for approval than is typical with most restorative projects. Restorative development usually shows a profit, even using our new-development–biased accounting systems.

> Sustain: to supply with necessities or nourishment to prevent from falling
> below a given threshold of health or vitality.
>   —author definition, compiled from various dictionaries

Calling for less dependence on sustainable development doesn't come easily to me. I almost choke on the words at times, because the people and organizations I most admire are usually sustainability advocates. But my jumping ship to restorative development is motivated by the same intense love of health, beauty, and wildness that initiated my involvement in both conservation and sustainable development.

Of course, the obvious response from levelheaded environmentalists is: "You've got to be kidding! We haven't even made any serious progress towards sustainability! How can we even think about raising the bar to restoration?" The fact is, restoration is actually a more realistic goal, short- and long-term, than sustainability. This is proved by the presence of over a trillion dollars per year of documentable restorative development, versus who-knows-how-much real sustainable development . . . maybe a hundred million, maybe none at all.

SUSTAINABLE DEVELOPMENT IS DEAD: LONG LIVE SUSTAINABLE DEVELOPMENT!

Two factors have stymied the progress of sustainable development, but they embody its salvation, as well:

1. Sustainable development encompasses all three modes of development: new development, maintenance/conservation, and restorative development. This confuses the perception of what sustainable development really is.
2. Sustainable development has been focusing too much attention on the most resistant mode, new development.

The good news is, as stated in item 1, sustainable development *already* includes restorative development. This makes the path to its future obvious. Focusing sustainability programs primarily (not exclusively) on restorative development will greatly accelerate progress towards that elusive Holy Grail, the "triple bottom line" development style that produces benefits to society, benefits to the environment, and company profits.

Thus, restorative development will likely be the savior of sustainable development, so we don't have to choose between them. Restorative development is already the most productive—and most measurable—part of sustainable development. But those exciting restorative projects often get stifled and muffled by being buried within the context of sustainability. Burying something so vital and dynamic as "restoration" under a label as passive and boring (not to all of us, but certainly to the general public) as "sustainability" does it a great disservice. Restoration should be the star, with the more demure, introspective sustainable development its protégé, who will one day come into its own.

Real sustainability, as regards new development, is still a dream. It won't become reality in time to save hundreds of species (not to mention millions of humans) so let's come to grips with the fact that pollution will be with us for some time to come. That being the case, we need to put less attention on improving new development (making it less damaging), and put more effort into replacing new development. We need to replace it with something that will not just do no new damage, but will repair old damage. In other words, restorative development.

This isn't to say that "greening" new development isn't worthwhile; it's vital, of course. The problem is that modestly improved—and still very damaging—forms of new development are being called "sustainable". We should call these forms what they are: greener, less polluting, less toxic, less wasteful, and less dependent on nonrenewable resources. Such claims are easy to measure and document, and don't overstate the progress. Calling greener forms of new development "sustainable" lulls us into thinking we've made far more progress than we really have.

Caution: Not All Restorative Development Is Sustainable

Sustainable development is often more about the built environment than it is about nature. Restoring the natural environment is obviously a "green" activity, but what about restoring the built environment? Restoring and reusing (i.e., recycling) a building is, by its very nature, "greener" than creating one from scratch. But that doesn't automatically confer environmental blessings on all restoration projects.

Despite all of its intrinsic "green" characteristics (such as reuse of assets), restorative development is not synonymous with ecologically sound development. Plenty of environmentally unwise activities qualify as restoration, either as a result of poor execution, old technology, or flaws in the project design. *All* (real) restorative development is more sustainable than new development, but that doesn't mean it's as ecologically sound as it could be.

Example: Infrastructure restoration firms often restore and protect old steel bridges with *lead*-based anticorrosion compounds. Fighting corrosion is a $350 billion-per-year industry in the United States alone, so greening this aspect of restoration and maintenance would be no small thing.

Restoring the Empire State Building reveals a different aspect of "green" restoration: Restoring the building back to its authentic original condition would regress it to a state of horrible energy inefficiency. It would force the contractors to ignore decades of advances in design, materials, and equipment. We must balance and integrate the purity of the aesthetic or historical agenda with the use of safer, cleaner modern tools and technologies.

Restorative development should be subject to the same sustainability guidelines that govern (or will govern) new development. Chemicals used in restorative work should be as nontoxic as possible, and products used in restoration should be recyclable and made of recycled materials whenever possible.

The broader restrictions of sustainability apply, too, such as "meeting our needs in a way that allows future generations to meet their needs." This would mean avoiding some of the destructive behaviors that are currently mistaken as forms of restoration, such as lip-service mitigation projects that destroy natural wetlands and replace them with poorly designed artificial wetlands located where no wetlands ever existed.

Mitigation projects are too often just a politically expedient method of allowing companies and communities to do whatever they want. Some mitigation is worthwhile, however, especially when the only alternative is new development *without* mitigation.

> . . . [P]lanners and ecologists [are presented] with a classic dilemma—is prevention better than cure? The precautionary principle enshrined at the heart of sustainability theory would argue in the affirmative, but, faced with present deforestation, actual loss of wetland, or the fait accompli of the Gulf War releases of oil, then no real choice is available. Cure appears to be the only reasonable response to continued degradation, and the choice is not whether to prevent or to cure, but at what scale and through what approach attempts at curing might be most feasible. A starting-point is then the challenge of overlapping strategies and related conflicting terminologies on offer to the planner . . . we find that there may be at least a temporary contention between the mission of substantive planetary restoration and the reality that, in practice, a multitude of more modest local goals may have more impact. It has to be acknowledged that the issue is both fundamental and complex. . . .
> —**Michael J. Clark,** "Ecological Restoration—The Magnitude of the Challenge:
> An Outsider's View," *Restoration Ecology and Sustainable Development,*
> K. M. Urbanska, Nigel R. Webb, and Peter J. Edwards, eds., 1998

In this book, I am broadly defining the Restoration Economy to include all activities that renew, redevelop, or replace. I am *not* restricting it only to the greener activities that contribute to restoring the Earth. For example, restoring an oil refinery that's been damaged by war is a legitimate form of restorative development, but it's hardly something that is going to revitalize the planet. This shows how a "sustainability filter" could improve restorative development. The damage to the oil refinery *could* be seen as an opportunity to restore the energy grid by removing the refinery and replacing it with a healthier, more modern technology, rather than just seeing it as an opportunity to restore the refinery.

Factors of scale, both spatial and chronological, can also confuse the issue: what's restorative at one scale can be destructive at another, and vice versa. An example of destruction leading to restoration is the ugly, disruptive work done by bulldozers and backhoes during the first stage of a stream restoration.

An example of restoration leading to destruction is the return of gribbles—wood borers—that are chewing up the wooden pier pilings in many restored harbors. Water pollution had driven them away (along with the fish), but watershed and brownfield restoration projects have restored the water quality, and the infrastructure is deteriorating as a result.

Taking some of the research and other resources currently devoted to making new development more sustainable, and reallocating them to making restorative development more sustainable, might produce a bigger bang for the buck.

Some Background Reading on the Relationship of Sustainable Development to Restorative Development

Sustainable development is far too complex a subject to deal with in detail here. I'll focus on just a few key aspects, and refer readers elsewhere to pursue it further.

The debate between the relative merits of sustainable development vs. restorative development reached a high point during the writing of this book, with the publication of *Restoration Ecology and Sustainable Development*, edited by K. M. Urbanska, Nigel R. Webb, and Peter J. Edwards (Cambridge University Press, 1998). As the title reveals, the dialogue was largely about the natural environment, restoration ecology, rather than the broader concept of restorative development, which includes the built environment.

The public's full awakening to restorative development might eventually be driven by government, citizens, academia, or business: all have substantial, fast-growing restoration components. National-level government agencies tend to lag behind the growth curve of many positive trends, but we've already seen two exceptions regarding restorative development. One is the previously described role of the U.S. Environmental Protection Agency in catalyzing and nurturing the brownfields restoration industry, and the other is the U.S. Park Service's key role in providing structure and "legitimacy" to the heritage restoration industry.

Here's another example of a government body's being on the leading edge of the Restoration Economy. In 1994, the National Science and
Technology Council (NSTC) published a report entitled "Technology
for a Sustainable Future." It identified four categories of needed technologies: avoidance, monitoring/assessment, control, and remediation/
restoration.

The council recommended that all four technologies be applied to the
rehabilitation and restoration of eight key areas:

1. Natural disaster reduction/recovery
2. Coastal/marine environments
3. Biodiversity/ecosystems
4. Water resources
5. Air quality
6. Energy efficiency/climate change
7. Toxic substances and hazardous/solid waste (industrial use of
   biological processes)
8. Resource use and management (including infrastructure
   reconstruction/restoration)

The NSTC published an applications-oriented follow-up report a
year later (1995) entitled "Bridge to a Sustainable Future: National Environmental Technology Strategy." Both are recommended reading for anyone wishing to see the United States secure its global industrial leadership position in the twenty-first century.

The NSTC's view of the twenty-first century was dominated by
restorative development, but little attention was paid to these forward-
thinking reports at that time. Part of the reason might have been the
titles' unfortunate, trendy use of "sustainable," which obscured the
reports' pioneering focus on restorative development. It's also likely that
the council was ahead of its time—maybe five years or so. In these days
of Internet connectivity, memes propagate like bunnies and paradigms
turn on a dime, so the universally appealing vision of restoring our world
is now spreading like wildfire. Those NSTC researchers are, no doubt,
thrilled to see that restoration's time has come.

No discussion of sustainable development's relationship to restorative development would be complete without references to Paul
Hawken's work, specifically, his groundbreaking *The Ecology of Commerce*
(1992) and the monumental *Natural Capitalism: Creating the Next Industrial
Revolution* (1999), the latter coauthored with fellow green giants Amory
and Hunter Lovins.

Both *The Ecology of Commerce* and *Natural Capitalism* are devoted to sustainable development, but the concept of restorative development bubbles throughout the texts. Because the sustainable development community doesn't generally differentiate between new development and restorative development, it's little wonder that "sustainable" and "restorative" are often used interchangeably in these texts.

Hawken and the Lovinses were certainly aware of active restoration, though. It was Amory Lovins who first pointed me towards Louisville, Kentucky, and Chattanooga, Tennessee, when I asked him for U.S. examples of restorative development. In the *Ecology of Commerce* chapter entitled "The Inestimable Gift of a Future," Hawken writes:

> It is not merely a question of stopping the cutting in the remaining ancient
> forests, it is literally the task of recreating the ancient forests of the future.
> 'Going forward' will someday mean *replacing what has been lost,* as well as
> *returning what should not have been taken* [emphasis added], not only in our
> forests and grasslands, but in our inner cities and rural backwaters, as well.

Earlier in the same chapter, Hawken says "The second issue is to restore and re-create some of what we have lost. The idea that we can bottom out in the next few years and achieve sustainable development is a popular but short-sighted ideal. Bottom out, yes." Given that Hawken says in this book that restoration must precede sustainability, why is 99 percent of *The Ecology of Commerce* about sustainable development? Because restorative development has mushroomed to an amazing degree in the decade between that book and this one.

> Sustainable development started out as a perfectly good term. Over time, as
> unfortunately happens with many good ideas, it gets co-opted,
> reinterpreted, and sadly distorted by many who flock to its use. [Paul]
> Hawken clearly had restorative economic activity in his book *The Ecology of
> Commerce,* and sustainability used to be much more meaningful before big
> business started using it and distorting the concept.
> —**Jeff Mendelsohn,** CEO, *New Leaf Paper,* March 2002
> [from his review of an early draft of the manuscript for this book]

Consider that Hawken probably researched that 1992 book for three to five years. Add a couple of years for writing and a year for publishing, and his data is pushed back into the mid-1980s. Much of the restorative activity I'm reporting in this book didn't exist in substantial quantities back then. Even so, Hawken *did* mention a military base redevelopment, a couple of examples of urban reforestation, a re-use of old buildings, and even a brownfields remediation (back at the very birth of the brownfields industry!). I am merely documenting an existing phenomenon; Hawken, though, was extrapolating from the earliest—almost ephemeral—dribbles of restorative development. *That* was truly visionary.

Integrating Restorative Development with Sustainable Development: We're Addicted to Growth, So Let's Grow in the Right Direction

> Sustainable development will not happen without financing and financing will not take place if sustainable development is not financeable. It [sustainable development] has to be brought into the mainstream of our economic behavior.
>
> —**Maurice Strong,** former Secretary-General of the United Nations Conference on Environment and Development

The marginal progress of sustainable new development's long, noble fight to become part of the economic mainstream—to become "financeable," as Strong puts it, above—has been eclipsed by the fact that restorative development already *is* the fastest-growing component of the economic mainstream.

Once restorative development is recognized and understood, many "sustainable development" organizations and resources will probably refocus in this more productive direction.

If sustainable development presently exists in reality, then it's in the form of restorative development. Sustainable *new* development might even turn out to be an oxymoron. Restorative development takes what already exists and makes it better, so by its very nature, it's mostly sustainable. New development, even the best "sustainable" examples, destroys what already exists, under the (often mistaken) assumption that the "new thing" will be better.

One caveat concerning sustainable maintenance/conservation: just as the ability to restore an ecosystem shouldn't be used as an excuse to forfeit conservation, so too should our ability to restore buildings and infrastructure not be used as an excuse to delay or underfund maintenance. Nor should the promise of eventual restoration become a substitute for high-quality initial construction.

ONE POSSIBLE SOLUTION

If we were to start differentiating the three modes of development in our dialogue—the trimodal development perspective—sustainability would take a major leap forward. Among other benefits, such differentiation allows community planners to specify development strategies that are, for instance, 45 percent restorative, 45 percent maintenance/conservation, and 10 percent new development. Without trimodal development language, that kind of clear specification is almost impossible.

The next step would be to stop trying to apply the uselessly broad term "sustainable development" to all forms of development. The language of sustainable development needs to be mapped to the trimodal development perspective. Doing so gives us "sustainable new development (SND)," "sustainable maintenance/conservation (SMC)," and "sustainable restorative development (SRD)."

The ultimate goal—sustainable development of all aspects of our world—would, in theory, automatically result from practicing all three modes of sustainable development. (Note: I'll use these three new terms [or their initials] in this chapter only.) In case you're wondering, SMC and SRD aren't as redundant as they might sound, for the three reasons already put forward:

1. Most forms of maintenance use toxic materials and large amounts of non-renewable energy.
2. Many forms of ecosystem conservation are not sustainable, whether due to unreliable funding, lack of integration with local communities, insufficient size, proximity of deleterious influences, or poor biological management.
3. Many unsustainable activities legitimately qualify as restorative development, and illegitimate ones sometimes masquerade as restorative development (such as some forms of mitigation).

If we don't break sustainable development down into these more manageable and clearly definable subsets, our future is likely to have more of the same: miniscule, incremental improvements in SND and SMC, plus exploding amounts of restorative development (both sustainable and otherwise). The restorative development will be wonderful, by and large, but it won't be as green as it could be. And sustainable development will continue to be stymied by its lack of trimodal clarity.

This more-specific terminology gives each of the three basic types of sustainability initiatives its own clearly defined focus. It allows SND, SMC, and SRD to each progress at their own natural pace. The faster ones (SMC and SRD) will no longer be hampered by the slow one (SND). What's more, SND will no longer be able to hide its foot-dragging behind SRD, which rightfully earns its favorable media attention.

The bad boy—new development—has dug itself in (for the most part) as the sworn enemy of everything green and sustainable. Some of the blame for this adverserial relationship can be accorded to combative environmental groups with holier-than-thou attitudes (mostly in the '70s and '80s), but the politically ensconced industries of new development are primarily to blame.

CLOSING THOUGHTS

Why is restorative development generally so lucrative, compared to sustainable new development, and even compared to much brown new development? One reason is that the results of restoration are usually both rapid and dramatically visible. Another is that the work is often both urgent and important—importance gets a project funded, and urgency increases the profit margins.

For example, landing a contract to build a new bridge is always nice, but a contract to rebuild a bridge destroyed in an earthquake can be a gold mine. Just ask the firms that rebuilt the roads and bridges after the 1994 Northridge earthquake: The Federal Highway Administration (one of the most innovative government agencies) used design-build, a more efficient but then still-controversial, construction delivery method. The design-build firm reopened all the vital roads in just 87 days and completed the entire rehabilitation in only 291 days, for a tab of $400,000,000: not bad for less than a year's work. The contract included bonuses for finishing ahead of schedule, which boosted profit margins even higher.

The public seldom decries such windfall profits, because the damaged asset—bridge, tunnel, power plant, fishery, watershed, or whatever—had been providing millions of dollars a day in commercial and societal convenience or other value, and the public wants it back . . . now! When people are hungry or thirsty—or when their business is going belly-up—they tend not to begrudge a handsome reward to whomever rescues them.

In contrast, the demand for companies to *sustain* anything in its current condition is far less urgent, even when the importance is equal. It's the combination of importance, urgency, and noticeable results that works such magic on restorative development's bottom line.

Unlike sustainable new development, the rewards of restorative development are perceivable on timescales relevant to humans, businesses, and governments. That single characteristic can make all the difference in budget and strategy decisions; thus, restorative development is an industry, whereas sustainable development remains a vision.

The greatest progress in sustainable new development might well come from "intermodal competition," as planners find they have more strategies from which to choose. New development's players (sustainable and otherwise) will increasingly find themselves trying to measure up to restorative development. That's a competition they can't win, but I'd love to see them try.

To recap: restorative development is the opposite of new development, whereas sustainable new development is "just" an improved version of new development. New development, whether sustainable or not, still expands our domain—and our domain on this planet has limits. We can't have too much restorative development—sustainable or not—but we can most assuredly have too much sustainable new development. It's like the difference between saying "there's no such thing as too high a quality of humans" and "there's no such thing as too high a quantity of humans."

Sustainable development has been the Next Big Thing among environmentalists and green politicians for some time now. But unless sustainable development focuses more on restorative development, it will probably remain the Next Big Thing forever.

Bermuda Case Study: The Unplanned Restoration of a Nation

Nonsuch Island is the most magical place in Bermuda.
> —**Graeme Outerbridge,** Environmental Resource Manager, Daniel's Head Village
> Eco-resort, Bermuda, personal conversation in February 2002

Bermuda lies about 570 nautical miles due east of North Carolina. However, it has a somewhat Caribbean environment, thanks to being deep within the Gulf Stream.

Bermuda is a good case study for many reasons, not the least of which is the fact that it effectively has zero land available for new development. You're about to make a happy discovery, one that I've been making in dozens of cities and countries: once we start looking for restorative development, we find ourselves surrounded by it . . . even when standing on the remains of an extinct volcano in the middle of the North Atlantic.

NONSUCH ISLAND

> To bring a species back from the brink of extinction is brilliant; to bring an entire island back is a miracle. . . .Over the years, Dr. Wingate has created a biological oasis by eliminating foreign plants and animals and reintroducing native species.
> —**Bob Friel,** Executive Editor, "Nonsuch Exists: An Island in Time,"
> *Caribbean Travel & Life* magazine, June/July 2001

At the mouth of Castle Harbour, just a few minutes by boat off the south-eastern corner of Bermuda's mainland, is a 15-acre speck called Nonsuch Island. In 1962, Nonsuch was an ecological disaster zone, and no one much cared about it.

Then, the discovery of an "extinct" bird altered the island's path: the island veered from its descent into ecological irrelevance, and (after 30 years of hard work with minimal funding) became the world's first living museum of restored pre-Columbian fauna and flora. What Nonsuch lacks in size, it now makes for up in importance, to the world at large, and to Bermuda in particular. In becoming a window on our ecological past, Nonsuch has became a window on our restored future.

This pattern could be considered the essence of restorative development: a mode of economic growth that restores our future by returning the worst of the present to a less damaged past, while enhancing the best of the present. Nonsuch is an extreme example, because only a tiny portion of the island's natural environment was in a condition worth retaining. This was a ground-up restoration (what automobile restorers would call a "frame-off" restoration).

The Bermuda Petrel (*Pterodroma cahow*), locally called the cahow, is a seabird that had been thought extinct for almost 300 years. It's estimated that a million cahows were in Bermuda (their only nesting site on the planet) in 1492. By 1620, they were considered extinct, the victims of European humans, plus their hogs, goats, and rats.

> the fat cahow, *our* mythic fowl. never seen men before. 1609, in scores
> on an unspoiled shore, sacrificed herselves to some preoccupied god. and
> let men feed from her limbs, her breast, and her eggs.
>
> vanished, unicorn with wings, children waited for her songs like faires
> that peep from behind hibiscus blossoms. now, she in pairs return.
>
> how, the bird glides out of our dreams and rests on the tales of our
> modern stuff?
>
> now, poems that i thought had begun to taste of sour obilvion, have flown
> back near bay. singing. she returns to nest in the limestone.
>
> i, with the wind, sing back . . . *now cahow now!*
>
> watch. words and feathers take flight.
>   —**Andra Simons**, poet, "Now, Cahow Now!" *The Bermudian*, February 2002

In the 1900s, lone cahows were occasionally encountered, but it wasn't until 1951 that the American Museum of Natural History sponsored an expedition to search them out, finding seven nesting pairs. By

1961, 18 mated pairs of cahows had been discovered barely clinging to life on a group of tiny, suboptimal islets within Castle Harbour in eastern Bermuda. (This story is told in *Bermuda Petrel: The Bird That Would Not Die* by Francine Jacobs [William Morrow & Co., 1981]; the book is out of print, but a few new copies are still available in Bermuda.)

A teenager was in that 1951 expedition, and he was inspired by the "second chance" being offered this species. What once was lost had now been found—an "amazing grace" if ever there was one. Ten years later, as the government conservation officer with the Bermuda Parks Department, Dr. David Wingate proposed that Nonsuch Island could support up to a thousand cahows.

Protected from development, invasive species, and excessive tourism, it would make, he felt, an ideal cahow reserve. But simply protecting the island wasn't enough: Few native species of any kind remained. Only by restoring native flora, fauna, and nesting sites could humans help the cahow to survive. The cahow restoration began by building artificial nesting sites, to replace the natural sites that had disappeared with the island's topsoil. Invasive plants and animals such as goats and rats ruled the island, and removing them was the next step.

Timing is critical in ecosystem restorations, and Wingate showed great forethought (this restoration started in 1962!) in realizing that it would be better to leave some of the invasive plants in place while the native species were getting reestablished. Invasive trees provided necessary windbreaks, shade, and soil stability, without which many native trees wouldn't have been able to reestablish themselves (the tabula rasa approach is often tempting, but not always appropriate.) Once the natives took hold, the horrendously labor-intensive job of removing the exotics began, the worst of them being the Brazilian pepper tree (*Schinus terebinthifolia*).

This wasn't a onetime job, either: Although one might think an island-based restoration would be free of renewed invasion, starlings (another invasive species) from the mainland constantly drop the seeds of Brazilian pepper (planted as an ornamental) in their feces. The restoration of mainland Bermuda would have to include educating and motivating all citizens to remove these floral infections from their gardens. Their eradication would make all other local Bermuda restoration projects, including Nonsuch, far easier.

The animal problem wasn't limited to goats and rats, either. The aggressive, native White-tailed Tropicbird was preventing the cahow from successfully nesting when the program began. The problem was

solved by making the entrance to the artificial nests smaller, thus restricting access by the larger Tropicbirds. (The fact that cahows are a ground-
nesting species made the restoration far more difficult, because restoring
their natural nesting behavior required topsoil, something that deforestation had left in very limited supply. Ground nesting also makes the
cahows vulnerable to pigs, dogs, and cats; three of the five (along with
goats and rats) "animal infections" introduced by sailors that have been
wiping out island flora and fauna around the globe for centuries.)

From the original 18 pairs of cahow, it's estimated that there are now
86 nesting couples, three-quarters of which use the artificial nests. This
growth was accomplished despite marginal funding and a number of set-
backs, such as Hurricane Hugo and the arrival of a vagrant snowy owl
that killed at least five young cahows. DDT almost rendered the cahow
extinct "again" in the '60s, but was banned just in time. (DDT wasn't used
in Bermuda; it apparently drifted from the pesticide-saturated United
States and was picked up from the fish the cahows ate in the open ocean.)

The Cahow Conservation Program (actually restoration, but that
term wasn't in use when the program was named) is one of the stellar
endangered-species recovery programs in the world. Many people throw
up their hands when one mentions restoring the world, saying it's impossible. But if one man can restore 15 acres, how many acres can six billion
people restore? (Hint: It's a lot more than is available for restoration—a
lot more.)

By the way, Bermuda's cahow success story is not unique: another
island nation, New Zealand, has pulled several endemic birds back from
the brink of extinction, including another ground-nesting bird, the
kakapo, a flightless parrot.

Wingate hopes to make Nonsuch, even though it's only one-
thousandth the land mass of Bermuda, an ecological microcosm of the
whole country, one that will eventually become the seedbed from which
all of Bermuda will be restored. Towards that end, Wingate has taken the
unusual step of adding wetlands areas that may never have existed on
the island. This enables him to conserve freshwater and brackish water
species that are in danger on the mainland—for example, Bermuda's
endemic killifish, whose only remaining habitats on the mainland are on
golf courses, where tons of herbicides, pesticides, and fertilizer flow into
their precious streams and ponds.

The dominant plant prior to the European invasion was the Bermuda
cedar (*Juniperus bermudiana*). The cedars were also the chief economic
attraction of the island, which led to Bermuda's ecological downfall as

shipwrecked sailors (the first arriving in 1612) chopped them down to build boats. Settlers later used the hardy cedar for furniture, homes, and just about anything else that could be made of wood.

This unrestricted harvesting was bad enough, but the coup de grâce was delivered when airport landscapers imported two tree diseases, oyster scale and juniper scale. By 1951, the infections had wiped out 85 percent of the remaining Bermuda cedars. No new ones grew—not even the few disease-resistant ones—because imported rats ate the seeds, and imported goats ate the few that sprouted. Luckily, a few did survive, but by then Nonsuch looked like a desert island. Then, the "Wingate miracle" happened; since then, Bermuda cedars are making a strong comeback. Some of the surviving cedars proved to be scale-resistant, and thirty years of planting from their seeds have restored healthy cedar groves to Bermuda.

By the mid-1980s, 95 percent of the mainland biomass consisted of invasive species. Hurricane Emily "helped" in 1987, by destroying about 35 percent of the mainland's mature trees, and up to 60 percent of the Australian pine (Casaurina), with gusts up to 125 miles per hour. Another 10 percent were lost in the subsequent cleanup process. As residents picked their way around the thousands of uprooted, nonnative trees, someone noticed that virtually every native tree on Nonsuch was still standing.

Locals began clamoring for native species that wouldn't damage their houses and cars every time a big wind blew. It also helped when Jeremy Madeiros, Wingate's handpicked successor as government conservation officer and warden of Nonsuch, accidentally helped restore an old Bermudian wedding tradition involving the planting of two seedling Bermuda cedars, believed to bless marriages with long life.

But a single canopy of cedar does not a forest make. A layer of endemic and native shrubs, along with ground cover plants, was needed if the animals and cedar seedlings were to become self-sufficient. To that end, Bermuda olivewood (Cassine laneana), buttonwood (Conocarpus erecta), and palmetto palms (Sabal bermudana) were planted on Nonsuch.

Some of the endemics (found nowhere but Bermuda), and even some of the natives (not exclusive to Bermuda), are extinct. Thus, a complete restoration of pre-Columbian conditions is impossible, but locally extinct natives have been restored from other countries. These include the Bermuda snowberry (Chiorocca bermudiana), Bermuda sedge (Carex bermudiana), white stopper (Eugenia axillaris), and forestiera (Forestiera segregata), as well as several fern species.

In a tragically poetic convergence, restoring Nonsuch has been personally restorative for David Wingate. His young wife burned to death in a house fire on the island when their two daughters were still quite young. He threw himself into restoring Nonsuch, in part to assuage his agony.

In turn, his restorative effects on the nation of Bermuda have been extensive. Between 1968 and 1978, Wingate was part of a project that took green sea turtle eggs from Costa Rica and planted them on protected Bermuda beaches. Sixteen thousand out of 23,000 hatched; one of Wingate's young daughters often swam with the babies as far as she could, trying to protect their dangerous ocean entry, when birds and fish often grab them.

The idea of the project was to restore green sea turtle breeding activity in Bermuda (they had been wiped out by overharvesting) by imprinting this new (old) location on the baby turtles. Those turtles should begin maturing around 2012, and Wingate lives for the day he sees the first one return to nest. (How many of us have made an investment of comparable value in our planet's future, or one that is likely to provide such an overwhelming feeling of satisfaction?)

[As my wife and I stood with Wingate and Madeiros on a Nonsuch cliff overlooking some turtle grass beds, three almost-mature green sea turtles rose to the surface simultaneously. No one could have been immune to the excitement that scene engendered.]

In 1982, Wingate reintroduced 86 West Indian topshells, a beautiful, cantaloupe-sized marine snail that had been rendered locally extinct by centuries of—you guessed it—overharvesting. An estimated 10,000 are now found around Bermuda coastlines. With proper management, the topshell might someday become fully restored, not just biologically, but commercially, as well. Although native Bermudans no longer eat topshell, it's suspected that immigrants from Caribbean countries, possibly unaware of its protected status, are illegally harvesting them. So the topshell restoration is probably contributing to the economy already (again), however illicitly.

On a different note, the story of the Bermuda sedge is a case study in unexpected synergies. This grasslike plant is endemic to Bermuda and had been completely eradicated from Nonsuch. It was barely hanging on in other parts of the country, again due to the introduced rats, which ate its seeds. Wingate brought some sedge over from the mainland after the rats had been exterminated from Nonsuch, but it still didn't do very well. Shortly after, he introduced herons to control the land crab population (see the "Issues and Insights" section of Chapter 7), and the sedge suddenly began to thrive.

It turns out the overpopulated land crabs had been eating the plants. Wingate had no idea that bringing in the herons would help the sedge, but such unexpected outcomes are exactly the sort of thing he expects. Wingate takes a dynamic, process-oriented approach to ecological restoration. Rather than trying to create an arbitrary, static "pre-Columbian condition" that experts dictate was what the first European explorers found, he tries only to recreate the ecosystem *processes* that were likely present at the time. The ebb and flow of particular species is thus largely uncontrolled, making for constant "surprises" like the sedge renaissance.

Along with the return of the sedge, another unexpected economic and environmental benefit resulted from Wingate's importation of that native heron analog. Wingate had won financial support for the project by hypothesizing that the herons might also help control land crabs on Bermuda's golf courses, where they were a major problem. His proposed solution worked out (to everyone's surprise) wonderfully well. Bermuda's wetlands and other wildlife also benefited, as the golf courses terminated their extensive land crab poisoning program.

NONSUCH INTO THE FUTURE

As the story of this remarkable achievement at Nonsuch Island has spread, Wingate has received high honors from the Dutch Crown and the British Crown, as well as an honorary Ph.D. from Clark University. He became the president of Bermuda Audubon and the Bermuda Conservation Officer of Parks. Now that Wingate has retired, the highly capable and personable Jeremy Madeiros has picked up the mantle. Madeiros shares Wingate's passion for restoration and is tirelessly continuing this world-class project into the twenty-first century.

Monitored on land by Jeremy Madeiros, and at sea by the Bermuda Marine Patrol, visitors to Nonsuch come by permit only. They are escorted, and are strictly warned against the taking of plants, the bringing of pets, walking off the trails, and the leaving of litter. This last isn't just for aesthetics: The native skink, known locally as Bermuda rock lizards, frequently get trapped and die in bottles and cans.

At 15 acres and with a strict restoration agenda, Nonsuch has limited carrying capacity for tourists, but it makes a wonderful educational laboratory for those who are fortunate enough to experience it. Younger generations, in particular, are desperate for evidence that we can undo the mess they are inheriting. Bermuda's got that evidence.

With careful planning, Bermuda could also turn the biological treasure that is Nonsuch into an economic treasure. Nonsuch Island's unique status as the world's only long-term, almost complete eco-restoration of a discrete land mass—if properly leveraged for both its scientific and PR value—could help reposition Bermuda (currently known primarily for golf, insurance, and shorts) in the eyes of the world. This would be especially true if other Bermudian landowners were to pick up the ball, extending the knowledge and techniques learned on Nonsuch to their own properties on the mainland.

The challenges faced during the Nonsuch restoration are shared by many Caribbean islands to the south. Most of them lost their topsoil as a direct result of Britain's losing the American Revolution: King George rewarded fleeing loyalists with gifts of Caribbean islands. The settlers promptly deforested them for agriculture, which allowed the topsoil to blow or wash away. They then abandoned the now-desert islands for others, and so continued their devastating march across the Caribbean. They repeatedly obliterated indigenous flora, fauna, and human cultures, never grasping the concept of sustainability, despite the plain-as-day cause-and-effect process staring them in the face.

If the United Nations does declare the twenty-first century "The Century of Restoration," the little country of Bermuda might well find itself with *two* UNESCO World Heritage Sites (the other being the town of St. George, which we'll discuss in a moment). Nonsuch would be an excellent start to a new category of World Heritage Sites dealing with the restored natural environment. Of course, a national economic rebirth based only on the rebirth of Nonsuch would be far-fetched. So, let's move on.

Wingate hasn't confined his activities to Nonsuch in recent years—he has also helped stimulate ecological restoration of mainland protected areas. These include native forest restoration experiments in Paget Marsh Nature Reserve, Bartram's Pond Nature Reserve, Morgan's Island Nature Reserve, and Walsingham Nature Reserve. And, he has consulted with commercial developments, such as . . . .

Daniel's Head Village

Our next stop combines restoration of both natural and built environments: the gorgeous Daniel's Head Village eco-resort. This story will serve several agendas. One agenda is that it allows me to offer a specific example of a wonderful restored property that's available for purchase by some lucky reader. The reason it's available is because it also fulfills my need to profile a failed project.

One of my frustrations in writing this book was the difficulty of finding examples of failed restorative business ventures. I'm sure there are others out there, but I couldn't find them, and business books are supposed to be balanced with cautionary tales. Daniel's Head Village rescued me by going out of business a few weeks after I visited (I don't think the two events were related). The resort thus allows me to offer an obvious caution: that the many inherent efficiencies and virtues of restorative development are not proof against undercapitalization, compromise of vision, or insufficient marketing, all of which afflicted Daniel's Head Village.

This isn't a hands-on manual of restorative development tactics and strategies, nor is this a collection of project case studies and company stories (that's the next book in my intended series), so we won't dissect the resort's failure here. Based on the reports I've cobbled together (the current owner didn't respond to inquiries) the story seems to be this:

1. Caribbean ecotourism pioneer Stanley Selengut (and his partner, Lew Geyser) had the original vision for the resort. They designed and built it, with some input from Wingate regarding restoration of flora and fauna. The high cost of everything in Bermuda was apparently underestimated, and they ran out of capital within a year, before launching a marketing campaign.

2. A California-based developer then bought the project. The firm had more money, but they compromised the ecological restoration agenda to such a degree that the restoration story was largely buried, and the resort lost many of its original champions. For instance, they hired a conventional landscaper who covered the place in exotic plants. They also put few dollars into marketing, so the resort was little known outside of Bermuda, and even had a low profile within Bermuda.

3. What's more, the developer reportedly failed to build strategic relationships with the other ecological destinations on the island (such as the Bermuda Biological Station for Research, which runs tours to Nonsuch) which could have funneled nature-oriented Bermuda visitors to the resort. Daniel's Head Village is isolated enough to require such relationships: there's no "walk-in" traffic, because no one drives past Daniel's Head (and wouldn't see it if they did).

That's the short story of what went wrong. Here's what was right about it. Daniel's Head Village was Bermuda's only eco-resort, but, more importantly, it combined more types of restorative development than any small commercial project I've encountered.

When Daniel's Head was first built (on a projected budget of $8 million), it was the first major new hotel development on Bermuda in a quarter-century, so hopes were high. The second owners started well, by hiring excellent managers. The gracious Richard Quinn, a Bermudan with extensive hospitality management experience, was their general manager.

Quinn hired a full-time environmental manager, Graeme Outerbridge, another highly qualified local. In Outerbridge, the resort didn't just get an ecologist: it got a restoration ecologist. He had worked closely with Wingate on Nonsuch over the years, and it shows in the restorative activities and plans at Daniel's Head Village.

One of Outerbridge's first restorative ecological activities was to install artificial igloo-style Tropicbird nests used by Wingate at Nonsuch. These nests were highly successful, and many were colonized in the first year. Selengut and Geyser had also consulted Wingate when they established a plan for restoring their two Bermuda rock lizard (skink) colonies. Daniel's Head set aside a small peninsula as skink restoration habitat for one colony, which was necessary, because an increasing population of domestic cats (fed from the resort's kitchen) was decimating the other colony. There's also a small island a hundred meters or so off the resort's coast, which the original owners had planned to restore to native forest.

The most recent owners were leading an effort to have a large portion of the surrounding waters declared a new national marine park. The shelf surrounding Bermuda—long the bane of sailors—is at least five times the size of the land mass (the whole country is basically a mid-ocean mountain top). Thus, Bermuda has great marine park potential. But Daniel's Head Village was a restorative development even before Graeme Outerbridge's arrival on the scene, and before many of these environmental restoration plans were put in place.

The entire resort is a redevelopment of a former Canadian military installation. All of the major buildings are renovated military structures (unfortunately, they have few redeeming architectural qualities) and the military nameplates remain above the doors in the headquarters building, as a reminder of its heritage. The reuse of this infrastructure alone makes Daniel's Head Village far less energy- and materials-intensive than many eco-resorts built from scratch.

Most of the guest quarters that are new structures are semipermanent, framed tent-like huts on stilts, which greatly reduces their ecological footprint. Solar power and solar hot water heaters are used in many buildings, though not to the extent originally envisioned. Some of the later nongreen compromises weren't the owner's fault, however. For example, they wanted composting toilets—which would have been perfect for a site like that, where both water and topsoil are in short supply—but inflexible, outdated Bermuda building codes forbade their installation.

DANIEL'S HEAD VILLAGE WAS FORTUNATE
TO HAVE INHERITED A CANADIAN MILITARY FACILITY

The resort was lucky that the site had been a Canadian—rather than U.S.—facility, and that it was only an electronic listening post. It's the only military base redevelopment project I've ever encountered that didn't involve brownfields remediation. On Bermuda's former British and (especially) U.S. bases, when a sergeant told a private to get rid of a barrel of water-contaminated jet fuel, rusting cans of paint thinner, or used engine oil, it would be dumped on the ground, or into a well or cave.

Witness Morgan's Point, where the U.S. military dumped thousands of gallons of oil and fuel into Bermuda's unique limestone caves. They also left behind a flood of raw sewage and tons of asbestos when they departed in 1995. In some places, like Bassett's Cave (possibly the largest in Bermuda), the oil from the old U.S. Naval Annex at Southampton forms a six-foot-thick layer on top of the underground lake.

These cave ecosystems are unique and contain wildlife communities that have yet to be studied. Dozens—possibly hundreds—of species were probably rendered extinct by the U.S. military, many before they were even named. At least 29 endemic (found nowhere else) species of cave shrimp alone have already been found. Bermuda's caves are, in fact, the only unexplored wildlife habitat in the nation, which is why conserving and restoring them is so vital.

It will cost an estimated $60 million to clean up the mess, but Pentagon officers are behaving more like vandals than gentlemen: the United States refuses to pay for cleanup, despite pleadings on Bermuda's behalf by Britain. We feebly defend this dereliction by pointing to the value of the transportation infrastructure we left behind (but we always improve roads around our bases, largely for our own military benefit). Especially galling for little Bermuda is the fact that the United States did pay for the cleanup of bases it abandoned in Canada. Bermuda wants to redevelop this former U.S. base into a leisure and housing complex, but the toxic mess adds hugely to the cost of doing so.

Daniel's Head Village was also doing a bit of heritage restoration on two quarter-century-old "fish wells." This technology consisted of stone-walled pits filled with sea water, designed to keep caught fish cool, fresh, and protected from sharks.

Daniel's Head Village thus combined five industries of restorative development: Military base redevelopment (part of the brownfields restoration industry), ecological restoration (skinks and island forest), heritage (fish wells); fishery restoration (marine park plan), and infrastructure (the military energy system was being reconstructed towards more use of solar power, and Outerbridge was investigating the use of a Living Machine-style wastewater treatment system, at my suggestion).

Visitors don't need to know about any of these restorative aspects in order to appreciate Daniel's Head Village, of course: just the ability to jump into the water and snorkel from one's front porch is enough, not to mention listening to the waves lapping at the pilings under one's room at night. If you're interested in taking advantage of this property's many inherent Restoration Economy characteristics, contact the Bermuda Department of Tourism, which is facilitating the sale of the property. What a perfect location it would be for the world's first restorative development "university" and corporate retreat.

ROYAL NAVAL DOCKYARDS:
THE BERMUDA MARITIME MUSEUM
AND THE WEST END DEVELOPMENT CORPORATION

> Preservation [heritage restoration] is now seen as being in the forefront of urban regeneration, often accomplishing what the urban renewal programs of twenty or thirty years ago so dismally failed to do.
> —James Marston Fitch, *Architectural Record*, March 1991

Just up the road from Daniel's Head Village is a massive British military complex, the Royal Naval Dockyards. On the far western tip of Bermuda, it commands an impressive view in all directions. Although many prominent local citizens were behind the idea of restoring and reusing the property, the mastermind was archaeologist Dr. Edward Harris, now the director of the Bermuda Maritime Museum, which occupies a major portion of the dockyards.

One of the most spectacular of the dockyard's restorations is that of the Commissioner's House, costing some $9,500,000. Erected in 1820, it is the oldest of the dockyard's buildings, and the astounding success of its restoration took the locals—even many of its supporters—by surprise. Most thought the Commissioner's House was beyond repair and that restoration would be a folly.

Now, it's universally prized as one of the country's greatest "new" assets. The Board Room of the Commissioner's House is Bermuda's most prestigious and memorable meeting facility. In recent years, queens, presidents, and prime ministers have gathered around its gorgeous 34-foot-long table.

The interior of the Commissioner's House has been turned into an extremely well-designed graphic museum of Bermuda's past, with each gallery corporately sponsored. The Bermuda Maritime Museum houses many restorations from across the country, such as the century-old "Dainty" racing yacht, restored at least three times during her life.

These restorations are themselves housed in eight restored structures, among the two dozen Royal Naval Dockyards' buildings and fortifications. In all, 18 of the 24 dockyards structures have been restored already. What's more, employees, researchers, and volunteers are constantly performing restoration on the premises. Restoration teams, many led by archaeologist Cliff Smith, bring back to life an astonishing array of artifacts, from cannons to entire centuries-old shipwrecks.

Thus, Bermuda's West End has restorations within restorations, and restorative projects within restorative projects. Despite its being the most geographically isolated of Bermuda's tourist attractions, the dockyards is one of its most popular and successful. Gift shops, pubs, and restaurants have sprung up within its restored walls, and hourly ferry service provides a scenic $4 boat trip to and from Hamilton, Bermuda's capital.

The Collision of Natural and Built

If Dr. David Wingate is Bermuda's restoration king of the natural environment, then Dr. Edward Harris is Bermuda's restoration king of the built environment. With almost poetic balance, their offices and main projects are diametrically opposed to each other: Nonsuch is in the extreme southeast corner of Bermuda, and Harris' office is in the extreme northwestern tip of the country. With any luck, the rest of the country will restore both built and natural environments in between.

Fortunately, the distance and diametrical opposition between Wingate and Harris is primarily geographic. David Wingate is primarily focused on ecological restoration, but he is quite holistic when it comes to the other aspects of restorative development. For instance, he fought long and hard to get the government to restore the three buildings left behind by the British military. That restoration of Nonsuch's human and architectural heritage continues to this day, closely connected to the ecological restoration. On the other hand, Wingate's primary concern is ecological restoration, so the archaeological agenda will take a backseat when there's a conflict.

Likewise, Edward Harris also loves nature. For instance, he feels zoos should exist solely for the rehabilitation of injured wildlife, and not as prisons for healthy captives. What's more, he takes great pleasure in naming the native plants as he takes visiting archaeologists on tours of the island. That said, archaeology clearly comes first, and Harris has butted heads with Wingate more than a few times as the restoration agenda for the built environment conflicted with that of the natural environment.

Harris's philosophy is that we can always grow another Bermuda cedar, but never another 300 year-old-fort. [Britain was determined to hang onto this vulnerable possession (Bermuda), and built 62 forts between 1612 and 1809, many of them intended as a defense against American invasion. By 1957, another 28 or so had been added by British, Canadian, and U.S. forces. Six have been restored so far, and several dozen are badly in need of restoration.]

As an academician and an archaeological purist, Harris will tolerate no trees or shrubs on his restored sites. He has three reasons for this seeming antinature approach. First is practicality: the fort sites need to be cleared for the archaeologists to do their initial dig and research. Second is historical accuracy: most of these sites are forts—and the garrisons would have removed all the trees to maintain a clear field of fire. Third is preservation: nothing destroys stone structures faster than roots that work their way into cracks.

Harris says he's quite happy to incorporate ecological restoration into his projects where it doesn't conflict with his mission. In fact, he caught onto this author's description of "integrated restoration" immediately and enthusiastically during our initial meeting. He's happy to have woodland areas and other ecosystems restored adjacent to historical sites, and is excited at the prospect of master-planning many forms of restoration together.

For example, Harris had already offered to allow Wingate to install artificial nests in the seaward walls of the Maritime Museum, to restore the endangered Bermuda Longtail. This location would render the nests invisible to tourists and inaccessible to predation by cats, rats, and dogs. (On the other hand, he's annoyed by the artificial Longtail nests installed in plain sight at some forts.) The Longtail (a.k.a. the White-tailed Tropicbird) lives in the air over the open ocean, returning only to Bermuda, and only to reproduce. Harris feels the museum visitors would enjoy watching them float in the air above the fort, their namesake tail plumes flowing gracefully.

Harris is also willing to entertain unusual adaptive reuses of historic sites, when the economic benefits outweigh the aesthetic clash. The old Naval Keepyard, for instance, is now a visually hidden (except for badly mismatched signage) dolphin encounter experience for tourists.

The stories of Wingate and Harris differ in other fundamental ways, as well. For instance, David Wingate is only now becoming well known outside of Bermuda, and even that is primarily within the fast-growing community of ecological restorationists. Wingate achieved most of his success at Nonsuch through decades of solitary work, with his skimpy funding requiring the help of many volunteers.

On the other hand, Harris, author of the impressive *Bermuda Forts 1612–1957* (1997), plus many research papers, has long been known worldwide (within his field of archaeology) as the inventor of the Harris Matrix. This stratigraphic analysis tool graphically represents the chronological data of digs, and is taught and practiced everywhere.

Harris has also been exceptionally successful at fundraising. With the help of the museum's trustees, Harris raised some $8,000,000 for the Commissioner's House restoration. This was no small feat on an island of fewer than 65,000 people, where heritage is nowhere near the top of most folks' priority lists.

Throughout this book, we've seen that economic revitalization often follows ecosystem restoration. We've also seen that such a revitalization is almost a sure thing in the aftermath of heritage restoration. But economic revitalization is virtually *guaranteed* when ecological restoration, brownfields remediation, infrastructure redevelopment, and heritage restoration are combined. As mentioned earlier, I searched long and hard for years—in vain—for examples of failed multifaceted restoration projects, only to be "saved" at the eleventh hour when Daniel's Head Village closed down. So far, integrated restoration seems like a near-bulletproof strategy. This is illustrated on Bermuda's west end, where the Bermuda Maritime Museum's development is intergrated with commercial development.

West End Development Corporation

An example of (somewhat) integrated restoration is taking place in the parts of the Royal Dockyards not occupied by the Bermuda Maritime

Museum. A for-profit company, the West End Development Corporation (WEDco) shares a restorative development agenda with a not-for-profit entity, the Bermuda Maritime Museum.

The vast, spectacularly scenic Royal Naval Dockyards would have easily qualified as a UNESCO World Heritage site, but WEDco's master plan required more flexibility in adaptively reusing the ancient buildings than UNESCO would probably have allowed. WEDco must tread that delicate line between conserving the architectural and cultural heritage of the site, and making it economically viable. As such, its plan includes virtually every form of use: single-family residences, multifamily residences, hotels, restaurants, museums, offices, marinas, cruise ship terminals, and parks. Two of those parks will be built on old military dumps and will possibly include a new aquarium.

I met with Lloyd Telford, WEDco's General Manager, in the company's Clock Tower Building offices. This breathtakingly cavernous structure is an adaptive reuse of a military warehouse. Solid stone on the outside, with huge Bermuda cedar beams on the inside, WEDco's second-floor space exudes an expansive, daylit charm. The first floor has become a mall of gift shops (hit hard by the post–9/11 downturn in U.S. visitors). Sitting by the wharf, the Clock Tower Building makes a picturesque welcome to arriving ferry passengers.

Lloyd Telford has been working closely with Edward Harris, and says they are usually able to arrive at mutually beneficial solutions concerning the balancing of commercial and archaeological agendas. Such harmonious resolution of conflicting constraints will hopefully become the norm as Bermuda maps out the restoration of its built environment, its natural environment, and its economy.

St. George

The 400-year-old town of St. George (Bermuda's original capital) is the oldest English-speaking community in the world, outside of Great Britain. On November 30, 2000, it became a UNESCO World Heritage Site. The coveted World Heritage Site designation resulted from years of hard work by the St. George's Foundation, with much help from the Bermuda National Trust, the Corporation of St. George, Bermuda's Parks Department and Department of Planning, and the Bermuda Maritime Museum.

The UNESCO designation has put a plan behind a spontaneous community restoration that had already begun. One example is Tabernius House, a mixed-use adaptive reuse of the historic Store Keeper's Cottage.

(On the fence around the construction site is a sign proclaiming it "A tasteful and sympathetic restoration of this historic waterfront property to luxurious condominium homes and office suites.") It's ideally located on the waterfront in the center of St. George, adjacent to the *Deliverance*. This ship was built of Bermuda cedar by British sailors in 1609 and 1610 after they were shipwrecked on their way to Jamestown, Virginia (the display is a 1968 reconstruction).

These words are being written from the tranquility of Aunt Nea's Inn (www.auntneas.com). Built in the 1700s, it's one of the few accommodations in the heart of St. George, and was once the residence of a U.S. consul. Starting in 1997, it was restored at a cost of over half a million dollars by the Robinson family, which has owned it since the early 1900s. With twelve lovely rooms plus beautiful gardens, it's now the most successful B&B in St. George. Maybe of more importance to Bermuda's restored future, Delaey Robinson, owner of Aunt Nea's, is a member of Parliament (MP).

BERMUDA'S RESTORED FUTURE?

Most people view Bermuda as a quiet place to play golf in the middle of the ocean, but other than SCUBA divers, few think of it in terms of wildlife. Bermuda has thus missed the boom in nature-based (and heritage) tourism. The country's population density (over five people per acre) contributes to the problem, along with the amount of land devoted to golf courses (fast closing in on 10 percent of the entire country). There is a potential upside, though: if the golf craze ends some day, those golf courses might be the only large tracts available for the country to restore some wildlife refuges and publicly accessible green space.

MP Robinson's potential key role in the government's ability to reposition itself in the Restoration Economy goes beyond his business skills, and even beyond his experience with historical restoration and adaptive reuse of buildings. As a doctoral student at the University of Guelph in Canada, Robinson's thesis was on the endangered Bermuda skink, and his research still contributes to skink restoration efforts. He worked closely with Wingate, who considered him a star student (and who was sorry to see science lose him to business and politics).

As a result of this background, Delaey (pronounced deLOY) Robinson qualifies as one of the few politicians this author has met who is literate in ecological restoration, heritage restoration, science, and business. He seems a reluctant, idealistic, noncareer politician though (the best kind, according to Thomas Jefferson)—thrust into the position when St. George's incumbent suddenly died—so I hope Bermuda appreciates his unique expertise while it has him in parliament.

But Bermuda isn't limited to ecosystem and heritage restoration. Despite the afore-mentioned irresponsible U.S. behavior, Bermuda boasts some success in the brownfields/military base restoration industry, as well. The country has remediated and redeveloped a defunct U.S. military base into a hurricane-proof business complex/tax-haven, largely devoted to Internet-based businesses.

Bermuda made a very smart move decades ago when it restricted rental vehicles to 50cc scooters (unfortunately, it forgot to ban 2-strokes, so the island is bathed in a shrill whine and blue smoke) and limited cars to one per resident family. Bermuda might be the most motorcycle-friendly country in the world, with free parking everywhere for two-wheelers, and only two-wheeled vehicles allowed on its ferries.

Bermuda does have a few restorative development challenges not faced by other countries. For instance, the tax-free status that attracts so many firms to Bermuda also robs the country of a valuable tool for guiding development: tax deductions and rebates. As a result, government is pretty much limited to handing out grants, a riskier and more labor-intensive undertaking.

Bermuda also has some distinct restorative development advantages, such as extreme isolation from other land masses. This makes it, at least in theory, far more able to sustain an ecological restoration of the entire country. Getting rid of all invasive species on its shores would be a monumental task, but keeping them off should be far easier for it than for most other countries.

Due to Bermuda's lack of coordinated planning, there are occasional missteps, where one form of restoration reduces the value of another. An example was the adaptive reuse of an old military parking lot as a noisy race track, directly across a narrow strait from peaceful Nonsuch.

Years ago, Bermuda also took the politically brave step of banning fish traps, a cruel and wasteful technology that had devastated local fisheries (they have been rebounding ever since). The new government (the first in about three decades) recently passed progressive legislation protecting one of the country's other submerged assets, its more than 400 shipwrecks. This legislation will make the wrecks available for future restoration, while continuing their present contribution to the nation's economy (they are the primary reason most snorkelers and SCUBA divers come to Bermuda).

CLOSING THOUGHTS

With its plethora of restorative activities (unplanned and uncoordinated as they are), and its convenient location, less than two hours from most east coast U.S. airports—and only 3 to 4 hours from Europe—Bermuda is well positioned to catch the rising tide of the Restoration Economy. Given the country's grassroots momentum in so many forms of restoration, its best next step, should it make a conscious commitment to restorative development as a national strategy, might be to establish the world's first federal Department of Restorative Development. Such a ministry would probably need to be led by a master facilitator, someone whose primary skills are in strategy, communication, conflict resolution, monitoring, and integration.

My choice of Bermuda as a discussion subject for this book was quite arbitrary, mostly an accident of timing. If I hadn't been there (investigating Nonsuch) just prior to finishing this book, I wouldn't have discovered the country's many other forms of restorative development. Other countries could have served just as well. Costa Rica would certainly have qualified; its projects have appeared throughout this book. In fact, dozens of nations or communities around the globe would have made excellent case studies, from St. Lucia and New Zealand to Havana, Singapore, and Louisville.

Conclusion

The extent of human-induced change and damage to Earth's ecosystems renders ecosystem repair an essential part of our future survival strategy, and this demands that restoration ecology provide effective conceptual and practical tools for this task. . . . If restoration ecology is to be successfully practiced as part of humanity's response to continued ecosystem change and degradation, restoration ecologists need to rise to the challenges of meshing science, practice and policy. Restoration ecology is likely to be one of the most important fields of the coming century.
—**R. J. Hobbs** and **J. A. Harris,** "Restoration Ecology: Repairing the Earth's Ecosystems in the New Millennium," *Restoration Ecology,* June 2001

Latter-day new development has been typified by activities that tend to diminish the *quality* of life, in order to make way for some new asset that's driven only by the *quantity* of human life. We destroy what we love to make room for what we think we need, only to find out later we could have had both in one package, at far less cost. Converting an attractive old warehouse into an apartment building serves the needs of a growing population, but it uses many existing resources (and thus far fewer new resources), not to mention zero additional real estate, so it's considered restorative development.

Of course, the quantity and type of restorative development varies from nation to nation, and from area to area, according to geography: newer coastal cities, for example, may have less heritage or infrastructure restoration on the agenda, but far more rebuilding efforts due to natural disasters like hurricanes.

In almost every successful case of urban revitalization, a focus on restoring green space has been a key ingredient. These projects are often based on historically significant sites, such as the private woodlands of industrial barons, and battlefields. Most battles were fought on farmland, meadows, or other open spaces offering a clear field of fire. Thus, battle-field restoration also helps battle a negative side effect of our recent decades' passion for reforestation: the loss of grassland ecosystems.

At Gettysburg National Military Park, for example, the National Park Service is restoring the battlefield's original open spaces, and doing so in such as way as to provide better habitat for native grassland wildlife species. Its restoration team has wisely collaborated with the U.S. Fish and Wildlife Service, the National Audubon Society, The Nature Conservancy, Pennsylvania's Game Commission, and researchers from Penn State University.

In a very large percentage of urban resurrection stories, the restoration of a waterfront has been the heart of the success. Throughout the industrial revolution, river, Great Lake, and bay frontage tended to be industrial zones, with the best neighborhoods as far away as possible. But people like to be around bodies of water, so cleaning up these frontages (often a brownfields project) and making them publicly accessible as parks, boardwalks, and shopping arcades is an element common to many successful downtown revitalizations. This key asset is available to many city planners, because we have traditionally built our cities near bodies of water.

Bottom line: bringing life back to the built environment often requires revitalizing the natural environment.

BUILT AND NATURAL ARE OFTEN HARD TO SEPARATE

Restoring our built heritage isn't always a matter of renewing bricks, mortar, paint, and pipes. Sometimes it involves restoring ambience and context, and that's often in the form of nature.

Like most tourists who have visited Stonehenge—England's most important archaeological treasure—in recent decades, I was appalled at the manner in which the British government had ruined the site. It built roads very close by (just a few yards at some points . . . I'm talking single digits!) on two sides, one of them the A303, a major highway and truck route. What should have been a contemplative, if not outright mystical, experience was turned into an irritating one. Annoyance at government "planners" competed strongly with the site's wonder for one's attention.

Good news, though: Even though Britain is still on an austerity budget, in 2001 it committed $225 million to "restore silence and solemnity" to this endlessly fascinating 5,000-year-old artifact. Doing so will involve restoring and rebuilding everything on and around the site, but the monoliths themselves will remain untouched.

The money will be spent burying a 1.25 mile stretch of the A303; removing the access road entirely and restoring its path with native grass; and moving the parking lot with associated buildings a full two miles away, thus necessitating an underground tram system. One of the challenges developers will face—because this tunnel will be a form of new development—is that the area surrounding Stonehenge is likely to contain many important burial sites and other ruins, which tunnel construction could disturb or destroy.

THE RESTORATION OF OUR NATURAL AND BUILT ENVIRONMENTS HAS BECOME THE GREATEST BUSINESS FRONTIER OF THE TWENTY-FIRST CENTURY

That headline might sound like a utopian dream, but it's a trillion-dollar-plus reality. Ours is the first *global* Restoration Economy. As common as the three crises of Constraint, Corrosion, and Contamination have been throughout history (on the local and national scales), this is the first time that any of them has been global, and the first time all three have occurred both globally and simultaneously.

It's only recently that we've reached the point where

- most of our cities have reached the limits of their expansion
- most of our built environment is not just aged, but in need of restoration
- most of our land is at least mildly contaminated, and much is heavily poisoned

Consider that the industrial revolution, itself a previously unseen phenomenon, accelerated (not just grew) continuously for a quarter of a millennium.

Consider that there are people alive today who grew up in a world with "only" 2 billion people (one-third of today's population).

Consider that all of these first-time-ever dynamics are being electronically connected in real time.

Considering all of this, it should come as no surprise that we are in uncharted waters. Every generation likes to think of itself as living during a crossroads in history—and every generation really *is* at a crossroads of some sort—but this is a Big One, folks.

Our Integrative Future

> We present the challenge to restoration practitioners and scientists alike to
> get our act together and devise and deliver effective restoration strategies
> and practices which can help repair the widespread ecological damage left
> to us from the last millennium. We need effective interaction between
> scientific analysis, land-user innovation and the development of principles.
> We need effective links between academics, practitioners and policy makers
> at all levels. We need the translation of research findings into action, and
> continuous feedback between users and researchers. We need to make sure
> that our actions are based on the best knowledge available now, and that
> our managers have up-to-date paradigms in their heads when they act. At
> the same time, we need to ensure that researchers ask questions that are
> relevant to the real world. It has been argued that this could form part of an
> on-going professional accreditation program.
> —R. J. Hobbs and J. A. Harris, "Restoration Ecology: Repairing the Earth's Ecosystems
> in the New Millennium," *Restoration Ecology,* June 2001

In April 2002, USEPA Administrator Christine Todd Whitman announced
a Bush administration initiative to clean up and restore the Great Lakes.
Over 30 million people get their drinking water from the Great Lakes, and
over 600 beaches front them on the U.S. side alone, making their recreational value not just significant, but vital to many local economies. As
with the European Community's multinational Danube River restoration,
the U.S. government is catching on to large-scale, integrated, international
restoration projects. Among the goals Whitman announced:

- reducing the introduction of additional invasive species
- reducing the levels of PCBs in walleye and lake trout by a quarter
  by 2007
- restoring 100,000 wetland acres by 2010
- accelerating the cleanup of contaminated sediment and complet-
  ing all brownfields remediation (including Great Lakes Superfund
  sites) by 2025

A partnership of federal, state, and tribal agencies—the Great Lakes
U.S. Policy Committee—actually wrote the plan. As such, it stands a
good chance of bringing a greater level of integration and synergy to the
multitude of current restoration projects. Among other integrative measures, the plan instructs federal agencies to work more closely with local
and state agencies. Canadian initiatives will also be crucial.

The good news is that many municipal and county-level Great Lakes
restoration initiatives are already integrative, because their goals usually
revolve around community revitalization. More good news: these current

projects include all eight restorative industries: ecosystem, fisheries, watershed, agricultural, brownfield, infrastructure, heritage, and disaster-related (primarily spills). Significant progress has already been made towards restoring what was once the most economically valuable fresh-water system on the planet.

The bad news is that increased synergies are all the agencies will have to rely on, because the Bush plan, despite its ambitious language, failed to budget a single new dollar to the effort. But don't underestimate the value of synergetic connections. Unlike new development, where each new unit often detracts from the value of existing units, as typified by gluts of office space, each restoration initiative tends to increase the value of other restorative projects in the area.

Witness historic downtown areas, which require a certain percentage of restored buildings to reach the "critical mass" needed to achieve des-tination status. Likewise with restored ecosystems: linking many of them can produce exponential increases in wildlife, and can also turn an area into a tourist destination. Despite the Bush administration's failure to throw any new money at the Great Lakes restoration (such a refusal to fund a restoration project is actually quite unusual), its commitment to better coordinate the billions of dollars of restorative efforts already underway is likely to spawn tremendous investment and business opportunities.

Many of the best growth opportunities will not be found within each restorative industry, but in the interstitial spaces among them. The leaders of the Restoration Economy will be the connective tissue that pulls "peripheral" restoration industries into each project. Several such integra-tive firms are already emerging—many of them already quite profitable—but they represent only a tiny handful of the "integrated restoration" com-panies that will soon exist.

STRATEGIC INTEGRATION GUIDE

If you are a corporate, NGO, or community leader planning a project—or a student planning a career—here are some suggestions on "mixing and matching" the eight restorative industries. This is only a general guide to predesign: Each project has its own unique agenda and characteristics.

The following matrix indicates the types of restorative projects that work best when integrated and performed *simultaneously.* (Note: Disaster/war is a wild card that can skew priorities swiftly and dramatically.)

(continued)

STRATEGIC INTEGRATION GUIDE *(continued)*

Core Project	Adjunct Restoration Projects
	(1 = Maximum potential synergy)
Ecosystem	1: Agricultural 2: Watershed 3: Brownfield 4: Infrastructure
Watershed	1: Fishery 2: Infrastructure 3: Farm 4: Ecosystem 5: Brownfield
Fishery	1: Watershed 2: Farm 3: Ecosystem 4: Infrastructure 5: Brownfield
Farm	1: Watershed 2: Ecosystem 3: Infrastructure 4: Heritage
Brownfield	1: Ecosystem 2: Watershed 3: Heritage 4: Infrastructure 5: Farm
Infrastructure	1: Watershed 2: Fishery 3: Farm 4: Ecosystem 5: Heritage
Heritage	1: Infrastructure 2: Brownfield 3: Farm 4: Ecosystem
Disaster/War	All, with priorities determined by the nature of the destruction

The following matrix indicates the types of restorative projects—and nonrestorative developments—that are often the most profitable or effective *sequels* to completed projects. (Note: Integration doesn't always need to take place "on the ground": Integration of marketing, fundraising, and postrestoration management all can achieve substantial results, even if the actual restoration projects are done in isolation from each other.)

Initial Project	Sets the Stage for
	(not in order of relevance)
Ecosystem	* Fishery restoration * Tourism * Housing * Office complexes
Watershed	* Ecosystem/Farm restoration * Tourism * Housing * Recreational industries
Fishery	* Ecosystem restoration (such as rivers and lakes used by migratory species)
Farm	* Fishery/Watershed/Ecosystem restoration * Rural community revitalization
Brownfield	* Fishery/Watershed/Ecosystem restoration * Residential/Commercial/Industrial redevelopment * Community revitalization
Infrastructure	* Watershed/Fishery/Farm/Heritage restoration * Community revitalization * Tourism
Heritage	* Infrastructure/Ecosystem restoration * Tourism * Community revitalization
Disaster/War	* All

Integrated restoration will be the next big thing. Each industry of restorative development has emerged independently of—and often oblivious to—the other restorative industries. At the time of this writing, I've not encountered any sense of community or shared purpose among, for instance, the restorers of brownfields, the restorers of cathedrals, and the restorers of fisheries. I hope one of the small contributions of this book will be to foster the emergence of such a community, or at least a multidisciplinary professional network.

One way an integrated restoration community could develop would be if those who sponsor conferences and/or trade shows related to the various restoration industries would work with each other to colocate. Properly coordinated, this should not only provide for wonderful inter-disciplinary networking and sharing of expertise, but should also produce some fringe benefits like cheaper hotel rooms and meeting space, thanks to combined bargaining power.

Imagine being at the first combined event, maybe bringing together the Restoration and Renovation show (commercial and residential buildings), one of the annual brownfields conferences, the American Fisheries Society, several of the hundreds of regional watershed and river restoration NGOs, the Society for Ecological Restoration, the National Trust for Historic Preservation, inner-city revitalization commissions, the Land Trust Alliance, the American (and the Royal) Society of Civil Engineers . . . well, you get the idea.

This list of potential professional and scientific societies, trade associations, NGOs, government agencies, international development banks and agencies, and commercial trade shows related to restoration numbers in the thousands. Universities could also play a key integrating role in the shared programs.

INVESTMENT OPPORTUNITIES

As illustrated earlier, new development-based economies, when excessively extended, destroy their past and depauperize their future in an increasingly frantic and futile pursuit of health, wealth, and security. There are at least two inherent ironies in our current situation: (1) restoring our "depauperized" future can be tremendously profitable, both for practitioners and investors; and (2) new development was supposed to be all about "progress" and "creating the future," but in its latter days, our New Development Economy mostly stole from the future, in a desperate attempt to hold a deteriorating present together.

No matter what political or economic changes occur, restorative development will continue to mushroom, and the necessary funds will (usually) appear. Public funding is subject to the usual ups and downs, of course, but the ebb and flow of support from Capitol Hill is far less vicious than that for new development and maintenance, because restoration is far more politically saleable. As with smart codes and the spawning of the brownfields restoration industry, sometimes it only takes minimal (well-directed) public efforts and funding to catalyze vast amounts of private investment in restoration.

At this early stage, though, it's investors who are likely to be among the biggest near-term beneficiaries of restorative development's growth. New technologies, new companies, and new projects all require financing, and precious few institutions have developed their expertise in this new investment frontier. Here's a quick review of three general categories of opportunities that pervaded these pages:

- **Restorative real estate investment** This is akin to the old fixer-upper scenario, but with more focus on intrinsic value and true restoration. It could be as "normal" as restoring a house with an interesting history. Or it could be more adventurous, such as buying degraded farmland, mildly polluted industrial property, or a clear-cut forest with ugly erosion scars that happens to be in a great location (a gorgeous tropical island?), and restoring it to health. Such investments could be the pinnacle of buy-low-sell-high, and the lifestyle enhancement, fringe, and tax benefits can be tremendous. Restorative land development is accessible to both private individuals and large corporations. One wealthy couple is restoring the oyster beds—which also brings back crabs and fish—offshore from their waterfront Chesapeake Bay home. Dee Hock, creator of the Visa credit card network, bought a tract of devastated land and restored it as a restorative therapy for himself, as he wound down from a high-stress business career. With experienced ecological restoration professionals guiding you—and an ability to trade time for capital—real estate restoration can be amazingly enjoyable, satisfying, and cost-effective.

- **Restorative mutual funds, REITs (real estate investment trusts), etc.** This is both a business opportunity for those owning the funds, and an investment opportunity for those who buy their shares. Many folks simply want to enrich their portfolio with investments that tap restorative development's energy, but they don't have the time or desire to research or get involved with specific projects. Restorative funds have already begun to emerge, and some are quite exotic, such as those dealing with water rights, wind farms, etc. (Note: The only business Enron owned that had significant real, physical assets—and real, bottom-line profits— was its wind energy business. Remember too that wind farms are increasingly being built on polluted land and former military bases, returning the land to economic productivity long before it has had time to heal ecologically. . . .)

• **Public infrastructure opportunities** Restoring public infrastructure can be expensive, and, as pointed out earlier, there's over a trillion-dollar backlog of this work in the United States alone. Innovative solutions are beginning to emerge, such as New York City's 2002 announcement that it was thinking of selling the Brooklyn Bridge (and others). The idea is that a company would purchase and restore the bridge, and then charge tolls to recoup its investment. This is similar to the design-build-operate model that has worked well in recent years for the building of *new* toll roads, water treatment facilities, etc. The emerging paradigms of the commercial and infrastructure construction industries will be design-restore (as opposed to design-build), design-restore-operate, etc.

We do not realize, I believe, what a portentous watershed in human history we are now treading. Civilization is a product of the increase in human control over environment. As our knowledge not only of nature but of man and society expands, we may get to the point where man comes not to be ruled by history but to rule it. He may be able to mold the unconscious dynamic which drives him to destroy his civilizations into a conscious dynamic which will empower him to perpetuate them indefinitely.
—**Kenneth E. Boulding,** economist, *Harvard Business Review*, May–June 1952

RESTORATIVE POLITICIANS

Without extensive restoration, this planet will be physically incapable of returning to a predominance of new development for many, many millennia (barring global cataclysm). Those political and industry leaders who still see new development as the sole path to progress need to either retire, or adapt to the new reality. Not doing so will doom their constituents or companies to following new development into decline.

This is mostly a business book, so I've tried to avoid excessive focus on politics. Restorative public leaders have been pointed out when appropriate, such as the current and previous mayors of Lisbon, Portugal, and Mayor Richard M. Daley in Chicago. Business and government restoring together is good for the economy, good for culture, and good for the environment: it's a still-rare but powerful thing.

Governmental support for small, emerging industries is often a double-edged sword: The young industry becomes too dependent on incentives and/or direct funding, and thus is vulnerable to shifting political winds. The U.S. solar industry is a perfect example: Jimmy Carter gave it a good kick in the pants and it took off like a rocket. Ronald Reagan and George H. W. Bush shot that rocket out of the sky, putting the United States way behind other countries in this crucial technology.

Fortunately, restorative development, although still emerging, certainly isn't small. Although most of the eight restorative industries receive large amounts of public funding, none except public infrastructure is totally dependent on it, and even that industry is becoming much more privatized. Politicians who protect distressed new-development industries could theoretically impede the Restoration Economy's progress, but this seldom seems to happen. There's no shortage of politicos who oppose conservation—and even sustainable development—but all seem to love restorative development.

Brownfields redevelopment is a rare example of a truly successful federal program. It might even be considered a "grassroots" government program, because it bubbled up from managers within the USEPA, rather than being mandated by legislation. They have been acting as facilitators for the many innovative state and municipal programs, and have provided a forum for sharing best practices.

Even regulators are partners in this process, something you almost never see in either new development or maintenance/conservation projects. This is a vital difference from the usual green initiative: brownfields redevelopers *usually* partner with the government, creating political pressure on regulators to expedite projects. The only way these officials can do their job properly under such time pressure is to get involved in the project at the earliest possible point, which means during the initial planning process. This is government at its best.

Christine Todd Whitman

Many Clinton-era conservation and sustainability initiatives were gutted by the George W. Bush administration, but the EPA's support of the brownfields program has continued unabated, because it was inherited by a true believer. Former EPA Administrator Carol Browner was at the helm when the brownfields initiative was created. She passed the reins to Christine Todd Whitman, who, as New Jersey's governor, was perhaps the brownfields redevelopment champion among U.S. state governors (despite her dismantling of many hard-won environmental legislative protections).

Via smart codes, Whitman pioneered innovative approaches to the adaptive reuse of old and/or historic buildings to revitalize blighted New Jersey cities. She was also active in river and coastal ecosystem restoration, and fisheries restoration. Her strongest competition for the title of "most restorative governor" might have been Maryland's Parris Glendening (for reasons documented in Chapters 7 and 11).

In the U.S. Congress, there are several examples of restorative legislators, but here I'll just choose the two (one from each party) who seem to be the leaders. Let's look at the Democratic example first: Senator Daniel Patrick Moynihan of New York.

Remember the discussion in Chapter 11, about the cities that demolished their heritage during the urban renewal craze of the '60s and '70s? Although most of the cities that survived that period with their heritage intact were those that were too poor to afford "renewal" at the time, not all were saved by serendipitous economic depression. Occasionally, farsighted leadership won out, but it was usually based on individual champions, not general enlightenment.

Daniel Patrick Moynihan

Washington, D.C., provides a perfect example. John F. Kennedy hired a celebrated architect, Nathaniel Owings, to plan the rebuilding of Pennsylvania Avenue. This is the central artery connecting the Capitol Building to the White House. In typical '60s fashion, Owings planned the demolition of a huge swath of the city's most beautiful buildings, including the Willard Hotel and the Washington Hotel, the National Press Club building, the Old Post Office (now a luxury hotel and shopping mall), the Old Patent Office (now Smithsonian museums), and more.

The man who almost single-handedly killed the plan, saved these buildings, and called for their restoration was Senator Daniel Patrick Moynihan. Fortunately, his commitment to restoring the city superceded political affiliations, and this Democrat went on to become Richard Nixon's urban affairs advisor. This post enabled Moynihan to provide critically important continuity, and the plan that finally emerged in 1972 followed his recommendations to a large degree.

Moynihan's vision was humane and, for its time, exceptionally urbane. "Care should be taken," he admonished, "not to line the north side with a solid phalanx of public and private office buildings which will close down completely at night and on weekends. . . . Pennsylvania Avenue should be lively, friendly, and inviting, as well as dignified and impressive." More than any other American politician of the second half of the 20th century, Moynihan has engaged the issues of architecture, urban design and infrastructure.

—**Benjamin Forgey,** "Moynihan's Legacy Is Written in Stone,"
Washington Post, October 7, 2000

The one building from Owings' original plan that did get built—the sterile, somewhat disturbing eyesore called the J. Edgar Hoover FBI Building—stands as evidence of how ugly Washington might be today were it not for Moynihan. His influence didn't end there, either: the fabulously restored Union Station is also one of "his" projects, as is the largest new building—the Ronald Reagan Building and International Trade Center—which is modern, beautiful, and architecturally appropriate.

Nor was his restorative hand at work only in D.C. In New York City, many restorations and redevelopments owe their existence to Moynihan, including Penn Station and the Alexander Hamilton U.S. Customs House in Battery Park. In 2001, the Urban Land Institute awarded him its second annual ULI/C. Nichols Prize for Visionary Urban Development.

Lincoln D. Chafee

Our Republican champion of restoration in the Senate is Lincoln D. Chafee from Rhode Island. The ranking Republican on the Superfund, Waste Control, and Risk Assessment subcommittee, Senator Chafee has amassed an impressive record of restorative leadership in the past decade:

- He sponsored the 2002 Brownfields Revitalization and Environmental Restoration Act.
- He sponsored The Estuary Restoration Act of 2000.
- He was executive director of the Northeast Corridor Initiative (now expanded to the National Corridor Initiative) which works to revitalize America's rail service.
- He was mayor of Warwick, Rhode Island, where he championed the revitalization of Greenwich Bay. Heavily contaminated with sewage when he became mayor in 1992, it's now one of the best places in the state for shellfishing.

Lest conservationists worry that the good senator is single-minded about restoration, it should be noted that Lincoln Chafee was one of the few Republicans brave enough to oppose oil drilling in the Arctic National Wildlife Refuge.

There are, no doubt, many other U.S. politicians who should have been mentioned here, such as California's Gov. Gray Davis, who recently signed an executive order requiring government agencies to reuse old buildings, or–if that's not possible–to reuse inner city land (which would often involve brownfields remediation). There's an even larger number of restorative politicians from other countries who have been ignored here. To them, I apologize. Suffice it to say that restorative development is a passion that is crossing all political boundaries. Keep an eye out for restorative candidates in your city, county, state, province, and country: they represent our restored future.

What To Do with This Knowledge

At the very least, I hope this book will get the subject of restorative development on the agenda of your next strategic planning or brainstorming session. Reading it should, I hope, give you a starting point for realigning your organization's mission with the threats and opportunities of this "backswing" of the economic pendulum.

"Backswing" sounds regressive, but everything in the universe runs in cycles. A grandfather clock stops running when its owner decides that only one swing of the pendulum is "good," and manually forces it in that one direction. Likewise, those organizations that continue straining towards new development will founder when they refuse to evolve— culturally, structurally, and strategically—in harmony with this natural, inevitable transition to restoring our world.

The United Nations currently predicts that the world population will eventually stabilize at between 10 and 11 billion by 2150. Based on trends "down here" at 6 billion, that's likely to be one ugly state of stability: Global ecosystems already can't service us adequately. Again, widespread restoration offers the *only* light on the horizon, unless a deadly pandemic of biblical proportions "rescues" us first. The United Nations does have a more optimistic alternative scenario: It shows world population declining to 3.6 billion by 2150. But even under that projection, world population will first double in the next 40 to 50 years, which is the only time period that matters for today's leaders and investors.

Even if the happiest of those predictions manifests, we still have to get from here to there with enough species remaining on the planet for it to function, and with our ecosystems strong enough to provide something approaching a "quality" of life. Absent wide-scale restorative development, things will get much, much worse before they (maybe) get better. Continuation of an economy based heavily on new development would guarantee that the path to 2150 would be the same resource-poor nightmare for "First Worlders" that it already is for many "Second and Third Worlders."

A FEW PARTING THOUGHTS

> What the American public always wants is a tragedy with a happy ending.
> —**William Dean Howells** (comment to Edith Wharton
> upon the failure of her play *House of Mirth*)

You've probably discovered in this book a lot of "trees" you never before heard of—or never noticed—but I hope your main takeaway from this book is a new perception of the "forest" they create.

Despite all my jumping up and down about "the Restoration Economy," we should remember that economies and societies are sloppy, complex, endlessly surprising organisms. Restorative development will no doubt be the overarching theme of the twenty-first century, but it certainly won't explain everything we do. Nor will it instantly end our lingering attachment to new development.

What we need more than anything else at this point is dialogue and contemplation, and to avoid charging ahead as if we already know what we're doing. Restorative development is complex because it's huge and diverse, but also because it involves human societies and economies, natural ecosystems, and a network of built systems (industrial, residential, commercial, infrastructure, etc.), each of which is, or is part of, a complex system.

Maybe I've overreached in my enthusiasm to wake readers to the work of the world's restorers. My definition of "restorative development" might be too broad for practicality, but my assumption was that the more people who are involved in this dialogue, the better. I hope that more capable researchers, practitioners, and writers will pick up the ball and run with it, taking it in more accurate and productive directions.

Simply dividing development activity into the three modes of new development, maintenance/conservation, and restorative development greatly increases our ability to have clear, practical dialogue about our past, present, and future. With luck, someone may build a useful economic model around this trimodal perspective. A sufficiently rigorous model might even develop into every economist's fantasy: a tool with at least a little predictive value.

Of course, there's nothing new about viewing economies from a closed-loop, life cycle perspective. The Scandinavians have led the world in life cycle economic planning for some time now—thanks to the pioneering work of Dr. Karl-Henrik Robèrt and his Natural Step program—and Paul Hawken has been that concept's primary champion in the United States. The trimodal development perspective is so obvious that I'll be amazed if readers don't flood me with reports of similar ideas published earlier, which somehow eluded my research.

Please Join Me in Better Documenting the Restoration Economy, Especially Its Best Practices and "Leading Lights"

> As the (restoration ecology) profession develops, it is inevitable that the issues associated with professional standards—ethical standards, quality definition, and control, acceptable and unacceptable practices, and the like—will become the topics for vigorous debate.
> —**Michael J. Clark,** "Ecological Restoration—The Magnitude of the Challenge: An Outsider's View," *Restoration Ecology and Sustainable Development,* K. M. Urbanska, Nigel R. Webb, and Peter J. Edwards, eds., 1998

For every organization and project mentioned in these pages, I was forced to ignore dozens for lack of space, and I'm probably altogether ignorant of far more. I became familiar with many of the nonprofit and community projects featured in these pages while setting up Restorica (www.restorica.org), a small charitable organization that's still forming. Restorica, Inc.'s mission is to better integrate the eight industries of restorative development via research, multidisciplinary networking, and community-based model projects.

The Restoration Economy focuses primarily on big-picture issues—concepts, technologies, and illustrative projects—rather than the companies, nonprofits, and people behind them. The business, investment, academic, and government leaders of restorative development will be profiled in a future book dedicated to success stories.

I'm collecting material for that work now, and would appreciate hearing from readers who know of exemplary research, firms, institutions, individuals, or restorative projects. You can contact me at storm@restorability.com. If you know of a deserving community or not-for-profit project that needs assistance connecting with resources of any kind (human, knowledge, monetary, material, etc.), please submit the request at www.restorica.org, or email me at storm@restorica.org. If your organization or community has a successful project you'd like me to publicize through my talks, I'm always looking for dramatic before-and-after photos.

Personal Restoration

I hope I've also motivated you to get involved in some form of restoration, if not professionally, then as a volunteer. Why? Because personal exposure to restoration has remarkable power to change our worldview, often in a way that puts new development into a dramatically new perspective (seldom a flattering one).

What's more, the act of restoration can be profoundly restorative on a personal basis. Wildlife rescue workers at oil spills often cite their days or weeks of cleaning beaches and de-oiling seabirds and otters as life-changing. They frequently extend a volunteered weekend into a month of leave from their jobs without pay. Many pray for the day when oil industry executives will be sentenced by the courts to partake hands-on in these efforts, the way vandals are often sentenced to removing graffiti. Nothing, they say, would more expeditiously end many of the socially and ecologically pathogenic practices of the increasingly dysfunctional realm of new development.

T. S. Eliot once said in *Tradition and the Individual Talent* (1922), "What happens when a new work of art is created is something that happens simultaneously to all works of art which preceded it. . . . For order to persist after the supervention of novelty, the *whole* existing order must be, if ever so slightly, altered; and so the relations, proportions, value of each work of art toward the whole are readjusted." So it is with the shift to a Restoration Economy: When we marvel at the results of a restorative development project, we simultaneously lose some of our previous infatuation with the wonders of new development. New development's destructive, wasteful, and/or toxic side effects—so easy to overlook when new development is the only game in town—suddenly appear shabby, even criminal, when viewed from a restorative development worldview.

There is always a place for *some* new development in any economy, but the growth of restorative development always comes at the expense of new development's slice of the pie. New development isn't going away. Remember that term "Restoration Economy" only refers to the dominant mode: the economic phase we're entering is putting significant power to all three development "wheels," but restorative development will be grabbing by far the most traction.

For the past three decades, progress has been impeded by the pervasive fallacy that a decline in new development equates to economic recession in general. We've believed the choice to be two-sided: the unsustainable path of new development vs. the sustainable—but less economically vigorous—path of maintenance/conservation.

Now, we're discovering that there's a third option, restorative development, which combines the economic power of new development with the sustainability of maintenance/conservation. Therein lies the twenty-first century's most extensive new universe of business and investment opportunities.

The past few decades also have been typified by a wealth of innovation in tools, along with a dearth of vision as to how to best put them to use. Restorative development is the vision we've been missing, the one that can make full and responsible use of the many technologies, such as genetic engineering, that have simultaneously been wooing and threatening us.

> [The $8 billion Comprehensive Everglades Restoration Plan] is the largest environmental project in American history. The plan is already the national model for future restorations, from a $15 billion proposal for Louisiana coastal wetlands to a $20 billion plan for California rivers and deltas. It is becoming the restoration blueprint for the world, studied in south Brazil's Pantanal and sub-Saharan Africa's Okavango Delta. And at a moment when partisanship reigned, the plan was an example of rare political unity in Florida and Washington. "We're here to talk about something that is going to be long-lasting, way past counting votes," Jeb Bush said [on December 11, 2000]. "This is the restoration of a treasure for our country."
>   But it's not remotely clear whether the Everglades restoration plan will actually restore the Everglades.
>   —**Michael Grunwald,** "The Swamp: Can $8 Billion Restore the Everglades?"
>   *Washington Post,* June 23, 2002

As witnessed by the above quote from Michael Grunwald's in-depth, four-part *Washington Post* series on the Everglades restoration, the dollars flowing into the Restoration Economy are vast, but so is the learning curve. The worst thing that can happen—and what *is* happening to a large extent in the Everglades—is for the people who created the need for restoration in the first place to be put in charge of the restoration, without first undergoing a thorough restoration of their own organizations, their component disciplines, their mindsets, and their body of knowledge. This need for increased knowledge, sensitivity, multidisciplinary approaches, and comfort with complexity also applies to restoration of the built environment—particularly the industries of heritage restoration and disaster/war reconstruction—though not to the same extent, since those who restore the built environment are usually not the ones who created the need.

Samuel Johnson said in his Preface to Shakespeare (*Mr. Johnson's Preface to His Edition of Shakespear's Plays*, 1765), "Of the first building that was raised, it might be with certainty determined that it was round or square, but whether it was spacious or lofty must have been referred to time." To apply the insight of the esteemed Mr. Johnson to our discussion: of any developing society, we can easily determine the amount of money or goods it produces, but whether that development was intelligent, just, or healthy will be determined in comparison to what comes after.

Individual restoration projects—even of a single building—often rate their own book (I've got dozens of such books). Community revitalization projects have so many stakeholders, factors, and agendas, that their stories are much lengthier. Ask the folks in Portland, Maine about their restored waterfront; ask Norfolk, Virginia about Diggs Town; ask Ponce, Puerto Rico about its Historic Center; or ask Los Angeles, California about restoring its Central Public Library. All deserve their own books.

Restoration-oriented laws and codes are emerging, restoration businesses are flourishing, and restorative mayors, governors, and presidents are entering office. It usually takes two terms for elected leaders to make a difference, which is just one of the reasons I'm projecting that restorative development will become the largest development sector sometime between 2012 and 2020.

Many folks are already actively restoring our world—built, natural, and social—in ways large and small, as professionals and as volunteers. They are all my heroes.

In Conclusion . . .

> Good restoration schools us in the graces of the old ways, freeing us to build anew. When we bring our loving attention to that which is old, it is not the past we are restoring but the future. Good restoration saves the future.
> —**Howard Mansfield,** *The Same Ax, Twice,* 2000

In this book, I've attempted a number of tasks:

1. Introducing the three modes of development and offering a brief taste of the eight industries of restorative development in both the built and natural environments.
2. Showcasing a few projects that demonstrate how the restoration of one portion of our world can synergistically affect the restoration of other portions.
3. Familiarizing you with some of the Restoration Economy's players. (Note: Many of these were in the public and not-for-profit sector; corporate players will get more coverage in this book's sequel.)

4. Inspiring the millions of people involved worldwide in the eight industries of restorative development to "look up and see each other." Hopefully, this will lead to more interdisciplinary collaboration, more standardization of terms/principles/agendas, and more multifaceted restoration project integration.

5. Hinting at important areas of needed research, organization, investment, and legislation that will accelerate the already-fast-growing Restoration Economy.

Is restoring our entire world utopian? Maybe. Is it achievable? Absolutely. Is it likely? That's up to you. As the old saying goes, "Anyone can make a living . . . I want to make a difference." Nothing makes a more dramatic difference than restoration. Our best possible world will come when every aspect of human endeavor has been imbued with the restorative dynamic, not just in our built and natural environments, but our social environment as well. One likely result would be the restoration of cultures, land, rights, and access to justice to those from whom such things have been lost, stolen, or denied.

> Sustainable use of the planet requires that ecological damage be prevented whenever possible and that it be restored when damage occurs. We must protect the planet's ecological life-support system. If we can ensure that the rate of restoration of ecosystems exceeds the rate of damage, future generations will hold us in their debt.
> —**John Cairns, Jr.,** Distinguished Prof. of Environmental Biology Emeritus, Virginia Polytechnic Institute (*Forum for Applied Research & Public Policy,* April 1, 2001)

The book was only a high-speed, high-altitude reconnaissance of a vast new territory. Its intent was to whet—not satiate—your appetite for knowledge about restorative development. In the process of researching this book, I accumulated enough material for at least four books.

Excising those in-depth explorations of the Restoration Economy's many fascinating subjects was painful but necessary, if this initial work was to fulfill its goal of being an overview, accessible to readers of almost any background and discipline. As you'll see in Restoration Readings, though, there is no shortage of excellent material already in print, ready to help you explore almost any facet of restoration in more detail.

Where We Go from Here

> A great investment opportunity occurs when a marvelous business encounters a one-time huge, but solvable, problem.
> —**Warren Buffett,** CEO, Berkshire Hathaway, *Berkshire Hathaway Business Principles,* 1989

Our evolution to restorative development is well begun.

Of the three modes of developing civilizations within our natural and built environments—new development, maintenance/conservation, and restorative development—only the latter is capable of being perpetuated indefinitely. Moral and spiritual evolution aside, if we have any chance of achieving the "indefinite perpetuation" of our civilizations, it will come from recognizing and embracing the "final" third of the societal life cycle: restoration.

We are finally maturing beyond the shortsighted, frontier-style, plundering mode of new development. We are finally ceasing our naive dependence on maintenance and conservation to balance new development's compulsive excesses. We are finally realizing that sustainability isn't based on limiting economic growth, but on making it restorative. Nature has demonstrated this for millions of years. We're finally displaying that same wisdom, and it's none too soon.

Restorative development is already a very substantial factor in our everyday lives, but we're in a rather awkward transitional period. It's awkward because we're not used to nice surprises. War, tragedy, and disaster seem to be the norm when it comes to unplanned major events. Discovering that we have a sure path to a brighter future, *and* that it's already roaring along with a good head of steam, seems downright strange. After a steady diet of political hype and corporate promises regarding "brighter futures," discovering that it has become reality feels, well, unreal.

This century shows every sign of going down in history as our proudest moment (warfare and crises, which have always been with us, notwithstanding.)

You should now be more prepared to perceive the economic growth opportunities that will make this global restoration happen. Welcome to the Restoration Economy!

Appendix
Trolling for Numbers

This section aggregates the significant monetary figures mentioned in this book. Its purpose is only to offer a taste of the Restoration Economy's size and potential, not to pose as a thorough accounting of any kind. These numbers represent only a small fraction of the current (completed projects not included) market and pent-up demand.

U.S. RESTORATION MARKETS AND BUDGETS
CITED IN THIS BOOK

- **$128 billion annually** in commercial building restoration (2000).
- $180 billion annually in residential building remodeling (we'll allocate just a third of that, **$60 billion per year,** to restoration, to be *very* conservative) (2001).
- The TEA-21 Restoration Act allocated $218 billion in federal funds into rebuilding the U.S. transportation infrastructure over a six-year period, which will be supplemented significantly by state funds, so let's call that about **$50 billion annually.**
- I don't have a public sector total on restoration of buildings and monuments in the book, but it is definitely over **$100 billion per year.**
- Over **$1 billion** of the U.S. Army Corps of Engineers' $4 billion budget goes to river and wetlands restoration each year, plus another **$1 billion** to brownfields restoration.
- The U.S. Forest Service and the Bureau of Land Management together spend **$75 million annually** to restore rivers and streams.
- **$200 million per year** in federal money alone for Pacific salmon restoration (not including related watershed restoration efforts).

(continued)

U.S. RESTORATION MARKETS AND BUDGETS
CITED IN THIS BOOK *(continued)*

- **$3,400,000 per year** for estuary restoration by the Restoration Center of the National Oceanic and Atmospheric Administration (NOAA).
- **$25 million per year** (for 10 years) from the state of Maryland for oyster restoration.
- **$11 billion per year** (for 5 years) committed by the Bush administration to restore water infrastructure.
- **$6.28 billion per year** (in 2000) in the United States were spent on contaminated site cleanup.

Total U.S. restoration budgets cited in this book
<u>$410 billion per year</u>

(This might be **half** of the restorative expenditures in the United States, and is [conservatively] less than 20 percent of what is spent worldwide each year. **Does not include** restorative agriculture, watershed restoration, ocean fisheries restoration, ecosystem restoration, art/museum/hobbyist restoration, or budgets under $25 million.)

Estimated total worldwide restoration expenditures
<u>$1.75 trillion per year</u>

(Conservatively estimated at only five times the incomplete U.S. total [above].)

RESTORATION BACKLOGS CITED IN THIS BOOK

- The EPA estimates a **$350 billion backlog** of contamination cleanup at U.S. military bases alone, and just those in the United States.
- **$1.3 trillion** backlog of public infrastructure renovation in the United States, as estimated by the American Society of Civil Engineers.
- **$4 billion** backlog of renovation in the U.S. National Parks.
- **$15 billion** proposed restoration of Louisiana coastal wetlands.
- **$20 billion** proposed restoration of California rivers and deltas.
- **$1 trillion** proposed Tokyo restoration project.

Total restoration backlogs cited in this book
<u>$2.689 trillion</u>

(These are the only compiled backlogs uncovered in my research. I found no backlog reports related to the restoration of ecosystems, watersheds, agriculture, fisheries, heritage, or disaster/war, which means this is a small fraction of the total restoration backlog. This is mostly U.S.: No reports seemed to be available on *worldwide* backlogs, and Tokyo is by no means the only non-U.S. city in need of a massive restoration.)

CURRENT (OR RECENTLY COMPLETED) WORLDWIDE PROJECTS CITED IN THIS BOOK

- **$12 billion** restoration of a single watershed in China.
- Hundreds of watersheds are being restored in the United States, such as the EPA's $359 million restoration of the Coeur D'Alene River watershed (projected to run **$1.3 billion** when completed), and New York City's over-**$1.5 billion** restoration of its Catskills watershed.
- **$950,000,000** over 5 years to rehabilitate Arkansas' interstate highways (all 50 states are primarily rebuilding, not building, highways).
- **$450,000,000** to restore Washington, D.C.'s National Airport.
- **$15 billion** to rebuild and restore Afghanistan (one of dozens of current or recently concluded conflicts that are, or soon will be, restored, but which aren't in this list).
- **$3 billion** to restore the Pentagon.
- **$2.5 billion** to replace the Washington, D.C.-area's Wilson Bridge.
- **$21 billion** to renovate the London Underground.
- **$52 billion per year** to restore natural disasters. (This does not include human-caused disasters such as oil spills, airplane/train/automobile crashes (mini-disasters), etc. This also does not include terrorism: Besides the thousands of lives lost in the events of September 11, 2001, at least $70 billion worth of damage was done.)
- **$100 million** to restore Angkor Wat, Cambodia.
- There are over a *hundred thousand* aging or useless dams in need of restoration or removal worldwide. Removal of average-sized dams often cost between $10 and $50 million, such as the $23 million Rogue River dam removal mentioned in these pages. We'll toss only **$100 million** into this total for the sake of being utterly conservative.
- **$110 million** U.S. Supreme Court Building restoration.
- **$225 million** to restore site around Stonehenge.
- **$9 billion** in disaster relief and rebuilding from 1998 Hurricane Mitch damage.
- **$1.5 billion** to restore damage from 2001 Seattle-Tacoma earthquake.
- **$3.1 billion** to launch first phase of Russian railway rehabilitation.
- **$72 million** to restore the historic Atlantic City Convention Hall.
- **$100 million** to launch first phase of Chesapeake Bay restoration.
- The 2002 Farm Security Act earmarked **$19 billion** for restoring Chesapeake Bay.
- **$352 million** to launch first phase of Los Angeles water infrastructure rehabilitation/integration project.
- **$500 million** to restore Istanbul's Golden Horn waterfront.

(continued)

CURRENT (OR RECENTLY COMPLETED) WORLDWIDE
PROJECTS CITED IN THIS BOOK *(continued)*

- **$100 million** restoration of the U.S. National Archives.
- **$100 million** first-phase funding for restoration of Black Sea.
- **$700 million** rebuilding of a single highway interchange (Springfield, Virginia).
- **$450 million** Mozambique restoration needs resulting from floods in 2000.
- **$60 million** Patuxent River spill of 110,000 gallons of oil in 2000 by Potomac Electric Power Company (just one—and not an especially large one—of thousands of spills annually that are not included in this list).
- **$3.5 billion** first-phase budget for Danube River basin restoration.
- **$7.8 billion** restoration of the Florida Everglades.
- Kobe, Japan, is still rebuilding from its **$100 billion** 1995 earthquake.
- The Estuary Restoration Act of 2000 (S. 835) allocated **$275 million** over five years to supplement state, local, and private budgets for restoring U.S. estuaries.

Total projects (worldwide) cited in this book
$1.888 trillion

(Includes only projects mentioned in this book that exceed $60 million. This total probably accounts for between 5 and 15 percent of actual restoration activity worldwide.)

Restoration Readings

Entries are listed in descending order of publication date to reflect the emergence of restorative development over the past decade. This sampling does not, for the most part, include subjects that have thousands of titles—such as war reconstruction, and the restoration of art, collectibles, antiques, vehicles, homes, etc.—or very specialized less important subjects, such as fence or golf course restoration. Due to publication deadlines for this book, many 2002 books are missing.

Jordan III, William R. *The Sunflower Forest: Ecological Restoration and the New Communion with Nature*. Berkeley: University of California Press, 2003.

Testa, Stephen M. *In-Situ Restoration of Metals-Contaminated Sites*. Boca Raton, FL: CRC Press, 2002.

Sproule-Jones, Mark. *Restoration of the Great Lakes: Promises, Practices, and Performances*. East Lansing, MI: Michigan State University Press, 2002.

Schultz, Dennis C., Dickerson, Scott, and Shultz, Dennis C. *To Save a River: Documenting the Natural History, Restoration, and Preservation of the Ducktrap River*. New York: Aperture, 2002.

Middleton, Beth A., editor, *Flood Pulsing in Wetlands: Restoring the Natural Hydrological Balance*. New York: John Wiley & Sons, 2002.

Perrow, Martin R., and Anthony J. Davy, editors. *Handbook of Ecological Restoration*, 2 vol. New York: Cambridge University Press, 2002.

Morrison, Michael L. *Wildlife Restoration: Techniques for Habitat Analysis and Animal Monitoring*. Washington: Island Press, 2002.

Lev, Esther. *Heroic Tales of Wetland Restoration*. Portland: Wetlands Conservancy, 2001.

Egan, Dave, and Evelyn Howell, editors. *The Historical Ecology Handbook: A Restorationist's Guide to Reference Ecosystems*. Washington: Island Press, 2001.

Maehr, David S., Reed F. Noss, and Jeffery L. Larkin, editors. *Large Mammal Restoration*. Washington: Island Press, 2001.

Allen, William. *Green Phoenix: Restoring the Tropical Forests of Costa Rica*. New York: Oxford University Press, 2001.

Restoration of Environments with Radioactive Residues. Vienna: International
    Atomic Energy Association, 2001.

Tomback, Diana F., Stephen F. Arno, and Robert E. Keane, editors. *Whitebark
    Pine Communities: Ecology and Restoration.* Washington: Island Press, 2001.

Liu, Gretchen. *Singapore Sketchbook: The Restoration of a City.* Boston:
    Tuttle, 2001.

Wend, Henry Burke. *Recovery & Restoration: U.S. Foreign Policy and the Politics
    of Reconstruction of West Germany's Shipbuilding Industry, 1945–1955.*
    New York: Praeger, 2001.

Kulchli, Christian. *Forests of Hope: Stories of Regeneration.* Vancouver:
    New Society, 2001.

Klyza, Christopher, editor. *Wilderness Comes Home: Rewilding the Northeast.*
    Hanover: University Press of New England, 2001.

O'Brien, Dan. *Buffalo for the Broken Heart: Restoring Life to a Black Hills Ranch.*
    New York: Random House, 2001.

Tung, Anthony M. *Preserving the World's Great Cities: The Destruction and Renewal
    of the Historic Metropolis.* New York: Clarkson Potter, 2001.

Mansfield, Howard. *The Same Ax, Twice: Restoration and Renewal in a Throwaway
    Age.* Hanover: University Press of New England, 2000.

Gobster, Paul H. and R. Bruce Hull, editors. *Restoring Nature: Perspectives from
    the Social Sciences & Humanities.* Washington: Island Press, 2000.

Zedler, Joy B. *Handbook for Restoring Tidal Wetlands.* Boca Raton, FL:
    CRC Press, 2000.

Harper-Lore, Bonnie and Maggie Wilson, editors. *Roadside Use of Native Plants.*
    Washington: Island Press. 2000.

Testa, Stephen M. and Duane L. Winegardner. *Restoration of Contaminated
    Aquifers.* Boca Raton, FL: Lewis, 2000.

Iskander, I. K., editor. *Environmental Restoration of Metals-contaminated Soils.*
    Boca Raton, FL: Lewis, 2000.

Rabun, Stanley J. *Structural Analysis of Historic Buildings.* New York:
    Wiley, 2000.

Stratton, Michael, editor. *Industrial Buildings: Conservation and Regeneration.*
    New York: Spon, 2000.

Kromer, John. *Neighborhood Recovery: Reinvestment Policy for New Hometowns.*
    New Brunswick: Rutgers University Press, 2000.

Swanke Hayden Connell Architects. *Historic Preservation: Project Planning &
    Estimating.* Kingston: R. S. Means, 2000.

Tyler, Norman. *Historic Preservation: An Introduction to Its History, Principles, and
    Practice.* New York: Norton, 2000.

Askins, Robert A. *Restoring North America's Birds.* New Haven: Yale University
    Press, 2000.

Throop, William, editor. *Environmental Restoration: Ethics, Theory & Practice.*
    Amherst, NY: Humanity Books, 2000.

Dobbs, David. *The Great Gulf: Fishermen, Scientists, and the Struggle to Revive the
    World's Greatest Fishery.* Washington: Island Press, 2000.

Young, Dwight. *Saving America's Treasures.* Washington: National Geographic
    Society, 2000.

Rafson, Harold J., and Robert N. Rafson. *Brownfields: Redeveloping Environmentally Distressed Properties.* New York: McGraw-Hill, 1999.

Streever, William. *An International Perspective on Wetland Rehabilitation.* Boston: Kluwer Academic, 1999.

Harker, Donald. *Landscape Restoration Handbook,* 2nd ed. Boca Raton, FL: Lewis, 1999.

Karr, James A., and Ellen W. Chu. *Restoring Life in Running Waters.* Washington: Island Press, 1999.

Hey, Donald L., and Nancy Phillipi. *A Case for Wetland Restoration.* New York: John Wiley, 1999.

Muddleton, Beth. *Wetland Restoration, Flood Pulsing and Disturbance Dynamics.* New York: John Wiley, 1999.

Whisenant, Steven G. *Repairing Damaged Wildlands.* New York: Cambridge University Press, 1999.

Hudnut, William III. *Cities on the Rebound: A Vision for Urban America.* Washington: Urban Land Institute, 1998.

Riley, Ann L. *Restoring Streams in Cities: Guide for Planners, Policy Makers, and Citizens.* Washington: Island Press, 1998.

Croci, Giorgio. *Conservation & Structural Restoration of Architectural Heritage.* Boston: Computational Mechanics Publications, 1998.

Simons, Robert. *Turning Brownfields into Greenbacks.* Washington: Urban Land Institute, 1998.

Hayes, Donald F. *Engineering Approaches to Ecosystem Restoration.* ASCE, 1998.

Dennison, Mark S. *Brownfield Redevelopment: Programs and Strategies for Contaminated Real Estate.* Rockville, MD: ABS Group, 1998.

Moore, Arthur Cotton. *The Powers of Preservation: New Life for Urban Historic Places.* New York: McGraw-Hill, 1998.

Loucks, Daniel P., editor. *Restoration of Degraded Rivers: Challenges, Issues, and Experiences.* Boston: Kluwer Academic, 1998.

Joyce, Chris, and P. Max Wade, editors. *European Wet Grasslands: Biodiversity, Management, Restoration.* New York: John Wiley, 1998.

Saur, Leslie Jones. *The Once & Future Forest: A Guide to Forest Restoration Strategies.* Washington: Island Press, 1998.

Gratz, Roberta Brandes, with Norman Mintz. *Cities back from the Edge: New Life for Downtown.* New York: John Wiley, 1998.

Greer, Nora, and Einhorn Prescott. *Architecture as Response: Preserving the Past, Designing the Future.* Rockport Publishers, 1998.

Marriott, Paul Daniel. *Saving Historic Roads: Design and Policy Guidelines.* New York: John Wiley, 1998.

Hutchins, Nigel, and Donna Hutchins. *Restoring Houses of Brick & Stone.* Toronto: Firefly Books, 1998.

Urbanska, Krystyna M., Nigel Webb, and Peter J. Edwards, editors. *Restoration Ecology and Sustainable Development.* New York: Cambridge, 1997.

Rast, Richard R. *Environmental Remediation Estimating Methods.* Kingston: RS Means, 1997.

Harris, James. *Land Restoration and Reclamation: Principles & Practice.* Boston: Addison-Wesley, 1997.

Clark, Tim W. *Averting Extinction: Reconstructing Endangered Species Recovery.* New Haven: Yale University Press, 1997.

Williams, Jack E., Christopher A. Wood, and Michael P. Dombeck, editors. *Watershed Restoration: Principles and Practices.* Bethesda: American Fisheries Society, 1997.

Foulks, William G. *Historic Building Facades: The Manual for Maintenance and Rehabilitation.* New York: John Wiley, 1997.

Friedman, Donald, and Nathaniel Oppenheimer. *The Design of Renovation.* New York: Norton, 1997.

Gutkowski, Richard M., and Tomasz Winnicki, editors. *Restoration of Forests.* Boston: Kluwer Academic, 1997.

Syms, Paul M. *Contaminated Land: The Practice and Economics of Redevelopment.* Malden, MA: Blackwell Science, 1997.

Murtagh, William J. *Keeping Time: The History and Theory of Preservation in America*, revised edition. New York: John Wiley, 1997.

Moe, Richard, and Carter Wilkie. *Changing Places: Rebuilding Community in the Age of Sprawl.* New York: Holt, 1997.

Weaver, Martin E., with F. G. Matero. *Conserving Buildings: A Manual of Techniques and Materials.* New York: Preservation Press, 1997.

Hutchins, Nigel, and Donna Hutchins. *Restoring Old Houses.* Toronto: Firefly, 1997.

Packard, Stephen, and Cornelia F. Mutel. *The Tallgrass Restoration Handbook.* Washington: Island Press, 1997.

McNamee, Thomas. *The Return of the Wolf to Yellowstone.* New York: Henry Holt, 1997.

Wright, James G. *Risks & Rewards of Brownfield Redevelopment.* Cambridge, MA: Lincoln Institute of Land Policy, 1997.

Phillips, Michael K., and Douglas W. Smith. *The Wolves of Yellowstone.* Stillwater, MN: Voyageur, 1996.

Ferguson, Gary. *The Yellowstone Wolves: The First Year.* Helena, MT: Falcon, 1996.

Briggs, Mark K. *Riparian Ecosystem Recovery in Arid Lands.* Tucson: University of Arizona, 1996.

Bowles, Marlin L., and Christopher J. Whelan, editors. *Restoration of Endangered Species.* New York: Cambridge University Press, 1996.

Falk, Donald A., Constance I. Millar, and Margaret Olwell, editors. *Restoring Diversity: Strategies for Reintroducing Endangered Plants.* Washington: Island Press, 1996.

Bucher, Ward, editor. *Dictionary of Building Preservation.* New York: John Wiley, 1996.

Cairns, John, Jr., editor. *Rehabilitating Damaged Ecosystems,* 2nd ed. Boca Raton, FL: Lewis, 1995.

Stevens, William K. *Miracle Under the Oaks: The Revival of Nature in America.* New York: Pocket Books, 1995.

Wheeler, Bryan D., editor. *Restoration of Temperate Wetlands.* New York: John Wiley, 1995.

Ferris-Kaan, Richard, editor. *The Ecology of Woodland Creation.* New York: John Wiley, 1995.

Friedman, Donald. *Historical Building Construction.* New York: Norton, 1995.

Mills, Stephanie. *In Service of the Wild: Restoring & Rehabilitating Damaged Land.* Boston: Beacon Press, 1995.

Highsmith, Carol M., and Ted Landphair. *America Restored.* Washington: Preservation Press, 1995.

Noss, Reed F., and Allen Y. Cooperrider. *Saving Nature's Legacy: Protecting and Restoring Biodiversity.* Washington: Island Press, 1994.

Gratz, Roberta Brandes. *The Living City: How America's Cities Are Being Revitalized.* Washington: Preservation Press, 1994.

Baldwin, A. Dwight, Jr., Judith DeLuce, and Carl Pletsch, editors. *Beyond Preservation: Restoring and Inventing Landscapes.* Minneapolis: University of Minnesota Press, 1994.

McRaven, Charles. *Building and Restoring the Hewn Log House.* Cincinnati: Betterway, 1994.

Kentula, Mary, editor. *Wetlands: An Approach to Improving Decision Making in Wetland Restoration and Creation.* Washington: Island Press, 1993.

Thayer, Gordon W., editor. *Restoring the Nation's Marine Environment.* College Park, MD: University of Maryland, 1992.

Matthews, Anne, *Where the Buffalo Roam.* New York: Grove Weidenfield, 1992.

Committee on Restoration Public Policy, *Restoration of Aquatic Ecosystems.* Washington: National Academy Press, 1992.

Nilson, Richard, editor. *Helping Nature Heal: An Introduction to Environmental Restoration.* Berkeley: Ten Speed Press, 1991.

Hunter, Christopher J. *Better Trout Habitat: A Guide to Stream Restoration and Management.* Washington: Island Press, 1991.

Fitch, James Marston. *Historic Preservation: Curatorial Management of the Built World.* Charlottesville: University Press of Virginia, 1990.

Kusler, Jon, and Mary Kentula. *Wetland Creation & Restoration: The Status of the Science.* Corvallis, OR: United States Environmental Agency, 1989.

Jordan, William R., Michael Gilpin, and John Alber. *Restoration Ecology.* New York: Cambridge University Press, 1987.

Other Books Needing Special Mention

Stewart Brand's near-genius *How Buildings Learn* laid so much groundwork for restorative development in 1994 that I hereby dedicate Chapter 13 to him. Here are a few other "nonrestoration" books that should be in your restoration library:

- Rolf Jensen's 1999 *The Dream Society: How the Shift from Information to Imagination Will Transform Business* (New York: McGraw-Hill, 1999) spoke of restorative futures.
- The Rocky Mountain Institute, et al. produced *Green Development: Integrating Ecology and Real Estate* (New York: John Wiley, 1998), which had much discussion of both integration and restoration.

- Richard C. Longworth's *Global Squeeze: The Coming Crisis for First-World Nations* (Lincolnwood, IL: Contemporary Books, 1998) is a good primer on some of the crises driving the growth of restorative development, and Marq DeVilliers' *Water: The Fate of Our Most Precious Resource* (Boston: Houghton Mifflin, 2001) does the same for a single particular crisis.
- In *Earth Odyssey: Around the World in Search of Our Environmental Future* (New York: Broadway Books, 1998), Mark Hertsgaard calls for global restoration.
- *The Ecology of Place* (Timothy Beatley) (Washington, DC: Island Press, 1997) has a chapter on restorative economies.
- Charlene Spretnak's *The Resurgence of the Real: Body, Nature, and Place in a Hypermodern World* (Reading MA: Addison-Wesley, 1997) explains some of the psychological and sociological drivers of the Restoration Economy.

If you're looking for a restoration book that's highly enjoyable to read and makes a great gift, you can't go wrong with Dan O'Brien's fun and emotionally gripping *Buffalo for the Broken Heart: Restoring Life to a Black Hills Ranch*. Another is Howard Mansfield's poetic and contemplative *The Same Ax, Twice: Restoration and Renewal in a Throwaway Age*. Both of those are listed above, but another fun read, Gene Lodgson's brief, modern-day fable *The Man Who Created Paradise* (Athens, OH: Ohio University Press, 2001) is not, because it's fiction (or is it?).

The year 2002 saw the publication of what might be the first children's book on ecological restoration: Meghan Nuttall Sayres' *The Shape of Betts Meadow: A Wetlands Story* (Brookfield, CT: Millbrook Press). At a third-grade level, the author tells how Gunnar Holmquist purchased 140 acres of arid former pasture and restored it to its original wetland condition. Discovering how beauty and wildlife were returned to this lifeless land is inspiring to young readers, and is a great (if a bit premature) preparation for one of the major investment trends of the twenty-first century: restorative real estate development.

Pamela Gordon's excellent *Lean and Green: Profit for Your Workplace and the Environment* (San Francisco: Berrett-Koehler, 2001) represents a newer breed of sustainable development books. Using 20 companies as successful examples, it combines profiting via environmentally sound practices, some of which involve renewing corporate culture via restorative activities.

And then there are the landmark books: *Ecology of Commerce* by Paul Hawken (New York: HarperBusiness, 1993) and *Natural Capitalism* by Paul Hawken, Amory Lovins, and L. Hunter Lovins (Boston: Little, Brown, 1999). Hawken was probably first to use the phrase "restorative economy." The *Ecology of Commerce* and *Natural Capitalism* are excellent roadmaps to slowing global degradation, which will allow passive restoration to occur. These are must-reads.

Finally, *The New Economy of Nature: The Quest to Make Conservation Profitable* by Gretchen C. Daily and Katherine Ellison (Washington, DC: Island Press, 2002) is about integrating public utilities and for-profit companies with the service aspect (such as water purification) of natural resources. It provides more detailed examples of integrating watershed restoration with drinking and wastewater management than I have here. Most chapters have restoration stories on just about every other page, making it a shame they didn't put "restoration" in the title. It's perfect follow-up reading to this book.

Restoration's growth is so strong that at least one publisher has launched a new line of books, solely on restoration. Island Press is a leading environmental publisher, so its new line focuses just on ecological restoration and is in partnership with the Society for Ecological Restoration. Island Press says, "*This series will compile a foundation of practical knowledge and scientific insight that will help ecological restoration become the powerful reparative and healing tool that the world so clearly needs.*"

Videos

Many videos have been produced on various hobbyist, art, and "non-business" aspects of restoration, but many come from obscure sources and have limited distribution. Restoring steam locomotives and other old rail equipment is one of the most popular subjects. Major historic building restorations often get their own documentary video. One of my favorites is *Return to Glory: The 13-Year Restoration of the Sistine Chapel* (1996), produced by the Nippon Television Network Corp. and available in the United States through CCC of America, Inc., Irving, TX (800-935-2222).

Given the startling before-and-after visuals of projects that restore streams, watersheds, ecosystems, neighborhoods, bridges, etc., there seems to be a lot of untapped video potential in the Restoration Economy. The slides I use in my talks always provoke "ooohs and ahhhs," so a high-quality video should convey even more dramatic impact, since they're able to capture the movement and sounds of returning wildlife and/or human activity, juxtaposed against the dead silence of the "before" condition. The good news is that some new restoration videos are on the way.

One of the less-glamorous sides of the Restoration Economy is now getting its time in the limelight. John W. Sutherlin, Ph.D., is producing and directing a 10-part series (not yet released as of this writing) entitled *Brownfields: Reclaiming America's Cities.* Included are over 150 interviews conducted across the United States during a two-year period with developers, citizens, regulators, engineers, planners, and elected and public officials. *Brownfields: Reclaiming America's Cities* is a part of *Our Urban Environment* video project being produced by the Urban Waste Management and Research Center (UWMRC) of the College of Engineering at the University of New Orleans [www.uno.edu/~engr/civil/uwmrc/videos-bf.html].

Resource Guide
Education, Memberships, Journals, and Events

This is a very small sampling of U.S. and (a few) non-U.S. restoration resources; it largely excludes regional and community resources because they number in the thousands, and new ones appear almost daily.

The free, constantly updated resource guide at www.restorica.org gives a more complete listing.

(Note: Lists are in alphabetical order. *Italicized copy* is from the organizations' own literature or websites.)

WHERE ARE THE FOR-PROFIT BUSINESSES?

With the exception of a few magazines, for-profit firms are not listed here. The next book in this series, tentatively titled *Leaders of the Restoration Economy,* will profile 8 top companies—one for each of the 8 restorative industries—and will list the 10 leading firms in each industry. Please contact the author at storm@restorability.com to nominate a firm you feel should be profiled (and to notify him of any errors or omissions you find in this book).

HIGHER EDUCATION

- The **New Academy for Nature and Culture,** in Evanston, Illinois, is a new national program being developed to provide college-level training for leaders of community-oriented conservation efforts. Their primary focus is on ecological restoration, which isn't surprising, considering that its president, William R. Jordan III, co-founded both the Society for Ecological Restoration and the journal

Ecological Restoration. New Academy is currently developing regional centers in Texas, Arizona, and California, and it works closely with the Society for Ecological Restoration.

Their first regional center is being established in Chicago, and courses have begun at two Chicago-area partner schools: Northeastern Illinois University and Loyola University. Contact Bill Jordan III at (847) 328-8389.

- **Ball State University** [www.bsu.edu/cap/arch/preservation/MA_Hist.html] offers a master of science degree in Historic Preservation. Contact: James A. Glass, Director, Graduate Program in Historic Preservation, College of Architecture and Planning, Ball State University, Muncie, IN; Tel: (765) 285-1900.

- **U.S. Environmental Protection Agency (USEPA)** offers a wide variety of training programs. As readers would expect, it has courses related to brownfields remediation, but many other subjects as well. For example, its Watershed Protection division has a site at www.epa.gov/owow/watershed/wacademy/corsched.htm which aggregates both EPA and non-EPA training programs related to watershed issues. Programs related to river and stream restoration appear frequently, such as this non-EPA sample: Oct. 15–24, 2002, *River Restoration and Natural Channel Design* (Wildland Hydrology, Tel: (970) 731-6100 [www.wildlandhydrology.com]). USEPA's River Corridor & Wetland Restoration site is www.epa.gov/owow/wetlands/restore.

- The **University of Maine's** Humboldt Field Research Institute offers a Certificate in Ecological Restoration [http://maine.maine.edu/~eaglhill/ECREDITS.html].

- **University of Vermont,** Master's Degree in Historic Preservation. Contact Thomas Visser, Historic Preservation Program, University of Vermont, Burlington, VT; (802) 656-3180; www.uvm.edu/histpres.

- **University of Victoria,** Division of Continuing Studies, PO Box 3030 STN CSC, Victoria, BC V8W 3N6, Canada [www.uvcs.uvic.ca/restore]. Restoration of Natural Systems is an accredited program created to disseminate information about environmental restoration and to provide practical background knowledge, training, and skill development for those working in areas related to the restoration of natural systems. The program is designed for those who need to study part-time.

- The **Arboretum at the University of Wisconsin–Madison** [http://wiscinfo.doit.wisc.edu/arboretum/] This is the mecca of ecological restoration in the United States, and it shows in many areas of the university's curriculum. For instance, the landscape architecture department has a heaver-than-usual focus on restoration ecology. In addition to a wide variety of related studies, the Arboretum publishes *Restoration Ecology* for the Society for Ecological Restoration, and is connected with the oldest ongoing ecological restoration projects in the United States (tallgrass prairies).

WEBSITES IN GENERAL

There are far too many websites (tens of thousands) related to restorative development to list here, and they change too often for inclusion in a book. As a sample, here are a few useful sites from one of the newer restoration industries: brownfields remediation.

- www.brownfields.com/env_newsltrs.cfm
- www.brownfieldstech.org
- www.epa.gov/brownfields
- www.nicole.org/nicole2/NICOLEindex.shtml
- www.dep.state.pa.us/hosting/phoenixawards/contacts/links.htm

NGOs, ASSOCIATIONS, GOVERNMENT AGENCIES, AND RELATED JOURNALS

- **American Society of Civil Engineers** 1801 Alexander Bell Dr., Reston, VA 20191-4400; Toll-free: (800) 548-2723, Tel: (703) 295-6300, Fax: (703) 295-6222 [www.asce.org]. Associate ASCE memberships are available for nonengineers. ASCE is the premiere U.S. association of civil engineers, but most developed countries have their own. The original is the U.K.'s **Institution of Civil Engineers** [www.ice.org.uk], established in 1818, which has over 80,000 member engineers worldwide. The younger ASCE (only 150 years old) publishes *Civil Engineering* magazine and produces many conferences. An example was the "Wetlands Engineering & River Restoration" conference in 2001, sponsored by ASCE's Environmental and Water Resource Institute (EWRI). EWRI is one of six semi-autonomous institutes recently founded by ASCE to promote greater integration of the engineering profession with other stakeholders and disciplines, such as contractors, architects, owners, etc. Another ASCE institute that deals with much restorative development is its Coastal Oceans, Ports, and Rivers Institute (COPRI).

- **Association of Specialists in Cleaning and Restoration (ASCR International)**   8229 Cloverleaf Dr., Suite 460, Millersville, MD 21108; Tel: (800) 272-7012, Fax: (410) 729-3603 [www.ascr.org]. Disasters come in all sizes, and so do the businesses that restore their damage. Ever since we moved out of caves, our buildings have been burning down, so ASCR represents one of the world's oldest restoration professions. Formed in 1946 (as a rug cleaning trade group), the growth of restoration in recent decades has forced ASCR to focus increasingly on that aspect of the business. ASCR is *"the leading trade association for cleaning and restoration professionals worldwide, and the foremost authority, trainer and educator in the industry. ASCR is a professional association comprising more than 1,300 member organizations, representing over 20,000 cleaning and restoration professionals who specialize in the cleaning, treatment and repair of damaged buildings and their contents."* ASCR publishes *Cleaning & Restoration* magazine.

- **Bioneers**   (Slogan: "Visionary and practical solutions for restoring the Earth.") 901 West San Mateo Rd., Suite L, Santa Fe, NM 87505; Tel: (505) 986-0366, Toll-free: (877) 246-6337, Fax: (505) 986-1644 [www.bioneers.org]. The Bioneers use the term "restoration" copiously, but their conferences and publications focus primarily on sustainability, human health, and spirituality. The "restorative" content is a mélange of green business, sustainable development, organic farming, and other activities that will passively restore the planet, not active restoration. However, interesting restorative technologies sometimes appear at their annual conference, and they work to actively restore heritage species of food crops, such as Iroquois White Corn. They even have a "Restorative Development Initiative (RDI)," and Bioneers' founder Kenny Ausubel can take credit for coining "restorative development" in the early '90s, though his usage is, again, mostly focused on agriculture. This book is re-coining "restorative development" as restoration (passive and active) of all aspects of the built and natural environments.

- **Congress for the New Urbanism**   The Hearst Building, 5 Third St., Suite 725, San Francisco, CA 94103; Tel: (415) 495-2255, Fax: (415) 495-1731 [www.cnu.org]. *"New Urbanism is an urban design movement that burst onto the scene in the late 1980s and early 1990s. New Urbanists aim to reform all aspects of real estate development."* Here are a few selections from CNU's "Principles of New Urbanism": *"The metropolitan region is a fundamental economic unit of the* *contemporary world. . . . Farmland and nature are as important to the metropolis as the garden is to the house. . . . Infill development within existing urban areas conserves environmental resources, economic investment, and social fabric, while reclaiming marginal and abandoned areas . . . renewal of historic buildings, districts, and landscapes affirm the continuity and evolution of urban society."*

- **Cultural Survival** 215 Prospect St., Cambridge, MA 02139; Tel: (617) 441-5400 [www.cs.org]. CS has been working hard, with very limited funds, for over three decades to preserve and restore threatened (mostly indigenous) human cultures, including their languages, customs, rights, and land. For example, the theme of *Cultural Survival Quarterly* (Vol. 25, No. 2) was "language revitalization programs."

- **Ducks Unlimited (USA)** One Waterfowl Way, Memphis, TN 38120; Toll-free: (800) 45-DUCKS, Tel: (901)758-3825 [www.ducks. org]. With more than one million supporters, hunting-oriented Ducks Unlimited is the world's largest wetland and waterfowl restoration and conservation group. For instance, Ducks Unlimited Canada [www.ducks.ca] boasts over 1,400 habitat rehabilitation projects. In an example of partnering between restoration groups, a 2002 press release stated, *"Representatives of the Ontario Great Lakes Renewal Foundation (OGLRF) and Ducks Unlimited Canada (DUC) announced an unparalleled $2 million funding agreement today based on their mutual recognition of the urgent need to restore degraded habitats in Areas of Concern around the Great Lakes."*

- **Mangrove Replenishment Initiative** P.O. Box 510312, Melbourne Beach, FL 32951 [www.mangrove.org]. A small restoration initiative that *"began as a local project along the central east coast of Florida; however, in the last few years it has contributed to a wide range of habitat creation and restoration programs that are international in scope."* It is included here as an example of the myriad tiny restoration organizations that are emerging from the passion and vision of single individuals.

- **National Brownfield Association** 5440 N. Cumberland Ave., Suite 238, Chicago, IL 60656; Tel: (773) 714-0407, Fax: (773) 714-0989 [www.brownfieldassociation.org]. As with everything else in the brownfields restoration industry, the not-for-profit National Brownfield Association is quite new, having been formed in 1999. Their members come from both the public and pirvate sector, and they publish the bimonthly *Brownfield News*.

- **National Trust for Historic Preservation** 1785 Massachusetts Ave., NW, Washington, DC 20036; Tel: (202) 588-6000 [www.nationaltrust.org]. This is the U.S. organization for the restoration of historic structures. Mostly focusing on buildings, *"The National Trust for Historic Preservation provides leadership, education and advocacy to save America's diverse historic places and revitalize our communities."* Most other countries—not just large ones—have their own national trusts. Some are very similar to the U.S. organization in structure and mission, while others differ significantly. In the United Kingdom, the premiere organization is the **National Trust** [www.nationaltrust.org.uk], but Scotland and Ireland each have several of their own, such as the **National Trust of Scotland** [www.nts.org.uk] and **An Taisce,** the National Trust for Ireland. The latter, An Taisce, is unusual in that, although it restores historic buildings and districts, the natural environment takes first priority.
- **The Nature Conservancy (TNC)** 4245 North Fairfax Dr., Suite 100, Arlington, VA 22203-1606; Tel: (800) 628-6860 [www.tnc.org *or* www.nature.org]. TNC probably performs more ecological restoration (including estuary, wetland, littoral, watershed, and more) annually than any other NGO on the planet. Its expertise in creating collaborative, innovative solutions positions TNC nicely to move into integrated restoration, should it ever wish to expand its mission into the built environment. Beautiful quarterly magazine.
- **Orion Society** 187 Main St., Great Barrington, MA 01230; Tel: (413) 528-4422, Toll free: (888) 909-6568, Fax: (413) 528-0676 [www.orionsociety.org]. A nontechnical, often philosophical lay forum in two forms:
  - *Orion:* A literary exploration of the more subjective side of restorative development, conservation, sustainable development, and living on the Earth.
  - *Orion Afield:* A practical, knowledge-based publication, with a greater emphasis on restoration than its more "artsy" sister magazine.
- **Restore America's Estuaries** 3801 N. Fairfax Dr., Suite 53, Arlington, VA 22203; Tel: (703) 524-0248, Fax: (703) 524-0287 [www.estuaries.org]. An alliance of regional, coastal community-based environmental organizations. *"Our mission is to preserve the nation's network of estuaries by protecting and restoring the lands and waters essential to the richness and diversity of coastal life."*

- **Society for Ecological Restoration** 1955 West Grant Rd., #150, Tucson, AZ 85745; Tel: (520) 622-5485, Fax: (520) 622-5491 [www.ser.org]. SER, although still young and small, is fast becoming one of the twenty-first century's most essential scientific societies. Its annual conference is a must-attend event. The conference is endlessly fascinating; as much for the diversity, passion, and professionalism of the presenters and attendees as for the presentations. The conference is also a great way to quickly get "up-to-speed" on environmental restoration, even if you have no background in ecology or biology. Two publications are available in conjunction with membership, though neither is published by SER:
  - *Restoration Ecology: The Journal of the Society for Ecological Restoration* Blackwell Science, Commerce Place, 350 Main St., Malden, MA 02148 [www.blackwellscience.com/rec] (subscription requests should go through SER). This quarterly peer-reviewed scientific and technical journal comes from a leading commercial journal publisher. SER members get a significant discount.
  - *Ecological Restoration* 1930 Monroe St., 3rd Floor, Madison, WI 53711-2059 [www.wisc.edu/wisconsinpress/journals2.html]. This quarterly is a publication of the University of Wisconsin Arboretum, and is more accessible to lay readers than is *Restoration Ecology*. Some of the more technical articles are peer-reviewed, but most are selected by editor Dave Egan, who does a superb job. Contents include *"progress reports on current restoration projects, topical and regional reviews of restoration activities, philosophical discourses on environmental ethics, descriptions of new restoration techniques, reviews of conferences and books, op-ed pieces, and letters from readers."*
- **The Wildlands Project** (Slogan: "Restore, reconnect, rewild.") P.O. Box 455, Richmond, VT 05477; Tel: (802) 434-4077, Fax: (802) 434-5980 [www.twp.org *or* www.wildlandsproject.org]. The Wildlands Project has been described earlier in this book. The project publishes *Wild Earth,* an excellent nontechnical magazine that explores the ethical, aesthetic, sociological, and strategic aspects of ecological restoration.
- **The Trust for Public Land** 116 New Montgomery St., 4th floor, San Francisco, CA 94105; Tel: (800) 714-LAND [www.tpl.org]. This well-funded, surprisingly low-profile organization is often a key player in restorative development. Like The Nature Conservancy

(TNC), TPL's primary focus is purchasing land. Unlike TNC, the properties are chosen for their value to humans (rather than wildlife), and ownership is always turned over to communities and public agencies. TPL's role is to facilitate acquisition, often buying land when it becomes available, and holding it in trust until communities have time to raise the funds. *"Founded in 1972, the Trust for Public Land is the only national nonprofit working exclusively to protect land for human enjoyment and well-being. TPL helps conserve land for recreation and spiritual nourishment and to improve the health and quality of life of American communities."* Its projects range from historic brownfields—such as its new Santa Fe, New Mexico, Railyard Park and Plaza—to disaster reconstruction sites. An example of the latter is Walton's Walk park in Ft. Walton Beach, Florida, where a fishing pier and commercial property, destroyed by a hurricane, are being redeveloped into a community park, in a region with precious few public waterfronts.

- **Urban Land Institute**   1025 Thomas Jefferson St., NW Suite 500 West, Washington, DC 20007; Tel: (202) 624-7000, Toll-free: (800) 321-5011, Fax: (202) 624-7140 [www.uli.org]. ULI is a unique, constantly surprising organization. It was *"founded in 1936, when many American cities were experiencing both suburban expansion and urban decay, with limited public sector planning and no guidance available to the private sector. No organization existed in the country to research, analyze, or encourage responsible patterns for long-term urban growth, or to conduct inquiries into what constitutes sound real estate development projects and practices."* I call ULI "surprising" because real estate developers—especially now, at the endpoint of new development's dominance—are often seen by the public (not without justification) as the "bad guys." ULI, especially as represented by its wonderful magazine, *Urban Land,* is at the forefront of restorative development. *Urban Land* articles about restorative development usually outnumber those dealing with new development by 2:1. But, as with many organizations born of new development, few ULI members have formally recognized this shift. It emerged from adaptive evolution—not revolution—because ULI's core members deal daily with the Three Global Crises: Constraint, Corrosion, and Contamination. ULI has over 15,000 members in 52 countries.
- **The Wetlands Conservancy**   P.O. Box 1195, Tualatin, OR 97065; Tel: (503) 691-1394, Fax: (503) 885-1084 [www.wetlandsconservancy. org].

This is an Oregon-only organization, included here for two purposes: (1) as an example of an excellent regional NGO, and (2) because it published (in 2001) *Heroic Tales of Wetland Restoration*, a book which *"tells of 12 rural landowners, who changed their farming practices to reclaim wetlands, streams and rivers."*

- **World Monuments Fund**   95 Madison Ave., 9th floor, New York, NY 10016; Tel: (646) 424-9594, Fax: (646) 424-9593 [www.wmf.org]. A private, nonprofit organization devoted to onsite restoration and conservation of monuments and heritage sites worldwide. Publishes an annual list of 100 Most Endangered Sites.

THE BASIC THREE MEMBERSHIPS

For newcomers wishing to gain a well-rounded orientation to—and a broad spectrum of networking connections within—the Restoration Economy, I recommend joining—at minimum—these three organizations:

- **The Society for Ecological Restoration** for issues related to restoring the natural environment.
- **The National Trust for Historic Preservation** (or the local equivalent if you're not in the United States) for issues related to restoring heritage.
- **The Urban Land Institute** for issues related to metropolitan redevelopment, including the restoration of infrastructure, brownfields, historic sites, watersheds, wetlands, and economies.

CONFERENCES AND TRADE SHOWS

- **Brownfields 2003** (name updated annually)   This is the premiere U.S. event in the brownfields industry, cosponsored and founded by the Engineers' Society of Western Pennsylvania. At the first conference, in 1996, 400 attendees were planned for, but 700 arrived. One thousand attended in 1997, 2,000 in 1998, 2,300 in 1999, and 3,073 in 2000. The conference was on track to break 4,000 in 2001, but it was just days after 9/11, so only 2,000 showed.
- **Restoration and Renovation Exhibition and Conference** Restore Media, LLC, 1000 Potomac St. N.W., Washington, DC 20007; Tel: (800) 982-6247 [www.restorationandrenovation.com]. Focuses primarily on historic restoration and adaptive reuse of residential and commercial buildings, with some art-, antique-, and museum-related restoration, and increasingly has sessions

dealing with community-level issues. Currently offering 60 seminars and 300 exhibitors, this show has a *lot* of growth potential, especially if expanded into other restorative industries.

- **RTM Communications, Inc.**   110 N. Royal St., Alexandria, VA 22314; Tel: (800) 966-7475 [www.RTMcomm.com]. RTM produces three annual conferences on brownfields, focused heavily on risk management. Its 2002 conference in Washington, DC, was titled "Contaminated Property Transactions—Converting Ruins to Rubies." It also has publications and research services related to the insurance and financing aspects of contaminated property redevelopment.
- **Inaugural National Conference on Coastal and Estuarine Habitat Restoration**   April 13–16, 2003, Baltimore, MD; Tel: (703) 524-0248 [www.estuaries.org]. Many new restoration-oriented conferences are emerging, focused on fast-growing activities that have never before had their own national or international events. This first-time-ever conference is a good example. It should be a well-integrated meeting: it's sponsored by Restore America's Estuaries, along with some two dozen federal and state agencies and other NGOs.

COMMERCIAL MAGAZINES

- *Engineering News Record* [www.enr.com]   McGraw-Hill's weekly news bible of the engineering world isn't about restoration, but it's hard to find an issue without a major wetlands, river, infrastructure, heritage, or building restoration project.
- *Environmental Business Journal*   4452 Park Blvd., Suite 306, San Diego, CA 92116; Tel: (619) 295-7685 [www.ebiusa.com]. Not overtly focused on restoration, this pricey ($495/year) "insider"-style journal (primarily for consulting engineers) reports on industry trends—plus the business ups and downs of key players—in fields such as brownfields remediation, water infrastructure (including integrated watershed management), solid waste, energy, etc.
- *Land and Water: The Magazine of Natural Resource Management and Restoration*   Land and Water, Inc., 918B First Avenue South, P.O. Box 1197, Fort Dodge, IA 50501-9925; Tel: (515) 576-3191 [www.landandwater.com]. Described earlier in this book, *Land &*

Water's readers are property owners, environmental engineers, and contractors. Its focus has been shifting from new development to restorative development for two decades, thanks to the explosive growth of mitigation, the increasing use of constructed wetlands to treat stormwater runoff, river and stream restoration, etc.

- **Old House Journal, Clem Labine's Traditional Building, and Period Homes** Restore Media, LLC, 1000 Potomac St. N.W., Washington, DC 20007; Tel.: (202) 339-0744. Restore Media, LLC was formed in 2000 to develop a media company serving the fields of building renovation and restoration. In less than two years, they acquired the *Restoration & Renovation Exhibition and Conference* (see above), as well as three magazines: *Old House Journal* [www.oldhousejournal.com], *Clem Labine's Traditional Building* [www.traditional-building.com] and *Clem Labine's Period Homes* [www.period-homes.com] magazines. They also publish *The Restoration Journal*, a buyer's guide to product and service providers.

- **Restoration Economy Leader** [www.restorability.com] Storm Cunningham's newsletter is the source of news and insight for leaders of organizations and communities desiring economic growth via restorative development. It covers the latest trends, new companies/associations/agencies/projects, success stories, profiles of leading firms, and an international calendar of events. Each issue has an in-depth feature article that is an advance peek at material from Storm's next book, giving subscribers a significant head start on the rest of the world. Free sample issue.

A NOTE TO ORGANIZATIONS, PUBLICATIONS, AND EVENTS NOT INCLUDED IN RESOURCE GUIDE

My apologies! Please go to www.integratedrestoration.org and list your nonprofit organization in the online database. The Alliance for Integrated Restoration (AIR) has been formed to help communities and nonprofits locate resources, projects, and partners, so your free listing can serve to both offer and recruit resources. A donation will eventually be requested to list for-profit firms. AIR's online resource guide should be considered a constantly expanded and updated version of this rudimentary print version.

Index

About the Author

Storm Cunningham was—from 1996 to 2002—Director, Strategic Initiatives at the Construction Specifications Institute, a 52-year-old association with 18,000 architects, engineers, contractors, and manufacturers. He was previously CEO of a small manufacturing company that developed commercial aquaculture systems based on a pioneering water purification technology invented at the Smithsonian Institution.

A former Green Beret SCUBA medic, Storm is now the founder of Restor*Ability*, an Alexandria, Virginia firm. Restor*Ability* provides strategic research and consulting services for corporations and government agencies desiring growth via integrated restoration strategies. He speaks publicly on the restoration of our organizations and our planet, and is also an avid SCUBA diver and amateur herpetologist, devoting much of his personal time to the restorative development of island nations and indigenous communities. He lives in Arlington, Virginia, with his wife Maria and a dozen Solomon Island skinks.

Photo by Maria Antonia MacKnight

Berrett-Koehler Publishers

BERRETT-KOEHLER is an independent publisher of books, periodicals, and other publications at the leading edge of new thinking and innovative practice on work, business, management, leadership, stewardship, career development, human resources, entrepreneurship, and global sustainability.

Since the company's founding in 1992, we have been committed to supporting the movement toward a more enlightened world of work by publishing books, periodicals, and other publications that help us to integrate our values with our work and work lives, and to create more humane and effective organizations.

We have chosen to focus on the areas of work, business, and organizations, because these are central elements in many people's lives today. Furthermore, the work world is going through tumultuous changes, from the decline of job security to the rise of new structures for organizing people and work. We believe that change is needed at all levels—individual, organizational, community, and global—and our publications address each of these levels.

We seek to create new lenses for understanding organizations, to legitimize topics that people care deeply about but that current business orthodoxy censors or considers secondary to bottom-line concerns, and to uncover new meaning, means, and ends for our work and work lives.

See next pages for other publications
from Berrett-Koehler Publishers

Macroshift
Navigating the Transformation to a Sustainable World

Ervin Laszlo

Preeminent futurist Ervin Laszlo confronts the global crisis and shows how we can shape our future. *Macroshift* informs readers about the dangers, opportunities, and choices we face—in business, in politics, and in our private lives—and motivates them to make informed and responsible lifestyle, civic, and professional choices. Laszlo expertly combines insights into the science of rapid and irreversible change with practical guidelines for managing that change.

Hardcover, 200 pages • ISBN 1-57675-163-5 • Item #51635-415 $24.95

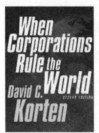

When Corporations Rule the World
Second Edition

David C. Korten

David Korten offers an alarming exposé of the devastating consequences of economic globalization and a passionate message of hope in this well reasoned, extensively researched analysis. He documents the human and environmental consequences of economic globalization and explains why human survival depends on a community-based, people-centered alternative.

Paperback, 400 pages • ISBN 1-887208-04-6 • Item #08046-415 $15.95

The Post-Corporate World
Life After Capitalism

David C. Korten

The Post-Corporate World presents readers with both a profound challenge and an empowering sense of hope. It is an extensively researched, powerfully argued, eye-opening critique of how today's corporate capitalism is destroying the things of real value in the world—like cancer destroys life—including practical alternatives that will help restore health to markets, democracy, and every day life.

Paperback, 300 pages • ISBN 1-887208-03-8
Item #08038-415 $19.95

Berrett-Koehler Publishers
PO Box 565, Williston, VT 05495-9900
Call toll-free! **800-929-2929** 7 am-9 pm Eastern Standard Time
Or fax your order to 802-864-7627
For fastest service order online: **www.bkconnection.com**

Affluenza
The All-Consuming Epidemic

John de Graaf, David Wann, Thomas H. Naylor

Based on two highly acclaimed PBS documentaries, *Affluenza* uses the metaphor of a disease to tackle a very serious subject: the damage done—to our health, our families, our communities, and our environment—by the obsessive quest for material gain that has been the core principle of the American Dream. The authors explore the origins of affluenza detail the symptoms of the disease, and describe number of treatments options that offer hope for recovery.

Hardcover, 275 pages • ISBN 1-57675-151-1 • Item #51511-415 $24.95

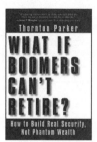

What If Boomers Can't Retire?
How to Build Real Security, Not Phantom Wealth

Thornton Parker

If you are one of the millions of Americans who are counting on stocks for your post-retirement security, Tip Parker's *What If Boomers Can't Retire?* is a wake-up call. In clear, jargon-free language, Parker reveals the flaws in the stocks-for-retirement cycle and shows how to cut through the glut of conflicting advice to make sound investment decisions, as well as prevent national economic disaster.

Hardcover, 280 pages • ISBN 1-57675-112-0 • Item #51120-415 $27.95

The Knowledge Engine
How to Create Fast Cycles of Knowledge-to-Performance and Performance-to-Knowledge

Lloyd Baird and John C. Henderson

The Knowledge Engine shows that in the new economy, knowledge must be captured from performance as it is happening and used to improve the next round of performance, integrating learning and performance into a continuous cycle. The authors show how to produce knowledge as part of the work process and quickly apply that learning back to performance to create a "knowledge engine" that drives ongoing performance improvement and adds value in every area of your organization.

Hardcover, 200 pages • ISBN 1-57675-104-X • Item #5104X-415 $27.95

Berrett-Koehler Publishers
PO Box 565, Williston, VT 05495-9900
Call toll-free! **800-929-2929** 7 am-9 pm Eastern Standard Time

Or fax your order to 802-864-7627
For fastest service order online: **www.bkconnection.com**

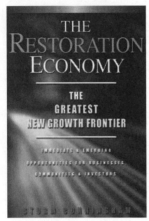